CHILDHOOD UNMASKED

The Agency of Brazil's Street and Working Children

Revised First Edition

By **Marcia Mikulak, Ph.D.**
University of North Dakota

Bassim Hamadeh, CEO and Publisher
Michael Simpson, Vice President of Acquisitions
Jamie Giganti, Senior Managing Editor
Miguel Macias, Graphic Designer
Mark Combes, Acquisitions Editor
Natalie Lakosil, Licensing Manager
Allie Kiekhofer, Interior Designer

Copyright © 2015 by Cognella, Inc. All rights reserved. No part of this publication may be reprinted, reproduced, transmitted, or utilized in any form or by any electronic, mechanical, or other means, now known or hereafter invented, including photocopying, microfilming, and recording, or in any information retrieval system without the written permission of Cognella, Inc.

First published in the United States of America in 2015 by Cognella, Inc.

Trademark Notice: Product or corporate names may be trademarks or registered trademarks, and are used only for identification and explanation without intent to infringe.

Cover image copyright © Depositphotos/alptraum.
    copyright © Maurizio Costanzo (CC by 2.0) at http://commons.wikimedia.org/wiki/File:Child_Labor_in_Morona_Santiago,_Ecuador_1990.jpg.
    copyright © Cauan Kaizen (CC BY-SA 3.0) at http://commons.wikimedia.org/wiki/File:Favela_dos_Trilhos_-_2009_-_Goi%C3%A2nia.JPG.

Printed in the United States of America

ISBN: 978-1-63487-470-0 (pbk) / 978-1-63487-471-7 (br)

CONTENTS

Abstract	ix
Dedication	xiii
List of figures	xv
List of tables	xv

INTRODUCTION   1

Street Children: Who Are They?	2
NGOs: Who Are They and What Do They Do?	5
Chapter Outline	7

CHAPTER 1: CHILDHOOD   11

Social Constructions of Childhood: Historical Framework	11
Administrative and Institutional Control of Children	20
Constructionist View of Childhood	23
History	24
Social Science Literature on Constructionist View of Childhood	25
Constructionist Theoretical Implications for the Reconstruction of Childhood	28
How Street Children View Themselves	29
NGOs	33

CHAPTER 2: BACKGROUND — 35
    Slavery — 39
    The Law of the Free Womb — 41
    Brazilian Economy and Inequity — 45
    Child Law and Child Rights — 48
    The City of Morro de Santana — 51

CHAPTER 3: METHODS — 53
    Methodology and Theory: Epistemology — 58
    Ethnographic Method and Grounded Theory — 59
    Practice Theory — 60
    Methods of Analysis: Research Methods — 63

CHAPTER 4: TWO CASE STUDIES — 67
    Case Study Number One: The Twins — 71
    Conclusion — 84
    Case Study Number Two: Mother of the Twins — 85
    Conclusion — 108

CHAPTER 5: STREET CHILDREN OF MORRO DE SANTANA — 111
    Daily Life: Children and Families and the Economy of Street Life — 111
    Economic Relationships Between Parents and Street Children — 112
    Household Income and Working Street Youth — 118
    General Data — 122
    Lack of Extra-Familial Support Networks in the Favelas — 129

CHAPTER 6: VIVA CRIANÇAS — 153

Roberto Silva: Historical Placement and the
Creation of Viva Crianças — 154

Viva Crianças: The Project — 160

The *Roda* — 161

Games in the *Rodas* — 173

The Kitchen and Garden — 176

Educational Activities — 186

Paper Making, Puppets, Theater, and Music, and Play — 193

Paper Making — 195

Puppets and Toy Making — 196

Theater Group — 199

Music Group — 202

Bornal de Jogos — 210

Bornal de Jogos: Teacher Workshops — 214

Conclusions — 221

CHAPTER 7: VIVA CRIANÇAS: COORDINATOR SELECTION PROCESS — 225

Workshops and Training — 228

The Coordinators' Views: Work and Viva Crianças — 237

Coordinators' Voices — 240

Sophie — 247

CHAPTER 8: FOUR ADDITIONAL PROJECTS — 257

Curumim — 257

Daily Activities — 260

Tutoring, Homework Assistance — 262

Games and Activities — 263

Nutrition and Gardening	265
Child Behavior: Home and Project	266
Popular Culture versus Technology	268
Citizens for Life Options (COV)	272
The COV Project	275
Associação de Pais e Amigos dos Excepcionais (APAE)	279
The Arts	284
Bom Jesus	287

CHAPTER 9: STREET LIFE AND SOCIAL RELATIONS — 293

Low Self-Esteem	293
Violence	302
Hunger	312
Living Conditions	322
Health, Illness, and Substandard Medical Care	331
Stereotypes of Danger and Immorality: *Pivetes e Ladrões* (Thieves and Bandits)	339

CHAPTER 10: SIGNIFICANCE OF FINDINGS — 353

Introduction	353
Contribution to Anthropological Research	355
Theoretical Contributions	357
Changing Established Ideas About Street Children	360
National Education Campaigns on Poverty and Race	361
Gaps Within Literature on Street Children	362
Suggestions for Changing NGO Practice and Policy	363
Differences Among NGOs	366

Contribution to NGO Practice and Policy
Regarding Street Children   368

Addressing Economic, Educational, and Racial Inequality   369

Computer Literacy and Exchange Programs   372

Right to Work   375

Discussion of Areas for Further Research   377

Conclusion   380

Endnotes   381

GLOSSARY: BRAZILIAN PORTUGUESE TERMS   395
BIBLIOGRAPHY   407
INDEX   437

ABSTRACT

This book explains how class-based definitions of childhood and constructions of race alienate and marginalize street and working children in Morro de Santana, Minas Gerais, Brazil. Middle-and upper-class definitions of "normal" childhood affect the life possibilities of street children, and these class-based assumptions in turn affect programs developed by non-governmental organizations (NGOs). Most Brazilian NGOs use the popular culture model to create race-and class-based programs, and in so doing, unwittingly reproduce the very negative social stereotypes and inferior educational opportunities that they purport to ameliorate.

I present an historical analysis of childhood and conclude that imported industrial notions of childhood as a time of innocence and protection from the adult world adversely affect street children. In addition, I argue that racism has a profound impact on street children. Racism is linked to Brazil's historical legacy of slavery, and few anthropologists have addressed and/or linked both race relations and social class to violence against street and working children in Brazil.

After linking constructions of childhood, race relations, and social class in Brazil, I discuss the daily life of street and working children and the economy of street life. Using interviews with child informants, I then discuss the daily lives of street youth, and present statistics on the incomes earned by street and working children in my sample. My research finds that street and working children who live at home but work on the streets make significant economic and emotional contributions to their families. The children talk about their daily life experiences in the following realms: self-esteem, violence, hunger, living conditions, health and illness, and negative stereotypes. I argue that the negative social stereotypes about street children are contrary to the actuality of their daily lives on the streets and at home.

I compare and contrast five NGOs in Morro de Santana, Minas Gerais, and argue that these organizations represent a cross-section of the various types of NGOs that work with street and working children in Brazil. The types of programs that these NGOs create, their institutional goals and ideologies, and the types of events that occur in each project on a daily basis are examined. Then, project coordinators and monitors (teachers and staff) talk about their conflicts with the NGOs where they work and the difficulties they experience with the children and youth with whom they work. I argue that NGOs need to create programs based on the expressed needs of their clientele (children and parents), and develop organizational structures that incorporate the ideas and needs of coordinators, monitors, and staff.

The conclusion discusses the implications of this study both for anthropological research about street and working children in particular and for research on children in general. I argue that social science needs to develop a new paradigm of childhood, one that redefines children's identities and activities using children as the main informants. Such research would approach children not as unformed and less-than-capable informants, but as full social actors capable of articulating their sense of self, their activities, their needs, and the strategies they use as they navigate through their world of peers and adults. I suggest that Brazilian NGOs need to reinvent themselves by changing currently used practices and policies that are based upon the popular culture model. I urge NGOs to address economic, educational, and racial inequality in Brazil in their programs for street and working youth. Finally, I argue for strong public educational programs that address the issues of race, social class, and social and economic inequality in Brazil, within the public and private primary and secondary educational systems, and within both federal and state university institutions.

DEDICATION

I dedicate this book to Celma, my Brazilian caretaker who loved me and rocked me to sleep when I was a child in Brazil, to the warmth and complexity of the Brazilian people, and to the street and working youth I came to know, love, and respect.

LIST OF FIGURES

Figure 1: Percentage of Job Types in the City Center
    Shot Clinic   121

LIST OF TABLES

Table 1: Income Distribution   121

Table 2: Street Youth Contributions to Household
    Express   122

Table 3: Types of Work Done by Working Children
    (Interviews with Working Street Youth)   124

Table 4: Survey of Working Children in Morro de
    Santana (Health Clinic Data)   125

Table 5: Children's Income Compared to Total Family
    Income (Health Clinic Data)   126

Table 6: How Earned Money Is Distributed
    (Interviews with Working Street Youth)   127

Table 7: General Working Data: Reasons for Working
    (Interviews with Working Street Youth)   127

Table 8: Viva Crianças Activities   185

INTRODUCTION

Rapid growth in the numbers of children living and working in the streets is a challenge to the international community. UNICEF estimates that there are between 25 and 40 million street children in Latin America alone, while Lusk and Mason estimate that half of these are in Brazil (Lusk and Mason 1994:159; Public Policy Statement 2007:235). Life on the street is insecure anywhere; in Brazil it is especially so. Between 1988 and 1990, 4,611 Brazilian children and youths were killed by death squads that were composed of police and civilians. In 2006 UNICEF reported that one third of the world's children lack adequate shelter. The victims are often described by the Brazilian media as filthy, degenerate, deviant, delinquent, or worse. Average citizens appear to be unmoved by their plight (Herringer 1997; Amnesty International 1994; Guadalupe 2008). Most importantly, a vast majority of children working the streets in Brazil are Afro-Brazilian, and as such, their plight magnifies Brazil's deep-seated and recalcitrant racism that further reduces their chances of gaining access to the minimal conditions necessary to live a life of dignity (Bandeira Beato 2004; Wood 2010).

This book seeks to illuminate the genesis of popular and official perceptions of street children and to compare those perceptions with the realities of street children. Specifically, my research examines the differing perspectives of Brazilian street children and five nongovernmental organizations (NGOs) that served them between 1998 and 2002. All names of NGOs, locations, and research participants have been changed to ensure anonymity. The relationship between these NGOs and street children in Brazil is problematic: the ideologies, policies, and programs of the former are often poorly suited to the needs of the latter, and both parties experience a complex set of social, economic, racial, and political constraints. I hope to demonstrate how and why NGOs dedicated to ameliorating the plight of street children often unwittingly fail to apprehend and address the needs of their clients.

Street Children: Who Are They?

As early as 1986, UNICEF formally recognized a distinction between two types of "street children": children *in* the streets (working street children) and children *of* the street (children living in the street). Lusk (1989) further subdivided this classification into four categories: 1) working children (family-based street-workers), 2) those living on the streets with their families, 3) those with no family ties, and 4) those dividing their time between living on the street and maintaining contact with their families. Definitions of who street children were during this time excluded recognition of Brazil's unique historical racism, child labor during slavery, and contemporary social and economic marginalization of Afro-Brazilians (Mikulak 2011).

The exact number of children currently working and/or living in Brazilian streets remains unknown, but even uncertain statistics are impressive. In 1992, Brazil had 59 million children (forty-two percent of the total population) under the age of 18, nearly two thirds of whom lived in abject poverty (IBGE 1992:11 and 14). Twenty-nine percent of Brazilian children under age 14 worked in the streets. Between ages 15 and 18, that figure rises to forty-eight percent (Leite and Esteves 1991). Furthermore, African descendants commonly begin working as children in Brazil; very few achieve the completion of secondary education, and even smaller numbers attend colleges or universities (Bandeira Beato 2004:773–4; Marcus 2012:1295).

In Brazil's cities, military police periodically sweep the streets of street children and place them in government institutions collectively known as FUNABEM (National Foundation for the Well-Being of the Minor). "Some 100,000 children are held in FUNABEM installations at any given time; of this total around eighty percent are simply poor children working on the street, nineteen percent are abandoned, and nineteen percent have committed some infraction" (Raphael and Berkman 1991:22; Amnesty International UK Blog 2013). Brazil in the 21st century has made strides to improve the lives of children who work on and/or inhabit the streets, yet much still needs to be done to improve their life chances, especially for Afro-Brazilian youth living in Brazil's famous *favelas* (Vargas 2006; UNICEF 2012; O'Connell 2013).

Most of the data in this research deal with children age seven to eighteen years living in the city of Morro de Santana in the state of Minas Gerais, Brazil. The majority live in some sort of family arrangement, but work on the streets; the majority attend school, and many receive services and benefits offered by NGOs. The children in this study are children "in the streets." Like Kilbride, Suda, and Njeru in *Street Children in Kenya*, I conceptualize street children as having more commonalties with the working poor and the homeless population in general than their status of "street children" and the stereotypes that define them imply. Street children break the stereotypes held about "normal" childhood in that they are resilient, resourceful, courageous, and independent. They function at remarkably high levels of efficiency on the streets both economically and emotionally, even though they earn pitiful incomes. They form strong bonds among themselves and with others in their communities, and they develop mature and emotionally sophisticated relationships among their peers. Finally, like the homeless in general, street children are part of a group of individuals whose life on the streets has a beginning and an end linked to their life's circumstances and their race (Robertson 1995; Abebe 2008). The transition into adulthood often moves them out of the category of "dangerous street children" into the category of the working poor or the homeless (Kilbride, Suda, Njeru 2000). Other researchers have cautioned against conceptualizing street children as "super" children, stressing that living on the streets among dirt, hunger, and fear is not sufficient to categorize them as such. While this research found children in the streets of Morro de Santana to be vigilant workers and important financial contributors to their families, they were not "super children." I postulate that they demonstrate capabilities that *seem* to be beyond the norm for children (Dodge and Raundalen 1991; Shanahan 2007; James 2007). Their life's actions and the abilities they possess have brought into question, for me, the constructions that currently define the capabilities of children in general. Indeed, the street children and youth I came to know in Morro de Santana far surpassed my expectations of them. In this sense, they appear to be performing tasks usually not attributed to children.

This study describes street children's personal lives, their family intimacies, and their difficulties. Street children want to be active participants in society and they desire and need to work within the adult world. Their stories indicate that they see themselves differently than their critics do. As they reveal themselves, their actions and their identities take on new meaning in the broader context of Brazilian society.

NGOs: Who Are They and What Do They Do?

A Non-Governmental Organization is a not-for-profit and non-partisan (not aligned with a political party) entity. The NGOs referred to in this research provide services specifically for street children and are generally funded by national and international agencies, mostly private. Brazilian social scientists Lucia do Prado Valladares and Flávia Impelizieri identify the following types of NGO programs offered to street children: daycare and schools, social assistance agencies, boarding homes, residents' associations, alternative education projects, job training projects, coordinating bodies, shelters, and centers for the defense of human rights (Valladares and Impelizieri 1992).

Statistics for 1994 state that wealthy Brazilians control 47.8 percent of the country's wealth, while the poor control 0.8 percent (Amnesty International 1994). In 1998, according to Brazilian economist Werner Baer, "ten percent of the population received 46 percent of the national income while the poorest 50 percent of Brazil's income groups received only 14 percent of the national income" (Baer 2001:4). The World Bank uses an indicator called the Gini coefficient to show the extent, on a scale of zero to 1, to which the distribution of income among households in an economy deviates from a perfectly equal distribution. A coefficient of 0 signifies "perfect equality" and a coefficient of 1 implies "perfect inequality." The Gini coefficient for Brazil has remained around 0.6 since the 1970s. Hence, Brazil has one of the highest coefficients of inequality in the world. Responding to the growing crises of poverty, social deterioration, and environmental degradation, the number of Brazilian NGOs working with street children has grown rapidly in the past two decades. Street children play pivotal roles in advocacy at the municipal and local levels, primarily in the fight for children's rights and their assistance in providing for the stability of their family's household income (Bandeira Beato 2004: Marteleto 2012; Emmerson and Knabb 2006: 421432).

The Brazilian NGOs in question were first created in the late 1970s and early 1980s as the military dictatorship came to a close. The transition to democracy brought serious economic problems to Brazil and increased public violence, shattering the structures that had effectively kept social classes safely apart. Anthropologist Nancy Scheper-Hughes states in a co-authored article with Daniel Hoffman that, "…suddenly, street children seemed to be everywhere" (Scheper-Hughes and Hoffman 1994:16). The history of Brazilian NGO culture is cogently outlined in a paper by Vera Sylvia Branco, from the University of Texas at Austin, Institute of Latin American Studies. Branco points out that the development and propagation of NGOs in Brazil delineates an important movement toward social justice in Brazilian society and a movement away from patron–client forms of "assistance" (Branco 2000; Reiter 2011).[1]

Although NGOs are highly visible in today's large urban centers such as Rio de Janeiro, there continues to be conflicting data about the actual number of NGOs that serve street children. *Invisible Action*, first published in 1991, documented the existence of over 600 NGOs and human rights groups functioning within the Rio de Janeiro area alone. In 1995, however, Brazilian researcher Flavia Impelizieri, in *Street Children and NGOs in Rio*, stated that there were no more than eighteen NGOs providing services to street children (Impelizieri 1995).

The research in this book was conducted mostly in 1997 (one year in the field). In 1999 and 2000 an additional four months (two months during each year) of fieldwork was conducted in Morro de Santana, Minas Gerais, a city of some 63,467 people (IBGE 1996), where there were nineteen registered projects working with street children. Ten percent of the total child population was registered by the city as attending one of these nineteen projects (*Conselho Municipal de Assistência Social de Morro de Santana 2000*). The primary data collected for this research came from Viva Crianças (Hurray Child Project), and comparative data were gathered from the following NGOs in Morro de Santana: Bom Jesus (The Good Jesus), Cidadania Opção de Vida (COV) (Citizens for Life Options), Associação de Pais e Amigos dos Excepcionais (APAE) (The Association of Parents and Friends of Those with Disabilities), and Curumim (no direct translation).

Chapter Outline

This book consists of ten chapters:

Chapter One contrasts post-industrial Western European conceptions of childhood as a time of innocence and separateness with the constructionist view, which describes children as active and viable social agents. I discuss how these two opposing theoretical notions of childhood continue to affect the ways in which street children are viewed. I draw upon the theoretical work of Philippe Ariès, who identified childhood as a distinct phase of life that is socially constructed and dependent on race, place, politics, religion, and other cultural factors. I argue that imported constructions of the innocence and purity of childhood affect the development of NGO programs and the kinds of services that are deemed important or necessary for street children.

Chapter Two provides historical background on Brazilian race relations and shows how the lives and labors of Brazilian street children today remain linked to the entangled legacies of slavery, racism, and economic inequality. I discuss the city of Morro de Santana, the site of my fieldwork, and demonstrate how the city is a living museum of inequity based on historic patron–client (master–slave) relations (Mikulak 2011).

Chapter Three presents the field methods I used while working with street children on the streets, in their homes, and in the NGO programs they attended. I discuss the types of interviews I conducted, the number of informants I worked with, and the analytical tools I used to generate a body of both qualitative and quantitative data. I position myself as an anthropologist who is also a friend and teacher to street children and NGO staff. I examine the complex variables that influenced my views and experiences within the field, and I discuss the challenges generated by my own biases.

Chapter Four discusses two case studies and argues my stance as an anthropologist in the field. I argue for the inclusion of my own impressions, sensations, and emotions in the data I present in this book. In this way, my personal data mediate the distance between the engagement necessary for work in the field and the self-effacement so often called for in writing ethnographies.

Chapter Five discusses the economic relations between street children and their parents by presenting data on the types of work street children do, how much time they spend working on the streets, and how much they earn and contribute to their families' household income. Street children, their families, and the coordinators at various projects discuss the lack of extra-familial support networks within the *favelas* (shantytowns) of Morro de Santana where most street children live.

Chapter Six begins with an historical and biographical sketch of Roberto Silva, the creator of Viva Crianças, and shows the theoretical and philosophical influences that directed the project's creation. This chapter describes the aims and goals of Viva Crianças, discusses the types of programmed activities offered to street children by Viva Crianças, and examines street children's reactions to these various activities.

Chapter Seven presents the views, feelings, and experiences of the coordinators who work directly with street children. The coordinators voice their conflicting reactions to the project's ideology and discuss what actually takes place in Viva Crianças on a day-to-day basis. They describe tensions and relations of power amongst themselves, the children they serve, and the project's administrative staff. They draw conceptual maps that illustrate the hierarchy of their organization.

Chapter Eight briefly presents and discusses the four additional projects I worked with during my fieldwork. All four have inherent similarities and differences, and they are discussed and compared to each other and to Viva Crianças.

Chapter Nine discusses data gathered from individual interviews with street children, coordinators, and parents to demonstrate how street children view and describe themselves and their lives. The major topics touched on in this chapter are self-esteem, violence, hunger, living conditions, health, and negative stereotypes.

Chapter Ten synthesizes and summarizes the important issues discussed in each chapter. I compare my findings with those of other anthropologists who have studied street children, NGOs, and the persistence of racism in Brazil. I offer suggestions and recommendations for the creation of NGO programs and social policy within local communities. Finally, I redefine street children and summarize their contributions to their families and communities.

CHAPTER ONE
CHILDHOOD

Social Constructions of Childhood: Historical Framework

The idea of childish innocence resulted in two kinds of attitude and behavior towards childhood: firstly, safeguarding it against pollution by life, and particularly by the sexuality tolerated if not approved of among adults; and secondly, strengthening it by developing character and reason. We may see a contradiction here, for on the one hand childhood is preserved and on the other hand it is made older than its years; but the contradiction exists only for us of the twentieth century. The association of childhood with primitivism and irrationalism or prelogicism characterizes our contemporary concept of childhood (Ariès 1962:119).

This chapter will compare and contrast post-industrial Western European conceptions of childhood as a time of innocence and separateness with the constructionist theoretical view, which describes children as active and viable social agents who construct knowledge of themselves and the world. The constructionist theory, also known as the constructivist theory, dramatically changes the ways in which child learning, and hence child abilities, are viewed by placing the child's own efforts to learn and understand experiences at the center of knowledge acquisition (Prawat 1992: 354–395; Baxter 2008:159–175). I discuss how these two opposing theoretical notions of childhood continue to affect the ways in which street children are viewed. I draw upon the theoretical work of Philippe Ariès[2], who identified childhood as a distinct phase of life that is socially constructed and dependent on race, place, politics, religion, and other cultural factors (Shanahan 2007:407–428). In addition, I discuss recent literature on constructionist theory. Finally, I argue that imported constructions of the innocence and purity of childhood affect the development of NGO programs and the kinds of services that are deemed important or necessary for street children.

In keeping with post-industrial Western European conceptions, most middle-and upper-class Brazilians view childhood as a time of innocence and protection. Because Brazilian street children view themselves as independent, knowledgeable, and necessary economic social actors, they do not fit into the upper-class definition of normal childhood. Therefore, they tend to be ignored, marginalized, and/or branded as delinquents.

Puritan writers during the Reformation had portrayed childhood as a state of original sin, where the child was born of evil, prone to sin, without moral knowledge, but with the potential and capacity to learn goodness. Hobbes (1588–1679) ascribed similar qualities to human nature at large. Locke (1632–1704), on the other hand, viewed the infant as a "tabula rasa" and as such subject to influence more by nurture than by nature. A century later, Rousseau, in *Emile* (1762), championed a more humanistic developmentalism, putting his faith in child-centered education and socialization based on developing Enlightenment notions of childhood (James and Prout 1997).

The industrial revolution in nineteenth century Western Europe culminated in the concentration and penetration of capital, which generated two distinct classes: the bourgeoisie and proletariat. Among the major transformations in economic and social relations that ensued was a redefinition of childhood. For the bourgeoisie, childhood came to be understood as distinct from adulthood in more than a biological sense: it was a special time of innocence and purity, requiring a degree of protection and guidance. In contrast, children of the proletariat did not often enjoy the same specialness and protection; most often they were viewed as miniature adult workers, a reserve labor pool. Philippe Ariès discusses how the concentration and penetration of capital impacted childhood in *Centuries of Childhood: A Social History of Family Life*. Ariès states that, "Henceforth it was recognized that the child was not ready for life, and that he had to be subjected to a special treatment, a sort of quarantine, before he was allowed to join the adult" (Ariès 1962:412). Hence, children of the proletariat and the middle and upper classes were removed from the adult world.

The industrial revolution also spawned a variety of theoretical definitions of childhood. Social reformers in the 1840s and 1850s warned that the children of the poor were wild animals inhabiting the streets of growing urban centers and endangering the future of society. In keeping with their conception of the evolutionary stages of mankind, anthropologists such as Sir John Lubbock, J. F. MacLennan, and E. B. Tylor defined childhood as a state of savagery regardless of class or geography (Stocking 1968:126). Christian missionaries viewed all primitive societies as proof of degeneration, while polygenists viewed them as evolving from inferior branches of the human race. Civilization, by contrast, embodied the bourgeois virtues developed in the Victorian era (James and Prout 1997; Ariès 1962). This historical reiteration is necessary here because it is linked to the recasting of childhood as a time of innocence and ignorance. After abolition in Brazil, freed African slaves constituted the majority of Brazil's poor and destitute. In Brazil, negative stereotyping of street children as degenerate savages has been linked to the innocence and ignorance of childhood as well as with the ongoing stereotypes of Afro-Brazilians as lower on the evolutionary scale. Such stereotypes produce a socially sanctioned discourse that describes street children as dangerous and immoral (Burdick 1998; Twine 1998; Skidmore 1993; Jahoda 1999; Reichmann 1999; Berndt 2009).[3] (See endnote for a discussion on race and racism in Brazil.) Street children in this research identified themselves using a variety of terms that included *moreno* (brown to dark brown), *preto* (black), *pardo* (brown), *mulato* (brown), *mulatinho* (little brown person), and Afro-Brazilian (Brazilians of African descent). I have chosen to use the term Afro-Brazilian because it was commonly used by the street children I knew who were consciously using the term to increase awareness of their ethnic links to Africa. Many times I was asked to talk about the black movement in America, and as I talked about the civil rights movement and affirmative action, street children were amazed and excited by my stories. It is my hope that by using the term Afro-Brazilian in reference to street children, this research will aid Brazil's burgeoning racial equality movement.

Ariès states that moralists, administrators, and churches in Western Europe successfully removed children from the everyday world of adults.

> Family and school together removed the child from adult society. The school shut up a childhood, which had hitherto been free within an increasingly severe disciplinary system, which culminated in the eighteenth and nineteenth centuries in the total claustration of the boarding school. The solicitude of family, church, moralists and administrators deprived the child of the freedom he had hitherto enjoyed among adults (Ariès 1962:413).

Schooling in Western European industrial countries successfully removed poor children from the streets while significantly improving their life possibilities. It is important to divert here and state that in the case of Brazil, street children (initially freed slave children and poor children of mixed blood) have not had their life possibilities significantly improved. Indeed they were "freed" from slavery, but forced to work in order to survive. Today, street children (as with their freed slave counterparts) must work in the streets while struggling to learn in an educational system with a high degree of inequality and an extremely high drop-out rate for poor children and youth. The public educational system in Brazil is notoriously dismal. For example, in 1998 sixty-seven percent of poor children dropped out of school before completing eight years of fundamental education (Ferreira 2000). A comprehensive assessment of Brazil's current educational system can be found in *Opportunity Foregone: Education in Brazil* (Birdsall and Sabot 1996). Schooling among non-whites (people of darker skin colors) in both rural and urban settings is significantly lower in Brazil, having on average only seventy percent of the schooling of their white counterparts. In general, the educational gap between poor youth and privileged youth is staggering: the median level of education for privileged youth is almost three times higher than that for poor youth (Kerstenetsky 2001; Marteleto

2012). Hence, placing Brazilian street children in schools has not successfully removed them from the streets, nor has it significantly improved their life possibilities.

The colonial project to civilize the world's primitive people through Christianity and capitalism also manifested itself in Europe's major cities, London in particular. The doctrine of the utility of poverty called for the masses to work cheaply for the benefit of the privileged. In this sense, the poor were put to work in the informal labor market, often performing arduous physical labor. In the same sense, child idleness (specifically for the children of the poor) was thought to be a great danger to society. As defined by the English Poor Laws of the 1800s, children of the poor were not cared for as a matter of charity (Fyfe 1989; Standing 1982). Rather, they were required to work for their upkeep. Research in archival records, by historian Hugh Cunningham, found that "The Poor Laws provided the legal and administrative framework within which the lives of the poor [and their children] could be monitored and controlled" (Cunningham 1991:29). Such notions about the colonial project also transferred to Brazil's poor as slavery ended and the push for industrialization began in earnest.

By the 1860s, the bourgeois class had come to worship childhood. According to Cunningham, childhood in this conception

> ...became the repository of good feelings and happy memories which could help the adult to live through the stickier patches of later life...it was both a place of refuge for those wearied by life's struggles and a source of renewal which would enable the adult to carry on. In effect, that is, childhood was a substitute for religion (1991:151–152).

In the latter part of the century, public schooling served to prolong childhood. Schools of the bourgeoisie became walled gardens where, "...within their bounds the Peter Pan fantasy came near to being a reality" (Cunningham 1991:154).

The proletarian childhood experience was decidedly different. In pre-capitalist modes of production, the extended family worked together as a productive unit. Under capitalism, the average proletarian nuclear family was supported principally by its adult male wage earner. Women and children generally entered the labor market in order to generate supplementary wages, but because their contributions were considered secondary, they constituted a class of even lower paid, super-exploited workers (Elson 1982; Diamond and DiIorio 1978). Karl Marx observed that while industrial capital paid the patriarchal head of households a "family wage" barely sufficient for survival, penetration of capital into all sectors of production forced lower wages and higher prices, leaving poor families no recourse but to send every member of the family to work, thereby further stratifying power relationships between state and individuals, men and women, and adults and children (Marx 1977:353–359). Similar processes occurred in Brazil, where poor families, especially freed slaves and their children, were forced to put every member to work as early as possible in order to ensure survival (Bieber 1994; Conrad 1984; Degeler 1986; Del Priore 1991).

As capitalism advanced and populations became concentrated in urban areas, poor children became more visible. Their presence was seen as a social problem to be solved by public policy and the benevolent efforts of religious and charitable societies. Such institutional control of children sought to provide the "right" environment for children in the eighteenth and nineteenth centuries. For the upper classes, notions of innocence and the need for guidance provided the motivation for childhood education. By contrast, schooling for the proletariat represented a deliberate movement to tighten control over the next generation of laborers. Industrial schools and reformatories flourished in mid-nineteenth century England (May 1973:7–29). As the social construction of childhood innocence spread into Brazil during the early 20th century, politicians, church organizations, and judicial sectors began making plans to develop policies that would define children who were on the streets as delinquent (Rizzini 1994).

During the eighteenth century, civil society, the church, and the state each had particular interests in redefining childhood and protecting children from the adverse effects of exposure to the adult world. Although the tendency in the early years of the industrial revolution had been to put the children of the poor to work, reformers called for the modification of child labor, insisting that children's work be tailored to their strength and capacity. Concern for the proper environment for children was expressed in sentimental arguments about religious and moral values. The religious and social reform forces feared that the working child was not being exposed to environments that would mold and form good character. Working (i.e., corrupted) children were seen as a potential threat to society. On the other hand, growing industrialism demanded an unimpeded cheap labor market (Cunningham 1991). The concerns about physical and moral hazards of child labor inevitably clashed with industry's demands and led to wide-ranging debates about the desirability and feasibility of controlling the child labor market.[4]

Labor reform focused on two kinds of "evil" thought to be particularly harmful to children: physical hardship and moral neglect. The bodies of working children suffered from long work hours in overheated and polluted mills. They were also often physically punished. From the perspective of the reformers, children lacked education and religious training, and they suffered from their immersion in the adult world. Together, these two concerns implied that the continuity of society was in danger, evidenced by the growing number of the working poor in urban centers. Religious leaders pleaded for the removal of children from the adult world in order to protect them from exposure to adult ways, mainly vulgar language and explicit sexual play. In the liberal imagination, poverty and crime were inextricably linked and youth were seen as powerless victims caught in a culture of poverty, vulgarity, and amorality.

The new conception of childhood as a time that ought to be characterized by innocence and guidance collided with the presence of poor children laboring in industrial settings. Historian Hugh Cunningham states, "If children in all ranks of society were perceived to be essentially the same, then the road was indeed open for an attack not only on child labor in the cotton mills, but on child labor of any kind" (1991:69). Historically, child labor had been protected by the practice of apprenticeship, but by the second decade of the nineteenth century, Cunningham points out that apprenticeship practices were seen as exploitative of children as well as "...an unjustified interference with the free operation of the market..." (1991:71), where increases in free labor were used in preference to apprenticed labor. It was recognized that child labor laws were a way to protect against a particular type of inhuman exploitation, as well as a way to remove children from the adult world of the streets.

While the first part of the nineteenth century in England witnessed a rise in concern for black slaves and for white child slaves, many privileged liberals who had campaigned for the former were blinded by their economic interests to rights of the latter. Researchers take a grim view of reformers and state that only when the market was glutted with cheap child labor did the battle for reform begin in earnest with the Child Labor and Education Acts of 1847 (Cunningham 1991; Brick-Panter and Smith 2000; Austin and Willard 1998).

Administrative and Institutional Control of Children

In England, the Factory and Education Acts of 1802 banned children under fourteen from factory employment. In 1851, thirty-seven percent of boys and twenty percent of girls between the ages of ten and fourteen were in the labor market. By 1911, those numbers had dropped to eighteen percent and ten percent, respectively (Cunningham 1991:166). Although reformers and bureaucrats could claim a successful moral victory in the removal of child labor from the work force, in reality children had been made superfluous by machinery and because (like foreign sweatshops today) they threatened the interests of adult male laborers.

The removal of children from the urban workforce transformed the nature of childhood in Europe. Within the family, children's economic contributions may have been curtailed, but their value in emotional and psychological gratification to their parents generally rose. From capitalist industry's standpoint, if they had lost a source of cheap labor, at least they had gained an enormous potential consumer market. Children were also a substantial new source of labor for adults in educational and juvenile justice systems, in that an entire system of government jobs came into being, requiring education, training, and hiring of scores of adults (Postman 1982; Zelizer 1985; James and James 2003). This new construction of children as economically useless, but emotionally priceless, was imported into Brazil and had grave implications for poor working children of color.

As the understanding of childhood as a protected, almost sacred province gained in popularity, so did the focus on the child's education, discipline, and potential pathologies. Freud, the "father" of developmental psychology and personality theory, expressed a vision of the

> ...diverse tensions in his culture (e.g. the savage child over the innocent child, the impulsive over the rational, the hidden face over the public face) and set others in perpetual tension (the biological and the social, the act and the wish, the real and the fantasy), molding the whole into a powerful mythology" (Stainton 1992:89).

Freud sexualized the child and defined a potpourri of undirected human drives that children, unless restrained, would unleash upon society (Stainton 1992). What is significant here is that only by external intervention could the individual be saved, through psychotherapy for the upper classes and social work (government social workers) for the lower classes. Such outward intervention resulted in a plethora of new professionals: psychologists, social workers, child protection agents, delinquent courts, and more.

Jean Piaget (1896–1980) is credited with "uncovering" the developmental processes of children through a model deeply embedded in the social values of his time, namely the progress from childhood (the primitive) to adulthood (modern enlightenment). His conception was similar to Freud's in that both see adulthood as the *goal* of childhood; the inferiority of the child's operational (logical) functions yields to the superior command of the adult mind. Susan Buck-Morss points out that "The abstract formalism of Piaget's cognitive structures reflects the abstract formalism of the social structure," thereby reflecting the social constructions that defined 20th century Western European behavioral sciences (Raskin, Bernstein, and Buck-Morss 1987; Watson 1928; Inhelder 1958).

B. F. Skinner's and J. B. Watson's behaviorism brought renewed attention to the nature vs. nurture debate (Rogers 1992; Morss 1990; Ozmon and Craver 1990). In their conception, children are products of their environment; their behavior can be correlated with their social, physical, and psychological history. Watson went so far as to assert that he could produce any kind of adult human being by controlling his or her environment (Watson 1928; Skinner 1974). In short, Watson and Skinner believed children could be trained to become model citizens. Their ideas had wide-ranging impact on social and educational policy throughout the western world, and sometimes fed the ambitions of totalitarian regimes. Stainton Rogers argues that,

> Behavior modification has taken on not a utopian cast, but a distinctly social control orientation in which "clients" often turn out to be the already oppressed and disadvantaged inmates of total environments.... (1992:100).

As the twentieth century began, the influence on Brazil of Western European and American theories of psychology, medicine, education, and justice were responsible for the creation of court systems dealing with a new species of child: the juvenile delinquent. Prior to the creation of the Minors' Code in 1923, that classification had not formally existed. Brazilian sociologists developed quasi-scientific tests to "diagnose" children who demonstrated "abnormal" or "deviant" behaviors. In most cases, the subjects of such testing were lower-class youths whose greatest deviation from the norm was in their living conditions, not necessarily their psychological or intellectual makeup. Affonso Louzada, in *O Problema da Criança: A Ação Social do Juízo de Menores* (*The Problem of the Child: The Social Action of the Judgment of Minors*) states that,

> ...one observes the growing importance ascribed to psychological, physical, social, and economic causes in explaining deviant behavior by minors. Moral causes, such as "bad habits," "loose morals," and "weakening of family authority" began to coexist with other causes,

such as "'physical and psychological disturbances,'" "hereditary factors," "urban overcrowding," "industrialization," and "impoverishment" (1940:18).

Today, even with the ratification of the Statute for Children and Adolescents, street children continue to be profiled according to social, economic, and racial attributes. In the following section I discuss the constructionist view of childhood and its theoretical implications on the study of children.

Constructionist View of Childhood

Childhood is not a universal condition of life. Humans, indeed most species, experience biological immaturity. But childhood is a uniquely human experience. It is the manner in which we understand and articulate the physical reality of biological immaturity. Viewed in this light, the "child" becomes a metaphor—a pattern of meaning—and childhood can be conceived of as socially specific sets of ideas, attitudes, and practices. Unlike gender or race, childhood is a temporary and temporal classification. But like race and gender, it acts as a set of power relationships revolving around different axes. Notions of "childhood" map implicit ideological (and moral) assumptions in the conceptualization of what it "is" to be a child as well as what it "ought" to be (Woodson 2000: http://bad.eserver.org/issues/2000/47/woodson.html).

History

If the nineteenth century gave birth to the notion of the innocence of childhood in Western Europe, the twentieth century can be said to have consigned and confined childhood within legal, medical, and educational institutions, isolating children from the everyday work world of adults. As technology advanced in the twentieth century, television became a common household item. Children from around the world were brought into the homes of all social classes in the US and Europe. Advertisements and programs presented by international organizations such as United Nations Children's Fund (UNICEF) and the World Health Organization (WHO) projected images of children living in conditions that utterly contradicted what the modern West (post-industrial Western Europeans) wanted to envision as the province of childhood. As James states,

> The consequences of famine, war, and poverty for children threw the very idea of childhood into stark relief. The "world's children" united "our" children and "their" children only to reveal the vast differences between them (1998:1).

Children in tattered clothes with distressed or blank expressions began to stare out of magazine covers and television screens. Agencies such as child protection and legal services grew in response to the recognition that childhood was a vulnerable and potentially devastating time. Public attention was drawn to child poverty, and the physical, psychological, and sexual abuse of children, not only in third-world countries, but also within the presumed protection of the developed West. The unpleasant images of children in distress heightened the tension between the idealized visions of childhood born of the West's affluence and the stark realities of an uncomfortable percentage of the world's poor children in industrializing countries.

Social Science Literature on Constructionist View of Childhood

My theoretical approach has been informed and influenced by various social scientists active in the formation of the social constructionist view of childhood. The constructionist view defines children as viable and cogent social agents. I discuss the significance of this new theoretical approach to childhood by reviewing the social science literature on the social constructionist view as it currently stands within the field of anthropology. Next, I illustrate and discuss how street children view themselves in accordance with the constructionist view. I conclude with a brief discussion of how conflicting views of childhood have kept society polarized about street children, and how these views impede the creation of NGOs, which are most often conceptualized, funded, and administered by middle-and upper-class elites who use Western constructions of childhood to create programs for street children. Frequently, such programs are ineffective in meeting the real-life needs of the children they seek to serve because they are based on notions of childhood that conflict with the social constructions that define childhood as it is experienced by poor children of color in Brazil.

During the 1970s and 80s, a growing body of literature about the dominant discourse on childhood grew from a need to redefine the ways in which childhood had been idealized, discussed, studied, and written about. During the 1990s social science and historical studies attempted to address the tension between the reality of childhood and the idealized constructions of it. Psychological literature criticized previous theories of child development and children's needs (Richards1974; Richards and Light 1986; James and James 2003). Martin Woodhead unpacked the vocabulary used to rationalize the efforts of social welfare workers, teachers, policy-makers, and parents. Woodhead states that:

> …by systematically analyzing the concept of "need," I hope to show that this seemingly innocuous and benign five-letter word [child] conceals in practice a complex of latent assumptions and judgments about children. Once revealed, these tell us as much about the cultural location and personal values of the user as about the nature of childhood" (1990:39).

Philippe Ariès (1962) introduced a historical perspective of the construction of childhood as an invention (meaning a social construction in anthropological terms), while other authors debated traditional social science theories about children and socialization (MacKay 1973).

Such scholarly debates eventually led to the development of a still-emerging paradigm concerning childhood and children's social relationships. This new paradigm views "…children as worthy of study in their own right, and not just in respect to their social construction by adults" (James et al 1998:4; James and James 2003). The constructionist view of childhood also informs the various disciplines of child psychology by going directly to children in order to gather data about their lives. The emergent paradigm redefines children as active social agents instead of passive subjects. In addition, the new paradigm assumes that concepts of childhood (who children are, what they do, what they are capable of saying and understanding, and how they are socially positioned) are dependent on culture, race, gender, and ethnicity rather than only on biological maturity.

Anne Solberg has written about the changing nature of Norwegian childhood by using empirical studies of changing roles of children within the family as she investigated their contributions to household management and division of labor within the home (1997). Solberg's work is an example of identifying and recasting the abilities of children. In her work, Solberg does not draw upon biological or developmental models to inform her on the abilities that children possess, but rather she draws upon experiences and events in the lives of her informants in her research. In this case, her informants are children.

In relationship to street children, there has been a significant amount of attention given to the social practice of removing them from the street. Some social scientists have developed and supported practices that remove children from the streets by building on the work of Roberto da Matta, who produced the seminal work on the symbology of street-versus-home in Brazilian society (da Matta 1985; Rizzini 1994; Impelizieri 1995). On the other hand, several social scientists have studied the way in which the street is viewed as a place of transition in order to move from one location to another and not as a place to live, sleep, and eat. Finally, other social scientists such as Benno Glauser, Judith Ennew, Nancy Scheper-Hughes, and Sharon Stephens have written about poor children in developing countries and the social constructions that define their childhood in terms of their inclusion in the adult world (Glauser B. 1997; Ennew, J. 1994b; Ennew, J. 1990; Scheper-Hughes 1989; Stephens, S. 1995). Ennew states that "One of the clearest cross-cultural findings in the 'Childhood as a Social Phenomenon' project is that, in developed countries, children inhabit spaces within an adult constructed world" (Ennew 1994a). Ennew has linked the intense organization of children's temporal experience (daycare, nursery school, pre-school, school, extra-curricular activities) to industrialization, where all time is commodified and conscripted, especially children's time. According to Ennew "free time" is related to idleness, which has no economic value. The idea of children governing their own time while they work in adult spaces and on public streets is viewed as posing a serious threat to society's interests. Ennew concludes her argument by stating that

> the purposelessness of "doing nothing" threatens collective representations: For this reason there exists a whole range of benevolent institutions precisely to give young people something to do. Thus, curiously, what little knowledge we have of what children do when they take control of their own time returns us to the economy (1994b:142)

Irma Rizzini has researched and written about the impact of Western notions of behavioral sciences on the development of the concept of the minor in the Brazilian court system. Children who were removed from the streets were frequently administered psychological and intelligence tests resulting in diagnoses that described them in negative stereotypes (Rizzini 1994:83–101). Today, despite the replacement of the Minors' Code with the Statute for Children and Adolescents, street children continue to be stigmatized, stereotyped, and incarcerated simply for having been on the street.

Constructionist Theoretical Implications for the Reconstruction of Childhood

During the 1980s, conferences headed by Judith Ennew and Jens Qvortrup on the sociology and ethnography of childhood were held in Cambridge, UK; Canada; Europe; and Zimbabwe, Africa. These conferences have stimulated the emergence of a new paradigm in the constructionist theory of childhood. Some of the predominant characteristics of the emerging paradigm include: 1) childhood is a social construction dependent on the criteria of culture, race, gender, and ethnicity, which form structural and cultural components in each location; 2) it is biological immaturity, not "childhood" that is a universal feature of all human groups; and 3) idealized social constructions of childhood that stress the innocence of children by removing them from the adult world are common to the middle and upper classes, while children of the poor are often stereotyped and stigmatized because they do not fit middle/upper-class notions of childhood. The new paradigm pays attention to the absence of children from official statistics and social accounting methods and recognizes how this absence marginalizes children and removes them from everyday agency. The new paradigm recognizes that in western cultures, children have become economically worthless, yet emotionally priceless (Postman 1982; Zelizer 1985; James and James 2003). The villainization of childhood labor is thus a consequence of the construction of childhood innocence. In the following section, I will discuss the ways in which Brazilian street children view themselves and compare these views with the constructionist theory of childhood.

How Street Children View Themselves

How Brazilian street children view themselves can be linked to the statistical data about them. Studies indicate that 83.5 percent of all street children live with their families (50 percent with both parents, 33.5 percent with one parent, usually the mother). Fewer than 10 percent of street children have severed all ties to their families (Rizzini 1986a; Oliveira 1989). These studies show that street children often work more than 40 hours a week on the street and that their labor provides on average 30 percent of their family's incomes. My own research in Morro de Santana found that street children contribute on average between 20 and 60 percent of family income.

My investigation supports the constructionist view. For example I found that street children saw themselves as important people, and that their ability to work and earn money is an integral part of their sense of self-worth. One street youth told me that his dream "…is to have a good home for my mother and my father, and to work and to study…so that they won't need to keep working like they are. [I want] to have money to pay them too." Street children commonly told me that working and earning an income made them into responsible people who were far from worthless. For them, working, paying bills, participating in household work and sibling care, and going to school were the accepted norm.

Working on the street, however, interferes with successful completion of education. Brazil's public primary school dropout rate is alarming. Seventeen percent of Brazilians over seven years of age are illiterate. Ayesha Vawda, in a report for The World Bank on the failure of Brazilian public education, wrote that,

> in 1990, the average schooling for the adult population was only 4 years, approximately the same as El Salvador, Guatemala and Nicaragua, countries with less than half the income level of Brazil. Brazil's low educational attainment rates are directly related to high repetition in primary education, particularly in the early grades. Each year over 50 percent of students in the first grade of primary school repeat, the highest first grade failure rate in Latin America. The average Brazilian student currently spends 7.7 years in primary school, longer than for any other Latin American country. Yet during

those 7.7 years, the average student does not even complete the fourth grade. According to a 1993 report, sixty-three percent of children drop out of primary school before completing it. One of the main reasons for such high dropout and repetition rates is the need for children to contribute to family income by working either for wages or on family enterprises. Currently, about seven million children work in Brazil (Vawda 1997).

Recent literature about the ways in which street children view themselves most frequently takes a constructionist view, focusing on the actual voices of street children as they talk about themselves and their lives. Patricia Márquez in *The Street Is My Home* explores how street youth in Caracas are brought together because of economic scarcity and social violence. She describes the ways in which street youth are able to gain financial resources and material wealth by creating meaningful experiences and relationships in their lives while describing the types of risks they face daily on the streets (Márquez 1999:2). Tobias Hecht, in *At Home in the Street* wonders why there are so few street children in Recife, in the Northeast of Brazil. Hecht views street children in Recife as being "...socially significant protagonists" who also bring "into focus the adult debates in which they are enmeshed" (Hecht 1998:4-6). Hecht's findings about the pride Recife's street children take in working and earning an income conforms with my own in Morro de Santana. Both of us found that street children's status within their family is enhanced in proportion to their successful economic enterprises on the street. Judith Ennew found that street children develop supportive networks and coping strategies by developing meaningful relationships with friends outside of the traditional adult supervision of the home (1994a). Sharon Stephens similarly noted in *Children and the*

Politics of Culture that street children "...develop their own social organizations, relatively stable attachments to territories, and support networks linked to the sharing of food and goods" (1995:12). Stephens links the negative stereotypes of street children to Mary Douglas' work *Purity and Danger*, where dirt is conceived as "matter out of place." Mary Douglas defined "dirt," a form of matter out of place, in this way:

> For us dirt is a kind of compendium category for all events which blur, smudge, contradict, or otherwise confuse accepted classifications. The underlying feeling is that a system of values which is habitually expressed in a given arrangement of things has been violated (1975:50–51).

In this sense then, I came to see that street youth blurred the boundaries between the social classes and their related constructions of childhood.

Street children, argues Stephens, are people out of place in that they defy the social consensus on what constitutes "normal" childhood (1995:12). Stephens suggests that as childhood is being redefined by children themselves and by the social, political, racial, and economic factors of their respective societies, childhood itself is being recast as dangerous. She calls on researchers

> ...to develop more powerful understandings of the role of the child in the structure of modernity, the historical processes by which these once localized Western constructions have been exported around the world, and the global political, economic, and cultural transformations that are currently rendering children so dangerous...the challenge is to grasp the specificity of childhood and children's experiences in different world

regions, national frameworks, and social contexts (1995:14).

Her call for an investigation into the contextual ways in which childhood is constructed is also a call for reassessing children in general by empowering them with social agency.

Taking a constructionist approach to childhood, I agree with Wacquant (1992:9), who asserts that social reality is a "contingent ongoing accomplishment of competent social actors who continually construct their social world via the organized artful practice of everyday life." In addition, alongside the development of the constructionist view of childhood, race, gender, and ethnicity simultaneously have come to be viewed as social constructions dependent on location. Everyday life in this sense includes consideration of the actual social, political, and economic conditions faced by street and working children from impoverished backgrounds. In addition, race, gender, and ethnicity are constructed in tandem with social, political, economic, and historical practices. Hence, I have taken street children as my main informants. Their own descriptions of daily life on the streets, in the NGOs, in schools, and in their homes form the body of my qualitative data.

NGOs

The conflicting constructions of childhood discussed earlier create difficulties in the creation of effective programs for street children in Brazil. NGOs are most often created, funded, and administered by people from the middle and upper classes who view childhood in their own class as a time of freedom from responsibility. Conversely, street children view themselves as viable social actors and as "acting adults." During the early 1990s, many NGOs, particularly in Brazil's large cities, attempted to offer programs directly on the streets where children worked and/or lived. In this sense, these NGOs at least acknowledged street children as living outside the social consensus of what constituted a "normal" childhood. Attempts were made to create moving classrooms in order to teach literacy and basic computational skills, while offering popular cultural activities such as *capoeira* (an Afro-Brazilian martial art), and street theater.

Other NGOs opened centers where street children came to receive food, blankets, medication, and some educational assistance. At the end of the day, these children returned to the streets. NGO attempts to encourage children off the streets and either back to their families or into various residential institutions have been largely unsuccessful. Factors involved in the lack of success in these programs include extreme family violence, alcoholism, and sexual abuse, not to mention economic stress. When street children have been asked what they most value in the NGO programs they participate in, they most often cite job training, leisure, respect of NGO staff who take the time to interact and talk to them, and nutritious meals (Impelizieri 1995). My data on street children in Morro de Santana concur with these observations.

The theoretical views of childhood discussed in this chapter affect how street children are perceived by the public at large and by the NGOs that seek to service them. More recent views of childhood, as a time of agency and self-directed learning and participation in society, may assist in the development of more effective programs for street children. In the next chapter, I discuss the historical background of Brazil's political economy and address how slavery, racism, social class, and educational and economic inequality act in tandem to limit the life possibilities of street and working children in the city of Morro de Santana.

CHAPTER TWO
BACKGROUND

In this chapter I provide a brief historical background on Brazilian politics and economy. In addition, I discuss Brazilian race relations and show how the lives and labors of Brazilian street children today remain linked to the entangled legacies of slavery, racism, and economic inequality. I discuss the city of Morro de Santana, the site of my fieldwork, and demonstrate how the city is a living museum of inequity based on historic patron–client (master–slave) relations.

Brazilian economist Celso Furtado illustrates the early economic history of Brazil by comparing it to that of the English colonies of North America. He points out that in Brazil, agriculture and the export of its products (principally sugar, coffee, and cotton) were dominated by large monocultural estates owned by a small number of powerful landowners, whereas in North America, land ownership was more evenly distributed and its various products more domestically consumed. These conditions, Furtado suggests, created the basis for independent commercial and industrial development in North America. In Brazil, by contrast, the concentration of land and capital led to internal markets of decreasing significance and, eventually, stagnation of Brazil's colonial economy (Baer 2001:12–13).

However, Barickman (1998) has suggested that because of the large slave-holding sugar plantations in the northeast of Brazil, the demand for *farinha* (manioc flour, a staple in the diet of slaves) fueled the internal economy rather than forestalling it. He postulates that the demand for *farinha* created a form of micro-industrialization in Minas Gerais. Likewise, historian Judy Bieber refers to recent scholarship that is reevaluating the economic history of 19th century Minas Gerais. She states that "…Minas has revealed a pattern of economic diversification and non-export-oriented trade. Following the decline of gold mining, Minas Gerais experienced a fairly widespread, silent, protoindustrial revolution in the form of cottage cloth production and small-scale iron foundries" (1998:21-22). The revolution was short-lived, however. In the late nineteenth century, railroads were built in Minas Gerais, reducing the price of imported goods, including cloth. Small cloth cottage industries and iron works succumbed to competition from cheaper imported goods. In short, Brazil's economy during the transition from slavery to early industrialization was fragile. Economists describe these fluctuations in Brazil's economic development as intrinsic to the classic pattern of boom–bust export cycles of sugar, gold, coffee, and rubber (Baronov 2000).

The sociological contours of Brazil's political economy described above reflect the complex interaction between Portugal's history of "royal absolutism" and the "incorporation of a Napoleonic legal system" founded on a "property-based class system" that incorporated latifundistic patterns of settlement (Dr. Jon Tolman, University of New Mexico Iberian Institute, personal communication 2001). By adopting the plantation production system as its economic engine, Brazil, like other oligarchic political systems, opted for a coerced labor system rooted in slavery. As the African slave trade neared its end (1850–1888), a labor crisis hit the Brazilian latifunda culture and slave distribution in Brazil shifted as slave owners in the North and Northeast sold their slaves to coffee growers in the South (including Minas Gerais). In the latter nineteenth century, cotton crops replaced sugar production in Northeastern Brazil. Unlike the United States, where cotton crops were worked by African slaves, cotton production in Brazil was enabled by "free" people.

> The Northeast, then, should have pioneered the experiment with agricultural wage labor in Brazil. In fact, it was the area where a colonial mode of production most tenaciously endured. The 1872 census, for instance, demonstrates that of the 15,104 slave and free who lived in the Paraiban municipality of Campina Grande, a mere five (0.03 percent) claimed to work for a daily wage (Meznar 1994:499).

Meznar found that in Northeast Brazil, freed slave children along with peasant children were "employed" for their cheap labor. These children aided in the transition from slave labor to free labor with negligible economic impact on the landed elite (1994: 499-515).[5] Meznar concludes that freed children of color and peasant children remained dependent on their "guardians" until adulthood

> ...since wards received no direct payment for their labor for many years. Guardians, who provided orphans with food, shelter, and clothing, were not likely to spend more than absolutely necessary for the upkeep of their wards. The decline of slavery coupled to an expanding export economy contributed to more tightly bind clients to patrons (1994: 511-512).

The marginalization of street children in Brazil can thus be, in part, tied to the world economic system, but particularly to Brazil's unique and partially successful patterns of dependent development. Between 1939 and 1973, the proportion of Brazil's wealth (GDP) from agriculture declined from 26 percent to 15 percent, while industry grew from 19 percent to 33 percent (Evans 1979:71; Evans, Rueschemeyer and Skocpol 1985). The transition from agriculture to industry was, in part, made possible by increasing dependence and indebtedness to core countries, principally the United States.[6] The drive for development in Brazil entailed the export of vast profits and failed to encourage the growth of local industries that could support poor urban migrants and their families. Brazilian "development" precluded nearly all investment in infrastructure and human capital formation, leaving in its wake millions of displaced people (usually of color) who created over the years the burgeoning *favelas* (shantytowns) that cover the hills and peripheries of Brazil's cities.[7]

That global economic systems have profound impact on huge populations of poor and disenfranchised people is obvious. Slightly less so is the power these broad affects have in determining varying constructions of childhood according to class, gender, and race. Consequently, the economic conditions and contributions of street and working children are related to economic trends at both the global (macro) as well as local (micro) ends of the spectrum. In Brazil, the dynamics of global processes of domination and exploitation in the name of economic development have contributed to a social construction of an entire class of "disposable" children, consequential when their energies are harnessed in the name of development but still considered superfluous by most. The legacy of slavery has potentiated this construction, as evidenced by ingrained linguistically negative symbology that still stigmatizes Brazil's darker-skinned children and youth. *Moleque* refers to "...a young black, usually a slave" or to a "black slave between 6 and 14 years of age" or again, to a "young or small black slave or servant; child of color" (Stephens1999:362). *Moleque* is perhaps one of the most common terms used to describe a street child. The term *mulato* or *mulata* identifies a "...person with any amount of African ancestry" (Stephens 1999:352). Most street children are *mulato*. Stronger terms frequently used to mark street children are *moleque ladrão* (small black boy who steals or is shameless) and *caipira preto* (*caipira* refers to a "hick" or "country bumpkin."). However, *caipira preto* is a term that refers to the offspring of black Africans who are illiterate and backward (Stephens 1999, 563). Another common term used to identify a street child is *pivete*, which translates roughly as "urchin or street urchin." *Criança de rua* (child of the street) is frequently used as a marker for street youth. Finally, many street children have been "adopted" by middle-and upper-class families. These children are most commonly called *filho de criação*. This term refers to "illegitimate offspring of a mulato or black mother and a white father" (Stephens 1999 583). It is not uncommon for such adopted children to serve as maids for their adoptive family. Simply put, street children of color are at high risk socially, economically, educationally, and politically. Their life pathways have been severely limited, with little opportunity for individual or collective agency.

Slavery

Indian and African slavery formed the basis of Brazil's colonial economic activities revolving around sugar, and later, coffee. During the 1600s, sugar for export to Europe was the principal source of wealth of the Portuguese colony; by 1627 there were over 230 *engenhos* (sugar mills) producing approximately twelve thousand tons of sugar yearly. Indigenous slave labor did not last long.

> The high death rate among the Indians exposed to European demands and diseases, their retreat into the interior, their amalgamation into the new Brazilian society through miscegenation, and the increasing importation of Africans to meet the growing labor needs…did more to solve the complex question of Indian-European relations than…the altruistic…legislation of the Portuguese Kings" (Burns 1993:41).

Forced migration of approximately 9 million Africans into the Americas began in the mid-sixteenth century and continued well into the nineteenth. In 1850, by conservative estimate, there were 3.5 million Black Africans enslaved in Brazil alone (Burns 1993).[8]

Life on the *latifúndios* (large landed estate) profoundly affected slave family structure. Essentially, the family existed in one of three forms: nuclear, matrifocal, or solitary (single parent with children). According to Alida Metcalf, the nuclear family constituted the most common form of family unit on large *fazendas* (large land holding used for growing sugar, coffee, cotton, etc.). "Given the ownership patterns of eighteenth-century Parnaíba, most slaves did not live on large *fazendas*" (1992:499). Smaller *fazendas* owned by white elites often owned up to eighty slaves, whose labor accounted for the production of sugar, coffee, cotton, and household maintenance. After abolition in 1883, freed slaves found themselves landless and without educational training to enter an industrialized market.

As Brazil moved toward modernization and industrialization, Afro-Brazilians (ex-slaves) continued to be marginalized, expressly so by the government's "whitening" policy (i.e., encouraging white European immigration) undertaken in order to reverse the effects of extensive miscegenation. While land, housing, and passage were offered to white European immigrants during this period,[9] freed blacks found themselves landless, homeless, and indigent. Brazilian historian Meznar found that in Campina Grande in northeastern Brazil during the mid-1800s, the number of landless peasants, which included large numbers of freed slaves and their children, reached approximately 85 percent of the free population (1994).

In 1945, the Brazilian dictator Getulio Vargas continued the policy of whitening via immigration by signing a law, which supported and regulated an open-door policy to European immigrants, citing "... the necessity to preserve and develop, in the ethnic composition of the population, the more desirable characteristics of its European ancestry" (Skidmore 1995:199). Henceforth, salaried labor belonged to White immigrants and not to freed Black slaves, who were rejected as a source of labor in the new economic system of paid labor.[10]

The Law of the Free Womb

Brazil's slave trade officially ended in 1850. On September 28, 1871, the *Lei do Ventre Livre* (Law of the Free Womb), promulgated by Princess Isabel of Portugal, declared that all children born to slaves were free; however, the *Lei do Ventre Livre* contained loopholes by which masters could prolong the servitude of child slaves. For example, slave children remained under the power and authority of their masters until eight years of age. At that age, the master had the option either to receive the *Estado a Indemnização* of 600.000.00 (six hundred *mil-reis*) or to continue using the child's services until the age of 21. If, at age eight, the child slave was deemed incompetent (slow-witted, dull, or rebellious) the master would most often settle for the money and free the child. Assuming slave children were deemed competent, many masters would be inclined to maintain their servitude to full term, which was, effectively, most of an Afro-Brazilian's productive life. The first Brazilian census wasn't conducted until the 1870s, making it difficult to say with certainty what the average life expectancy was among Brazilian slaves. However, Conrad cites archival documents stating that "not more than 25 or 30 percent of the children [slave children] reach the age of eight" (Conrad 1984:100).

Life for freed slave children was not much different from what they experienced under slavery. Brazilian law required that orphans be placed under the care of *tutores* (guardians), who were to provide food, clothing, and shelter. Most often, orphans were put to work on small *sítios* (farms) or in homes as domestic servants. Children's labor was viewed as recompense for their "care and shelter," while the government, in recognition of the value of child labor, required foster parents to deposit in the municipal treasury a prearranged yearly sum, called a *soldada*. This sum was to be transferred to the orphan once he was declared emancipated by reaching the age of 21 or by marrying prior to the age of 21. However, it was highly unlikely that these children received the monthly deposits meant for them once they came of age (Meznar 1994: 504–507).

Brazilian historians tend to agree that the *Lei do Ventre Livre* did nothing to assist slave children and adolescents in the transformation from slave labor to paid labor (Mattoso 1991). The great majority of slave owners continued to use the services of freed slave children (Conrad 1984:341–350; Del Priore and de Mello e Souza 1991). Of the 400,000 children of slaves registered in 1885, just 118 had been liberated.[11] This figure constitutes less than 0.1 percent of slave children (Del Priore 1991). Furthermore, the sale of children born to slave women continued until 1884, demonstrating that slave owners did not see these children in a much different light than they saw their slaves.

When the abolition of slavery was approved in Brazil, on May 13, 1888, the 20 percent of the African population that was still indentured had to create economic activities, many of which were informal. Part of this informal economy included freed black children, who now had to find ways of generating income to ensure family survival. Those who were not used as apprentices were "thrown into the streets after emancipation, becoming the ancestors of our numerous street children" (da Silva 2009, webpage article).

During the 1700s, public institutions such as the *Santa Casa da Misericórdia* had been created in order to "care" for the increase in abandoned children, whose mortality was between 50 and 70 percent (Del Priore 1991:67). Those who survived were sent to *criadeiras* (nannies) to be raised until they were seven years old. *Criadeiras* were paid by the *Santa Casa da Misericórdia*. After they were seven years old the children were sent to "adoptive families," or to the marines if they were boys, or to a "real and proper" orphanage in the case of girls. In whatever situation, wherever they went, these children had to work for free for seven years in exchange for having a place to sleep and being fed. After they were 14, they could find a job and receive wages (Del Priore 1991: 67).

Abdias do Nascimento, a Brazilian Black activist, found that freed slaves were left unemployed and their presence on the streets gave them the name *desocupado* or *vadio*;

> ...a pejorative term used for so-called free Africans, ex-slaves to whom the right to life by free labor was denied. Expelled by the dominant society, their strength having been exhausted in the enrichment of that same society, they were cast into a kind of slow death by hunger and all sorts of destitution. An inexorable extermination without drawing blood: very convenient for the system (1995:246).[12]

As the number of freed slaves grew, the number of the unemployed increased.

After abolition it became common practice to pick up freed slave children and place them into orphanages. In 1874, just three years after the passage of the Law of the Free Womb, the *Colônia Orfanológica da Isabel* (a school for all orphaned children, who were primarily freed slave children) was created in Recife. The primary purpose of the orphans' school was to keep the freed children of slave women in agricultural work under the guise of rehabilitating them as peaceful and moral citizens (Higgins 1985:63). But orphanages were not universally popular. The orphanage houses were reducing the cities and the interior of the country into a depository of idle beggars and parasites (Del Priore 1991:70).

Echoes of these patterns linger today in Brazil. Young girls are often given to families where, in exchange for long work hours, they receive an abysmal wage and some second-hand clothes and school supplies. Boys are usually initiated into the streets and the informal marketplace often by the age of seven, where they are expected to work in a variety of activities. Hence today, Brazil's poor children of color are most often expected to work for a living, while attending school and supporting the needs of the families for whom they work. Children identified as vagrant are frequently institutionalized in FUNABEM institutions (Wood, de Carvalho, and Guimarães 2010).

The legacy of slavery can also be seen in contemporary family relations among Black Brazilians, where households headed by single mothers are common. Brazilian researcher Thales Azevedo attributes the "incomplete" and "disorganized" Afro-Brazilian family to the legacy of slavery: women of color, the descendants of slaves, continue to reproduce family relations common to slaves. He asserts that these fractured homes are the result of Brazilian slaving practices that discouraged marriage and separated husbands, wives, and children. Azevedo states that the "taboo of virginity" has traditionally been strong among the poor (black) population because of "the enduring effects of the slave regime" as well as the hardships of poverty among Brazilian Blacks (Degeler 1986:175; Azevedo 1966:121–23). The states with the largest numbers of Negroes and mulatos also have the highest proportion of unmarried mothers (Degeler 1986; Barros, Fox, and Mendonça 1997).[13]

Finally, the growth of Brazilian cities exploded with modernization. In 1920, about 25 percent of the population lived in urban areas; by 1940, that number grew to 31 percent. By the 1970s, over 50 percent of the population had migrated into urban settings, and by 1980, over 68 percent of Brazil's total population lived in urban cities (Burns 1993; Bacha and Klein 1989:16). During the same period, the growth of non-agricultural employment within the economically active population increased from 40 to 71 percent. The transition from slave to paid labor, and the migration from rural to urban areas are intricately linked. Historian Thomas Skidmore argues that,

> These immigrants helped create the notion of a Brazilian "melting pot," where ethnic differences would be dissolved in the creation of a single nationality. Missing from this optimistic picture, which the elite liked to promote, was the huge population living in Brazil before the immigrants arrived. Italian immigrants might find assimilation easy, but what about the illiterate, unskilled Brazilians, overwhelmingly of color? (1999:71).

Brazilian Economy and Inequity

Brazil's plantation economy of the 1600s accentuated the social, economic, and political differences between masters and slaves, patriarchs and laborers, fostering class and race distinctions that produced extreme inequalities (Da Costa 1985). Flemish and Dutch money fueled the Brazilian sugar industry by funding the development of plantations. The sugar industry in Brazil was a capital-intensive operation, using all available land for the development and exportation of a single crop, making the plantation owner an agrarian capitalist with unlimited power over his slaves and dependents. To this day, Brazil reflects the complex web of this early patron–client relationship stratified by color and class. Brazil's sugar plantations and their economic structure pioneered the

> ...agrarian export economy that would become the way in which most of the Americas were inserted into the global economic order...create[ing] an economy dependent on foreign markets beyond American control [with] boom and bust cycles [as] harbinger[s] of things to come (Winn 1992:73).

Brazil has long been called a "racial democracy," despite years of convincing evidence to the contrary (Skidmore 1993; Azevedo 1975; Freyre 1946). Brazil had the largest number of slaves brought into any Latin American country, at least 3.65 million by some estimates (Skidmore 1999:17). By the late 1700s, the population was more than 50 percent black (Skidmore 1994:38-77).[14] By the 1890s, the Brazilian census recorded the black population as less than 15 percent, while whites accounted for over 40 percent, and by the 1950s, whites constituted over 60 percent of the population with blacks accounting for only 10 percent (Degeler 1986). Such census data demonstrate the degree to which people defer on the side of declaring themselves white. However, it is important to point out that the terms for race in Brazil have varied enormously over time: One era's *cafusos* (offspring of a black and a *mulato*) and mulatos became the next era's *brancos* (whites) (Stephens 1999:561). This changing semantic arena makes these kinds of percentages extremely misleading. Therefore, it is even more important to take into consideration the dominant cultural somatic discourse on race throughout Brazil's history (Mikulak 2011).

Brazil's whitening continues today. The 1990 census stated that only 5 percent of Brazil's population was *negro* (black) while over 55 percent was white, with 39 percent as *pardo* (brown or *mulato*) (IBGE 1992). The 2000 census recorded 5.7 percent as *negro* (black), and 39.5 percent *pardo* (brownish, *mulato*). Together, these last two figures represent 45.2 percent of Brazil's population, or more than 70 million people of African descent (*Almanaque Abril 2000*:76). Nigeria is currently the only country with a larger population of Blacks in the world (Kuperman 2001:1–4). Finally, the 2008 Brazilian census reveals how Brazilians identify according to skin color; 49% of individuals 15 years or older identify as white, 7.9% identify as Negra (Negro), 1.4% as Preta (black—a pejorative indicator), and 13.6% identify as Parda (dark brown). Only 21.7% identify as Morena (light brown) (IBGE 2008). These figures reflect Brazilians' continued proclivity to whiten themselves. The Brazilian government has in the past paid attention to poverty, but not racism. However, it is important to note that Brazil has signed international human rights conventions and currently stands on the cutting edge of anti-racist legislation. Yet, making racism a crime is not the solution. In this sense, my findings as well as the authors already cited, concur with journalist and writer Kevin Hall: "...outlawing racism is not enough. Regardless of their color, Brazilians must take action to raise each individual's awareness of social injustice, and incite everyone to help wipe out inequality" (Hall:2002; Da Silva et al. 2004).[15]

Race relations in Brazil have traditionally been silenced by morphing race relations into class relations by the Brazilian mythology of a racial democracy. Hasenbalg has described this mythology of racial democracy as "the most powerful integrative symbol created to demobilize blacks and legitimate the racial inequalities prevailing since the end of slavery" (Hasenbalg 1979:8). Such inequalities produce both symbolic and social violence against Afro-Brazilians, particularly street children in large cities. Penha-Lopes writes that,

> The massacres of destitute children bring to the fore not only the substandard social conditions faced by a large proportion of the population, but also the perilous position many Brazilian Blacks and mulattos occupy today (1997:150).

Child Law and Child Rights

During the 1970s and 1980s, a variety of social movements emerged in Brazil that challenged official government policies affecting the poor. "Political repression of these movements resulted in the imprisonment, torture, and death of many young people in this period of Brazilian history" (IBASE 1992:7). During this burst of social advocacy, activists began the process of defining basic civil and legal rights for children. This in turn gave rise to the street children's movement and created the now-infamous National Foundation for the Well-Being of the Minor (FUNABEM) (Raphael and Berkman 1991:22–33). The Minors' Code, which directed the creation of FUNABEM, stated that children in the street could be detained against their will and placed in institutions if their parents were deemed unable to care for them. Unfortunately, FUNABEM treated all street children as if they were delinquents. Some 100,000 children have been held in FUNABEM institutions. An estimated 80 percent of these are simply poor children working on the street. Ten percent are abandoned, and 19 percent have committed some minor infraction. It is estimated that about 95 percent of all youth incarcerated in FUNABEM are black or mulato (Raphael and Berkman 1991:22).

Recent statistics state that wealthy Brazilians control 47.8 percent of the country's wealth, while the poor own only 0.8 percent (Amnesty International 1994). Because of the growing threefold crisis of poverty, social deterioration, and environmental degradation, the number of Brazilian NGOs has grown rapidly in the past decade. They have played pivotal roles in advocacy at the municipal and local levels, primarily in the fight for children's rights. NGO programs were developed with the intention of rehabilitating "at-risk" street children into functioning citizens so they could be returned to society at large.

In 1985, with the help of NGOs, Brazilian street children founded an organization called The National Movement for Street Children (MNMMR). The MNMMR asserts that children are human beings deserving of rights enabling them to participate as citizens in decision-making that affects their lives. It has been street children themselves who have called for changes related to the rights of children and youth in Brazil. Raising their own consciousness about their legal and human rights, street children are addressing the discriminations that alienate them from participation within their society. In 1986, the first of two National Street Children's Congresses was held in Brasilia (Amnesty International 1994; NACLA 1995). Organized, directed, and publicized by street children, they gave voice to their serious life-threatening issues, speaking for themselves in a public forum and exercising their rights to citizenship. In this forum, the children amazed politicians and the general public with their clear and insightful critique of their social, economic, and political situation. By gaining the attention of the national and international press, they began to pave the way for their biggest victory to date: The Act for Children's and Adolescents' Rights (ECA) (the *Estatuto da Criança e do Adolescente 1990*). In 1990 the ECA, the most progressive children's rights document in the world, replaced the 1920s Minors' Code and demonstrated to the world that grassroots activism by children and for children working alongside national and international NGOs was possible. The street children I came to know during my fieldwork were consistently aware of the term *direitos humanos* (human rights) as it applied to children's rights.

The old Minors' Code stated that children in the street could be forcefully removed and placed in institutions if their parents were deemed unable to care for them. An important contribution of the ECA was the establishment of a legal clause stating that children can be arrested *only* if they are caught in a criminal act and that they have the right to legal counsel and legal proceedings. The ECA additionally states that children have the right to know what they are charged with and it is now illegal for children to be incarcerated with adults (Raphael and Berkman 1991:24). In spite of the ECA, children continue to be arrested simply for being on the street, and they continue to be incarcerated with adult criminals, while being profiled as juvenile delinquents because of their poverty and their Afro-Brazilian heritage (Amnesty International 1998).

Despite these laws, public perceptions and popular media persist in the use of derogatory names to define street children. In so doing, the basic civil rights of street children as defined by the ECA are ignored. Popular newscasts and local newspapers fuel hatred for street children and often advocate their elimination by the repeated use of such terms as *pivete* (thief), *trombadinha* (pickpocket), *maluqueiro* (street delinquent), *menor* (juvenile delinquent), and *marginal* (criminal). Furthermore, most NGO programs were and continue to be punitive and have failed to transform street children into the hegemonic version of "productive" and socially "normal" children.

The City of Morro de Santana

Morro de Santana is a mid-size city whose population in 2001 was 58,829 (with a total municipal population of 67,141). At first glance, it appears still to be part of colonial Brazil, with many old buildings renovated and still standing along the wide central avenues. The Municipality of Morro de Santana occupies an area of 3,193 square kilometers and ranges in elevation from 1,021 meters (in the *Serra do Crioulo*) to 540 meters (in *Foz do Corrego Estreito*).

The geography of Morro de Santana is typical of tropical savannas in Brazil, which are characterized by hot and humid summers and mild, dry winters. The median annual rainfall is 16 inches a year, with the driest time of the year occurring during the June–October winter season. The median annual temperature is 24 degrees C (75 degrees Fahrenheit). During the cold months, the median minimum temperature is 16 degrees C (60 degrees Fahrenheit), and 29 degrees C (84 degrees Fahrenheit) during the hottest months. Humidity fluctuates between 20 and 60 percent, depending on the season and the amount of rainfall.

The original vegetation of the area was savanna-like grassland with scattered shrubs and small trees that, in some areas, is still well preserved. Intensive charcoal production and cattle grazing have changed most of the original ecosystem into an area of sparse vegetation, dominated by wild grasses and weeds. In the regions that are most intensively used for agriculture, the original terrain has given way to pasture lands and planted fields. In these areas, the land has been greatly degraded (Durigan 1997).

Morro de Santana is surrounded by small farms. Child agricultural labor as well as domestic service is common in the surrounding rural areas. Such work reflects the same types of ethno-labor performed by child slaves prior to abolition. Within city limits, various types of informal labor are performed by poor children: selling ice cream, shining shoes, gardening, caring for household animals in wealthy homes, domestic service, driving carts, loading and carrying stones for street repair, begging, and petty thievery. Like their ancestors, most poor, darker-skinned children begin to labor at the age of seven, when they are initiated into the streets and encouraged to work in order to supplement family incomes.

I have demonstrated how Brazil's political economy impacted Afro-Brazilians in the past and present. Social inequality and silent racism have created real and symbolic violence against street children. The creation of the ECA and the development of the NGO movement have been vitally important in bringing to the attention of the general public the plight of street youth. However, the lack of organized, anti-racism campaigns and government-supported civil rights laws continue to ensure future oppression of street children. The city of Morro de Santana is a typical example of a semi-rural, semi-urban city in the interior of Brazil, where constructions of race and class intermingle to create the social, economic, and educational oppression of street children and their families.

The following chapter will discuss my field methods and the theoretical positions that have directed and informed this research.

CHAPTER THREE
METHODS

In this chapter, I present the field methods I used while working with street children on the streets, in their homes, and in the NGO programs they attended. I will discuss the types of interviews I conducted, the number of informants I worked with, and the analytical tools I used to generate a body of both qualitative and quantitative data. In addition, I position myself as an anthropologist who is also a friend and teacher to the street children I worked with. I examine the complex variables that influenced my views and experiences within the field, and I discuss the challenges generated by my own biases. Finally, I discuss the theoretical and methodological approaches upon which my fieldwork is built.

I spent two months in 1994 in Rio de Janeiro, participating with and observing two NGOs that work with street youth: *Se Essa Rua Fosse Minha* (If This Street Were Mine), and a small NGO in Vargem Grande, a small town in the countryside outside of Rio de Janeiro. In addition, I assisted a woman whose work is well known in Rio. An independently wealthy woman, she uses her own resources to provide food, guidance, and emotional support for street youth throughout the city. I accompanied this woman for several weeks during my stay in Rio, visiting garbage dumps, abandoned buildings, and cardboard mini-cities under over-passes, to provide the children in these places with vitamins, bread, milk, and medicines.

During my preliminary fieldwork in Rio, I interviewed people on the streets, in businesses, and those providing services in the streets (street vendors, bus drivers, police) in the upper-class neighborhoods of Copacabana, Ipanema, and Leblon, and in the middle-class area of Cosmo Velho, as well as in the favelas of Rosinha and Vidigal. I used a prepared questionnaire that focused on people's perceptions of street children: where street children come from, what they do, how many there are, whether or not they are violent, whether or not they have been abused, and what they or their government could do to help. During this time, I also traveled to Sabará, a rural town in Minas Gerais, to observe various other NGOs. In the end, I decided it was more realistic for me to work in a smaller city than Rio.

During my preliminary fieldwork in Rio, my interactions with street youth were an initiation into the world of the streets. I arrived well-stocked with the researchers' tools: video camera, tape recorder, camera, laptop computer, and other, less technical equipment. I instinctively felt that I was not accepted or welcomed by the youth, who I know had been researched to death (almost literally) by other social scientists, both foreign and Brazilian. I also knew that my technology and my presence in the projects accentuated the inequalities that separated us, and I didn't want to be part of the continuing deluge of researchers that exploited street children for personal gain—a dilemma with which I still struggle as I write.

Against my better judgment, I used my video camera in a very delicate situation, one that called for respect of privacy before all other concerns. I had arrived at the project by mid-morning and the atmosphere was charged with tension. Elaine, the project director, was sitting in the inner courtyard in front of a group of about thirty youth. Elaine struggled to tell them why she refused entrance into the project to certain street youth, while the boys seated in front of her screamed in disapproval, accusing her of authoritarian behavior based on her privileged social position. Who was she to say who could come in and who couldn't?

> *Project Director*: These boys who wanted in, they are drug users, and they will only bring trouble. This project is a place for you to be safe and to have a chance to change your life. You can study here….
> *Street Youth*: You lie! You want to be in control of everything! This is our project, not yours!

So the argument went, until I began to videotape the event. I'd been given permission to use my camera, but what I didn't understand was that I needed to ask, each time I wanted to use it, before I began taping. An explosion erupted, and every youth seated on the ground ran at me. The project teachers stepped in and took my video camera, and the boys shouted insults at me. They told me that I had to ask them, not anyone else, if I could use my camera. They pointed out to me that they were not there for me to research them. They would help me, or not, depending on the kind of person I showed myself to be. Their sense of justice was articulate, astute, and powerful. They were very well versed in the ways in which social injustice worked, in the ways in which they were exploited and controlled. I learned, face to face, what hegemony meant and how I, despite my superior educational opportunities (or perhaps because of them), participated in its ongoing processes.

In 1997, I returned to Brazil, but this time to Morro de Santana, a mid-sized city in Minas Gerais. Viva Crianças, originated in the *periferia* (outskirts) of Morro de Santana (the word *periferia* is often used in place of the word *favela* [slum] in smaller urban centers). Socially, Morro de Santana is a microcosm of larger, urban centers such as Rio de Janeiro and São Paulo, with similar economic inequalities, and racial bifurcations. It also echoes the layout of larger cities: a city center and financial hub amid a ring of deep poverty.

The NGOs serving street youth in Morro de Santana are roughly representative of those in Brazil as a whole. Throughout 1997, I observed and worked with five of them: Viva Crianças (Hurray Children), APAE, (The Association of Parents and Friends of Those with Disabilities), Curumim (literally, Curumim refers to *caboclo*, an acculturated Brazilian Indian or "mixed race" who is copper colored), COV (*Comite de Cidadania Contra A Miseria e a Fome: Cidadania Opcao de Vida*, loosely translated means Citizens Against Misery and Hunger: Citizens for Life Options), and Bom Jesus (Good Jesus). I also spent a brief time in Belo Horizonte, accompanying a spiritualist group, *Grupo de Fraternidade Irmão Luizinho* (GFIL, The Fraternity Group of Brother Luizinho) on Saturdays as they gave bread and water to street youth.

In Morro de Santana, I worked daily at Viva Crianças for nine months and in the four additional NGOs mentioned above for a total of six months. Between 1997 and 2000, I collected fourteen life history interviews from project youth in Morro de Santana, and twenty-one informal interviews from project coordinators and project staff. Each project director was interviewed in 1997, 1998, and 2000. In addition, I conducted seven staff interviews of at least two hours' duration. I also conducted ten informal interviews with parents of children in the projects, five with local business owners, and five with professionals (a lawyer, doctor, dentist, physical therapist, and psychologist). My qualitative database is composed of 1,000 pages of transcribed interviews and several hundred pages of field notes.

I collected fifty surveys of street youth in the various plazas and markets in Morro de Santana, and 550 cross-section household surveys in the *favela*s and the city center. Data included the number of residents per household, number of working children per household, parents' income per household, and working children's income per household (See Chapter Five, The Economy of Street Life).

I interviewed fourteen children, most of whom were involved with my music classes; some were more eager than others to be interviewed. I interviewed those more than once. Other children, more reluctant to participate in interviews in the beginning, became interested in talking with me as we developed closer friendships. The children often invited me to their homes, and I met their parents and came to know their neighborhoods within the various *favelas*. I found that after a few months in the field, I had more children wanting to participate than I was able to include in my formal sample. In these cases, I became an attentive listener and a good friend, and my field notes are filled with the stories they told me.

Interviews with project coordinators/monitors (teachers) were scheduled after I had been working at the various projects for a period of two to three months. I often went to the homes of the coordinators and met their families and had dinner with them. My formal interviews and frequent discussions with coordinators constitute several hundred pages of the qualitative data. In addition, I attended training workshops for coordinators and participated in the activities and discussions. I tape-recorded these workshops for subsequent note-taking. I found that by participating in workshops and discussions, I was able to feel more closely aligned with the coordinators and the frequent difficulties they experienced between project ideologies and actual daily occurrences within the project, as well as gaining an understanding of the kinds of relationships they had with the project youth.

After six months in Morro de Santana, I became a part of the local community. I frequently sat with friends at outdoor tables during hot evenings, drinking a beer or eating ice cream. Many times I joined co-workers from various projects at the plaza, where we would sit and talk. I bought products from the local pharmacies and purchased my food at the local supermarkets or the various weekend produce markets. As I came to know some of the owners of these various businesses, I would invariably be asked about my work and why I was in Morro de Santana. In this way, many business people became interested in discussing the problems of unemployment, crime, and street children, and our talks often continued late into the night. Eventually, I arranged informal interviews with local business owners. Each conversational interview took its unique form and direction. I often probed for their feelings, perceptions, and descriptions of poverty, inequality, racism, and the Brazilian way of life.

Methodology and Theory: Epistemology

Street and working children are deeply involved in the NGO system in that their behaviors, attitudes, appearances, needs, and resistance all help to form the programs that are developed for their supposed benefit. Yet the formation of programs is also intricately linked to what NGO directors, staff, and funding agencies (both national and international) perceive as within the bounds of correct activities, occupations, and knowledge for children and youth. Bringing these two worlds together (street children and their needs and NGO directors and staff) in order to examine the contradictions and similarities that exist between them has been greatly assisted by borrowing from grounded theory and practice theory methods in this research. Principally, though, my research is ethnographic in method while being inductively guided. The ethnographic method placed me firmly in the field among my subjects, while practice theory assisted me epistemologically, forcing me to ask how I conceptualized my subjects and their life processes. In this way, practice theory is a way of looking at the world, and a way of becoming informed about the world, by reflecting on my own cognitive processes: biases, fears, reactive responses, and logical and illogical internal dialogues.

Ethnographic Method and Grounded Theory

My field methodology is based on the ethnographic method, which is inductively derived by immersing myself in the lives of my informants and studying the phenomenon at hand. In short, my theory has been discovered, developed, and verified by systematically collecting data in the field and analyzing them as I proceeded. By working inductively, I proceeded from specific observations to broader generalizations while looking for patterns and irregularities. On the other hand, even though grounded theory is also an inductive process, grounded theory separates life experiences into discrete categories and can be seen as both a theory and a method that is based on objective processes. By assuming that "...there is a world out there that can be known to some extent and that we can get at it by successive approximations," grounded theory can be seen as continuously "tested" theory (Dr. Jane Hood, University of New Mexico, Sociology Department 2002: personal communication). Both the ethnographic method and grounded theory processes allowed for the collection of data, ongoing analysis, and the generation of theory to be linked in a reciprocal relationship (Strauss and Corbin 1990). It has been my intention to let the data I collected (life history interviews, focus groups, and to some extent, structured surveys) reveal themselves, rather than starting with a firm theoretical premise, or deductive premise. It was through the use of and borrowing from grounded theory analysis that I developed theoretical categories based on thematic coding.

By allowing the data I collected to guide me, I was by no means working from a purely random set of events as they unfolded. Rather,

I worked systematically, developing interview questions from my daily interactions with street youth, their families, the NGO staff where I worked, and local residents. My research findings, therefore, constitute a theoretical formulation of the realities of street youth within projects as I witnessed and investigated them. In this way, information obtained from informants and across populations (street youth, parents, NGO staff, and local residents of varying social and economic classes) intermingled and cross-fertilized, producing a multi-layered analysis of the complex issues facing all people involved in the daily life of street youth. Hence, within my data, even the populations least likely to have direct contact with street youth, namely the Brazilian elite, are intricately connected to the lives of street youth. It became clear that the indifference frequently expressed by the elite toward poor children was linked to the various assumptions of social class, race, and gender.

Practice Theory

This research is also based on practice theory, conceptualized and developed by French anthropologist Pierre Bourdieu, whose work attempts to bridge the divisions between objectivist and subjectivist positions in social science practice and in the everyday world constituted by individual agents (Bourdieu 1980; 1984). Practice theory has guided my methods by forcing me to pay attention to the differences between the ways in which I, as an anthropologist, foreigner, and woman, think about street youth and how NGOs and Brazilian society at large view them. The tricky business of generating models or theoretical schemes tends to separate the very act of daily life as it unfolds into a reconstructed non-reality. I believe that society and history are governed by organizational and evaluative schemes that encompass institutional, symbolic, and material factors. Taken together, these factors constitute a system. However, unlike systems theory, which tries to break the system down into discrete chunks, practice theory recognizes that a unit may at once represent several tightly interwoven processes, such as social relations, economic relations, political processes, cultural categories, norms, values, ideals, emotional patterns, and so on. Moreover, relations between units may be asymmetric, unequal, and/or dominating; processes may be simultaneous, multi-directional, and/or reversible.

Bourdieu puts the dilemma of bridging the gap between the privileged social scientist, the creation of theory and text that attempts to discuss observed events, and the act of living (practice) this way:

> The shift from the practical scheme to the theoretical schema, constructed after the event, from practical sense to the theoretical model, which can be read either as a project, plan or method, or as a mechanical program, a mysterious ordering mysteriously reconstructed by the analyst, lets slip everything that makes the temporal reality of practice in process (1980:81).

Hence, the struggle to link theory, method, practice, and ethnography into a seamless unit. In perhaps a more clearly stated example, Bourdieu refers to music as a way to discuss the dense correlation of time, physical and temporal structure, intentions, and synchronicity involved in doing fieldwork and utilizing practice theory:

> Practice unfolds in time and it has all the correlative properties, such as irreversibility, that synchronization destroys. Its temporal structure, that is, its rhythm, its tempo, and above all its directionality, is constitutive of its meaning. As with music, any manipulation of this structure, even a simple change in tempo, either acceleration or slowing down, subjects it to a

destructuration that is irreducible to a simple change in an axis of reference. In short, because it is entirely immersed in the current of time, practice is inseparable from temporality, not only because it is played out in time, but also because it plays strategically with time and especially with tempo (1980:81).

When practice theory is understood in this light, it cannot be separated from method or from "being in the field." To do so would be to sever the interchanging and interrelating correlations that occur while in the field, doing what anthropologists do, which is relating, discussing, feeling, participating, interacting, and conceptualizing. Indeed practice theory and grounded theory are both theory <u>and</u> method when combined with the ethnographic method used by anthropologists. After reflection and dissection, the processes and analytical procedures I used refused to separate actual life experiences into discrete categories (which ground theory on its own does). Rather, the combination of all three methods used in this study seek to unite anthropologist, informant, data, and experience into a unified, cyclical, and hence, multidirectional and permeable membrane of experience.

Practice is ultimately concerned with actions taken by ordinary people (often referred to as actors), who live within society, or the "system," which is often powerful and constraining. Yet, as anthropologist Sherry Ortner points out, "...the system can be made and unmade through human action and interaction" (1984:159). Indeed, human action and interaction generate dialogue, and through dialogue, the potential for change that can dramatically affect peoples' lives is increased, especially if the anthropologist listens to what informants say, and decides to become involved rather than simply create yet another theoretical text (Scheer 2012).

It is understood in practice theory that individuals, as actors, weigh options, make choices, and negotiate on a continual basis within the arena of a dominant and imposing social space, which I have termed "the system." Yet, what people do, say, and act on is often inconsistent. The system sets rules and laws with the aim of consistency, yet the system is also inconsistent, varying according to class, race, gender, and age, to name but a few variables. The complex web of non-linear action/reaction events between individuals and systems, therefore, allows for a variety of influences and modifications. Though the system often shapes individual actors, those actors who resist the hegemonic powers of the system (often artists, poets, writers, and other individuals on the fringe of social norms—including street children) at times shift the balance of social norms, bringing often unpredictable social change (Scheer 2012).

Methods of Analysis: Research Methods

Since I worked from the ethnographic method and borrowed from grounded theory/practice theory approaches, I analyzed my data on a weekly basis, looking for patterns of similarities and differences in interview responses. I often asked varying informants (children, parents, NGO staff, business owners) the same questions, until the answers I received achieved a certain predictability. Then I knew that it was time to look for the next set of questions. Often, it was the eccentric piece of information provided by an informant that would inform the next set of interview questions.

Prior to analyzing my data, I transcribed and translated the majority of my interviews from Portuguese to English in order to revisit each interview and meditate on the meaning of my data. This afforded me an intimate review of the information. Once all my data were transcribed and formatted, I began entering them into a data-analysis program. In order to analyze the density of my qualitative data, I chose to work with Atlas TI, a qualitative data-analysis program that allows for model building and conceptualization based on the generation of codes that emerge from the data itself. I eventually created over 150 codes, delineating the major themes that emerged from interviews and field notes.

Qualitative data analysis can be overwhelming and labor intensive, and it is frequently easy to become lost in a maze of codes and become blinded to the larger patterns being revealed by the coding process. In order to grab hold of and preserve thoughts and interconnections that often arose from coding, I made copious use of memos, which could also be coded for the development of conceptual maps. It was the codes themselves and the conceptual maps generated from my memos that revealed the issues discussed in this research.

Once all interviews and field notes had been formatted, entered, and coded in Atlas TI, the program's query tool proved extremely valuable, allowing for the retrieval of coded text. Using simple Boolean operators (binary and unary) allowed me to filter for codes that were interrelated. For example, I came to see that child abuse, unemployment, and alcoholism were causally linked across interview samples. Such tools greatly assisted in organizing and tracking my data, allowing me to create specific files dealing with conceptual ideas. In this way, the chapters of this book emerged: grounded theory methods and procedures generated raw data; new concepts from saturated field data produced new interview instruments; open coding led to axial coding (putting data back together again in new ways after open coding); concepts and identification of theories followed coding processes; and linkage with existing theories and creation of new theories emerged from analysis after the coding process.

An anticipated outcome of the analysis of my qualitative data was the generation of conceptual typologies that could, in part, reveal the ways in which views about street children are socially constructed in both the NGO and societal setting of Morro de Santana. The qualitative data-analysis techniques already discussed assisted me in examining the social interactions and relationships that construct negative stereotypes about street youth that result in symbolic and actual violence against them.

This chapter has discussed the methods and theoretical perspectives that have guided this research. The goal of this research has been to discover how the social worlds of street youth, their families, NGOs, and Brazilian society are all interlinked within the system, and how through the actions and interactions of human agency these worlds reproduce and reinvent themselves. Taken together, these field experiences, and the data derived from them, provided the empirical base for analysis using the constructionist theoretical perspective.

The next chapter presents two cases studies in the form of two dialogues: one with twin boys who worked in the streets and attended Viva Crianças, and the other with their mother. I argue for a dialogic and reflexive approach as an anthropologist and conclude each case study with a summary of the significance of my informants' stories (Sangren 2007). I discuss how their lives explicate the nature of people living in poverty in Morro de Santana.

CHAPTER FOUR
TWO CASE STUDIES

This chapter consists of two case studies: one with twins, two of Stefany's children; and one with Stefany, the mother of the twins. I selected these two interviews as case studies because they clearly describe and represent the life histories of many of my informants. I wrote the following interviews as dialogues that are verbatim from the taped interviews of Stefany and her sons. While I wanted to represent my informants in as accurate a manner as possible, I also felt it was important to include my own thoughts and emotions during the interviews.

Ruth Behar in *The Vulnerable Observer: Anthropology That Breaks the Heart* states that;

> Always as an anthropologist, you go elsewhere, but the voyage is never simply about making a trip.... Loss, mourning, the longing for memory, the desire to enter into the world around you and having no idea how to do it, the fear of observing too coldly or too distractedly or

> too raggedly, the rage of cowardice, the insight that is always arriving late, as defiant hindsight, a sense of the utter uselessness of writing anything and yet the burning desire to write something, are the stopping places along the way. At the end of the voyage, if you are lucky, you catch a glimpse of a lighthouse, and you are grateful (1996:2-3).

By putting aside my fear of observing too closely or too coldly, I have chosen to include my own shocked and, at times, emotionally loaded thoughts about the difficulties of my informants' lives. In presenting the voice of my informants along with my own inner voice, I hope to expose the complexity of the processes I faced while working with poverty, racism, and inequality.

Including my thoughts throughout the two case studies presented here reflects the concerns of Rosaldo in *Culture and Truth*. There, Rosaldo (1989) argues that culture is learned and not genetically encoded. Hence, learning about the culture of the "other" requires the anthropologist to be aware of their own reactions to everyday events, often in very unfamiliar territories, which can shock, dismay, or create prolonged despair in the anthropologist. Placing reactions in textual dialogues that reflect the anthropologists' thoughts and the informants' words increases the richness of the data, because the anthropologists' thoughts and words are included in analysis. In addition, my reactions (seen or felt) are in tandem with my informant, and generate additional dialogue, either for good or for bad. Finally, my reactions as a participant observer can reveal various aspects of my theoretical and methodological biases as well as exposing how I think, process, and write about my informants. In this way, fieldwork can be seen as an orchestra that is conducted by interchanging conductors, instead of one overarching conductor, which traditionally has been the anthropologist.

Rosaldo points out that since the end of the 1960s, the field of anthropology has been involved in a creative process of redefinition that exposes the fallacy of impartiality for anthropologists, who are, after final analysis, also people with embedded agendas, systems of beliefs, feelings, theoretical biases, and much more. "The shift in social thought has made questions of conflict, change, and inequality increasingly urgent.... Borderlands surface not only at the boundaries of officially recognized cultural units, but also at less formal intersections, such as those of gender, age, status, and distinctive life experiences" (Rosaldo 1989:24–45; See also Marcus 1992; Clifford and Marcus 1986; Clifford 1988).[16] Clifford addresses the hegemony of anthropological abstractions based on the academy's certification and sanction of qualified social science scholars. Such academic practices resulted in specific textual results that placed the anthropologist in extremely powerful positions of social, political, and cultural authority without necessarily exposing their mental, intellectual, and emotional biases. In the case studies presented here, the life circumstances of my informants reflect their extreme poverty and the social inequalities they face every day, while my responses reflect my culturally privileged stance as a liberal, American, middle-class, white, Anglo-Saxon, female anthropologist. Showing the collision of these two worlds through the narrative inclusion of my own thoughts and reactions, despite my anthropological training to achieve a modicum of objectivity, is a textual tool that can reveal a great deal about my biases and my interactions with my informants while remaining true to their words, thoughts, and experiences.

As Rosaldo points out, the ethnographer of the past was imbued with the agendas of imperialism and an unquestioned notion of objectivism. These ethnographies created a body of anthropological knowledge that could be produced only by the academic elite, who shared a naïve collective ideology of the superiority of Western

European society and its "sciences." It is this naïveté that has undergone extensive literary investigation in anthropology. James Clifford states

> ...that the West can no longer present itself as the unique purveyor of anthropological knowledge about others, it has become necessary to imagine a world of generalized ethnography. With expanded communication and intercultural influence, people interpret others, and themselves, in a bewildering diversity of idioms, a global condition of what Mikhail Bakhtin (1953) called "heteroglossia" (1988:22).

Even without considering expanded communication technologies, the anthropologist in the field, with or without technological tools, no longer can ignore their own interpretations of what they see, feel, react to, think, and hence write about. It is possible, perhaps, to liken my textual treatment of these two case histories to the posthumously published diaries of Malinowski, except I chose to place my thoughts alongside my data. When anthropologists read Malinowski's published diaries for the first time, some reacted with a sense of outrage and recognition. We all react, we all censure our reactions so that others may see what we want them to see about us. The anthropologist should know better, and let the chips fall where they may by exposing themselves, as well as their informants, in their writing. Erving Goffman's work in the 1970s explicated how, as anthropologists, we must become aware of multiple realities if we are to have any hope of capturing the complexities of qualitative experiences (1974; 1959). It is in this spirit that I have chosen to present the following case studies in the form of a dialogue infused with my impressions and thoughts. My intention is to present these two interviews as a literal record, with myself as the contextualized "other."

In this way, I take a stand as an anthropologist by exposing my biases as a human being responding to very physically difficult and emotionally draining situations, as a social scientist trying to distance myself but finding it an impossible task, and as a woman who is in touch with and responds to her emotions. I feel that I must be as honest with my own feelings as my informants are with theirs. In these interviews, Stefany and two of her sons share their life stories with clarity, honesty, and emotion while they reveal the prevalence of alcoholism, abuse, racism, and the daily struggle for survival they face among the poor in Morro de Santana.

CASE STUDY NUMBER ONE
The Twins: A Narrated Life History of Twelve-Year-Old Twins
Enzo and Vitor

"I usually do interviews with only one person, but today we'll work together because you are twins, right?" "Yes, we are twins," Enzo answers for both himself and Vitor. "Could you tell me your names, please?" "Our complete names?" Enzo asks. "Yes, your complete name," I say. "My name is Enzo da Araújo." "And how old are you?" I ask. "I am twelve years old." "And Vitor?" I ask, turning to the other boy. "Vitor da Araújo, twelve years as well," Vitor stated, looking down at the ground. I ask, "And you're boys, right?" "We are," stated Enzo. No one laughs except me. "Not girls…and in your family how many children are there…in your house? How many boys and girls?" I ask. Both twins spoke at once, in unison. "We have, we have, we have…Murilo, one boy is called Murilo."

The twins were sitting far away from me in a cement shack we used for our music class. I chose to have our conversation here so we could have some privacy and a little quiet. Viva Crianças was always echoing with the thunder of shouting and yelling. It was truly deafening. My music shack was next to a wood-cutting business. The noise at times rivaled the project when the whine of the saws cut through hard woods. "Come closer," I say. *They scoot their metal stools close to me and lean over to talk into the microphone.* Vitor continues, "Boy…girl, we have one. In the house there are four men, that includes us. The other man is called Davi and the girl is called Sabrina. "Uh-huh," I say. "How old are they?" I ask. "Sabrina is ten, Davi is eight, and Murilo is seven," says Vitor. "OK, so there are a total of five, right?" I ask. "Yes, five people…six with my mother."

"Do you live with your father also?" I ask. "No, no…he separated from my mother because he drank a lot, and then he suffered a hemorrhage in his brain and then he went to live with my Aunt," *Enzo and Vitor answer in unison again. It's uncanny how in sync they are.* "He had…what did you say?" I ask. "He had a cerebral hemorrhage," Enzo said. I still wasn't sure so I ask, "Did he fall?" "No, he broke because he drank a lot," Enzo says matter-of-factly. "Ah! Because of alcohol," I say. "Yes, yes," the twins answer jointly. I tell them, "My mother drank too, now she doesn't drink because she's dead. But I think that when a person drinks, it's very difficult. Was your father violent when he drank?" *I confess and ask at the same time.*

"He was aggressive, hitting my mother, and one time…the last time that he was there he almost yanked her hair completely out," Enzo says. "Did she go to the hospital?" I ask. "No, no…because then he kept pulling her hair and it didn't want to come out. When it was the next day my mother was combing her hair and a lot of hair fell out. She had to cut her hair because he pulled and pulled. He never pulled out blood from her, no." "Did he hit you all too?" I ask. "When he drank?" Enzo asks me. "Uh-huh," I say, nodding. "He one time…he tried to hit…but…," Enzo began, but let his words trail off. Vitor continued, "On our birthday, he wanted to hit our mother, but we begged him, and he kicked me with his boot!" Vitor said. "Now since he's not drinking it's very good." *Enzo finished his brother's account with an attempt at being positive.* "Do you see him?" I ask. "Yes, more or less. Almost every Sunday we go and visit with him at my Aunt's house," again the twins answer together. "Does your aunt live in Morro de Santana?" I ask. "Yes, in *Jardim Paraíso* (Paradise Gardens)." "What kind of work did he do?" "He was a tractor driver, he was everything, but he was mainly a tractor driver," Enzo and Vitor each took parts of the sentence, looking at each other and nodding. "He drove...," says Enzo, "Farm equipment," finished Vitor.

"OK, what type of work does your mother do?" Vitor looks at his brother and then at me. "My mother was a domestic maid, including she left her work yesterday because the people didn't pay her right. So she left her work." "Did she work in the city center?" I ask. "Yes, in the center of the city," says Vitor. "She worked in only one house, in the house of only one family. She began working every day at seven o'clock, each day she arrived at this house at this time. And she arrived at home about six o'clock more or less. She worked only from Monday to Saturday."

"Do you know how much money she made?" Both boys answered, "$R120...but the *dona* didn't pay her right, so she left yesterday." *I had met the twins on the street the other day. They'd been selling ice cream. I ask them how long they've been selling on the streets.* "I began selling ice cream in the cart on Tuesday. I have worked for these ice cream businesses many times, but I've been working now for three days. "How long do you think you'll work selling ice cream this time?" I ask. "I don't know...because my mother quit her job and we need to sell ice cream. I didn't want to work...to stop going to the project," says Vitor. "I can't work and go to the project because we go to school in the morning and in the afternoon we go to the project or we sell icecream."

"How much money do you make a day selling ice cream?" Vitor tells me, "the day before yesterday, he got $R1.00 and I got $R2.00." "So you got a total of $R3.00?" "No," Vitor says, "We had a total of $R5.30. The money that we make…the *dona* takes out almost half. We get the rest." Enzo says, "I took home one real and…" Vitor finishes the sentence saying, "and I took home two real. And the other days that we've been working Enzo was making about $R2.95. And then he made one more and I made two. That's about $R5.00. Yesterday I made $R.95." "OK," I say. "So, for example, if you both make $R6.00, you must give her almost $R3.00?" Vitor says, "She takes almost half for herself and gives us the other half."

"Do you give the money you make to your mother?" I want to know. "Everything to our mother," nods Vitor. "Is your mother, is she loving with you?" I ask. The twins reply together, "Yes, very." "Do you think that your mother is a friend to you?" "I think she is, yes I think so," they nod. They often talk about a thought as if it belongs to both of them. "How often does she hit you?" I ask bluntly. "No…it's very hard for her to hit us. She only hits us when we really need it," both twins say, nodding. *In the homes of the upper class, I haven't seen children and adolescents held responsible for working and earning money, nor have I seen them hit for not being responsible for their siblings or for cleaning the house.* "Enzo and Vitor," I want to say, "you need to know how different your life is to those who classify you as deviant." *Is it that we live so completely within our own reality that we can't see injustice as it tears at our fabric, pushing us to try harder, harder, harder…? Why aren't these youths angry? Why aren't they enraged at their poverty? Do they know the degree of their poverty? Are they angry? If so, why don't they scream at me? Where is their anger kept?*

"How many days per week do you go to Viva Crianças?" I ask. Vitor asks, "how many times per week?" I nod. "One time, because the rest of the days we are working and helping at home." Enzo looks at me, "Cleaning house, washing clothes, these things, making beans." I ask, "If you didn't need to work—" I wasn't able to finish my question. Enzo asked, "You mean, need to sell ice cream?" "Yes," I reply. "Ah, then, we'd go every day," Vitor stated. "Even though you have to help at home?" I ask. "Uh-huh." To Vitor, helping at home isn't work, it's what he does every day. Again I ask, "What kind of work do you do every day to help your mother?" "We clean the house, wash clothes, wash dishes, make lunch, if we—" Startled, I ask, "You make lunch?" "We make breakfast too," the twins say. I ask them what kinds of food they eat every day. "We only have coffee…we don't have a very good life. Sometimes coffee with bread," Enzo replies. I ask if their coffee is black or if they put milk into their coffee. "Sometimes…where my mother worked, she got one liter of milk a day and she'd bring that home for us. But she left this work, remember? They didn't pay her right," Vitor tells me. "So we eat bread, salt bread and sometimes we get some *cana de açúcar* (sugar cane) to suck on." I ask, "And what do you eat for lunch?" "Every Sunday when our mother is here, we have rice, beans, a little potatoes and maybe some chicken. She cooks this for us. During the week, Monday through Friday we make the food and sometimes on Saturdays we cook too," Vitor tells me. I want to know what they have for dinner. "We make what we have left over from lunch. For example…today I will come home and I'll make dinner. Today's dinner will also be tomorrow's lunch for my other brothers and sister. So, I'll go to the project, when I can, and I'll eat at the project," Vitor explains. *What I came to know is that the twins usually ate rice and beans. There was no other food except what they were able to get as a snack at school or what they ate at Viva Crianças for lunch when they were able to go.*

I ask, "Do you get to take food home from the project?" "No," both boys answer. "Sometimes at home we have some vegetables and macaroni, but we don't like to eat it. We eat it when we don't have anything else, or we just eat rice and beans. Usually we drink water or coffee…sometimes my mother buys juice and we make it and drink it," said Vitor. "OK," I say. "So you don't have any milk to drink, just to put in your coffee?" "That's right," says Vitor, "now the milk we were able to have every day is gone."

I return to the subject of Viva Crianças. I want to know how many children in their family go to the project every day. "At times I go, and Enzo, and Sabrina, but mostly it's just Enzo and I. My sister stays home more to help my mother. We usually come home after school or from working in the streets or going to the project around 6:00 pm. Then we start to help our mother until about 7:00 pm. That's when dinner is ready. So between six and seven we help her clean the house every day. Everything is divided because there's a lot of people and if everything was done by just one person, that person wouldn't have time to do it all. So sometimes we wash the clothes and other times it's my mother or our brothers or sister. But mostly it's us," Enzo and Vitor tell me, taking turns as they talk.

Usually the twins and their siblings are in school every day for four hours. The twins go to school in the mornings from 7:15 to 11:15. They told me they usually don't have a lot of homework because the teachers don't have enough books and materials. Usually everyone has to do their work, what there is of it, in school. Both twins could read and write and do basic mathematics. Both boys told me they liked to read comics and books with illustrations. They also liked reading stories and playing games, especially futebol (soccer).

"Your mother, does she read?" I ask. "No…she's illiterate. She never had the opportunity to learn to read. She doesn't know how to read or write. She didn't go to school. She just knows how to write this way: we write her name on a piece of paper and give it to her to copy. She can write out the letters like that. She doesn't know any math, but she knows everything about money," the twins tell me. I ask them to tell me about their mother, about her life and their life with her.

"Our mother was born in *Govia*...," says Enzo, who is interrupted by Vitor. "No, *Govia* is where her sister lives. My mother didn't really know her brothers and sisters. When she was little, they were all separated. Her mother and father died and they (all the children) were given to different people. We didn't know our grandparents... they died early, very early when our mother was a little girl. They died from some kind of disease. We don't know what kind. One...my grandmother died because of the heart...but my grandfather, I don't know what he died from." The twins are sharing the story; one talks for a while and then the other begins.

"Our mother lived with her stepfather and stepmother, but her stepmother was more than a stepmother. She made her into a housemaid, a servant, and demanded that she clean the house. It was a very big house. Today this woman who made her clean her house is my godmother," says Vitor. "And it was when my mother was about six years old that she began to work. She first stayed for a while with these people, but when she was six, she began to work for her stepmother, cleaning the house, washing the clothes, ironing the clothes," continued Enzo.

"She had a very hard life. Very few people were kind to her and they were only kind for a little while. Because the people who came into that house stayed away from our kind of pain. My mother's name is Stefany. She is now 33 years old," Enzo tells me. Vitor continues, "We began, my brother and I, going to school when were about seven. We went to school in the Alto Bom Jesus to a school called The Municipal School of Good Adventures. Now we go to the State Municipal School."

"When we were little, what I remember is that my brother and I and my other brothers and sister had a lot of illnesses. Kinds of infections. Because of our blood…it was very bad. When we were very little my mother saw many flies and mosquitoes in the bedroom. She went into the bedroom and saw that my brother was full of insects. He had all these sores on his head and the insects were laying eggs in his sores. She didn't go to the hospital because my father didn't want to take him…no. My mother tried many kinds of medicines (*I later learned that she had tried many popular herbs*) until they were all used up. He didn't want to take him to the doctor…I think because he was drinking and was drunk. He was sleeping and didn't want to wake up. We know many fathers, fathers of our friends that drink. They don't drink a lot or a little. They just drink. The same as our father…he drank a lot until one day, he stopped. *It's common to drink in the favelas. It's perhaps one form of relief from the pain of poverty and the hunger of poverty. It's an escape from the cries of hungry children, angry wives, and desperate fears.*

"Our father is stupid in his head now…he doesn't recognize or know anyone. He stopped drinking when he had his cerebral hemorrhage. A majority of fathers drink. We know a man here who drinks a whole lot. There is a lot of violence against women too. Principally we are talking about the man who drinks a lot. His children hit him now because they are all men now. Or his wife hits him because he ruined everything with his drinking. My cousin drinks a lot. Everyone begins to fight, everyone fights. One time one person threw another into a ditch. And one time one person cut the head of another person. We are afraid a lot of the time. Of the streets in our *favela*." Enzo is afraid of the streets in his *favela*, but Vitor isn't. "At night we don't stay on the street. I don't feel a lot of fear. I'm not afraid that the fight will take me," says Vitor.

I ask, "When your father was yelling at your mother and was hitting her, what did you do?" "We were crying, because we were very little, and we just cried, screaming for my cousin to help and to stop my father. We tried to separate them but my mother would order us out of the room so we wouldn't be traumatized. But nothing we did helped. He hit us when we got close," Vitor said. "When he was drinking and fighting we were really afraid of him," Vitor and Enzo agreed, nodding. "When he was hitting us and our mother, he yelled a lot. He also spoke *palavrões*...horrible, coarse words to us and to our mother. He called her a girl...told her she wasn't a woman...told her she was a woman of the night. This was all very difficult to hear. My cousin's wife, when she is drunk, she says absurd things and no one wants to be around her. A person that is strong isn't like this," said Enzo thoughtfully.

Vitor remembered a time when he was very sick. "I couldn't even take water. I couldn't run a lot. I couldn't, for example, if I left home without eating...I didn't have the strength to walk. I felt really bad. I couldn't get enough air. I was about eight or nine. I coughed a lot and at times it seemed that everything would explode." Enzo tells me that they use herbs to try to control their head lice. "We've had lots of them. We cut our hair a lot and take out the lice. We use herbs for them too, but we also use a soap (*the project makes an herbal soap that isn't very effective for head lice*) and a small comb. Head lice are normal here," says Enzo. "There's lots of head lice in the schools." *There are lots of head lice in the public schools and in the favelas and in the projects. The poor are used to them.*

"Can you tell me about your house?" I ask. "There are two bedrooms, one for my mother and ours, where I and Vitor and my other brother sleep on a single bed. My mother sleeps with my sister on a newer bed, a double bed. We're used to sleeping with three in a single bed," Enzo tells me. *When I visited their home, I saw the beds, including the "newer" double bed. These were old used mattresses, full of holes and stains.* "We don't have a bathroom in the house. We use the bushes. We take a bath in cold water...we have to get it and then splash it because we don't have a bath or a shower." *I learned later that it was common for the twins and their siblings to bathe in the polluted streams and rivers not far from where they lived in the Alto Bom Jesus.* "We try to take a bath about three times a week," Enzo told me.

The twins told me they liked going to Viva Crianças because they learned how to make things like soap and paper. They liked the project also because they were learning something about gardening. It was at the project that they ate foods they normally wouldn't have, like vegetables and a little meat and margarine. They could play soccer too. The project wasn't so good in some ways. The older boys were often violent and hit the younger boys. The coordinators didn't do anything about such fights. The twins also felt that the project wasn't preparing them to get a job. Like most working street youth, getting a better job was a priority without hope.

I ask the twins about the violence they experience at Viva Crianças. Since the coordinators didn't do anything to control the older youth and their violence, I wanted to know if they felt the coordinators should talk to the older youth about their behavior. "I think it would be much better, because whenever we go and talk to Alana, Maria Vitória, or Giovanni they don't go with us and talk to the older boys. They don't talk to these boys. And, if they did, the older boys would invent lots of things about us. We think that the adolescents at the project have too much liberty, without responsibility," both Enzo and Vitor agree. When I ask them what they thought should be done, Vitor responded, "If it was up to me, I wouldn't put them in the same place as a servant, but they need to do some service and work at the project, because it shouldn't be just a place to play and fight. There have to be consequences. If it was up to me, I would say this, if they don't stop acting this way, hitting small boys, then they have to leave the project and be isolated from the project," Vitor says emphatically. "Then I'd make a meeting with their parents and talk to them."

I ask the twins what kind of work they want to do in the future. "I want to work in a firm. If I could, I would like to work and let my mother stay at home. This is one of the things I would change to make a better life for us now," says Vitor. Enzo adds, "I too would do almost the same thing...help people. If I had an opportunity to make my life better, I would like to buy a better house and find a way to have my mother stay at home and relieve her suffering so she won't have to suffer as much as she has in the past."

Vitor says, "The more I hear about how people are assaulted by a thief, the more fear I have of this." "Me too," says Enzo. "We don't have a house with any security. I'm afraid too." *The twins lived in a house without glass or metal coverings over their windows. They were covered only with a piece of cloth. The door was an old piece of wood, broken and frayed, jagged with splinters.* "We're afraid also of being homeless, and afraid of losing our mother. We're really afraid of that." The twins nod. "We don't have any relatives that would help us. I think that my mother has a lot of responsibility. If we arrived at some point where we are begging in the streets it would be because there was absolutely no other way, no other way," Vitor says. Enzo continues, "We were talking about relatives...they abandoned my mother... my mother works so she won't lose us, and they never come and help us, never!" Vitor cuts in, "In the case that we wouldn't have a house and have to beg on the streets, we would find one of our aunts or go to a farm where we'd work." I ask if they would go to the project and ask them for help. Enzo and Vitor both shake their heads no. "Why?" I ask. "Because I'd have lots of shame," Vitor replied.

"Who do you have the most trust in?" I ask. "I have the most trust in myself and my mother," says Vitor. "We're Catholic but we only go to church once in a while because we don't have time...we do talk to God. Many times," says Vitor, "when we lie down we have to pray and ask God for health." *I don't know why, but at this point I ask the twins what the worst thing is a person could say against them.* Vitor tells me, "To curse my mother…to call her a *rapariga* (a girl without responsibility) or a *puta* (a prostitute), these kinds of things."

The twins didn't seem to be aware of the notion of "rights" and the significance of them for children until I prompted them. As our discussion continued to explore what "rights" meant, they demonstrated an increased and heightened awareness about rights within their own lives. "There are rights to go away and to come," Enzo tells me. "Everyone needs to have rights," says Vitor. "Children need to have the same rights as adults," both Enzo and Vitor say. "We need to have the right to work so that we can help our mother…and the right to study…to play. But adults need to play as well," the twins say. "But they don't have the time as adults, to play." Vitor tells me, "If they (adults) had time every once in a while to play with us, for example, if we were the only children of my mother—I would really like it if my mother would have time to play with us."

"I think it's a good idea that children work in the streets and earn money selling things," the twins say. Vitor continues, "I think it is, how do you say…like the other day, a free space to have the freedom to sell. I think we need to grow up and become an adult, not to be a thief or a person who smokes dope." Enzo adds, "I too, I think the same as him. To give a little hand and help. I think it's good to go to school and to do light work, work that doesn't exploit us. I don't agree with putting kids into places to make charcoal…that's bad work." Vitor adds, "I think a child should get half the salary of an adult, about $R5 a day to give to their mother. Certain kids use their money on silly things."

Our interview came to an end at this point. But I was to talk many times with the twins over the next year and a half. They continued to work both at home and in the streets while struggling to stay in school and encouraging their siblings to do the same. One day, the boys told me they wished they could afford to take a computer course because it would help them get a better job. It was also a dream of their mother's. It will never happen for them unless they find a benefactor. I came to understand that poor youth viewed idleness as dangerous. The end result of idleness was crime and degeneration. Ironic. Wealthy youth perceived poor working youth as dangerous and immoral. Such inversions sustain the separation between classes and "races," while creating stereotypes about the darker-skinned poor that foster social inequalities. How stunning, how revealing to comprehend the power of perceptions. I keep coming back to the arc of history, to slavery. The twins are still enslaved by social injustice, by class divisions based on racial inferiority. Jean-Bertrand Aristide (Haiti's president in 1994) wrote:

> In Haitian iconography the zombie is one whose soul has been stolen in order to enslave his body to his master. The powerful fear evoked by the fate of the Zombie in Haitian consciousness stems from the collective memory of slavery. To wake the zombie, to free his soul, you must give him a taste of salt. (2000:53).

For the Haitian, "a taste of salt" implies a return to native intelligence and a severance from the enslavement of the master/slave relation. There is a reminiscent call here. This time to a recent past, to the work of Paulo Freire. Yet, the "pedagogy of the oppressed" can't compete with globalization.

Viva Crianças embraced Freire's work and ideologies by rooting its programs in popular culture. The twins, along with more than one hundred other youths, spent their days making toys from recyclables found in the garbage, planting in the project's garden seeds their parents can't afford to buy, creating theater from Grimm's fairytales, and playing soccer while they dream of being another Pele—their chances are slim, at best.

Conclusion

Vitor and Enzo were selected as a case study because their life story is descriptive of and similar to that of most of the children studied in my formal sample. In addition, Vitor and Enzo became close friends of mine and were eager to share their life story and family life with me. Finally, their mother Stefany (case study number two) and I developed a close friendship during my fieldwork. Stefany is a clear and articulate woman whose life story is sadly representative of many poor women in Morro de Santana and other rural and/or urban areas.

I did not find any exceptions to poor families' working relationships with their employers; the patron–client system was universally true in my formal sample of street children, their parents, and of other poor families I came to know.

While it was the norm for the street children in my sample to experience alcoholism and various forms of abuse (physical, emotional, and sexual) in their families, they were loved by their parents, who demonstrated their affection in ways that were unfamiliar to me; usually with a pat on the shoulder as a greeting, a short acknowledgment in the form of a greeting, or what seemed to me to be in a harsh tone of voice. Hitting was normal and frequent, as was the expectation of obedience. The street youth I knew who had left home did so because of extreme abuse, either from an older sibling (usually an older brother) or an alcoholic mother or father.

One exception existed in my sample of street youth and their parents. In this family, the boy, age nine in 1997, lived with his mother, stepfather, and brother. Discussions with the mother and observations over time during visits to their home revealed behaviors more similar to middle- and upper-class treatment of children. The mother often talked to her son about his day and discussed issues of importance with him regularly. She was often affectionate and hugged her children frequently. She and her husband were non-drinkers and they both worked: she as a maid and he as a truck driver.

The twins' desire to work and their keen sense of children's rights were common among my formal sample of street youth. They often discussed issues of human rights and abuses of human rights with a highly developed emotional intelligence, using concepts frequently not considered part of a child's intellectual and emotional vocabulary.

The second case history presented next is the story of Stefany. The difficulties faced by Stefany and her children unfortunately reflect the norm for the children and their families in my sample.

CASE STUDY NUMBER TWO
Mother of the Twins

"*What would I change? What would I change?*" *Stefany repeats the question. Did I really ask her this—surely I must be joking?* "Ah Marcia, everything" (Field interview).

>It was a hot evening. Dust drifted down on us in an unceasing cloud as the wind, cars, foot traffic, dogs, and running adolescents passed us by. We must have looked suspicious…or rather I must have, with my Sony professional recorder on my lap and my high-tech microphone in hand. I sat on a tree stump; Stefany sat on an overturned bucket, and Ricardo, her lean neighbor, squatted on his heels. Above the *favela* Bom Jesus we came together to talk, about life, hardship, abuse,

ignorance, and love. Stefany and I had planned this meeting; Ricardo just happened along.

"In my country, the US, we have a lot of corruption, too. We have inequality, racism…but the laws that we have don't just stay on paper. There's more equality there, at least on the surface, when compared to Brazil," I say.

"There's inequality there?" Stefany asks. And I reply, "I'm certain of it."

"Well, it's very difficult for us to talk about a country that we don't know," Ricardo interjects.

"Yeah, it's difficult…I know," I say.

"Because we sometimes see things on the TV, that something happened in this or that country. Sometimes it's something good, or sometimes something bad happens and that's put on too. Therefore, the way it's presented, as good or bad, affects us, tells us how to think about a country. We don't know if *favelas* (shantytowns, slums) exist in other countries," Ricardo says.

"Oh yes, they exist," I say. "It's a problem throughout the entire world."

Ricardo explodes in rapid speech, "We have a community here that is very poor, all the money we give in taxes will be taken away to some other place and thrown away, while our community stays in need. The hospital has many needs…they are shutting down! There are so many necessities that aren't being attended to because we don't have any money. What are we going to do? How can we study this problem?" *There's a kind of pleading anger in Ricardo's voice, and his astute awareness is common, rather than rare. Yet, I'm frustrated. How can people be aware of the causes of their misery and do nothing, especially if they are the majority? In Morro de Santana, the poor outnumber the middle and upper classes.*

"But Brazil needs to pay attention to its people. I know that it's been only a little over ten years since the military regime, and that you don't have a strong history of fighting against racism and oppression and winning. But if these things are to change, you have to fight against them, every day." *My voice sounds to me as if it's holding at bay a flood of potential violence, and I wonder at the visions of holocaust that seem to come frequently to my imagination when I think about Brazil and civil rights.* "Ha!" I say, "Laws in Brazil exist, but they stay on the paper!"

"It's not law, it's money! A law!" Ricardo spits out his contempt. "For example, to put it simply, if you are arrested and you go to jail, you're free if you pay money to some policeman, you're set free and nothing has been corrected. So, the 'law' wasn't worth anything, there's no law. The law is just easy to replace with money. Many things that we see in our country are divided like this. We actually have an unwritten law that sanctions killing. Do you understand the problem? For example, because a person is poor and has no way to survive and steals, he can easily die. e will be an example for the rest of the poor. You understand the problem? The funny question is this: Who would want to exchange death for life without having a way to live? So, I decide I'm going to do what I want…either way it's the same." *As I heard Ricardo talk about his perception of police impunity, I tried to understand such brutality in theoretical terms. Witnessing the hard poverty of Brazil, I have at times longed to understand economic violence and social inequality in divine terms, searching for religious or spiritual metaphors or parables that might explain the source of inequality, brutality, and suffering. Are we working it out? It doesn't seem so.*

Ricardo is like the dust: he drifts away and leaves us sitting on the stump and bucket, blinking the grit deeper into our eyes. Stefany coughs, I sneeze.

"The other day, your children told me about their reality. I want to know about yours. I'll begin by asking you things that are easy… like, how old are you?" *I probe (please, I beg, I suppose of myself. How do I do this? It's so, so, fragile poking into the private places of people's lives).*

"I'm 34. I was born in *Costa Sena*, it's close to *Morro de Santana*. It's a lot hotter there," Stefany says. "There were, if we all lived, there were ten of us altogether. God took two…no it was three. There are five women and two men now. One was born with a problem and the others died after they were older from different kinds of diseases that made them bloat and swell. We lived on a *roça* (a plot of land without resources, where the rural poor eke out a living, often by caring for rich people's land and animals for one minimum salary or less a month). We didn't have any medicine, we didn't have any resources. Understand? There wasn't anything, where I was living, there wasn't anything. My brother was very young when he died, one or two years old when he died. I saw my brothers and sister die, I came home and saw it, but I was very young. I didn't understand those things. I didn't understand that my mother had just lost a child."

"Yes," I nod. "You can't cry a lot, because you have to survive," I say.

"No, you can't, huh, Marcia?" says Stefany. "But we didn't have the same things, the same problems with people being killed or the things that happen in the *favela*. We were very poor, but we didn't have the same things happen to us as in the big city," she continues. *I blink, my eyes hurt, and I see little difference between the death on the roça and death in the favela, but I say nothing, nodding.*

"My mother died when I was very young. First my father died. He was about 30, I think, and soon after my mother died. I'm not sure, but I think my father may have died of alcoholism and my mother from childbirth. My parents didn't hit us, I don't remember that, but my father hit my mother. I don't know where they were from, where they were born. The people that mistreated me were the people that raised me.

"When my parents died, I was left with all my brothers and sisters, who were also very young. One day, a man from Villa Nova came. He was newly married and he took me with him from the house of another woman who lived on the *roça* too. My other brothers and sisters…well, one stayed on the *roça* alone. The rest, well… we lost contact. I don't know if some are still living or not. I only have contact with one who lives in Gouveia," Stefany tells me this, fluidly. *Firecrackers explode close by, very powerful ones and, even though I'm used to them by now, I hunch over the safety of my tape recorder, my link to some sense of illusory and privileged living, as if it could transport me to safety, to a world where longevity has a chance. (Brazil has a passion for soccer, and it's a year-round event accompanied by exploding sounds, announcing a "Gooooooal!")* "Where's Gouveia?" I ask, while Stefany and I wipe our eyes with dirty fingers, digging the grit from our tear ducts.

"It's past Inimutaba," Stefany says. "In Minas, right?" I ask. "That's right," she says.

"I grew up in Morro de Santana. The family that raised me lives in Morro de Santana. I mean they lived in Cosa Siena and then we moved to Morro de Santana. I was very little. The wife of this man that took me was a teacher…she was a woman like a policeman! She taught me how to cook by putting a small bench in front of the oven, and I learned how to cook that way."

One of the twins interrupts us. "But, he is really not feeling good."

"No, we aren't going now. Sit here and keep quiet," says Stefany.

"What's happening?" I ask. "Oh, a person on the road isn't feeling good and he wants me to go," Stefany says, *and without missing a breath, continues with her story. Life is like that here, it doesn't miss a beat, and if it does, it simply changes rhythms from common time to syncopated multi-rhythms...always moving on. It's just the way it is.*

"When I arrived there, the woman who raised me treated me very badly. She put me in school at night so I could work during the day, but I had to clean the house every day."

"Was she white or black, rich or what?" I ask.

"Ah, she was white and rich. She was upper class. I don't remember too well how old I was. It was the time when my mother died, I was very little. I was taken in by others, and then by this woman. I think I was about four maybe, but I don't remember when I started working...I was very young. She had children of her own and they are all grown up now and are so tall and strong...so strong that they couldn't pass through my doorway. I raised them all. She was a professor and she never arranged her time so that she could say 'let me help you with your homework.' I was the youngest, and she put me in school. She did it in a way that was acid...she always arranged things in such a way that I couldn't study at night. I was the last to arrive at school and the first to leave. She always came and got me early. And then she made up stories that I was cutting school, watching *novelas* (similar to an American TV soap opera), and when I became an adolescent, she said that I cut classes so I could meet boyfriends. So, I was never able to get through the first year of school. I never cut classes, not for anything, Marcia! Not for anything! But, her children, they cut classes. She used to hit me a lot...understand? I have a revolt inside me against her. She hit me a lot and drew blood...using her hand, a broom, a chair...."

"A chair?" I ask—*did I hear her say* a chair*?*

"Yes, a chair. She took it and hit me with it. It had a red pillow, like this." Stefany makes a round, puffy shape with her hands. "I don't know if you remember these—they had little tiny feet made of iron. One time, she commanded me to get that chair and bring it over to her…a simple thing. I was ironing clothes for her sister because she needed them to go to a party. It was very late…after 11:00 pm. I was falling asleep and almost burned myself. I often ironed late into the night. Well, her boy came up to me and was hanging on my arm and I was so tired I couldn't stand and I began to fall over. He fell away when I swayed on my feet. She saw that and started to hit me, saying that I tried to hurt her son. She came at me like a panther, and she picked up that chair and hit me in the mouth, and cut my mouth. It was swollen and full of blood. I was splattered with blood all over my clothes. My arms were bruised, like this Marcia. I looked like I had a sickness of the skin and body—all because of her rage. I was red and bruised. She had long nails and she grabbed my ear and her nail was so long it cut my ear inside and it began to bleed and drip over my clothes, like this. She was a professor and she gave classes. My life, it has never had anything good," *Stefany states, matter-of-factly. Another car passes, throws sheets of dust over us. We're silent as we let the dust settle.*

"She turned everything into confusion. She did this with everything—she'd say, 'get the scissors' and I'd do it and then she'd grab me where my hair was tied up and hit me in the head with the scissors. Many times I'd be working on the weekend in the house, making *pão de queijo* (cheese bread) and cleaning the house, washing the cans that coffee comes in. She'd arrive at the house in the afternoon and just take a bath, or eat all the cookies, or drink coffee, or take a small lunch before going to church. She would watch me all the time and she'd hit me horribly, a lot, all the time. I never liked to stay in the house, but I couldn't go out. She threw hot coffee in my face, hot coffee—this is the woman who raised me."

"How did you meet her?" I ask again. "I told you, my mother died and left us—the girls, well—people knew that they could use us to work in their homes. This woman's husband came and took me.

He told me that they would care for me, that I'd be like a daughter to them, but it was just the opposite. They just came and took me. That's it. I didn't have anything to give her. I didn't have any clothes or anything at that time. He told me his wife was a professor and that she wanted a girl to raise. But really, she raised me for only one year—then I became her maid.

"After a while, I had a boyfriend with a good face, and I felt that life was a little better. She told me that I couldn't have a boyfriend. Her sister had a boyfriend, but he was white and rich, but I was black and ugly. Then, one day, she told me that I would never get married and leave her house because I was a maid and I was black and ugly, just like a dog. She said these things to me. She was a religious person. How can it be? So—I stayed like this, wanting to run away. I couldn't receive a message or anything from anyone. I couldn't do anything, you know? I thought about running away, but I didn't know how. When she would go out she would lock all the doors and keep the key. I stayed locked in like a prisoner while she would visit a friend, or whatever. I didn't start school until I was eleven—I couldn't learn anything. I had to wash, iron, make cookies for them, do everything. I woke up at 4:30 every day. I never slept any later than that. Sometimes I had to wake up earlier. Until today, I wake up, ready at this hour. I worked every day, Sundays too. She eventually chose my husband for me—he was poor and an alcoholic."

"Was she a professor in public or private school?" I ask, as if this will explain her behavior.

"I think it was a public school, but I don't remember. I don't know if it's like this everywhere. The rich have the ability to get things—all of us don't have this ability. Now, I don't know if I'm being swindled or not. I can't tell. I only went to one year of school. I can't read or write. Really, it was less than one month that I was in school. She called me out of school almost every time I arrived there.

"After I married, I became pregnant with the twins with a very big stomach. I worked for a woman who lived in front of the project—I've just kept these things in my head. I wasn't born with these horrible things in my head; it was her that put them there. My head isn't very good. It's not a good head," Stefany tells me, shaking her head.

"But you don't have a problem with your mind," *I say, angry now.*

"I don't?" She asks. "But I can't remember things. One time, I was thrown off a horse, me and my brother—there were three of us on the horse. Two of us hit our head. I was dizzy for a long time. I had a lot of headaches. How do you talk about a life that isn't a life? I don't have a way to explain my life." Stefany is crying.

"Yes, but you have your children, even though it's hard with so few resources," I say. *Michael Foucault suggests that punishment, within punitive systems such as prisons, can be regarded as a political tactic (1984:170-178). Here, dividing practices within social systems, such as social classes and racial categories, can be viewed as techniques of domination that are used on the marginal classes. Hence, dividing practices and punishment systems are used together to create oppression. Oppression has a way of regenerating itself, of taking on the character originally imposed upon the oppressed by the oppressor. Stefany assumes that her life "isn't a life." She is at a loss to explain the causes of her suffering and it seems that she assumes responsibility for her suffering.*

"I have a bad mind. I couldn't learn anything because I haven't had any opportunities. I don't know how to write, just my name. If you write out numbers, I can copy them by watching you. I can't read, not a single word." *It's with such finality that Stefany states her case, her lack of mental prowess. It's a huge period at the end of a tiny sentence—I am nothing.*

"I worked in a house in Morro de Santana as a maid, for five years and eight months. I never received a holiday, and I never received money when I worked more than eight hours a day. I never received anything extra. In the end, the *dona* just made my final payment. In the end, cleaning up my accounts there were many pages like these (pointing to my notebook), but the pages were colored. There were red, yellow, blue—there were many pages for me to sign. *(This is a workbook given to domestic servants and other lay laborers who are registered and will eventually receive the equivalent of social security. By law, ironically, it is the maid's responsibility to make sure that everything is signed. Ironic in the light of the rate of illiteracy.)* There was one page that was white, and the woman at the *prefeitura* (mayor's office) told me that I needed to sign it so I could get my benefits. I gave my book to the boys (the twins) to help me find where I needed to sign. I signed it, but not correctly. I signed my name alone, not with my last name. So, they told me that I had to come back. They said that I had to sign it correctly. They wanted to take all my benefits away," Stefany recounts.

"There are times that I get money back after I buy something and I will try to analyze it. I'll go over it. How much did I give and how much did I get back. I'll try to understand if they gave me the wrong change. I'll go back to the store and look and see how much something costs, but I don't know anything about numbers or math." *Further proof to Stefany that she is unequal.*

"Are you married now?" I ask.

"Yes, I'm married. I was 21 when I got married. We were married in a civil and religious ceremony (everything needs to be correct for the upper class. She was raised by the upper class and a good show needs a good performance). My stepmother (*madrasta*) knew that he wouldn't be a good husband because he drank and worked in menial jobs. She knew that he was bad. She wanted me to be with someone who would beat me. She wanted to slap me in my face. She was a witch.

"Now I have five children, my first were the twins, Enzo and Vitor. I went to the hospital to give birth. I didn't have any help while I was pregnant—" I interrupt her and ask if her husband helped her out during this time. "Ha! Marcia—he helped with nothing. It was like this. We are poor and don't have anything, don't have any rights. The INPS (*Instituto Nacional de Presidência Social*, a governmental, low-quality health care system, similar to Medicare in the US, but very slow with very unequal quality of health services and care), they took care of us. With the twins I had problems. I was very swollen and my blood pressure was very high. I stayed in the hospital for one week for observation. I had a caesarian. After, the boys and I stayed one week so they could control my blood pressure. Now, this one here, she almost died," Stefany says, pointing to her daughter. "I wanted to give birth normally. I didn't have a good passage (her pelvis wasn't wide enough), I never did. I stayed one week going and coming from the hospital. I'd go to the hospital and they'd tell me that I wasn't in labor, even though I'd be rolling in pain. They told me to go home. Day after day it was like this. Then they kept me for observation at the hospital and they gave me some serum. All the pain stopped when I was in the hospital, but nothing was happening. Then I was released and went home. On a Saturday or Sunday, I started having pain again, and I was tired of going and having exams and being told that it wasn't time yet. When Saturday came, my water broke and my stomach became small and the baby stayed like this at the top. I kept losing water all night, and I was having sharp pains. She didn't drop down or come out. The water bag was hanging outside me, and the baby stayed on top. She hurt her face and that's when she almost died. Me too—I almost died. After I left the hospital and went home, I got an infection. In all, I gave birth five times. The rest were OK.

"I didn't take any pills (birth control) because I was afraid they would go hungry if I didn't breastfeed them. Their father wouldn't buy any milk for them and I didn't have an invoice (given by the state) to buy milk, and I couldn't buy any. The pill is difficult to get and people said if I take it, your milk will dry up and they will need a bottle, they told me that I wouldn't get pregnant if I was breastfeeding.

"I was pregnant with Sabrina and I didn't know it. I wanted my tubes tied, but it's difficult to arrange this. I don't know if it was a political issue at the time, but you have to have money to have something like that done. So I didn't have it done. I got my papers in order to try to get my tubes tied, and went in to get them tied, but when they cut me open they saw that I was pregnant. After my fifth child, they finally tied my tubes.

"Enzo had problems with his lungs. He had pneumonia. At times he feels pain, usually on the left side of his chest. The doctor says it isn't anything—it's worms. So, they are taking medicines. When he had pneumonia, he was in the hospital. Vitor had the same exam (to check for worms) and he had three kinds of worms, and Davi he had many furious worms. Sabrina was feeling very bad and my husband took her to see the doctor, and he said she had malnutrition. He told us we needed to give her better food to control her growth, to fatten her up. Yes, fruit, vegetables, meat, milk, but how do I get these things? Those that have, they don't give them. I would go out and buy these things but I don't have any money. We don't have a refrigerator, running water, toilet. I work outside the home, Monday through Friday, and get home late on Friday afternoon. I'm working now, planting trees. It's a long way out of the city, and I can't afford to come home after work, so I stay at work during the week. The twins take care of everything. They are responsible for their younger brothers and sister. They have a lot of responsibility. At work, there is a kind of lodge, a kind of barracks where there are ten beds. They have a cook and a dining room. The conditions on the farm are good. There's a bed and we bring our own bedclothes and there's good food. They don't mistreat anyone. I work from 7 in the morning to 5 in the evening (ten hours a day), and I make one minimum salary ($R130 per month), but they take out money each month for my living expenses ($R20.00). I have about $R110 each month."

"You raise your children on $R110 a month?" I ask. "Yes, this month, this week for example, if the director of the group here lays me off for a day or takes a day off, I will not have any money to leave with the boys to buy food. I don't have any money and I can't buy things on credit or trust. This is how it is. For example, another house where I worked, I quit after a short time. For two months I did a lot of work there, and she hasn't paid me yet. I was really nervous today because I saw the woman, the owner of a shop where I owe money. I didn't know if she'd ask me for the money I owe her or not. I gave my boss two months' work, and she hasn't paid me yet. The owner of the store stopped me in the street. She didn't need to do this. I owe her $R30."

"Wait," I say, "during the week, your children stay in the house alone?" "Yes, that's right," Stefany answers. "So, during the week your children are living here alone?" I ask. "Alone," she says. "There's a neighbor, not a relative that lives on the other side of our house. They go to her if there is a problem." *The firecrackers are really blasting away. Someone, somewhere made a goal.* "They (the twins) wake up early and they make coffee for everyone. They go to school, and they also work. This woman wants me to pay her what I owe her, and she says that I won't pay because I'm just a vagabond. I have been very nervous because she says many things about me. I'm waiting to get some money so I can pay her—the money from the other woman I worked for. Logically, the store won't let me have any more credit because I'm so late in my payment. I don't know. It's difficult." *Stefany lets her voice trail off. More firecrackers explode, and a dust devil twists by us, throwing more grit in our faces. We've given up trying to* get it out of our eyes, and we just let them fill with tears that run down our faces.

"What do your children usually eat every day?" I ask. "Rice, beans, they don't like macaroni very much (no one likes it—it's a stigma, a mark of poverty and it's bland and slimy). They eat vegetables only at Viva Crianças. *The irony of the name adds to the irritation and pain in my eyes. How is it that projects in Brazil tend to isolate poor children into such an idealistic world, when their reality forces them into the world of adult indifference? I know I expect too much from projects, but giving children garbage to make toys is not helping them to improve their lives.*

It's as if childhood is a construction that offers refuge to the very adults who created it as an escape from the hardships and realities of indifference, of economic accumulation, of the ever-insistent rush of global forces that seek to insulate human vulnerability. How is it that the images so common to childhood seem to be applied only to the children of the economically privileged? I am discovering in Morro de Santana that the numerous projects created since the 1970s have unintentionally acted as an effective shield against economic, racial, and political change for the children of the poor. Indeed, a child of which class, of which location, of which lucky or unlucky inheritance?

Viva Crianças's ideology seeks to alter the sensibilities of the poor children they work with to match those of the middle-and upper-class staff who design and implement the project. As I talked with Stefany and she revealed to me the extent of her children's hunger, I told her of the following dialogue I had with the project's gardener. "I talked with Sr. Levi first, without talking to Alana (the main coordinator). I went directly to him and I said, 'Look, I talked with two boys. They are twins here at the project and they have a lot of responsibility. They are hungry a lot of the time. I think it would be a good idea if they could take home some vegetables from the project's garden.' I had been told about the project's ideology, about their policy of giving vegetables to the children to take home if they needed it. When I talked with Alana, the director, she laughed, 'Ah, Marcia. They're eating well. They get everything here at the project. They don't need anything. You don't need to worry about them.'

"*Olha só!*" (This means roughly, "How about that!"). "It's really difficult, isn't it? So, what are we going to do? They (the project) know about our situation. They could take what they throw away, and they could give it to the kids who need it. How can we live?" Stefany looks at her hands, studying them and shaking her head. "This is their way. So, I buy what I can, rice, beans, macaroni, oil, soap for head lice, some coffee...we often don't have sugar—but the thing that we need and don't have is meat and vegetables."

I ask, "Do you have milk?"

"No, we don't have any," she says. *I ask if they sometimes buy cheese, and then remember that cheese is more expensive than milk.* "Your children, they work in the streets selling ice cream to help you. They told me that they had to work so they could help, that they wanted to help you, and they told me that they usually get about $R3 a day."

"Sometimes. They have never brought home $R3. It's usually $R2 or less than that. Sometimes it's very little. It's always like this, they never earn more than this. When I'm here, I send them out to sell and they give me what they earn. Now, they go to the project and go to school in the mornings. They come home for lunch or eat at the project. Sometimes they sell on the streets and other times they don't."

At this rate, the twins are earning approximately 35 percent of the household income (Stefany=$R100, twins=$R40–45, @$R2 per day, five days a week. According to the twins they are working every day now, while their mother works at the tree-planting company. Parents are reluctant to talk about how much their underage children work).

Stefany looks tired and drawn and I ask her if she's tired. "Really tired, but no I don't want to stop," she says. "My boys go to the project every day, Monday through Friday. I heard from other people that it was a good place, where they could play. There are boys from the neighborhood that also go there and they say that they like it. But this one here (pointing to one of the twins) sometimes he doesn't like the project, and he doesn't go."

"They told me that there are times that the older boys hit them," I say.

"Yes, that's right. This one doesn't go back now," Stefany tells me. I ask her to tell me what things the project is doing that she thinks are good. "The music is good for them, teaching them how to do simple work is good—homework, they don't bring their homework to the project. They bring it home and when they have a problem, they take it to the project. The food, at times they say it's good, other times they say it's bad. I think working in the vegetable garden is good, learning how to grow a garden. If God wills, someday we can have a garden here. Everything that they can learn about work, how to do things is good. It's also good to play, but it's also more important to learn a profession."

"About the things that are problematic for them, what can you say about that in relation to the project?" I ask. "Sometimes the boys come home saying that the others hit them, and that they told the coordinators and that they didn't do anything. These problems seem to be constant, but just this. Sometimes the work is not good, like cleaning the old bathrooms that have snakes and poisonous insects. There are times that they don't tell me what's happening—and other times they tell me how bad it is with the older boys, because they let everyone run around free. I'm certain that the project could do more. They have the conditions to do more (money), they could buy computers. It wouldn't cost them much. The boys just play football.

They could be learning how to use computers. If they did this, it would be a really good thing, it would be the best thing they could do for our children. Because they could be learning how to use the computer—instead, they will have to find a way to take a course in computers after they leave the project, and this won't happen." *This is the way it is for the poor. Those who have, get, and those who don't, don't. Stefany shakes her head and continues to study her hands.*

"So," I ask "do you think the project is preparing the boys to enter the work world?"

"Ah, Marcia, I don't think so," she says, shaking her head.

"Do you think that the project—would you like the idea, if the project would work with your children and other youth to help your *favela*? For example, to get better conditions, like sewage, do you think this would be a good idea?" I ask, interrupting her.

"I think it's a great idea. For me, it's a great idea. Here in our *favela*, there doesn't exist a community. No one looks out for us here or helps us," says Stefany. "You don't have a community group?" I ask. *I've been told how each favela has a community group that represents them and petitions the mayor's office for services.* "We don't have anything," she says emphatically. "Nothing is done here. We have a city government, we have the *vereadores* (like a city councilwoman or councilman) that comes here during political campaigns, going to all the houses, and after the elections are over, it's over. We could fall down in front of them and go hungry. I walked into town and asked them to help me fix my house. With one minimum salary. Look at my house and my back yard—my back yard is completely open." *They don't have windows, they're open to the street. No running water or indoor toilet, no refrigerator.* "When it rains, it all comes into the house from the roof gutter. Here, on this wall, it infiltrates inside the wall, it's falling down, (the wall), and here too, in the bedroom of the children."

"Your neighbors won't help you?" I ask. "No! With nothing. They've never helped me with anything," Stefany mumbled. *I remember the social network described by Janice Perlman, in the favelas in Rio de Janeiro. Perlman shows that in the urban setting of favela life in Rio de Janeiro, favelados are well organized "...making wide use of the urban milieu and its institutions" (1976:242-243). By contrast, I found the favelas of Morro de Santana to be unorganized, and de-politicized. Yet, like Perlman, I found that poor and racially dark-skinned favelados have similar aspirations for themselves and their children as the middle and upper classes have. In the favelas of Morro de Santana, the poor rely on the hierarchical exchange that occurs in clientelism, the actions and events that create relations of dependence between the rich and poor, and between the poor and the poor. With its origins in the countryside, clientelism was born of relations between lords and vassals, imported by the Portuguese as they colonized Brazil. Its vestiges are evident everywhere in Morro de Santana, as is populism, how votes are won by politicians. Promises are made by the political elite to "marginal" groups, who almost never receive the goods promised them (Gay 1994; Perlman 1976).*

"There's no solidarity here. The majority, if they see me with this blouse, they want to take it. They'd take it from me. That's the way it is here." *Stefany talks as if she is so used to her words that they have no effect on her. Her voice seems to be devoid of emotion. Firecrackers explode somewhere near us, behind us, and we feel them through our feet and bodies, but we are no longer startled by them.*

"Why aren't you working as a maid in someone's house in Morro de Santana?" I ask, wondering why she would choose to be so far away from her children during the week.

"For this reason, because generally to do the work of a maid, you have to work in the kitchen—the stove, everything. Most of the time, the boss doesn't have the patience to teach me how to use these things. (Stefany can't read or write.) If you show me one time, so that I can see it, I will soon learn. But, most of these *patroas* don't have patience. They want me to make cakes, cookies, fish, everything. I need to know how to read, understand? If I knew how to read, I could do all these things. They could leave me with a recipe and I'd do it. Another thing, the majority of the houses where I've worked, where I've been given lots and lots of work to do, they don't pay you. The house that I told you about, that I left, this woman owes me $R126.40. While I'm waiting for this money, the owner of the shop where I have credit, she's wanting me to pay her. I can't pay her because of this woman."

I ask Stefany if she can get a legal process going to get her money. "There is, there's the *ministéria*. I'd have to go there with her and then she's supposed to pay me. It's difficult because a majority of the people say you don't want to do this, because they will (the *patroa*) will 'dirty' your name, so you won't get another job. I have to do something, but I don't know what, and I think about it day and night, every day."

I ask Stefany about her husband. "Could you talk about this, your marriage? How many years ago did he leave?" I ask. "About five years ago, about that. When he left I had all five of my children. He drank a lot! Most of the time he was here at home, and I had to go to work. I worked in a *cozinha* (kitchen). Sometimes I would come home and find dinner ready, and hot water for a bath. Other times I would find him dizzy drunk, fighting, fighting a lot. He hit me, he yanked out a lot of my hair. I went to the *Delegacia de Mulheres* (Delegation for Women). I had a physical exam—he hurt me a lot. When I was pregnant with Davi, he hit me. I don't think it was in the stomach, but I know that he hit me, things like this were normal. He did many, many bad things! He said *palavrões* (very degrading things to her like whore, bitch, etc.), all the *palavrões* that exist, he said to me.

Everything. There was a time that he worked at a little grocery store up the street. I was in the house and we didn't have anything, didn't have any gas to cook with. My neighbors didn't have any to loan me. When I was looking for something to make, the boys came inside this house, it's really a shack, to hunt for some pieces of wood to light to make a fire. I owe this woman money (the one mentioned, whom she has credit with), and only God can take care of this debt and pay it. Heloísa (her name), I don't know if you heard me talking about her, she is the owner of these stores that you see around here. I owe her money, and has said that only God will pay it for me. I went for my husband and told him that we didn't have anything to eat and that the children were hungry and that we didn't have any gas. I took the boys—the woman at the store told me that I can't ask anything without my husband's authorization. He was working in this place (this other store). She said that we couldn't get anything to eat without his authorization. I went and told him this. He told me that he told her not to give me any food, that I wasn't to bring anything home and that everyone should die of hunger. So, I began to insult him. 'OK, you stay here with your children. You're working in a place that has food and I don't have any, and I don't have anything to take and give to the children to eat. So, stay with the children, and I'll go and hunt for work somehow.'

"I came to this bridge (metaphorically) with my children lined up like a staircase behind me, one behind the other. So, I talked with Heloísa and she bought food for us and gas so we could kill the hunger of my children. I am taking this generosity of Heloísa and other people too, like the godmother of Sabrina (her daughter). She is great to me, but she doesn't have the means to help me.

"My husband, he didn't leave me with any longing for him. Today he's in a wheelchair. He can't talk, he doesn't know anyone, and he used to say things and then forget what he said. He eats with his hands, he doesn't eat right (with utensils). He had difficulty eating with his mouth. He doesn't get up and he doesn't walk any more. He just stays a little bit on his feet. He used to feed the birds. Now he can't do even this anymore. He had a type of stroke. The doctor didn't say it was a stroke, but it probably was because one side of his body doesn't work. His left side, his left hand is swollen. You can't touch his left hand or take it because he will scream."

We're both quiet for a while. Another car passes and the dust, now orange in the setting sun, continues drifting. I feel like the "Woman of the Dunes." There is so much of it, it's so constant that it's useless to fight it. One learns to adjust to it, and to feel that it's normal to be covered with it. The dirt becomes a symbol to me of poverty and racism.

I ask Stefany about her children—did they see the fights, did they try to intervene, were they afraid? "Yes, all the time, all of them tried to help me. They were afraid, they screamed a lot, and at times they came at him. They weren't hurt because at times when we were fighting and hitting, other people would come in and break up the fight and separate us. I didn't let him touch them, and at times he would hit me more because I wouldn't let him hurt them."

Stefany tells me that she is religious, but that "the religions that I am practicing now, I want to say this. They don't worship any saints. They are different because they don't adore a dead Jesus. They adore a living Jesus. Understand? So, for them a church doesn't exist. They have a book of music. Understand? They have been doing many good things for me. I had three unpaid bills, the company was going to cut off my water. I had two water bills and I think one light bill. They went and paid them for me. Our rice ran out. They bought more for me. Sometimes I don't have eggs. When I buy them they go soon because the boys are hungry. I and my children talked with them and they bought more for my boys. It's like this kind of trust. When I'm not here during the week, they come by to see if the boys need anything. They offered in the moment to take Murilo to the doctor. They asked to bring his prescription to him and to buy the medicine for him. I told them that I wasn't feeling good, and they took me to the clinic to get a prescription and they paid for the medicine. This is the way they are. They are helping me, and Vitor and the others said that they were preparing a surprise for me. Now what it is, I don't know. I just know that there is a surprise. I would like for you to meet them. They are very loving people."

It's almost dark and I need to go. I'm on foot and it's a long way down the hill to the center of the city. I ask her about rights. Does she know what human rights are? "Marcia, I don't know. I would think that everyone must have the right, like this—to have a good house, and that those who are the most powerful should help those who are weaker. For example, if I have a very old refrigerator that still works, and I'm going to get a new one, I should give it to the poorest because in all these ways, I should be helping. So, like this. Many other things need to happen," Stefany says.

"Do you want to go inside? The dust is really bad here," Stefany says, starting to stand up. "It's OK," I say. She sits down again and continues: "And health. Because there are times Marcia, that health is a thing very difficult for the poor, because it's like this. Many times, for example, the other day, I met a friend of mine, last Sunday who was passing by. I was going to church and she was going home. She was a few months pregnant, and she was losing blood, not a lot, but some. At the clinic they wouldn't see her. She returned home feeling pain and losing blood. She was very afraid she was going to lose the baby. They didn't want to see her. So, she went to the clinic and a friend of hers called the doctor and they told her they needed to see her, and that she needed to take medicines. Yet, they didn't do anything. So, sometimes we go to INPS to get an appointment. They say something like this, 'To get an appointment you must wait until the next week.' So, it's very difficult. I don't know if she lost the baby because I haven't seen her again."

We're nearing the end of our discussion; it's almost too dark to see. Walking down from the favela Bom Jesus after dark is dangerous, but not for the reasons one would think. Pedestrians are an endangered group of people in Brazil, and in Morro de Santana, where a good number of streets are still paved with the broken stone laid by slaves, the hazards increase. They are uneven, filled with deep ruts, and the drivers of cars love velocity. I ask her one last question.

"What about children's rights? Should they have the same rights as adults?" I ask.

"If adults and children should have the same rights?" Stefany repeats my question. "Yes, they must have the same rights. They must. Yes, I think they must, because if they are working and don't get the same pay, they are being exploited. The thing we have the most of in Brazil is the exploitation of minors. My stepmother, looking at the other side, she didn't care about me. She took boys like the ones on the street to peel garlic and then she'd give them a plate of food for their work. This is what happens with the maid too. She will hit the boys if they don't do enough or do it fast enough. Yes, they are abusing them. The same rights because everyone is a human being. Children should have the right to work and go to school. I think it's very important, because that's what I didn't have as a young girl. I want my children to have that. No one can take their schooling and what they know and learn away from them."

I ask Stefany what she hopes for her children, for their future. The movements around us become calmer, fewer cars and running adolescents, but the fireworks continue. "My hopes for my children?" she asks. "For them to study, for them to get through the year, that they become young men and a young woman who are good people, working honestly and to have a good profession. The only hope that someday I'll have something is to see my children raised and working. I can hope for this, but more than that, no."

The light is almost gone now, and the dust has begun to settle, until another car passes or running feet kick it up again. I have so many questions I want to ask Stefany. We promise to talk more soon, but I must ask her one more thing. What would she change to make her life better?

"What would I change? What would I change?" *Stefany repeats the question. Did I really ask her this—surely I must be joking?* "Ah Marcia, everything. I just wouldn't change my dignity. There's nothing that matches it. That I have and it's worth a lot. My children wouldn't want me to change that, but if I could change things it would be for the better, for the better. To have a better little house, with more comfort for me and my children. My little house doesn't offer them any comfort—not for them, not for me, or for anyone. Just these kinds of things." I ask, "Do you think you will have these things someday?" "Ah yes, certainly. When God helps. This is how I'll live until then. When my children are working, I think it will happen."

Our interview comes to an end; I pack up my tape recorder and begin coughing again. "Marcia, let's go and ask my neighbor for some cold water and she will give us a package of juice, grape juice. Do you like grape juice, Marcia?" Stefany asks. "Grape juice? I like it," I say. *We get water from her neighbor and pour in the grape juice powder. We drink it, grateful for a means to wash the dust from our throats. In the dark, I feel my way down the Alto Bom Jesus.*

Conclusion

I came to see from interviewing other parents of street children in my sample that Stefany's story is a familiar one. Her life began in poverty with many siblings, some of whom died. She was taken in as an "adopted" child and used as a child maid. Her education became an impossibility because of her long work days and the interference of her *patroa*. While the frequency of physical abuse suffered by Stefany is more intense than that experienced by other mothers of street children I interviewed, the long work hours and constant dependency on a *patroa* were universally experienced. Further study is needed in order to determine the frequency, intensity, and type of abuse experienced by women from their employers. Her poverty, lack of food and lack of support networks, and her struggle with poor health were also common experiences shared by all the mothers of street children in my sample.

Despite the hardships of daily life, both Stefany and her children shared a sense of hope for the future and the determination to work hard for a better life. For the twins, playing soccer filled them with joy. Many days after school, project attendance, and/or working, I watched them play vigorous games of soccer as they ran, whooped, and laughed. The twins have a strong sense of respect and love for their mother in spite of the harsh physical punishments (hitting and slapping) she at times enforced on them. Stefany did not drink or smoke and she tried to instill in her children the importance of going to school. However, because of their poverty, she did encourage her children to work when they could.

Why present an interview as a narrative? As Renato Rosaldo (1989:130–131) stated, "social analysis should attempt to reveal not historical laws but an understanding of what happened in a specific place at a particular time, and under certain circumstances." It is my hope that by presenting the case histories of the twins and their mother, the reader will receive a dialogic pictorial experience of the places and circumstances that constitute a portion of their lives. The next chapter (Chapter Five) discusses the daily lives of street children and their families, and addresses the economy of street life.

CHAPTER FIVE
STREET CHILDREN OF MORRO DE SANTANA

Daily Life: Children and Families and the Economy of Street Life

This chapter discusses the economic relations between street children and their parents by presenting data on the types of work street children do, how much time they spend working on the streets, and how much they earn and contribute to their families' household income. Street children, their families, and the coordinators at various projects discuss the lack of extra-familial support networks within the favelas (shantytowns) of Morro de Santana where most street children live.

My work at Viva Crianças was to design and implement a children's experimental music group. My research goal, however, was to become familiar with and, where possible, integrated into Viva Crianças's activities and programs. My role of music teacher provided me with a direct link to the children, as well as an accepted position in the organization. Over time, the children in the projects came to accept me. Though I continued to be "*aquela americana antropóloga*" ("that American anthropologist"), I became well acquainted with many of the students, visited their homes, and got to know their parents. I considered the children my friends and in turn, they befriended me.

From the standpoint of studying street children, Morro de Santana is distinct from larger Brazilian cities in a number of significant ways. Most of the children working on the streets in Morro de Santana still live with their families. Compared to the extremes in Rio de Janeiro, São Paulo, Brasilia, and other large Brazilian cities, violence against street children in Morro de Santana is low, as is membership in street gangs. Nevertheless, research by Brazilian social scientists on the structural causes of urban poverty, homelessness, and working children is still germane in Morro de Santana.

Economic Relationships Between Parents and Street Children

I selected the street children and families I worked with based on both the recommendations of coordinators in the projects where I worked and on the willingness of the children at the projects to participate in my research. As discussed in the methods chapter, developing friendships with children and their families was crucial to gaining trust of and access to the lives of my informants. I became friends with several children only after working as a music instructor for several months in the projects. It was at that time that I approached the children about interviews with them and their parents.

In families where both parents are working, street children in Morro de Santana generate on average, 20 percent of the family's income. Where only one parent is working, the working child may provide 50 percent or more of the family income. My surveys found that of 107 families, 51 percent were supported by the work of fathers and children, 12 percent by the work of mothers and children. Those families supported by income earned by mothers and their children tended to generate higher incomes than those supported by the earnings of fathers and their children. This could be a reflection of the slightly higher wages paid to men who often incorporate their male children into their jobs, increasing the amount of work completed in a given day. When children help their fathers at work, the child is often not paid. Mothers and their children, on the other hand, tend to earn their money independently of each other. Hence, the combined income of mother and child is slightly higher than that of father and child.

Resourceful and economically successful children are highly valued. Sister Irmã Heloisa from Bom Jesus explains it this way:

> There are times where the parents don't have enough to give their kids anything, so the child becomes preoccupied with selling popsicles, so that they can help their mothers. They say to me, "Ai, Irmã Heloisa, I'm not coming here today, or I'm going to leave here early today, so I can go and sell popsicles and help my mother, because the money that my father makes isn't enough." So the little that they get, they give to their parents and they feel that they are valued at home. So in reality they are valued because they also produce income—for what they contribute to their families. And where rich kids receive everything, poor kids fight to give what they can to their families.

Many of my informants took on the arduous task of being their parents' future hope for some semblance of economic security and well-being. When I asked Claudeti (an adolescent girl working as a domestic servant) what her long-term vision for herself was, she exemplified the attitude of many street children I interviewed:

> My dream, my dream is to have a good home for my mother and my father, and to work and to study so they won't need to keep working like they are, to have money to pay them too.

Out of the fourteen life history interviews with project children, more than three quarters stated that they felt the need to provide for their parents. Here, we can see how many street youth see themselves as "parenting the parent." The responsibility of work is linked both economically and emotionally to their parents and to their younger siblings. This was a common theme among the street children I came to know in Morro de Santana. Further research needs to be compiled on relations of care and responsibility felt by street children for their parents. One girl of 13 years of age told me about her most constant worries:

> It's like this, more or less. I don't know from day to day what is going to happen to me, what's going to happen to my family. I'm worried about my brothers and sisters and about myself. I am more worried and afraid that I'll lose my mother. That we'll be homeless, because we have two tax bills that we can't pay. I'm most worried about these things, with my house and how to help my mother at home with money. I worry about my little sister and how to take care of her. When I grow up, I need to be more competent, I'll need to take care of the house because my mother won't be able to work anymore, and nor will my father, understand?

When asked whose idea it was that they should start working in order to help support the family, most children replied that it was their own. However, in further conversation many admitted that their parents' need for them to work was very strong and heavily influenced their desire to work and contribute. The need to be respected as an integral part of the family is a major component part of a young person's identity. By being economically valuable, a child can earn the respect of his parents, siblings, peers, and neighbors (Veloso 2012). Despite these close identifications with family, home life frequently involves surprisingly little non-essential interaction. Family relations are often circumscribed by the hardships of daily life, especially the lack of leisure. I asked eighteen of my informants from three projects (Viva Crianças, COV, and Curumim: five girls and thirteen boys whose average age was 13) if they spent time each day talking with their parents. In all cases, I was told that this did not occur in their family. Commonly, children and adolescents came home at the end of the day to an empty shack where they began to prepare dinner or look after and discipline their younger siblings. When the parents came home, affection was usually expressed by a pat on the shoulder. Children were not coddled or given special treatment. Instead they were expected to participate in whatever needed to be done in order to maintain the household. Indeed, they were expected to be tough and were treated accordingly, perhaps as a way to prepare them for their early entrance into the harsh reality of daily life.

Girls especially reported that when they were at home, they were working all the time: washing, cleaning, preparing meals, and caring for younger siblings. At one point, a group of children in my music class at Viva Crianças laughed when I asked them about talking with their parents about their daily activities or their feelings. My field notes state:

> They looked confused and thought my questions strange and funny, they laughed. "No," they said, "my parents don't talk to me when I come home from school. I usually begin to do my chores or go to work selling *picolé* (popsicles)."

While working at Curumim, I was told by Melissa, a monitor at the project, about the aggressive nature of the children and youth: "The children are naturally aggressive because no one at home respects them as individuals, and two-way discussions are rare. Instead they are hit, yelled at, ridiculed, and beaten." On the other hand, the children of the rich are often coddled and indeed, quite often play a large part in determining the activities of their families. While living with three families, two within the upper-middle class and one in the upper class, I observed the social constructions that define the daily life of privileged children in Morro de Santana. Their life consists of school and play, with no household responsibilities. Leisure and play are intermingled with mild attention to schoolwork. In contrast, the conditions that define the lives of poor children favor tough and aggressive individuals who work the streets and are willing to fight for what they want. In my observation, those who yelled the loudest and who were the most persistent and aggressive often succeeded in getting what they wanted. The angelic child (clean, cute, and dependent) had no clout here.

Most of the projects where I worked presented almost weekly theatrical productions. The children and the monitors created the themes and eventual dialogues for each play based on the real-life events of the children. One day I watched as the youth at Curumim rehearsed for an upcoming production.

> The play begins with the mother who says: "Hey kid, go get a bottle of *pinga* (cane alcohol) for me, you

moleque (street kid)." The boy always does what he is told. A girl enters on stage and says, "Every child has the right to protection." Another child enters on stage and announces that the boy is nine years old and has never been to school and his mother doesn't know what's up or how he will survive in the future. "How will he matriculate?" the child asks. The mother says, "School, why do you want to go to school?" Her son responds, "But mother!" he cries, "All my friends are in school!" The son says his friends' names. The mother responds by yelling, "Look here, boy! I'm old, I never went to school! I work all the time doing services for others. I never needed school! Get out of here and go get the clothes for me to wash, now!"

After rehearsing their parts, the children and monitors stop to discuss the meaning of the themes. The rights of the children are outlined and detailed: the right of every child to go to school, specifically. I ask the youth in the theater if the story is accurate, if they know kids who live this reality, and I'm told by five out of six youth that they know friends who must stay at home helping their mothers instead of going to school. They tell me, "It's a bad thing. It's very difficult for these kids. They need both things, because they learn one thing at home and another at school. They need school to be able to survive in the world, but they need to help at home or they won't survive at all." The youth attending Curumim are frequently absent from the project, sometimes months at a time, because they must work the streets selling ice cream and shining shoes, or they are needed to work alongside their father or mother in order to generate additional income during extremely hard times.

Household Income and Working Street Youth

There were no official statistics in 2002 collected by the city government of Morro de Santana on the number of homeless street youth, nor were there any official statistics on the numbers of youth working in the streets. Hence, I conducted my own survey of fifty street youth who worked in the center of the city, shining shoes or selling ice cream or various homemade foods and sweets. I used a prepared survey instrument with standardized questions that included a section for qualitative data focusing on the kinds of work their parents performed and the household income of their families. After several months of observation on the plazas where street children worked during the day, I selected the plaza in the middle of Morro de Santana most often used by street children. Over a period of one week, during the summer (the most active working period for children selling ice cream and working on the street) a field assistant and I interviewed fifty working street youth, approaching each working youth and asking for their permission to interview them. On any given day I counted on average ten street children in the central plaza between 12:00 pm and 6:00 pm. This six-hour period is the peak time for vending and working on the streets. This sample of working street youth also includes children who did not attend projects.

In addition, I collected data from 557 households throughout the city. There are eighteen *favelas* in Morro de Santana. The total population of Morro de Santana in the year 2002 was 67,512 (luiscarlos@ibge.gov.br). In 1997, the year of my fieldwork, the total population of Morro de Santana was 67,141. From the total population in 1997, I selected eight *favelas*. Currently, there are no census data on the populations within *favelas* in Morro de Santana. Hence, the population for each *favela* in the city is not known. The selected *favelas* represent the areas in which the children lived who attended the various projects where I worked. The following eight *favelas* were surveyed:

Ponte Nova I, Ponte Nova II, Ipiranga, Santa Cruz, Bandeirante I, Bandeirante II, São Ricardo, and the Alto Bom Jesus. A sample was gathered for household income data on poor families by purposively selecting three health clinics that served the eight selected *favelas*. Local health nurses at the clinics pulled fifty charts from clinic files on each of the eight *favelas*, totaling 401 households. For each household they recorded the following household data:

1. Number of people in household
2. Father employed and amount of salary
3. Mother employed and amount of salary
4. Number of children employed and amount of salary

Out of the 401 households, 107 reported children working (see tables 4 and 5). Data from parents about their working children may well be incorrect due to the stigma attached to street children and their activities, economic or otherwise, on the streets. This stigma is discussed in more detail in Table 7.

In order to analyze middle-class household income data, I collected an additional purposive sample of 156 short survey forms (completing the total of 557 households) with the assistance of the hospital head nurse during a public health clinic immunization event over a two-day period in the neighborhood of the city center. Typically, shot clinics in the city center are used by the middle to upper-middle classes in Morro de Santana, and as such are a fairly reliable representation of these classes. In this survey I collected information on the kinds of professions most commonly performed by middle-and upper-class Courvelians and the monthly incomes they received. Of the 156 people interviewed at the shot clinic, 111 described the type of work they performed and the income they received. The additional forty-five declined to talk about their profession and/or their income.

Table 1 and Figure 1 represent a table and a bar graph of income distribution. These data categories are ranked in order of income levels, and as such represent a simple categorization of social class in Morro de Santana based on ranked income levels from the immunization clinic discussed. This sample may not be representative of the population of the city center (middle to upper-middle classes), but probably does capture the range of working- to upper-middle class occupations present in that population. Such a classification is used here in order to demonstrate the high level of income inequality in Morro de Santana. The unemployed earn an average income of less than one minimum salary monthly, whereas professionals frequently make $R10,000 and above per month. One minimum salary represents $R130 per month, and in 1997 the real (the Brazilian currency) was roughly equal to the US dollar. One minimum salary would not have enough purchasing power to buy enough rice, beans, salt, coffee, and bread for a family of four people each month.

As we can see from Figure 1, out of 111 cases where job types were recorded from the clinic data described, informal labor market jobs **and** blue collar jobs that pay from $R60 to $R400 per month (informal labor: street sellers, street workers, charcoal makers, etc.; and blue collar jobs: public service workers such as stone cutters for street work, stone layers for street work, factory workers, clothes washers, taxi drivers) comprise 72 percent of my sample. Professionals, defined here as the middle class, are composed of those who earn from $R1,000 to $R10,000 or more per month (dentists, doctors, lawyers, professors, scientists, and large business owners) and comprise only 15 percent.[17] Since my sample from the immunization clinic consisted mainly of families with children, wealthier individuals in the upper classes who do not take their children to shot clinics are probably not represented. Hence, this convenience sample may or may not be representative of the population and cannot be used to estimate the percentage of professionals in the population at large. Hence, this sample compares working-and middle-to upper-middle-class families to the very poor families of street children.

Table 1. Income Distribution

TYPE OF JOB	INCOME LEVEL	PERCENTAGE
Blue Collar/Informal	$R120–450 per month	72
Professional	$R2,000–6,000 per month	15

Total is less than 100 because retired, unemployed, and military are not included

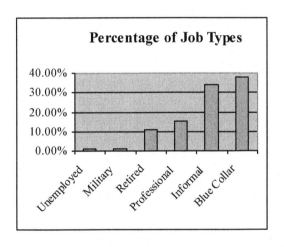

Figure 1. Percentage of Job Types in the City Center Shot Clinic Sample N = 111

General Data

Working Street Children

The median age of the fifty working children interviewed on the streets in Morro de Santana was 15 years (age range was 7–18). The median grade in school was 6th series. Only three of these youth stated that they worked because their parents forced them, whereas the remaining forty-seven stated that they worked because they wanted to. The most common reasons to work were the need to help their family (82 percent), and the need to have their own personal money to buy their own things (18 percent). These numbers correspond with the ways in which the children decided how their money was distributed or spent: 84 percent of the children contributed to household expenses (ten percent put all their income to household expenses), while only 16 percent kept all of their income for themselves. Of those who earned money in order to help their families, 52 percent used their money to buy food, 34 percent to pay household bills, (most commonly light and water bills), 30 percent to buy needed household goods, and ten percent to buy medicines.

Table 2. Street Youth Contributions to Household Expenses
N = 50
(Total is more than 100 percent due to more than one individual reporting in more than one category)

NUMBER OF STREET YOUTH	PERCENT OF STREET YOUTH	TYPE OF BILL PAID
26	52 percent	Food
17	34 percent	Household Bills/Water and Light Bills
15	30 percent	Household Goods/Soap/Rags
5	10 percent	Medicines

When children used some of their money for their own needs (90 percent of the children did use a portion for their own needs) it was used to play video games, pay for soccer fees, buy clothes, buy school supplies, and to buy personal things (toys, candy, bread). When asked if children and youth should have the right to work, 86 percent responded "yes" while 14 percent stated they "didn't know" how to answer the question. The 86 percent who responded positively to my question regarding their right to work knew that in Brazil, children over 14 years of age had the legal right to work. In this sense, they understood what a right to work meant in terms of a child's right to work. The children and youth stated various reasons that they considered it appropriate for them to work. The most common reasons were as follows: "It's good to have responsibilities," "I need to help my family survive," "I want to be responsible and earn my own money so that I can be responsible for myself." One child stated that he worked so that "I won't be worthless." Several children said that they worked in order to buy clothes and school supplies that their parents couldn't buy for them. Others felt that working gave them more opportunities in the world and made them wiser and shrewder. One boy told me "I need to work so that I can get a bank account...so I can have a future." Finally, one youth honestly stated, "I work so that I can have my own money so that I don't have to rob or steal."

I would like to note an important finding in my fieldwork related to parents of street children in Morro de Santana. Many parents told me that they were not willing to state that their underage (less than fourteen years of age) children worked, and others stated that they wanted to hide the reality of their poverty by avoiding the social stigma attached to having a child who worked the streets.[18] Indeed, in the early months of my work in the projects, children frequently denied that they worked and earned an income in any form. Among *favelados*, I found that working children are understood to be an asset and a symbol of pride and respect. However, I also found that among the middle and upper classes, working children are perceived as *pivetes* (thieving street children), *ladrões* (robbers), and *vagabundos* (vagabonds). Hence, many *favelados* publicly hide the fact that their children work. Middle-and upper-class norms of childhood define working children as *crianças de rua* (children of the streets), a title that renders the children as deviants and sees their parents as lazy and irresponsible.

Table 3. Types of Work Done by Working Children (Interviews with Working Street Youth)

N = 50

TYPE OF WORK	FREQUENCY	PERCENT
Gardening	2	4
Selling Ice Cream	38	76
Farm Labor	1	2
Masonry	1	2
Street Seller (Foods)	1	2
Raising Frogs	1	2
Begging in Streets	2	4
Shoe Shine	2	4
Domestic Servant	1	2
Laying Stones in Streets	1	2

Table 4. Survey of Working Children in Morro de Santana (Health Clinic Data)

N = 107

DESCRIPTION	NUMBER OF FAMILIES	CHILD PERCENT OF INCOME	AVERAGE CHILD INCOME	AVERAGE FATHER INCOME	AVERAGE MOTHER INCOME	MEDIAN INCOME CHILD	MEDIAN INCOME FATHER	MEDIAN INCOME MOTHER	AVERAGE NUMBER IN FAMILY
Only Child Working	18	100 percent	$R188	-0-	-0-	$R130	-0-	-0-	6.33
Father and Child Work	55	51 percent	$R159	$R163	-0-	$R130	$R130	-0-	6.9
Mother and Child Work	13	12 percent	$R195	-0-	$R120	$R130	-0-	$R130	6.66
All Work	21	20 percent	$R132	$R158	$R108	$R130	$R130	$R130	5.9

* "Child" refers to children in household working. Exact number of working children in each household is unknown. Data sample collected by nurses from files in health clinics from each *favela*.

* Eight *favelas* were surveyed: Ponte Nova I, Ponte Nova II, São Ricardo, Bandeirante I, Bandeirante II, Santa Cruz, Ipiranga, and Bom Jesus:
- Fifty households from each of the seven *favelas*
- Fifty-one households from one *favela*
- Total households 401
- Out of 401 households, 107 reported children working

Table 5. Children's Income Compared to Total Family Income (Health Clinic Data)

N = 107

DESCRIPTION	AVERAGE TOTAL FAMILY INCOME	MEDIAN TOTAL FAMILY INCOME	PERCENTAGE OF AVERAGE CHILDREN'S INCOME TO TOTAL FAMILY INCOME	PERCENTAGE OF MEDIAN CHILDREN'S INCOME TO TOTAL FAMILY INCOME
Only Children Working	$R188	$R130	100 percent	100 percent
Father and Children Working	$R322	$R260	49 percent	50 percent
Mother and Children Working	$R315	$R260	62 percent	50 percent
All Work	$R399	$R338	33 percent	38 percent

Table 6. How Earned Money Is Distributed (Interviews with Working Street Youth)

N = 50

MONEY USED FOR	PERCENTAGE
Food	52
Household Bills (Light and Water)	34
Household Items	30
Medications	10
Own Needs (Video Games, Soccer Fees)	4
Own Needs (Clothes)	12
Own Needs (School Supplies)	8
Own Needs (Toys, Candy, Bread)	7.5
	147.5 total is > 100 because children used money in more than one way

Table 7. General Working Data: Reasons for Working (Interviews with Working Street Youth)

N = 50

WORKS/ WANTS TO WORK	WORKS/MADE TO WORK	RIGHT TO WORK: YES	RIGHT TO WORK: DOESN'T KNOW	USES MONEY TO HELP FAMILY VS. OWN NEEDS
94% (47)	6% (3)	86% (43)	14% (7)	82% (41)

* Right to work yes and no refers to the street youth's stated belief that he/she should have or should not have the right to work.

It was very difficult to gather any credible data on the numbers of working children in Morro de Santana. When I asked this question of working youth themselves, 48 percent (24/50) responded. Of this number 58 percent (14/24) didn't have any idea about the number of working youth, 21 percent (5/24) stated that there were approximately 50 to 60 working youth, and 21 percent (5/24) stated that there were many working youth in Morro de Santana. No matter what the actual numbers are, it is a growing phenomenon in Morro de Santana, where the unemployment rate continues to remain fairly high, reflecting the national unemployment rate overall (in 2000, there was close to 7 percent overall unemployment in Brazil according to IBGE 2001 <www1.ibge.gov.br>). In Minas Gerais, 32.7 percent of families with children between the ages of 0 and 6 years of age lived on a monthly income of one half a minimum salary, with 28 percent living on 1.5 minimum salaries per month. Only 3.4 percent of families with children of the same ages lived on more than five minimum salaries per month (IBGE 2000 <www2.ibge.gov.br>).

All of the working children interviewed on the streets were males between seven and nineteen years of age. It is very rare to see a girl selling goods on the streets, unless she is involved in prostitution. There are apparently a fair number of young girls in Morro de Santana involved in informal prostitution who sell their bodies from their own homes or from local brothels. I accompanied a doctor on several visits to local houses of prostitution and informally talked with adolescent girls who had decided it was more lucrative to sell their bodies than their labor as domestic servants. Indeed, they can make over R$1,000 per month as prostitutes working four to six hours a night instead of $R130 per month working ten hours a day as domestic servants. Young women who do prostitute themselves often have children of their own, and several prostitutes told me that they sent their children to private schools, something they would never be able to do on the salary a domestic servant earns.

Morality and sexuality are intricately linked for women in Brazil where the body of the mother is tied to notions of purity and religious virtue (Patai 1993; Burdick 1998; Da Silva 1997). At times, however, prostitution can be a means out of poverty if the woman is "attractive" and "discreet." I met a young woman of 23 who had consciously decided to become a prostitute in order to provide her daughter with opportunities that would otherwise have been impossible for her. She worked only at night, hired domestic servants and women for childcare, put her child in an exclusive daycare center, and was saving money for her daughter's education at private schools.

During an interview with Lorena, a social worker in Morro de Santana, the topic of prostitution as related to poverty became a central issue. During our conversation Lorena told me that as a social worker she often heard from young female prostitutes that "Ah—I make $R5, $R10, $R15 per program (per man served). When Lorena asks how many men a prostitute might serve a night, she was told "Ah, I do three or four a night." Many young women confided in her that they make more money doing this, and they could never rise out of poverty by performing the respectable "slave labor" that poor women of color do to survive in Morro de Santana. To them, it is preferable to sacrifice their values and traditional gendered morals in order to gain financial freedom.

Lack of Extra-Familial Support Networks in the Favelas

The kinds of social welfare systems existing in the *favela*s surrounding Rio de Janeiro described by Janice Perlman in "The Myth of Marginality" are minimal if not completely nonexistent in Morro de

Santana (1976).[19] When I asked who would help out the family if they were unable to bring home supplemental income, my informants replied, "No one." Occasionally, a near relative, such as an aunt, would be mentioned, but further conversation revealed that such support was seldom forthcoming from extended family. Instead, they would mention a *tia*, which would normally mean their mother's patron or another ex-employer or perhaps a teacher. I interviewed sixteen mothers who had children attending one of the five projects where I worked. All sixteen mothers stated that they did not rely on help from friends or neighbors, nor did they have support systems within their immediate families. All their friends and neighbors were too preoccupied with the survival of their own families to offer any help to them.

I found that poor children and their families in Morro de Santana held similar attitudes about their lack of resources, as did Mexican peasant communities studied by George Foster (1967, 122–152). Foster's model of "cognitive orientation" describes the ways in which *Tzintzuntzenos* constructed a set of basic values and attitudes based on their belief that resources exist in limited quantities. Foster developed a model, which he named the

> Image of Limited Good, where…behavior…is patterned in such [a] fashion as to suggest that *Tzintzuntzenos* see their social, economic, and natural universes—their total environment—as one in which almost all desired things in life such as land, other forms of wealth, health, friendship, love, manliness, honor, respect, power, influence, security, and safety *exist in absolute quantities insufficient to fill even minimal needs of villagers* (1967:123).

I find Foster's model useful here in that, goodness (defined here as material goods and services such as medical, nutritional, and educational needs) is not conceptualized as a resource that can be shared. When goodness appears, it by necessity must be taken from another, whose need can be as severe as the recipient. I observed this kind of static economic immobility within the *favela* communities in Morro de Santana, where poverty is dealt with as a constant companion. Indeed, Foster's model of limited good has been widely applied to not only peasant societies, but to developing countries as well, where upward economic mobility and the researcher's perceived notion of "peasant inertia" are commonly not found together. In other words, peasants stay poor and are excluded from upward economic income trends commonly found in the middle and upper classes whose access to education and job markets ensures their upward mobility (Hammel and Nader 1979).

Foster's model is intrinsically psychological and is based on his model of cognitive orientation. Here, people behave (unconsciously) in ways that produce mistrust, jealousy, fear, and animosity. Such behaviors are seen to be directly linked to the economic stagnation that poverty in and of itself creates. However, I see Foster's model as more useful when seen through both a structural and a psychological lens. Upward mobility is not even considered by Morro de Santana's poor *favelados*, nor is civil protest a viable option for possible change when considered in light of Brazil's political history.[20]

Unlike Oscar Lewis'Culture of Poverty and other marginality theories, Foster's model of Limited Good can, as a structural phenomenon, be linked to inherent social inequality and political corruption. Where Lewis points to the poor as the architects of personality traits that perpetuate their poverty, I argue that in Brazil, social, racial, and economic inequalities begin within the hierarchy of social/racial class, where poverty and skin color often mark those living in poverty as socially marginalized.

It is interesting to juxtapose Bourdieu's discussion of the good-faith economy and the market economy (Bourdieu 1980:114–121) with Foster's notion of limited good. Bourdieu compares the "man of good faith" to the man of the market. As individuals within groups become less united through genealogy, each becomes less of the man of good faith and more the market man. What I came to see in Morro de Santana was Bourdieu's description of symbolic capital between "patrons and clients," and not reciprocity between *favelados*. The symbolic capital, economically played out between patrons and clients, is based on the ability of the patron to mobilize capital (money, medicines, clothes, emotional and perceptual values) in order to determine the rules of employment and the significance and meaning of the work performed by their clients. In this way, hierarchies of control and privilege become naturalized and absorbed both psychologically and physically. Symbolic capital helps to ensure that the rules of relations of power remain the same and are clearly understood, most often in nonverbal forms of communication. Where Perlman found *favelados* to be internally linked through networks of trust and unity (Bourdieu's good-faith economy), I found *favelados* in Morro de Santana to be mistrustful and disjointed among themselves, precisely because their good-faith economy of friendly networks has been crumbling for some time under the pressure of the global market economy and Brazil's longstanding index of economic inequality. Neighbors were not to be relied upon in times of crisis (such as the illness of a child, lack of food, or domestic and child abuse). In addition, contrary to Perlman's assertions, *favelados* in Morro de Santana were not linked to the city's larger economic and political activities. I was told on many occasions that taking any public stance against the mayor's policies on the allocation of funds in Morro de Santana (sewer development, road improvement, allocation of funds for education and health care) was futile and laughable. People essentially struggled on their own, relying as little as possible on neighbors or public assistance, which had so consistently ignored their needs in the past. Indeed, I found that *favelados* in Morro de Santana turned to their patron as a source of potential help and assistance and were more likely to ask them for the necessities they lacked. It is this symbolic capital that acted as a currency in times of need.[21]

During a conversation with Clemenson, who was at the time a graduate student in linguistics at the *Universidade Federal* in *Belo Horizonte, Minas Gerais*, the subject of patron–client relations became the center of our discussion. Clemenson was born into a lower-middle-class family. More fortunate than many of his social class, he has passed the vestibular (something like our SATs), received his bachelor's degree, earned his master's, and his Ph.D. in linguistics. His personal experience with poverty and his observations of class exploitation and the reality of everyday racism led him to make the following statement:

> The relations of dependency between patrons and maids in Brazil are more complex than you can imagine. It's very common to hear maids saying that their *patroas* are "truly mothers and friends." This is because these *patroas*, we could say, have sustained an "intimate" place in the lives of their maids. Some *patroas* have participated in the private lives of their maids, in the raising and formation of their children, in the maintenance of their house and their health. This apparent relation of cooperation that happens a lot is praiseworthy, and doesn't necessarily have to result in relations of power and submission between domestics and their bosses. However, this situation causes the relations between *patroas* and maids to be based on a system of exchanged exploitation: when the *patroa*

interferes directly in the personal life of her maid she automatically is having access and control in the life of this maid. If we think about it, we are repeating what happened on the large *fazendas* and urban centers during the time of slavery: the masters were owners of the lives and destinies of their slaves. And this relation of slavery is repeated again.

Clemenson's observations were confirmed by my fieldwork experiences among poor children and their families. I postulate that the most common form of extra-familial support for poor children of color and their families is through the relations that occur between them and their *patroas*. I align myself with Bourdieu's theoretical notions about the three-tiered structure of capital and its linkage to social class. All three notions of capital are based on social relations that are mediated through symbolic means that create relations of power. By maintaining congenial relations with one's patron (which requires being willing to work many extra hours without extra pay), it is possible to receive financial help with medicines, food, clothing, education, and such. It was not uncommon for my informants to tell me (seven coordinators and six children) that by working for a *boa patroa* (good boss) their ability to go to school, buy books, eat well, and acquire school clothes was significantly increased. *Boa patroas* financially helped their child maids while in school.[22] Of course such help is dependent upon the mood of the *patroa*, and usually any monetary help is eventually taken back in extra work or taken out of future pay. The patron–client system is also fueled by the *patroa's* need to maintain status as a *boa patroa* in order to gain the reputation that they are someone worth working for. In addition, patrons often work hard to maintain their religious reputations and obligations to help the poor. Whatever mistreatment a *patroa* might inflict on her domestics is forgiven if the *patroa* comes through financially for her servants. The following interview with a woman (whom I'll call Marta) who was no longer working (she was in her 70s and had severe arthritis in her feet) exemplifies this tradition of forgiveness for *patroas*:

> *Marcia*: But how did you feel when you worked so, so, so, much for people, in their houses, where they had everything?
> *Marta*: Ah! My girl, it's hard. But they were really good to me, right girl?
> *Marcia*: Your *patroas*?
> *Marta*: Yes, they were really good.
> *Marcia*: They were really good?
> *Marta*: Yes, they were good people!
> *Marcia*: What do you mean?
> *Marta*: Yes, they were good, they gave us things! You didn't get a lot of money but you got food and clothes.
> *Marcia*: So, they gave you things?
> *Marta*: Yes.
> *Marcia*: What other kinds of things did they give you?
> *Marta*: They gave us medicines when I'd get sick and show up to work, for me and for the girls, everything.
> *Marcia*: Would they take you and your kids to get a medical consultation (to see a doctor)?
> *Marta*: Yes.
> *Marcia*: They'd give you medicines?
> *Marta*: Yes.

When I asked Marta whether she would rather have money for her extra work or things from her patroa she said, "I'd choose the things, right? I'd prefer to have the material things in my hands than the money."

The idea of receiving a fair wage for a fixed number of hours and then receiving extra pay was completely foreign to Marta, and to most of the mothers I came to know. The working poor would rather keep their good reputation as hard workers with their patroas than be paid a fair wage for the long hours they work each week. In exchange for their hard work and extra hours, their *patroas*' generosity was considered fair. For these women, one minimum salary of $R130 per month is the only reality available to them. They are hardworking women who are up at the crack of dawn six days a week, working ten to twelve hours a day at hard labor. They are responsible and reliable women who have learned to survive in a system that keeps them dependent and tied to ignorance and deprivation. Hence, their children are expected to help at home, continuing the cycle of poverty that often requires them to leave school in order to work. At best, the children of the poor must work and go to inferior public schools, where even if they complete the Brazilian equivalent of high school, they have very little hope of passing the vestibular and continuing on for higher education. The most common support systems I found in Morro de Santana were linked to patron–client relations and the contributions of children and adolescents to family income and maintenance (childcare, housework; i.e., working for parents). A young child left at home while parents work and older siblings attend school might be shooed off the street by a friendly neighbor, but would not be taken care of otherwise. Many times, as I walked through the *favela*s on my way to work at the projects, I'd hear neighbors calling to children on the street, "Hey boy! Go get some water for me. Here take this bottle, go!" Or, "Hey! *Moleque*! I need you to do some work for me!" Children were seen as potential chore-doers not only within the family, but also by anyone in the vicinity.

Bianca told me this story about a woman who lived in extreme poverty and had several children. Bianca, a lower-middle-class woman, was always helping her, giving her clothes, food, and medical help. In particular, she wanted to help the daughter of this woman. She bought her school supplies, clothes, and medications when she was sick. When the daughter grew up, she turned to prostitution, became pregnant, and had two small children. Eventually she became pregnant again and wanted to get an abortion but didn't have any way to do it with certainty. She took herbs to abort the baby, but instead of losing the baby, she became very, very sick with diarrhea, vomiting, and fever. She lived in squalor in a one-room mud shack. For one week she stayed in bed, vomiting into a big pan and passing diarrhea into it as well. She didn't bathe or eat and her two young children were in the room with her, without food or anyone to care for their hygiene. Eventually, a neighbor came to Bianca and told her about the daughter's condition. Again Bianca took action. She arrived and took the young woman out of bed, who was screaming in pain and crying loudly. She took off her soiled clothes and put her on a chair in the shower and bathed her. Then she dressed her and took her to the hospital. The hospital said they couldn't treat the woman without payment. Bianca had only $R20, and it was going to cost $R40, so she went to her church (another common source of patronage) and begged for money to help this woman. Her request was successful and she gave her own money and the church's money to the hospital. The woman recovered, maintained the pregnancy, and had the baby, but apparently never thanked her. The daughter's neighbors were yelling to Bianca to "leave her…she's a prostitute. She should die! Leave her children to die too!" This story is an example of the detachment experienced by my informants who lived in the *favelas* of Morro de Santana.

All the children I came to know in the projects and on the streets worked at home as well. Cecilia, a girl of twelve, told me how she works at home on a daily basis and then goes to school in the afternoons.

> *Cecilia*: I began helping my parents at home when I was five years old. I help them clean the house at home, in the morning. This week, I am cleaning the house when I wake up. I don't know how many hours a day I help them. I usually wake up around 6:00 in the morning and I help out until about 9:00. I clean the house, wash the dishes, clean me and my brother's room.
> *Marcia*: Do you work with either of your parents in the streets?
> *Cecilia*: No. I work, doing some work in the *favela* of Bela Vista.

When I pushed Cecilia to talk about the kinds of work she did in her *favela*, she eventually told me that she worked at times as a maid, helping her mother in the homes of her *patroa*. Children working alongside their parents in Morro de Santana is a common phenomenon. Children often work with their fathers or relatives in the rural areas where their parents are hired (for one minimum salary) to work on small farms called *sítios*. The labor of children significantly impacts the labor output of the parent they are assisting, and in this way, children are also increasing their families' monthly labor output, even though the parent receives no increase in remuneration for their child's labor. Rather, children who assist their parents by working with them increase the amount of labor completed, often leading to the acquisition of more jobs in the informal economy for the parent.

As I came to work more closely with the children, they began to tell me about the things that worried them the most. Many children were afraid of losing their mothers, who were often the only supporting parent. It was also very common for a youth to express desire to care for, protect, and support a parent. When an eleven-year-old girl named Milena I had befriended was absent from Viva Crianças, I began to ask the coordinators about her. Where was she? Was she ill? I was told that she was probably helping her mother, that when she could, she would return to the project. A few days later I ran into Milena and several of her family members in the streets where they were begging:

> I met Milena on the streets the next day as I was passing by Celme's house (the house of a friend of mine). She had a nine-month-old baby in her arms, her sister was with her (she seemed to be mentally disabled), and three other children accompanied her. They were all very dirty and certainly seemed to be in need of assistance. Milena came running to me, greeting me with hugs and holding my hand. I asked if her mother was with her and she informed me that the woman across the street was her aunt and that her mother was down the street. I crossed the street with her and introduced myself to her aunt. Shortly after, her mother joined us. I told her that I had been worried about Milena, she hadn't been at the project for several weeks and that we missed her in the music group. She was very apologetic, explaining that she had to work a lot, washing clothes, that there wasn't any money. Milena had been helping her mother wash clothes and begging in the streets.

Milena and I had become close after working together in my music class for several months. She was ashamed of begging in the streets, but she knew that I was a friend who would understand that she was working to help her family survive. She was deeply connected to her mother, even though her mother was an alcoholic who had often abused her. Milena even went to jail with her mother when they lived in São Paulo. In the following section on home abuse, Milena's story will be included with the stories of other children who lived in abusive homes, but whose loyalty to their parents was unswerving.

Lack of support networks among *favelados* and close family members was further evidenced in the discussions I had with coordinators and monitors at various projects where I worked. Children talked about lack of support networks in very similar ways, agreeing with their parents, coordinators, and monitors at the projects, and with my field notes and observations.

My notes on various discussions with adults concerned with children in Morro de Santana are presented here. I begin with Natália, who was a coordinator at Viva Crianças and who as a child was given to a *patroa*:

> When she was eleven her mother had to give her away, or rather hire her out, because she didn't have the financial means to take care of her and more importantly to assure her a future with an education. She was sent to work for a woman with more means than her mother, who paid for her clothes, food, and education and paid her less than one minimum salary per month. She didn't actually become a domestic servant until she was twelve, at which time she did all the housecleaning, cooking, washing and went to school in the evenings. Like Marta (another young woman I met and became friends with, who had been a child domestic servant), she has had a hard life. She went on to tell me that her *patroa* was never satisfied with her work, that if there was any dust left on the furniture she would scream

at her. She was always following her around, checking her work and always finding things wrong with what she did.

I postulate that in this way many coordinators at Viva Crianças found that they were in conflict with the ideology of the project that constructs childhood as a time of innocence, where play and freedom from responsibility are key ingredients for a healthy and normal childhood.

One day I visited a household of women in Ipiranga, a very poor *favela* in Morro de Santana. Present were a grandmother, one of her daughters, and five grandchildren by various mothers. Their shack consisted of one room and one bed (where they all slept), and a bathroom with sink and a toilet that didn't flush. The room was ripe with the smell of raw sewage. There was a cacophony of voices as each woman and several of the children competed for vocal space within the small room.

Eight-year-old Bruna shouted to me, "There are lots of kids that stay on the street from here! They don't have anything to eat—that don't ever go home, that eat by begging at the doors of others here. When they don't have a house, they go out into the streets, and just come by here to sleep." The grandmother tells me that they are not able to control them or handle the constant needs of these children. Bruna tells me that one of the kids who was just here was one of those who frequently sleep on their doorstep. I ask if these children go door to door begging for food because they don't have homes of their own, and Bruna replies, "Why, I think they do—yes they have homes." The grandmother continues for Bruna, explaining that "They have homes, but they live in a lot of poverty and there's nothing to eat, and their families don't have anything to give them, to give them what they need. So, they go to the streets to beg—they beg for food. Sometimes they're given bread and they say, "No, I don't want bread, I want real food." They say, "If a senhora has a little meat, please give me a little meat. They knock on the doors. Here at my house we get a lot of these kids." These women with so many children to care for don't have the means to give much in the way of help. They didn't want extras sleeping on their doorstep. Their poverty is so overwhelming, they feel themselves being crushed from within by their own ceaseless pangs of hunger and fear, and from without by the endless and unquenchable needs of the multitudes of poor who surrounded them. I quote further from this interview when I commented:

> You know that many times, when I've walked through the center of the city, I've seen and heard the owners of stores talking about "street kids." One day while I was in front of a store owned by a woman she said that she didn't like these kids "hanging around" and she was always telling them, "Ah, go get a job one way or another." So, what do you think about this?" Eight-year-old Bruna said, "Ah, I'm dying of pain for these kids….

Yet the grandmother flatly stated that she felt these begging *meninos* should work. Indeed, she said that the ideal situation would be "if there was an institution, right, that collects these children in this place and then they give them food and teach them a profession so they can work and earn some money." I asked if the *meninos* would live at these institutions and she replied, "No, they wouldn't live there. If they studied in the morning, they'd go to school first or if they studied in the afternoon they'd go to the streets right after. Then they'd learn a trade and then work doing various things—light work for them to do, and get a little money to help at home and they'd be learning a 'trade' at the same time."

Two mothers from Bom Jesus, Stella and Eduarda, told me that support systems were absent not because people didn't care about their neighbors, but because they were so exhausted and ashamed by their own poverty that they had reached a point of not asking for help. I include the long discussion that followed in order to allow the full meaning intended by the mothers as they spoke to me about the issues of poverty and assistance networks:

> *Marcia*: Do you think that people who have very little money have a kind of social system to help each other?
> *Stella*: No.
> *Marcia*: Do you think that if you don't have money, you have relatives that will help you, or friends? Do you think that you will be able to survive?
> *Eduarda*: I think if they know I am in need, or I'm hungry, then if they get together in a community—for example, a person needs so much help. If a group gets together, and unites and takes it on together then it's OK. But just one person bailing the other person out, that's hard. If you have a group, it's OK. But, here in my *favela* I've never seen this. This kind of help isn't common, I've never seen it. I think that when people don't have the things to survive, they stay in the house and don't say anything.
> *Stella*: Yes, they just stay hungry.
> *Marcia*: They don't say anything?
> *Eduarda*: That's right, they don't say anything.
> *Marcia*: They just stay hungry?
> *Eduarda*: They stay hungry. They don't say anything. Now, this is what I've seen—this is what happens.
> *Stella*: That's right. My mother-in-law is missing lots of things she needs, and if I have some of these things,

CHAPTER FIVE 143

I'd give them to her but she doesn't ask. She won't say anything.

Marcia: Why do you think that people don't say anything?

Stella: Ah, because they are ashamed to ask to eat.

Marcia: But, if you're going to die, it's better to have shame than to die isn't it?

Eduarda: Sometimes, they will ask for a little something, they'll take it but they won't ask for more.

Marcia: What about the government in the city, the mayor. They have programs to help, don't they?

Eduarda: Now, they aren't helping anymore.

Stella: There was a time that they did help, but not anymore.

Eduarda: The other day, at home, my sister, she just had a baby. There wasn't anything to eat in the house. I went to the *prefeitura* to ask for help and didn't get anything. I went there to ask for her and didn't get any help. One time, I got help and the next time I didn't.

Marcia: Have you been able to help her?

Eduarda: I took things to her house for her from my house. But at the end of the month it was all gone again.

Marcia: What types of things did you take her?

Eduarda: I took everything to her, whatever I had, I gave it to her. She was hungry.

Marcia: But normally, is it true when a person is hungry it's just their relatives that help them, or do their neighbors help too?

Eduarda: I don't think that the neighbors help, no.

In this discussion, we see the strain put upon a destitute family trying to help relatives. Giving what you can is only a temporary kind of help and the need is so constant that in the end, begging in the streets may be the only option left to a mother with hungry children.

My music assistant at Viva Crianças, a 21-year-old black woman named Catrina, talked about the harshness of life in the *favela*s as producing a sense of hopelessness and isolation, where everyone is so poor that they can only, in reality, take care of themselves.

> *Marcia*: What do you think about this saying?
> *Catrina*: About this phrase, *a vida é um osso duro de roer*? (Life is a bone that's hard to chew.)
> *Marcia*: Do you think that this phrase has anything to do with why people don't help others, why they think of only themselves?
> *Catrina*: Eh—this phrase is more, it's like a cross that I must drag. You know? It's a hard struggle every day, understand? Many people want to escape from this, because life is always hard and tight here. You know, so life is—you can't think about anyone else. You're always pushing or shoving, you know? Sometimes you try to hope and imagine. You know? Do you know what it means to be *desesperado*? (A desperate person.) This means that you wish you could be a criminal. This is how I feel a lot of times. How am I going to pay for my tuition at the *faculdade*? I say "Oh my God, I haven't paid the university!" I have to help my mother. I divide what I make for food that we're going to eat, and I despair.
> *Marcia*: You are saying that your life and the lives of others are very hard and it's so difficult that it takes up all your attention? It's difficult to worry about anyone else?

> *Catrina*: Yes, it's difficult. If I don't pay for what I need, nobody else is going to pay it for me! (laughter) Understand? Many times it's like this. But it's like I said, for people to just survive, the situation stays the way it is. Understand? Maybe—I don't know what to say—but myself and all the people I know have a lot of problems.

Support systems within poverty-stricken *favela*s are almost nonexistent. Hungry children are shooed away from the doorways of destitute mothers, grandmothers, and daughters who are themselves living with the constant hunger and filth that poverty forces upon them. Support systems come from the children and youth themselves. Nicolas, a nine-year-old brain-injured boy who attended Viva Crianças and APAE, provides a clear example of the kinds of support expected from the children of the poor by their families who struggle to keep order and cleanliness within their shacks.

> *Nicolas:* I bring in the brush and clean everything. I wash the dishes, then I clean the house, after I clean the house, I make the beds, and after I take the sofa, and put it on top of the other sofa, and then I get the table that's in the living room and put it on top of the sofas, and then I go and get the squeegee and cloth and put water in the house.
> *Marcia*: Do you do this every day or what?
> *Nicolas*: Almost every day.

One day, several mothers at Bom Jesus told me about the support they expect from their children. I was intrigued and asked if they'd be specific about the kinds of help that their children (daughters, in this instance) were required to provide for them on a daily basis. One mother gave the following litany of chores her daughter did each day:

Rayssa: She helps me make dinners, wash clothes, clean the house, all these things.
Marcia: Is she helping out with the care of the other children.
Rayssa: Yes, she helps me! Wow, she really helps me.
Marcia: She helps you a lot. If you had to pay someone to help you with your other children, there's no way you could do that is there? To help you at home?
Rayssa: Me, to help me? You can't raise a child without them helping you because when they grow up to be a woman, she won't want to do anything. You can't be that way!

When the realities of childhood in poverty are compared with those of the middle and upper classes, the ideological differences that separate the children of the poor from the children of the privileged are starkly visible. The following is an excerpt from a discussion I had with Professor Ricardo, an upper-class man living in the city center in Morro de Santana. I asked him if his children worked:

Professor Ricardo: They work now, the older ones (they are in the *Universidade Federal* in *Belo Horizonte*).
Marcia: And the younger one? (Who's nine years old).
Professor Ricardo: No, he doesn't work.
Marcia: If he wanted to work would you help him do that, or give your consent?
Professor Ricardo: I don't know how to respond to this. It depends on what kind of work he wanted to do.
Marcia: If he wanted to work at something so that he could buy a bicycle for example.
Professor Ricardo: Yeah. It depends—I think it depends on how conscious he is.
Marcia: If he wanted to sell ice cream?

Professor Ricardo: I don't think that I'd agree to that because this kind of work isn't very proper in the scheme of our lives.

Marcia: Because it has to do with your social class?

Professor Ricardo: Yes. I think so. Because it determines what your social place will be. So, in my structure (social place) many times I can say that I agree or would agree, depending on the work, but, deep down, I don't agree.

Marcia: Thank you for your honesty. I was asking because I have been very involved in the daily life of economically poor children and youth here in Morro de Santana for some time now. Many of these children have to work.

Professor Ricardo: Right. If I had a boy that wanted to work to earn money, and he wanted to sell ice cream, I think I would think about my social position. The situation isn't just about social class, it's about your *situaçao proprio* (individual characteristics, your proper personal place within your community). It's different from the situation of work in the US—the situation of work in Brazil. It's like a person that does domestic work. Here in Brazil it reveals a lot about our mentality (concerning the mind, intellectualism, spiritualism). And we take action according to our mentality.

Marcia: So, you'd be afraid that he'll (your son) hurt his reputation or that his life would be more difficult because of this (selling ice cream on the streets)?

Professor Ricardo: No. It's that I haven't considered the fact that he'd begin to work at nine years of age,

> because I don't understand this. I don't understand the need to have young children working.
> *Marcia*: It's not part of your reality, right?
> *Professor Ricardo*: Right. I don't understand why a child at nine years of age would have to work.

Here, we can see the great divide between the social constructions that define the childhood for the poor and for the elite. Historically, child labor was expected from the children of slaves, and indeed has continued as a rite of passage for children of color, and for children who are poor and of the lower social classes, regardless of skin color. Dark skin simply deepens the stigma of poverty and low social class. In addition, Professor Ricardo can't conceive of a young child working, because to him, childhood is not a time for labor, worry, or earning an income.

A mother named Bárbara, who worked as a domestic servant most of her life, with a history of alcoholism and violent home abuse by her husband, moved to São Paulo to try to start over again. She didn't have a support system to help her, so she used her older daughter (eleven-year-old Milena, whom I've discussed) to work in her place in order to extinguish the debts she owed for their room and board.

> *Bárbara*: I went to take them (her two daughters) to São Paulo and when we arrived there I broke my leg. I was there, unemployed with my two daughters. I had a broken leg, I was unemployed, without a place to stay, and without the ability to work. The work that I would have done for my friend, my daughter (Milena) did, and this one (the younger daughter) stayed in school.
> *Marcia*: So Milena is having to repeat a grade?
> *Bárbara*: There wasn't any other way. It was difficult. We have to let it pass. It was a terrible thing. I feel really badly about this.

Another example is Benício who began working at the age of ten, helping his father at his cooking job. Benício, even though he wasn't paid for his labor, significantly added to his family's income by securing his father's position by increasing his productivity. During this time, Benício dropped out of school in order to help his father.

>*Marcia*: How many hours a day did you work with him?
>*Benício*: I worked six hours a day with him.
>*Marcia*: Did you receive a salary or were you paid for your work?
>*Benício*: No, I wasn't paid, no. I was just helping him.
>*Marcia*: So, was he able to do more work with you than without you?
>*Benício*: Yes, that's right, he could finish his work faster with me helping him.

The above examples are a commonplace event for the children of the poor in Morro de Santana. While Brazil in general has an illiteracy rate of 16.7 percent, Morro de Santana has had school drop-out rates (in the public schools where poor children of color are educated) as high as 70 percent, where after the first grade, children frequently hit the streets in order to work and help support their families (Roberto Silva, director, Viva Crianças, 1997, personal communication).

All the projects I worked with included horticulture as a part of their daily routine. At some projects, vegetable gardens were lush and beautiful and provided most, if not all, of the fresh produce used each day to feed the children. Aside from a lack of support by immediate family due to their inability to buy seeds, tools, and fertilizer, children found that their attempts to supplement their families' nutrition by planting small gardens (using techniques they learned at the projects they attended) were also unproductive within the *favela*s. It was common for small family gardens to be raided by neighbors. Indeed, Viva Crianças kept a dense jungle of foliage around the project garden as a way to keep out people who often steal food from any garden that has open access.

I have discussed the absence of support networks and support systems among *favelados* in Morro de Santana, and have demonstrated how important working street children are to the survival of their parents. Their labor, both at home and on the streets, often makes the difference between survival and starvation, between having a shack or the street as a place to wander and sleep. Considering the reality of their lives, the stereotypes that define them as vagabonds, thieves, and worthless riff-raff are deplorable. In Brazil the children of the economically privileged classes are seen as cute, cuddly, and clean children who are to stay innocent and protected for as long as possible, removed from the adult world where responsibilities or worries are a reality. If a child looks dirty, isn't cute, is lean and muscular from labor and hunger, he is seen as spoiled goods. The mostly dark-skinned children of the poor are frequently perceived as deviant by most in the upper classes, who often speak as if these children should be removed from sight, despite the fact that they are not only supporting their own independence, but also the very survival of their families.

The miserable conditions of everyday life create a shame so deep that the poor act against each other. This is not to blame the poor for their poverty. Indeed, like the "gaps and fissures...portions of histories that get suppressed in the later reconstruction of History..." described by Louise Lamphere in *Work and the Production of Silence*, the poor in Brazil have, in part, come to know themselves and their history through the eyes of those who have repressed them (Lamphere 1997:263). Instead of questioning the social, racial, and economic conditions that perpetuate their poverty, the poor Afro-Brazilian often absorbs the deprecating and demeaning stereotypes constructed and used by the elite to describe them. Robin Sheriff cogently describes this process in this way:

> I assert that in focusing on salient discourses, contested cultural domains, and public forms of conflict and power, cultural and linguistic anthropologists, and other social scientists, have overlooked the significance of communal forms of silence in shaping the social and political landscape. I argue that such customary silences constitute "cultural censorship," which, unlike state-sponsored censorship, is practiced in the absence of explicit coercion or enforcement…cultural censorship tends to be constituted through, and circumscribed by, the political interests of dominant groups (Sheriff 2000:114–132).

In this way the darker-skinned poor collaborate in keeping themselves in poverty. This is part of the cycle that keeps the native intelligence battling itself, enmeshed within an endless web of ignorance, poverty, anger, and immobility.

In Chapter Six I address Viva Crianças and its creator and director, Roberto Silva. A brief historical and biographical sketch of Silva's life is presented and the political and historical influences that impacted him are discussed. It is during Silva's childhood and adolescences that his political ideologies were formed, and it is these ideas that were to direct the creation and generation of Viva Crianças.

CHAPTER SIX
VIVA CRIANÇAS

In this chapter I present a historical and biographical sketch of Roberto Silva, the creator of Viva Crianças, and show the theoretical and philosophical influences that directed the project's creation. This chapter describes the aims and goals of Viva Crianças, as I understood them, and discusses the types of programmed activities offered to street children by Viva Crianças. Finally, this chapter examines street children's reactions to these various activities.

In 1997, nearly a third of Morro de Santana's 60,000 citizens were under the age of fourteen. Roughly ten percent of this age group was registered by the city as attending one of the nineteen NGO projects established to help poor children (*Conselho Municipal de Assistência Social de Morro de Santana, Controle Social e Participação Popular, 27 de janeiro de 2.000* (Municipal Council of Social Assistance of Morro de Santana, Popular Participation and Social Control). Eleven of these projects served children up to age six; the remaining primarily served youth up to fifteen years old.

The first project to be discussed here has its roots in the folk-culture of Minas Gerais. Viva Crianças is a project with over fifteen years of active operation in the city of Morro de Santana. Developed and directed by Roberto Silva, an anthropologist with a focus on popular culture, Viva Crianças's diverse ideology combines elements of Brazilian folklore, imported constructions of childhood, and the free school movement of the 1960s in the US.

Roberto Silva: Historical Placement and the Creation of Viva Crianças

In order to discuss the project Viva Crianças and its ideological base, placing it and its creator, Roberto Silva, within Brazil's political history is essential, for this will help to explain the wide gap that I found between the project's ideology and its actual day-by-day practice.

Silva's ideological foundations were laid during his childhood, in the Brazil of the 1940s. Then, Brazil was still a largely underdeveloped country with widespread disease, nearly nonexistent medical care, and an overall life expectancy of 46 years. Its economy was still dependent primarily on the production and exportation of coffee. The massive push for industrialization, the proliferation of political parties during this era, the fear of communism, the huge rural-to-urban migration, and the inequality and oppressive nature of an educational system that validated Brazil's historical roots to Portugal and the monarchy all contributed to Silva's ideological development.

In Brazil, one is a mixture of Portuguese, Indigenous, and Black African. Although race and its definition are difficult to categorize, having a strong Black African resemblance is rarely a matter of pride. For Roberto Silva, his roots, especially those that led back to his *Tía Gorda* (fat aunt), proved to be extremely important, leading him to pursue studies in history, anthropology, and folklore. The following story from *"Folclore: Roteiro de Pesquisa"* ("Folklore: Summary of Research") relates Silva's concern about his historical roots:

> I was seven years old, entering school for the first time in Belo Horizonte. On the first day of class, a very gentle teacher took us to the library to introduce us to words. She opened the book of the most beautiful stories and began to read, pausing: "There was a place very far away, where there lived a king and a queen." I was enchanted with what I was hearing and immediately interrupted and said, "Teacher, I have an aunt that is a queen!" So, she calmly responded, "Be a little quiet and listen. This is a little false history, a false story. These kings and queens did not really exist." And she continued to read. But, one more time I insisted, "But I have an aunt that is a queen, it is true." After my third attempt to intervene, the teacher ordered me to *cala a boca* (shut your mouth). At the end of my first day of class I was sent to the room of the *direitora* (director) like a *menino problema* (problem child). Never again, during all my grade school years did I talk about this fact (1991, 1997).

When Silva was in high school, he attempted to talk about his *Tía Gorda* for a second time. His teacher, a history professor, refused to let him speak and told him, "Shut your mouth, stop saying this nonsense, and pay attention in class. I am talking about the kings and queens, important people. Here in Brazil, we've never had these. You cannot possibly have a royal family, look at your name, look at your color." Silva (who is *moreno*) vowed never to bring up this subject again.

However, after graduation from high school Silva found himself in Ouro Preto where he had gone to work with his brothers who had opened a business.

> At the end of high school, I went to Ouro Preto and one day, I was reading *To the Unknown God*, by John Steinbeck, sitting in the depths of the church cemetery of São José and I began to observe and think about the many buildings and walls of the buildings that were around me. "Who were these made for? Why? How, and when?" I discovered in that instant that I could not say anything about this and many other questions, simply because I did not know the history of our people. "These people, do they not have the same history of my origins?" It was on this day that I resolved to attend to history. During four years I had studied the life and trajectory of the kings, queens, and important persons of all that came here. But where could I study my history and the history of my ancestors' roots that continued to be hidden and in limbo? Where could I study about my origins?

Silva returned to Belo Horizonte (where he was born) and entered the university to study anthropology, where he eventually specialized in folklore.

> Today, as I reach the middle of my life, I believe that I've been able to reveal a large part of these unknown issues. The university is a society that wanted me to be a professor. I wanted to go much deeper. I wanted more. I became an educator. This is the prime or principal material of my work…culture.

Silva told me later that his *Tía Gorda* was *the Rainha Perpétua do Congado*, the (Perpetual Queen of the *Congado*), part of the secret brotherhoods developed by Black African Slaves in Minas Gerais (Kiddy 1998). The *Rainha Perpétua do Congado* is a key figure in a pantomimic folk dance of African origin. She is revered by dancing and by fights performed by the guards of the *Moçambiques, Congos*, sailors, villains, *catapões*, and *caboclinhos*. To Silva, this story is what led him "...to what I do nowadays. I became an educator due to an existential necessity and also because I believe that this is the only way to give back—through a practical and educational way—all the privileges that I've had" and it is a way to be part of the privileged people with whom he now works (personal communication 1997).

During the 1970s, Silva began working with SENAC (National Society for Education, Arts, and Culture) in the area of tourism and he began conducting research about craftspeople and popular culture for the hotel school for which he worked in tourism. He was contacted by a colleague working for a project called *Centro Nacional de Preferência Cultural* (The National Center for Cultural Preference), who wanted to develop a project that could identify both popular Brazilian cultural roots and the origins of Brazil's persistent problems of unemployment and low household income. In a 1997 interview, Silva told me,

> In 1975 we had a *roda* (talk circle) to discuss with friends in Brasilia the ideas of developing work around popular culture—there were politicians there that began to talk in a restaurant and each one arrived and asked the waiter for something. "Bring some French wine" or "bring some Swiss cheese," or "I want some Spanish Cognac," and here we were getting together to talk about the problems of Brazilians. And then, the person from the Ministry of Industrial Commerce was

there and he provoked everyone by saying, "Look, it is funny that we're here to talk about Brazilian problems and each one has asked for something from another country."

It was Silva's fierce pride of being Brazilian and his frustration with foreign influences in the marketplace within the Brazilian economy that led him to develop *Dedos de Gentes* (Fingers of the People), the cooperatives that form part of the NGO that houses Viva Crianças.

This *roda* and subsequent ones reinforced Silva's emerging ideas about popular culture and gave him the opportunity to begin thinking about the creation of an NGO that would work with children and youth in the areas of education, popular culture, and development. By 1982, Silva and a few interested friends began to develop their ideas for their larger organization and Viva Crianças. Silva and his friends created

> ...a model, an operational model of culture that we could work with. This model needed to utilize and test in practice our ideas of popular culture. We had a lot of problems because [it was hard to work] with the bureaucratic processes [and to get] the people in the communities [to comprehend our visions], so that we could get our projects up and running.

By 1984 Viva Crianças had become an NGO. The essential ideological base of Viva Crianças is constructed around three principal areas: education, culture, and development. According to Silva, popular culture is the essence of culture and exists in innumerable definitions, all of which are rooted in *o folclore do povo* (the folklore of the people). Here, people (across class, race, gender, and age) are the most important element; they make folklore possible in the first place. In Brazil, folklore is traditionally understood to be the symbolic and superstitious world of the backward and ignorant peasant. For Silva, who reverses the traditional usage of folklore, it is also true that the carriers of folklore are the intellectuals and scholars, who adopt and recycle (often unknowingly) folk traditions whose origins are from the people. According to Silva, "Starting with this premise, all of us, wanting to or not, are part of the people and are therefore, producers and consumers of culture, which is dominated by traditional aspects."

As the ideological framework for Viva Crianças began to take shape, tradition became a tool by which the children and youth participating in Viva Crianças came to be identified. At Viva Crianças, tradition is linked to social facts and elements (materials in the environment and social and spiritual [religious] practices) that have been passed down from generation to generation via actual experience or as folklore. Here, tradition embodies the character and cohesion of the people who came before you via games, stories, traditional herbal medical knowledge, curative folk traditions, and other ingrained practices. In this sense, tradition is valued as the history of the present that is alive and in constant transmission from one generation to another. This is the source of the educational foundations that Viva Crianças practices.

Silva's definition of folklore and popular culture is as follows: "Everything that people do, think, feel, and express is intimately related and integrated to their work and to their day-to-day social, material, and spiritual existence—[these things] do not exist just to exist but to attend to daily responses and necessities in local social groups and in regional and national arenas."

With this background in place, we can now begin investigating the various programs I participated in during my fieldwork. The following sections outline the ideological gaps at Viva Crianças, where the daily practice experienced by the children and the coordinators differed widely from the written and spoken propaganda used to describe the project.

Viva Crianças: The Project

In *Street Children and NGOs in Rio,* Flavia Impelizieri provides a good overview of the types of NGOs common in urban settings. She breaks them down into categories: **shelters** (serving children and youth who are on the streets almost permanently), **street-education projects** (street educators who go to street youth on the streets), and NGO projects often referred to as **day-centers** (serving street children who often live at home but are poor and underprivileged) (1995:69–73).

Viva Crianças fit into the day-center category of NGOs. Daily attendance averaged between 80 and 100 individuals who were spread over two sessions, one in the morning from 7:30 to 11:30, and the other from 12:30 to 4:30 in the afternoon. Morning and afternoon sessions generally served between 35 and 45 children each, although the project advertised itself in community fliers and grant reports as serving 180 children daily (Silva 1991). Viva Crianças began each morning and each afternoon session with a *roda grande* (large circle) where the day's events would be presented, announcements made (by children, adolescents, and coordinators), and where problems were discussed. The *roda* was symbolically presented to me by Roberto Silva and the main coordinator "Alana" as the hub of all activity, the place where the project revolved and evolved. The *roda* is where the culture of the children and their community was, according to Silva, to be found and expressed. In reality, the *roda* expressed not only the local popular culture (where games and stories were sometimes played and told), but also the aggression and anger, the frustration and social and economic oppression street children experienced on a daily basis. Ironically Viva Crianças's ideology lacked the economic and political awareness to address the daily life issues of the children they intended to serve.

The *Roda*

When I first started working at Viva Crianças in January of 1997, I was under the impression from the literature provided by Roberto Silva that this project was conceived and organized with the needs of the children and their families in mind. In other words, I assumed it was built from the ground up rather than the top down.

I arrived at the project each day around noon and would often eat with the children and other coordinators. The noon lunch was usually quite good and included fresh vegetables grown in the project garden, rice, beans, juice (mixed from powder), and occasionally chicken. After lunch, the noon group formed the *roda grande*, where we would spend most of an hour attempting to discuss issues of importance. The *roda grande* began with a great deal of confusion. The coordinator leading the *roda* was instructed by Alana to sit without saying anything until the circle became quiet of its own accord. Usually this took about 20 minutes or more, and sometimes quiet would never come. The *roda* actually began when the assigned coordinator (coordinators rotated each week to lead the *roda*) initiated the discussion by bringing up problems that had occurred in the project the previous day. In addition, it was a common practice for the children to write notes to friends and coordinators, congratulating them on birthdays or expressing warm or friendly feelings. The notes were a big success and everyone liked getting them. Discussions of problems tended to be frantic and noisy, and at times they were filled with aggression (shouting of obscenities and slapping, hitting, or punching). Each *roda grande* ended with circle games and songs that attempted to bring everyone together again after the tensions and anger brought out during discussion of problems. It was very rare for a problem that occurred in the project (such as robberies, violence, abuse of materials, or infractions of the rules) to be resolved at this time. However, later, the children gathered in their individual groups of approximately three to eight children. Each *roda pequena* was named by the children and their coordinators to represent some quality agreed upon by every participant in the group. Examples of names for these groups included "The Lions" and "The Champion Readers." The smaller groups discussed interests, problems, and project rules. Compared to the *roda grande*, coordinators and youth worked more intimately with each other in the *rodas pequenas*, which allowed for more in-depth discussions and often led to a more successful resolution of problems.

One day in my music group, I asked Diego (nine years old) what he felt about the *roda grande*. I wanted to know what he felt the *roda* was about and if he felt that he was being heard when he brought up problems to be discussed.

> *Marcia*: Do you like the *roda*?
> *Diego*: The big *roda*? No.
> *Marcia*: Why?
> *Diego*: The boys are *zombeteiro* (tempting, teasing), they scream at you. They fight with the other boys, and if you sit close to them they try to get you to talk. It is hard to not talk to them and get in trouble.
> *Marcia*: Why do you think they scream and fight?
> *Diego*: I do not know.
> *Marcia*: Do you like the small *roda*?
> *Diego*: No, I do not like it either. Because the kids leave the group, talking all the time, fighting all the time, hitting.

Marcia: In both the big and small *roda*?
Diego: Yes.
Marcia: OK, can you tell me what you like about the *roda*? What things are important to you in the *roda*?
Diego: Yes, I like the notes that are saying good things that we write to each other.
Marcia: Why do you like them?
Diego: Because they are very happy things for us. You have the opportunity to say things that are very good to other people. Like the first day that you came. We gave you those notes.

Diego's statement about aggression in the *roda* is reflected by many other youth, particularly the younger prepubescent boys who were the constant victims of the aggressions of the more combative adolescent boys. It is also interesting to note that Diego stated that talking in the *rodas* would get one in trouble, "It is hard to not talk to them and get in trouble." Yet, both adolescents and children, male and female, appreciated the "good news cards." It was one of the few times when positive statements about themselves could be heard and exchanged. The twins Vitor and Enzo were more articulate about their experiences in the *roda* when I asked them if they felt that problems were solved in either the *roda grande* or the *roda pequena*. They observed that problems are talked about, but not resolved.

Enzo: This is what I wanted to say, that there in the *roda*, almost all the problems are **not** solved. They are only resolvable in the group (the group that each child belongs to).
Marcia: OK, the small group?
Enzo: The small group that they belong to.
Vitor: Yeah, in the small *roda*.
Marcia: Do you agree Vitor?

> *Vitor*: I agree, yes.
> *Marcia*: You think you are resolving the problems with the adolescents in the small *rodas*?
> *Vitor and Enzo*: No, no…
> *Marcia*: (laugh) OK, let's begin again.
> *Enzo*: The adolescents are another problem…right?
> *Vitor*: Ah…there, anything I do they are hitting me (the older boys), André, Luan, Diogo, Lago, Calebe, Felipe, or Edim…these guys.
> *Marcia*: How old are they?
> *Vitor*: About 15 years old, more or less. Some of them must be 17 or less.

Enzo and Vitor echo Diego when they tell me about the aggression and violence of the adolescent boys against them. However, both Enzo and Vitor felt, at least part of the time, that problems were solved by discussion in the smaller *roda*. Nonetheless, according to the twins, the *roda pequena* did not resolve the issues of aggression between adolescents and younger children. My field notes of April 1997 concur:

> Problems in the *Roda*. Problems during the day, problems in small groups, problems between people are resolved or attempted to be resolved during the *roda* itself. The *roda* represents a symbolic form of community and unity. Today the *roda* was difficult. Alana called the group back, after we waited for about twenty minutes for them to stop talking and shouting. Finally we began the discussion that ends each day. It is a time to talk about problems and to evaluate the day's work. Alana talked about the fighting that occurred today, disruptions, disorder, screaming, not listening.

> The small groups before the large *roda* met today to try to resolve the problems. The representatives of each group presented their group's ideas. Very difficult process.

While the ideology of Viva Crianças created this idealized notion of the meaning of the *roda grande* and the *roda pequena*, the on-the-ground reality of the *roda* experienced by the children and the coordinators was quite different. I was frequently told by Catrina and by Roberto Silva that the *roda* was the heart of the project, where words were turned into discussions, and discussions led to resolutions. Roberto Silva was deeply influenced by Paulo Freire and his writings, particularly the *Pedagogy of the Oppressed.* In this text Freire articulates how words embody both reflection and action, and in this sense, words and discussions are praxis in action (Freire 1970:75–118).

> Dialogue is the encounter between men, mediated by the world, in order to name the world. Hence, dialogue cannot occur between those who want to name the world and those who do not wish this naming—between those who deny other men the right to speak their word and those whose right to speak has been denied them. Those who have been denied their primordial right to speak their word must first reclaim this right and prevent the continuation of this dehumanizing aggression (1970:77).

Ironically, the idealism of the project prevented the development of practices that could address the everyday reality of the poverty and misery lived by the children *outside* of the project. While the technique of dialoguing is essential for successful communication in all aspects of daily life, what transpired in the *rodas* did not address the limitations of poverty experienced on a daily basis by the children and their families. Indeed, the subjects of poverty, disease, inequality, racism, and hunger were never addressed throughout my entire year at the project. The premise of the project was to focus on the popular culture rooted within the historical legacies of poor Afro-Brazilian children, yet the focus on popular culture eliminated the discussion of racism, while idealizing the life of the poor and perpetuating folk traditions that kept them in poverty. Social and racial inequalities were flatly ignored. I was told that the responsibility for resolving the problems of aggression, robberies, and damaging property was placed upon the children. Hence, such problems continued to exist because the essential issues that make life so harsh and fragile for the youth were not addressed. Learning how to be discursive is not a solution to poverty in and of itself. Effective activism requires many skills, including an effective education system that works together with social services that can offer some relief from the grind of poverty. NGOs are beginning to address the real-life circumstances of street children. Indeed, there is a growing movement among NGOs and governmental bodies in Brazil to provide effective vocational training to youth attending NGO programs in order to assist them as they enter the job market. Impelizieri found that job training and educational tutoring were among the most appreciated (by street children) types of assistance provided by NGOs (1995:101–103).

An example of the ways in which dissent was dismissed at the project concerned the cook, Bárbara. The children and adolescents liked working with Bárbara. She was fun, happy, and welcomed their participation in the daily kitchen tasks. While working in the kitchen, jokes and laughter were common. Serious discussions also surfaced and there were moments of truly creative dialogues where children and youth brainstormed on health, hunger, and poverty. Bárbara's kitchen seemed a place of liberty, a place where the children displayed less aggression and competition than I normally observed in the rest of the project. One day Bárbara told me she was leaving the project.

> Alana (the main coordinator) did not want Bárbara, the cook, to work at the project any longer. As I listened, I came to understand that to Bárbara, the reason she was fired had to do with authority and control. Alana did not want the children to have freedom and liberty and in Bárbara's kitchen the children had liberty. Several children were in the kitchen and they were visibly angry, and several said that if Bárbara was going, so were they. They wanted a voice and felt that their voice was not being heard. It has been interesting to watch how the project really functions on a daily basis and to see how the children's feelings have been addressed or not addressed. Yesterday in the *roda*, Alana had to wait a long time for the children to become silent. This is not in itself unusual. Once she began to speak, she was interrupted by a few angry boys who seemed to be the more aggressive children in the project. I did not witness girls expressing the kind of explosive anger I have talked about above. At one point she said "I have to talk really loud because X will not shut his mouth, eh?" Scattered between her attempts to speak, during which time she said, "Today I received many notes, some good and some not so good. I would like to start with the good notes." "No!" shouted the leaders of the protest, "Begin with the horrible ones!" they shouted. Alana said that there were no horrible notes, only ones that were not so good. "Begin with them!" they demanded. It was only minutes into the *roda* that Alana dismissed them into groups for activities to be done that day,

and I also sensed that such extreme dissent from the children was not encouraged. I am surprised that the ideology of Viva Crianças, based on Paulo Freire's notions of self-liberation and self-responsibility, ignored the dissent of the children they worked for.

The project fired Bárbara, and many children were upset. I was told by several children, both girls and boys, that they wished they could prevent the project from firing Bárbara, but they told me nothing they said would influence the "people at the top."

On another occasion, interpersonal trouble arose during my music class between several boys who began a fight over what instruments they wanted to play. Catrina (the coordinator assigned to work with me) and I followed the policy of the project and formed our small *roda*. I watched as Catrina began the *roda*. I wrote the following in my field notes:

> My music group, which is also the group that Catrina has every day in the project, had some personal problems between individuals that had to be solved in a small *roda*. The small *roda* began in what I have come to see as a typical pattern, with Catrina doing most of the talking, which went something like this: "Look, all this aggression has to stop. How do you expect to get anything done? In the large *roda*, everyone talks over everyone else. This is disrespectful. I do not agree with it. You do not have any respect for each other or for us (the coordinators)."

As this example demonstrates, aggressions are strictly controlled and admonished while the youth remain voiceless. The *roda* ended without discussion, the fight and its cause left unexplored and unanswered.

Throughout my work at Viva Crianças, I came to see that robberies were a constant problem. Supplies would disappear, children would lose their school materials (most of which cost them and their parents several days' salary), shoes and clothes were stolen. Over a period of days several robberies occurred and three adolescents were suspected of committing the thefts. A small *roda* was arranged and I asked if I could join them. By this time I had been at the project for six months and was an accepted part of the daily routine. Again, I draw extensively from my field notes:

> Today was very important; it was a day in which I was able to see how the project deals with problems of robbery. The subject was brought up during the large *roda* and taken to a small *roda* run by Maria Vitória, Giovanni, Letícia, and Catrina (coordinators at the project). Children from the large *roda* were told to come to the small *roda* who were witness to the incident of the thievery or who knew anything about it. In this way the children are encouraged to "tell on each other," dividing them and creating conflicts between them. Those who are responsible for creating difficulties do not take responsibility for revealing their actions. Often, while working with the children, I am struck by the quickness of their anger and their expressions of violence toward one another. I have witnessed what appears to be the need to grab quickly what you want because the chance to get it may never come again. There is almost no discussion of personal feelings, no exploration of the feelings of others.
>
> Four boys had taken matte knives from Maria Vitória's work area, new knives that she uses to cut cardboard and other material to make the games for

the *Bornal de Jogos* (Bag of Games). After the children who knew anything about the robbery had reported what they had heard or what they saw, they were dismissed from the *roda*, leaving only the four accused boys and us adults. Maria Vitória seemed to be leading the group. Catrina and I were observers. Maria Vitória tells them that robbery is a crime that the police would come to your house and take you to prison to resolve such crimes. Giovanni tells them that if you know about a crime and do not say anything about it you are also committing a crime. There is no talk about WHY they steal. I find this very interesting and curious. Motive is not important. Maria Vitória tells them that they are also robbing the very people (the project) who help them. Their actions reflect on their parents as well and on the image of the project. To rob a place that just wants to help you, that trusts you, that is here to do things for you, is unbelievable. If you rob small things, you will move on to robbery of bigger things. The boys say that the police rob and murder. Giovanni asks if this is a reason to do it as well. Here is an opportunity to talk about social injustice in the country and in their lives and an opportunity to affirm the difficulties of their lives and how to change such inequality, but there is no discussion about social injustice or corruption, or about social responsibility or about how you can positively use your civil rights to change oppression.

The *roda* described above ended by sending the adolescents home to retrieve the stolen objects and bring them back to the project within an hour. Their parents were not called, their poverty was not addressed, and they left feeling angry and frustrated. I later talked with the four boys about the thefts. One boy, whom I will call Calebe, told me,

> Look, we do not have anything, right? I do not have money to buy a matte knife and I needed one to do some work, and I need things for school. So I take what I need. At home, anything I have is taken by others. I do not have anything that I can keep.

Nine-year-old Nicolas stated that he did not like the aggression of the older boys. "I do not like the boys that hit other kids. The big kids hit the smaller ones.... There are times when the big kids are exploiting the younger ones."

Sarah's response was uncommon, as she described how she perceived the *roda* and the resolution of problems:

> *Marcia*: Do you like the *roda*?
> *Sarah*: Yes
> *Marcia*: Why?
> *Sarah*: Because in the *roda* we discuss the things that we are going to do, we discuss what we cannot do...
> *Marcia*: About? How? For example?
> *Sarah*: For example, a boy is making trouble, so we go and talk in the circle about us not doing these kinds of things, and when someone has a birthday we announce it in the *roda*.
> *Marcia*: Do you think that problems are resolved in the *roda*?
> *Sarah*: Yes, they are, but there are some people who are really difficult that make a lot of work for others, that do many difficult things to people.
> *Marcia*: Do you think it is possible for these kids to change their behavior?

Sarah: Yes, it is possible.
Marcia: How?
Sarah: For example, they did something wrong, and he sees that he did something wrong. Then he gets the kid—he saw the kid do something wrong so he calls the kid and then they talk and resolve it.
Marcia: The coordinators, they will help in this?
Sarah: Yes, they help.
Marcia: For example, if you have a problem with another kid, will you go and talk to a coordinator? And after, will the coordinator go and help you all?
Sarah: We will go and make a *roda*.
Marcia: Ah! With you all.
Sarah: Yes…
Marcia: With you, the person you were having problems with, and the coordinator?
Sarah: Yes.
Marcia: And will you then talk about the problem?
Sarah: Yes, we talk.
Marcia: Sometimes, do people end up crying?
Sarah: In the *roda* yes.
Marcia: Or get angry?
Sarah: They cry more than they get angry.
Marcia: Why, do you think?
Sarah: Because getting angry makes you cry, and it's the better way to express anger. It doesn't get you in trouble.

Based on my observations of the *roda*, girls tended to be less verbally combative and expressive, although there were exceptions. Luiza, a very strong-willed and combative girl of 15 years, is one example of aggression in girls. It was common for her to jump up in the *roda grande* and physically grab a boy her size and hit him. Sarah, unlike Luiza, was a shy girl by nature, and her comment may reflect more on her own emotional makeup than as a reliable statement about gender differences related to expressing emotions. Indeed, on several occasions I witnessed boys, usually preadolescents, breaking into tears during an argument or a fight (with another boy) in both the *roda* and in the project environment. I would like to speculate that Sarah's comments about anger generating crying may convey the sense of helplessness I often witnessed in the children at the project, and one of the strategies they used in order to find expression for their feelings. At home, crying often produced more anger and aggression from frustrated parents and older siblings, while at the project, crying often brought the attention of a sympathetic coordinator. In this sense, crying could be the result of the project's environment that allowed the children and youth to express their emotions, if not their thoughts. Remember that Viva Crianças embraced the ideology of childhood as a time of protection and as a time of sensitivity. Even though the coordinators found that their own childhoods conflicted with the project's ideology, they were nonetheless initially enchanted with such notions of the purity and innocence of childhood.

Games in the *Rodas*

One aspect of the *roda grande* that everyone enjoyed, including the coordinators, was the games that took place at the end of every meeting. During the games, which were introduced by the children and youth as well as by the coordinators, all participants shared the opportunity to switch roles and to shift power relations. Since most games had a leader and followers, the leaders found themselves to be not only the center of attention, but also somewhat godlike. Choosing themes, selecting people for special roles, hiding objects, were common tasks assigned to leaders as well as the sometimes-heroic task of locating hidden objects or guessing words or gestures by focusing attention on subtle body language and facial signals. One game that called on one's powers of observation went as follows:

> One person is sent out of the circle and called back in. Someone in the circle begins a new move, pulling their ears, or tapping their elbow…the person in the center must pay attention to who instigated the movement. If they can find the person, another person is chosen.

Word games were also common. My field notes describe one event that included coordinators and the parents of the youth.

> Alana explained that singing and word games are often played during the circle and demonstrated a circle game, asking the coordinators to begin, later asking the parents to join in and take part. This game was a word and body game. Different gestures, such as snapping your fingers or stomping your feet or wiggling your hips, were selected by the leader, who demonstrated what movements the rest of the circle were to follow.

I was most impressed with the word-rhythm games because they required a great deal of skill and attention to perform. Indeed, there were many times that order and harmony came into the *roda* simply by playing these games, but particularly the games where music and body gesture were incorporated. My field notes detailed one such *roda* performance:

> We ended the session with them teaching me circle dances with body gestures and rhythms. An example follows with the game called tic-key-tac, tic-key-tac,

> tic-key-tac, pom, pom. A large circle is formed, one person is selected to begin the game by choosing a body gesture and saying "tic-key-tac, tic-key-tac, tic-key-tac, pom, pom." The person directly to the right of the chosen person copies their gesture. The first person continues to perform their gesture and sounds while the person next to them imitates their sounds and gesture, and so on around the circle. When performed really well, which requires intense observation and quick responses, the circle produces an intricate and beautiful vocal band with body shuffling rhythms. They demonstrated another game, where heads are put together while standing in a circle and arms are put around each other. A footstep is used and a song is sung. As the circle moves around slowly, the song ends and one only hears the delicate shuffling of the foot rhythm as it continues after the end of the song.

Brazilian folk culture has been well documented and is beyond the scope of this research. Yet, it is important to state here that the *roda* in the various projects I was involved in served an important function as it linked the coordinators and youth together in a common purpose that reinforced and validated local traditions through games, songs, and dance in a forum designed to enhance fun, trust, and unity. This said, it is also important to state that the *roda* did not function as a place for the resolution of problems, nor did it provide a venue for the voices of the youth, who often felt frustrated and unheard.

The Kitchen and Garden

As stated above, Viva Crianças opens its gates five days a week from seven-thirty in the morning to four-thirty in the afternoon. Two sessions were offered, one in the morning and a second in the afternoon, with lunch served in between for both sessions. Viva Crianças had an extensive garden that provided all of the lunch vegetables. The city of Morro de Santana provided additional nutritional needs that included powdered juice mixes, white bread, powdered milk, eggs, beans, white rice, garlic, and other spices. I was always impressed with the food at Viva Crianças. Not only was it grown by the project (with the help of the children), but it was always freshly picked the day it was used. I quote from my field notes:

> Large bowls of fresh vegetables, carrots, lettuce, *mandioca* (a root vegetable), and onions sat on the ledges of the short walls that separate the kitchen from the front porch. The day was cloudy and intermittent rays of sunlight spread across the faces of the youth as they helped prepare the day's lunch. Peeling chunks of *mandioca* with large knives was an easy task for them, and those who were small used knives that fit their hands. If you are careful and cut to just the right depth, you can pull the tough outer skin off with a few twists of your wrist, using the knife as a wedge. On the stove, a large utility stove made for industrial use or for restaurants, sat a huge cooking pot filled with floating and bobbing pieces of *mandioca*. This root is a staple of Brazilian diet, with a wide array of recipes that turns the root into different kinds of cuisine…into a paste, or mashed, or cut into small pieces that are boiled and then fried, ground into the popular flour known as *farinha*, or

another popular dish as *farofa*. Here, manioc flour is toasted in butter or olive oil. You can fill the stomach of a hungry child with *mandioca*, for it's almost pure starch. My friend Celme told me that poor families fill the stomachs of their children with small amounts of *mandioca*. The root expands in the stomach and the child feels full, feels *satisfieta*.

I would, at times, go with the coordinators and children to the garden and bring up large quantities of fruits and vegetables. One day we went to the garden and we picked several huge bundles of bananas, 98 lemons, and some *acidrola*, a small red, sour fruit full of vitamin C. In the garden they have rows of lettuce, carrots, radishes, *quiabo* (okra), squash, sweet potatoes, mangos, papayas, *mandioca*, oranges, and more. One of the greatest services provided by Viva Crianças is its nutritional contribution to the children and youth who otherwise would probably be malnourished. Indeed, the garden was so prized and cherished that a virtual jungle surrounded it on all three potentially open sides. One day, Alana (the main coordinator) and I and a group of youth in my music class went looking for bamboo in the dense forest surrounding the garden. I was following the gardener, Seu Levi, as he entered the forest, when Alana took my arm and held me back. She told me it would be better to let Seu Levi cut a path for us because there are snakes living in the dense growth and sharp leaves that cut your skin. Before she could stop me I put my foot down into the thick grasses. I was wearing sandals and before I could pull my foot up it was covered with stinging ants. Alana told me that "the growth acts as a protection from beggars and thieves who would otherwise enter the garden and take the vegetables grown by the project."

During my first few months at the project I spent a great deal of my time in the kitchen helping prepare food for lunches. It was in the kitchen that I came to know many of the children, some of whom were to join my music class. The kitchen was a place where the division of labor was somewhat relaxed, where each person decided what task they liked doing and then proceeded to work on it. It was the children who taught me how to cut *mandioca*:

I helped cut and peel *mandioca* today. The children taught me how to cut it. If the piece of *mandioca* is small, hold it in your hand and cut off the ends (easier said than done: *mandioca* is a tough root with a thick bark-like skin). Then hold the root in your hand and plunge a heavy knife into the root (again easier said than done: if you plunge too hard, the knife will cut your hand; too soft and you have not broken through the tough outer bark). Then you wiggle the knife free from the root and peel the bark away. Under the bark is a pink skin, which I learned must also be removed. If you do it just right, the skin comes off very easily. If you find a long root, you hold it in your hand and use the knife like a machete and slice off sections, letting them fall onto the table.

Another horticultural goal for Viva Crianças was to plant and cultivate an extensive medicinal herb garden to create a natural pharmacy that would be used at the project and eventually taken into the community and sold to the public. During my tenure at Viva Crianças, the natural pharmacy project never materialized, even though the topic was embraced by several coordinators at the project (discussed below). At present, Viva Crianças grows a small number of herbs used to treat colds, fevers, head lice, stomach ailments, various rashes, and allergies. Part of Roberto Silva's philosophy is that the medical profession provides inadequate health care for the poor. Here, he believes, folk culture provides the answers for street youth.

Marcia: Do you use medicinal herbs for medicine?
Vitor: We do.

> *Marcia:* What type of herbs do you use? What do you use for medicine?
> *Enzo*: We use aloe vera to put on cuts, make a tea out of it, boil it and put it on a piece of cloth and put it on the cut.
> Marcia: Do you have or have you had head lice?
> *Enzo and Vitor:* Yes, we've had lots of them also. We cut our hair a lot and take out the lice.
> *Marcia:* Do you use herbs as well for head lice?
> *Enzo:* Yes, herbs for them too.

Yet, it is clear that folk culture and folk remedies are not the ultimate solution for a better quality of health care for the poor in Brazil. Herbs and herbal medications can take a long time to be effective, and in many cases herbal remedies are ineffective and at times harmful, in that they can delay the diagnosis of serious disease. The following excerpt from my field notes is an example of the pressures put on the coordinators by the upper staff at Viva Crianças to practice the ideology of the project:

> We (several coordinators and I) were talking about natural herbs and a project that Roberto Silva is trying to initiate where the *favela*s develop alternative medicine through the use of herbs so they will not be dependent on western medicine. A very worthy idea and interesting, but it becomes a kind of oppressive alternative. Pointing to Catrina's feet where each toe was wrapped in white medical tape, Alana asked her why they were bandaged. Catrina showed her the deep and painful corns on each of her toes and explained that it was difficult to walk each day the miles that she needed to travel to get to work at the project. Catrina had

> decided to go to the doctor to get them removed. Alana looked at me, shaking her head, explaining to me that the project had herbs Catrina could use but typically, Catrina went to the doctor. "Why?" Alana demanded of Catrina. Catrina explained that the herbs took a long time and that the doctors used medicine that would work in a few days. It had become too painful for her to walk the two hours each day to the project.

Health care in Brazil has an extensive literature, which cannot be addressed here. However, there is a general consensus among researchers that Brazil's pervasive clientelism has prevented health care reform, especially for the poor. Institutional obstacles, bureaucratic politics, and stubborn opposition to eliminate clientelist networks have resulted in few improvements in health care reform for the poor (Weyland 1995; Atkinson, Medeiros, and Lima 2000:619–36). Hence, Silva's attempts to provide basic medical care through locally grown herbs are admirable. It is unlikely that Brazil's health care system will radically change within the next century.

Despite the benefits that Viva Crianças's extensive gardens provided, it was also an area of contention for some of the youth at the project, according to several coordinators who frequently complained of having to argue with the youth in order to get them to go and work in the garden. In addition, Seu Levi complained about the lack of respect and care the children had when working with the plants. I recorded the following discussion I had with Seu Levi in my field notes:

> I talked with Seu Levi, the majestic and well-respected gardener at the project yesterday. I asked him, as he pulled carrots, cabbage, lettuce, herbs, and more for me to take home, if he worked with the children in

the garden. He told me that it was not possible; it was very difficult to work with the children because they do not have any patience, do not pay attention, and do not like to work if it is difficult. Another coordinator (Sophie) said that she has the same problems...that at home the parents do not pay any attention to their kids, just order them to do chores and then want them to get out of the house. Seu Levi said the same thing...the project was like a big creche or daycare center because the parents did not know what to do with their kids... they just want to keep them off the streets.

Getting the children to work in the garden was described by some of the coordinators as a difficult task. Morro de Santana, even though it is considered to be a mild climate for Brazil, often reaches the high nineties in the summer with moderate to high humidity. Laboring in the sun is often very tiring and many of the children resisted the hard work of weeding, hoeing, and digging in the garden. Two coordinators, Mirella and Sophie, described it this way:

Mirella: No one wants to go, and when they go, they mess up the garden. I could talk all I wanted to them... but I'm the one who is wrong (meaning that the project would not listen and Alana would blame them for not inspiring the youth to work in the garden). I started (working at Viva Crianças) in April 1996. I was a coordinator to assist the children to develop activities. I thought that I would say, "Well, today we will make toys," and everyone would go with no objections. But it did not happen. For example, I would say, "Today we will go to the vegetable garden," and everybody would say, "Oh great! No! I do not want to go. Oh, it is a pain

CHAPTER SIX 181

to go. I'm not going. No!" Then I have to say, "No, you're going!" If a boy went into the *horta* (vegetable garden) and stepped on the vegetables, it is all my fault. The fault is not the boy's, no, it is mine. It is because of your group—yes, that's what it is. And I think that this is wrong. It is wrong for sure. There is no doubt about it. It is not she (Alana)—Oh my God—I do not know, she preaches freedom, but the boy, you have to stay, you have to keep on watching him. He is there all day long, being watched. That's not freedom.

Marcia: The food, too; many children that I interviewed do not have much to eat at home.
Sophie: No, they do not.
Marcia: The only food that they eat that is nourishing for them is the food that they eat at the project.
Sophie: Yeah, generally.
Marcia: Do you think that the children like to and want to work in the vegetable garden?
Sophie: No. The majority do not want to. No, no, they do not want to. Something they should have at the project is to change all the types of work. Because the work that the youth are doing, they are not interested in (kitchen, gardening, weeding, cleaning the bathroom, garbage duty, recycling materials and organizing them, paper making, glue making). They should do something more, something bigger. But, close to the reality of their everyday lives. That's it. One thing I think that they could do is they could work with adults in the outskirts of the city…with their grandfathers, grandmothers, picking herbs. Then they could study them and then they would learn how to turn them into

medicines, and then they could sell them. This way they would be developing a job and the need for these medicines is great. They could make money.
Marcia: Yes, that's an interesting possibility that they could do.
Sophie: This is what I'm telling you, to do some type of work that will give them money and responsibility. There is more reality with their life this way, that the kids can use afterwards if they want to. That way they are going to learn something.

Aside from their distress at the resistance the children and youth demonstrated toward working in the garden, it is also clear that these two coordinators hold constructions of childhood that radically differ from the middle-and upper-class views of childhood, where children are expected to be free from the responsibilities and cares of the adult world. In this sense, Viva Crianças conflated these two constructions of childhood. On the one hand, to be a child means to have freedom and liberty, to play and be free from responsibility. On the other hand, to be a child of the poor means that work and responsibility must be addressed and realized at an early age. Such dichotomies were common for the children and youth at Viva Crianças, and as we have seen, the *roda* was one arena where such conflicts were demonstrated but not addressed.

Yet when I surveyed ten children at Viva Crianças about their favorite and least favorite activities in the project, I found that half of my informants stated that they liked working in the garden, and one-third listed gardening as their favorite activity. I can offer some possible suggestions as to why the children listed garden work as their favorite activity when several coordinators stated the opposite. First of all, working in the garden, which was very large (at least five acres), provided the children with a degree of freedom from supervision. I speculate that in this way the children and youth were practicing a form of resistance toward the coordinators, and perhaps toward the project's ideology that so conflicted with their daily reality. It was not difficult to disappear into a tree (tree climbing was a favorite activity) with a friend and hide and talk in the cool shade provided by the canopy of the tree. Secondly, the garden always had some vegetable or fruit that was ripe and ready to pick, and eating while weeding was also a strategy to increase one's nutrition and cut one's hunger. Finally, when I went to the garden with the children they did take pride in picking large amounts of fruits and vegetables and carrying them in rusty wagons or pulling them on large sheets of cardboard up the hill and into the project. All the children would run and gather around the food, licking their lips in anxious anticipation of their lunch. All fruits and vegetables were picked within two hours of each lunch period. In addition, all the children attending Viva Crianças ate with vigor, and were often scolded for taking more than they could eat.

When interviewing street children, I left the question of favorite activities open and without prompts. I simply asked, "What is the activity that you like to do most at the project?" Since I was the music instructor, the frequency of students who stated music as their favorite activity should be discounted, allowing for bias and their desire to please me. My experience at the project and my observations of activities that were most frequently initiated by the youth are to some extent supported by my small sample. Working in the kitchen, with Bárbara, was indeed a favorite activity. Soccer, especially with the boys, was an all-time favorite. Every day, during free time and often during scheduled activities, boys would break away from their groups to form informal soccer matches. Paper-making was also an enjoyable activity, especially during the hot and humid days of summer and fall. In order to make paper, water is an essential ingredient in all phases of the process, especially rinsing the wire mesh trays that held the paper pulp. It was refreshing and many times I found myself assisting in making paper with the youth in order to cool off and joke and have a good time. The chart below shows the favorite activities of the ten children who volunteered to participate in a survey on their favorite project activities. Eight of the children were in my music class, while two additional children from the project in general asked to be included in the survey. The favorite activities listed and the number of children who listed them were music (4), kitchen (3), garden (3), collecting recyclables (1), play (1), soccer (2), drawing (1), washing floors (1), making things (2).

Table 8. Viva Crianças Activities
N = 10

NAME	AGE	GARDEN	FAVORITE ACTIVITY
Diego	9	No	Music/Kitchen
Lais	14	Yes	Music/Kitchen/Recycling (sucata)
Enzo	12	Yes	Garden/Making Things/Soccer
Gustavo	11	Yes	Music/Paper Making/Soccer
Isabelle	10	No	Music/Paper Making/Soccer
Vitor	12	No	Soccer
Joana	11	No	Play, Draw
Maria Sophia	14	No	Music/Paper Making
Lucca	12	Yes	Garden/Make Things/Soccer
Nicolas	9	Yes	Garden/Play/Kitchen/Wash Floors
10	Average age 11.4	5 yes, 5 no	

CHAPTER SIX   185

Educational Activities

Before discussing the educational activities offered by Viva Crianças, a description of the physical layout and appearance of the project will be helpful in conceptualizing how the project looked and functioned within its open-air environment. Viva Crianças is located behind a famous church, the *Basílica São Ricardo*, and is fronted by a long wall that runs the length of the facility, in roughly a straight line for a distance of about one city block. There are no identifying marks, plaques, or banners that announce the project. Once inside the project, immediately to the right is an L-shaped building housing the wood shop and storage and working spaces. To the left is the long I-shaped building that runs the length of the outer wall. The actual structure that houses Viva Crianças is made from cinderblocks and is open on one side, which faces out onto a long expansive grass field about the length of a *futebol* (soccer) field. At each end of the field are large trees that provide shade during the hot summers. This long building is divided into several sections with a total of six rooms on the lower floor. An upper floor runs half the length of the structure and is accessed by a series of concrete steps. These upper rooms are particularly hot and stuffy during the summer and fall and house the toy-making workshop. Since the building itself was once a storage facility for the *Basílica São Ricardo*, they were not constructed as classrooms. The rooms were poorly lit and unventilated. The roof is corrugated tin and acts like a furnace that conducts heat into the upper rooms. The downstairs rooms are walled, enclosed on three sides only, with the front part open to the air. Below, the rooms are separated by a partial wall, waist high, running the length of the building, with sections of open space in the wall for entering and leaving.

The room closest to the entrance gate is the room where the project makes its own paper and where it has its *sucata* (recycling center).

Hence, this room is full of materials gathered from the community (cardboard boxes, bags of scrap cloth, cardboard tubes, cans, glass bottles, etc...). In the next room Alana has a desk and phone and some metal lockers for storage. Next to her desk are concrete steps leading to the upper level of the building, where the toy workshop is located. Behind Alana's desk is the room where the colorful *bornal de jogos* are made by Maria Vitória. This room is fairly large and is also one of the areas where homework is done. These special bags hang on the walls. Next to Maria Vitória's workspace are two bookshelves stacked with cardboard boxes that store the completed games. These games are available for use by the children at the project.

My early impressions of Viva Crianças took note of the participation of the children in the daily maintenance of the project, particularly the ways in which the responsibility for cleaning and straightening up were placed upon them. It is clear that the notions about responsibility for the care of the environment are an attempt to emulate the work of Maria Montessori, whose work paid close attention to the "prepared environment." In a Montessori prepared environment, all furniture is miniaturized and adapted for the various physical heights of young children, as are the bathroom and kitchen areas. Such adaptations were made by Montessori in order to encourage children to participate in the activities of daily life.

> I have noticed that the environment is set up in a way that allows the children to have responsibility for its care. They wash all the tables and clean the grounds every day; they help in the kitchen (peeling squash, other veggies), wash the veggies, cut veggies, wash dishes, and wash the kitchen floor daily. They have different colored trashcans for paper, wood, metal, plastic, etc. They reuse everything.

The area designated for homework and study was, like all areas in the project, filled with noise and confusion. The architecture in the project was such that voices were amplified by high ceilings and large open rooms. Hence, concentration was often difficult to achieve. In this room, there were children doing homework as well as general socializing and helping Maria Vitória with cutting, gluing, and pasting paper onto various states of constructing game boards. The ambiance of the room, in fact all the space at Viva Crianças is filled with echoes…loud and reverberating echoes. The children are constantly talking loud, at times yelling in order to be heard, and at times it seems that the sheer noise itself induces fighting. The noise level is difficult for me, but the children seem not to be bothered by it (perhaps they have come to accept and expect it) but I sense that their concentration is weak. Concentrating on homework is difficult. In addition, I see many children guarding their belongings (pencils, erasers, and paper are precious items that are not easy to get). They are preoccupied by concern for them. When I ask them why they are so worried about their things, they tell me that they cannot afford to buy more of them if they lose them. Their parents will beat them if they come home without them. It is common to see a fight break out over the disappearance of a pencil or some other school supply. I came to see that if they lost these coveted items, they would simply go without them. However, they usually found a way to "take" someone else's supplies, a kind of "replenishing" of their stolen items. Every time they begin to involve themselves in a project, something distracts them.

One of my activities at the project was to assist children in their homework, particularly their English homework; however, there were many times that I found myself working with both individuals and groups in math. One instance stands out in my mind as an example of the ways in which the Brazilian public schools taught math.

> At one of the tables was a young boy I have worked with before on math. He was again doing math and working on word problems. This problem went something like this: Jane has 92 balls and Sue has two times as many. How many balls are there together? Hi began to solve the problem by writing 92 × 2, but then instead of multiplying the 2 and then the 9 by 2, he made stick marks on the paper, writing out ninety lines, then two lines and counting them. I could not believe it. I asked him what 2 × 2 was and he told me 4, and then 2 × 9 and he told me 18. When I showed him how to do the problem by simple multiplication, he immediately got it. But why did he not make the connection for himself? Is it possible that he really did not know this, especially since he knew how to multiply? I was fascinated by this and asked Alana and she told me that he is used to reading the numbers as if they were words, and then separately studying multiplication and that he had never put the two processes together! Indeed, neither did the coordinators at the project.

Another tutoring session brought to my attention the similarity between teaching and learning processes based on rote and memorization in the public schools.

I moved to another table and worked with the adolescent girl who is studying English in school and often has homework in English. She had several phrases to translate into English from Portuguese. We worked on the translations, and again I noticed that phonetics was not used to spell words. Memorization and rote were the tools she used most often in trying to learn to write in English. I tried again to present the sounds of the letters. I had asked that we move to a quiet location, it is almost impossible to hear each other talk; the space is really difficult for the children.

In comparing Brazil to other Latin American countries such as Chile, Argentina, or Uruguay, one sees that Brazil still lags behind in the quality and equality of its educational system (Birdsall and Sabot 1996:7–44). According to Cláudio de Moura Castro, economist with the International Labor Office in Geneva, patterns experienced by industrializing countries do not apply to Brazil. Normally, these patterns reveal that once a certain degree of saturation has been obtained at one level of education, growth rates at this level tend to decline and growth begins to climb at the next higher level of education (de Moura Castro 1989:523–552). Since the elites in Brazil successfully benefited from the system of elementary and secondary education (public funding for private education), their priorities moved to the development of undergraduate and graduate education for their offspring. I quote extensively from *Opportunity Forgone: Education in Brazil*, where authors Plank, Birdsall and Sabot note that

> ...private schools receive large quantities of public money through direct and indirect transfers from federal and state governments. On the other hand, the fees that private schools charge parents are subject to

regulation by public authorities. In concert, these policies serve to ensure the survival of a large number of private schools and to guarantee the "right" of parents to send their children to them. At the same time, these policies contribute to the further deterioration of the public schools, both by depriving them of potential revenues and by encouraging the flight of parents who might provide an articulate and effective voice in favor of school recuperation. As a result, the public schools are widely and accurately perceived to be schools for the poor, of no immediate concern to anyone other than those condemned to attend or work in them. (Birdsall and Sabot 1996:124).

This process continues to exist in Brazil, where the elite develop an educational system that meets their needs while their privileged policies do not trickle down to the lower classes. In this way, lower classes are always kept in a social position of subservience, accepting the limits of their knowledge, their technology, their poverty, and their social position without question because they have never had the opportunity to experience higher levels of satisfaction in most social service areas. Educational inequality serves as a mirror that reflects the political, social, and economic stagnation that exists in Brazil (de Moura Castro 1989; Baer 2001).

Brazil has an illiteracy rate of 15.8 percent compared to 3 percent in the United States. This is the second-highest rate of illiteracy in South America, second to Bolivia, where 16.9 percent of the population cannot read. In addition, more than one third of the Brazilian population is functionally illiterate, defined here as possessing the capacity to write one's name as well as possessing a superficial knowledge of the alphabet (*Almanaque Abril 2000 Brasil*).

Viva Crianças provided assistance with homework, but at the same time perpetuated the learning-by-rote techniques of Brazilian public school pedagogy. In most cases, the coordinators working with the children were raised in Morro de Santana and attended the same public schools as the children they tried to help. Their reading, writing, and math skills tended to be rather low (based on my observation of the tutoring abilities, especially in math and reading). Indeed, there was a general feeling among the coordinators that the children attending the project had few opportunities for upward mobility in their future and that the project was not helping them prepare to enter the adult world. It was surprising how many coordinators felt that the children should be taught a trade in order to earn money now, accepting the notion that poor Afro-Brazilian children indeed are different from the children of the elite because they need to work to support themselves and their families. While the coordinators expressed their support for teaching the youth a trade, their feelings were in contradiction to the project ideology of Viva Crianças. This conflict was apparent in the frustration they felt in trying to carry out the project's goals of providing games and craft activities for the youth, who openly displayed their disinterest in and anger at the project. Most of the children attending Viva Crianças were not able to enter other projects because of long waiting lists. I was told by a few children that even though they were dissatisfied and frustrated with the project, they were used to it and had many friends there. Leaving the project would mean leaving their friends. In addition, the youth, especially the adolescents, found the repetitive activities of school homework to be boring and inconsequential to their lives. I wrote in my field notes:

> The model of Brazilian public school education is one that eliminates creative thinking and encourages repetitive learning. Children from the primary grades on

spend a great deal of time copying out homework. They receive mimeograph pages that they must cut out, paste into their notebooks, and then re-copy them in writing. I suspect that there is this idea that copying equals learning. The ideology of Viva Crianças is based on the notion that local culture is full of learning experiences and if you give a child the opportunity to participate and work with the materials (culture) in their environment (paper, newspapers, magazines, boxes, cartons, plastic containers, tubes, etc.), they will learn how to read, how to create, how to use their hands and their intelligence. People think the work at Viva Crianças is *bonita de mais* (really pretty) but it is not really learning, it is good for the poor children, who after all, will never enter the job market and compete with the children of the elite.

As we shall see in the section on coordinators and their views about Viva Crianças and its ideology, project children were often viewed as argumentative, deviant, and untrustworthy. It was often the coordinators, who themselves were poor women of color, who perpetuated a perception of project clients as marginal contributors to society. It was as difficult for them to accept the ideology of Viva Crianças as it was for the children themselves to alter their sensibilities and become like the privileged children of the elite.

Paper Making, Puppets, Theater, and Music, and Play

I have learned to do many things there, make paper, soap to kill head lice, detergent....

Vitor, Twelve Years Old

"How do you make detergent" I asked Vitor, the twelve-year-old boy who had become a good friend and informant to me. "Well," he said, "you have to have a kind of acid, now the rest you put, you have to put in the place of the acid (lemon), water, grated coconut soap, powdered soap…herbs." Interested, I asked what days the project made detergent. "I've never seen it being made there," Vitor replied. "Oh, we only made it one time, I made it with my group one time." I was disappointed, but I was beginning to see that many of the activities at Viva Crianças were sporadic and often one-time occurrences. It was difficult for the project to maintain a stated objective that was outside the basic parameters of their intended dual purpose of providing daycare and a place for the children and youth to play and hang out. In this sense, there were many times that I felt the project's ideology and practice were far apart, and that the professed ideologies described by Roberto Silva were used primarily to procure funding. While detergent- and soap-making were infrequent events (and while I was there, I never heard about or participated in the production of such items), puppets, toy making, theater, and music were offered on a continual basis. The music group and the music program was created as a way for me to integrate into Viva Crianças, and as such, was the first time the project offered a continued program for musical improvisation and musical performance of various types of *roda* songs.

This said, it is important to mention the areas where the project was consistent, principally in the daily provision of a nutritional diet to the youth who would otherwise have been undernourished or malnourished. In addition, the project provided daily assistance with schoolwork as well as access to learning about gardening techniques.

Paper Making

The children are making paper again today. They have designed a swift team. Several children shred newspaper into a large basin while others prepare the huge blender used to mix the paper, water, and juice from okra. Another fills the large metal container with water. They know just how much water to put into the container before it becomes too heavy for them to carry. It is as though an invisible signal travels throughout the group, each busy circle recognizing when it is time to begin the next stage of paper making. Suddenly, the huge pile of shredded paper is put into the can and water is added. It takes two children to carry the large can, about two feet in diameter and about three feet tall, to the table where the large blender stands assembled and waiting. Another child appears, unasked, to assist in hoisting the heavy container onto the table. Three children stand on the table and lift the can, pouring in the contents. They are careful not to plug in the blender until the improvised lid is in place. I noticed that on a few occasions some child was ready to plug in the gigantic machine, unaware that the children on the table were not ready. However, there is always some child aware of the right time; timing seems to be natural here because the children work as a coordinated team. The lid is a large piece of tin held in place by the older and taller children as they lean their weight against it. The blender is turned on and a deafening roar chokes the air. At various intervals, it is turned off by the child who stands by the plug and pulls it from the wall, and other children test the thickness of the mixture. Usually, they do this several times until it is a kind of grainy, thick batter, which is poured into a large basin in the sink. Paper-making is a favorite activity at Viva Crianças. It is an activity that assures participants will be cool on hot humid days, and the teamwork provides one of the few activities that spontaneously seem to lead to an energetic and collaborative activity, devoid of anger, fighting, and competition.

The completed paper is used to write notes to each other in the *roda grande*, to make cards for their parents, and to use in a variety of art projects. My music group used the paper to cover their puppets used in the musical theater group and the paper was used to cover board games and playing pieces in the *Bornal de Jogos*.

To make the actual sheets of paper, the children use wire mesh frames they constructed, which are approximately 15 × 10 inches. The wire mesh is made from window screening. With balletic grace, they dip, tip the frame up and down, and swish it sideways until an even layer of paper pulp is dispersed onto the window screening. Each child examines his/her tray once it is lifted out of the water while excess water runs off. If the layer is thick enough and even enough for the kind of paper they want to make (gross or fine), they carry the drained frame over the waist-high cement wall and quickly and adroitly flip the frame onto a smooth cloth they have placed on the concrete surface. With a damp cloth, they mop up the excess water in the paper, which is on the other side of the screen and is protected by the screen from being pushed or disrupted. When the water that is held by the tiny particles of paper is removed, the cloth is peeled off the frame and hung with clothespins on a line that extends diagonally the length of the room.

Puppets and Toy Making

Toy making and puppet design did occur on a weekly basis. However, Giovanni (the only male coordinator, who was also responsible for working in the creative arts with the children) often found himself making the toys and puppets intended as work for the children, who lost interest in making simple toys such as whirly-gigs, toy cars from plastic soda bottles with caps for wheels, or straw-stuffed toys such as ducks and dogs. These items were often photographed and displayed as items made by the children, and as such these toys brought a lot of attention to the project from the media and the surrounding community. Hence, the project's reputation as *um lugar bonito* (a pretty place, meaning the project did nice things for poor children) was based on the propaganda of the project's ideology.

Presenting the youth with activities that encouraged creative thinking and concentration was an impossible task at the projects where I worked. I digress here to point out that my own ideology about the creativity of children plays a role in my critique of this project. However, I also observed the children attempting to focus their attention on various tasks (art projects to schoolwork), only to find that the noise level and lack of personal work space caused them to give up. The environments of the projects are architecturally designed to be open spaces, with high ceilings that produce strong echoes. In addition, long tables are placed close together, making the task of homework difficult. When combined with the low level of Brazil's public primary school education, its focus on rote and memorization, and the aggressive and independent nature (encouraged by poor families) of street children, projects tend to exacerbate the potential for confrontation such as stealing, hitting, cursing, grabbing, and aggressively loud speech. Hence, the project's ideology of personal freedom expressed as unsupervised play posed many problems, among the most serious of which was the lack of actual training in skills that could help prepare the youth for adult life. Unlike youth from the middle and upper classes, poor youth rarely experience freedom from life's responsibilities. The contradiction between the project's notions about childhood, borrowed from the social constructions that define the innocence and freedom of childhood for the elite, and the reality of poverty and the hardships of work often produced a kind of confused and frantic energy among the project youth. Furthermore, the project tended to direct and dictate the activities the youth engaged in. In doing so, the youth lost an important opportunity to acquire critical skills. Such skills could have included the ability to problem-solve and think creatively. However, the youth were not allowed to invent their own projects, and when presented with the projects offered by Viva Crianças (such as making cars from plastic bottles or puppets from tin cans), the children and youth often opted not to participate at all. One coordinator at the project told me in no uncertain terms that the toys and puppets presented to me and to the public as the invention and handiwork of the children was just "propaganda that was a lie." "But," I protested, "When I got to the project and I saw the puppets and toys...everyone told me that the children made them."

> *Coordinator*: It is not true...Giovanni...the coordinators, it was the coordinators...Giovanni...and also Alana and Natália. They made the marionettes and they made the costumes for the marionettes.
> *Marcia*: But they told me that the children had made them and the clothes.
> *Coordinator*: Well, this is what I say. Everyone that comes to the project as a visitor is from somewhere else. They are told, "Ah, the children made all this" and they believe it. And now you see it is a lie. You believed it...but now that you're part of this...you see that it is not true."

It is true that procuring a more appropriate space where work on a more individual level would occur, where instruction and mentoring in drawing, design, building, and computer science were offered, would be very difficult to find and to fund. Although such a project is not outside the realm of possibility, it would require commitment to a very different kind of construction of childhood as well as development of a model based on the real-life needs of the children and youth involved. Such a project would also require a different social and economic order, one that recognizes and seeks solutions to extreme racial, economic, educational, and social equality.

The *brinquedoteca* ("a toy room") at Viva Crianças offered the youth fun and innovative ways to take used materials and turn them into toys, despite the fact that many of the children and youth did not participate. Giovanni, a young man in his early twenties, was the coordinator in charge of the *brinquedoteca*. He was a somewhat shy but always calm and reserved young man who had an easygoing manner with the project youth. Being the only male coordinator at the project, he worked well with the thirteen women coordinators. His almost heroic patience often astounded me. Of all the coordinators, Giovanni was the most sympathetic when working with the youth, especially in problem areas such as robberies, rights, and general disputes. Older boys' shouts and aggressive displays were often aimed at Giovanni, who remained calm and patient. Indeed, it was Giovanni's ability to remain somewhat neutral that seemed to open a way for some project youth to express their anger. Many times the anger expressed at Giovanni was not a focused anger, but a kind of generalized anger born of frustration about their lives. When I discussed the anger I observed with the children in my music group, I was told that many youth were just rebelling because they are so hungry and filled with fear. When I asked what they were afraid of, I was told that they were afraid of having to live on the streets, of starving or dying from illness, or of losing their parents.

Theater Group

Theater is a valued art in Brazil and is a big part of most popular culture NGOs. The theater group at Viva Crianças was a successful and continual part of the project's activities. Here, children often re-enacted fairy tales (Grimm's) or created theater pieces based on stories with strongly stated morality (that stealing was wrong, that honesty and hard work were valued, that wealth did not bring happiness). In addition, the theater frequently produced a weekly "news program" imitating the nightly news on television. The children and theater coordinator, Luna, created the weekly news performance in the form of a semi-comedy, but at times also produced some serious commentary, especially about police corruption and environmental issues. It was not uncommon for the actors to mingle among their peers during the week and collect informal interviews from their friends about their feelings on a variety of issues. These interviews would be included in the news program performance. The news program was one of the children's favorite activities.

The weekly theater was a very popular activity at Viva Crianças, with as many as fifteen to twenty youths participating at any given time. The costumes and makeup were donated to the project or collected from friends of the coordinators or from charity organizations. The props were made by the youth, who commonly constructed walls, landscape scenes, doors, etc., from large pieces of donated cardboard. In this instance, the project youth fully participated in, and at times were solely responsible for, entire theater productions. Paints and other set materials were all donated or made from found objects.

On a few occasions, my music group provided improvisational music and sound effects. However, our career in musical theater was cut short when the students in my group produced a piece of rap music based on their experience of being in the streets, and their perceptions and thoughts about street children. The performance of the music group's rap piece, *Preciso de Amor* (*I Need Love*), in the weekly *roda* caused Alana to try to censor our future work. We were invited by a neighboring project to bring our group to their facilities for a performance. Despite Alana's attempts to perform more appropriate music, the youth insisted that their composition be performed. As mentioned, the project sanctioned the use of fairy tales and morality stories, and traditional children's songs. I came to see that the project was not interested in the voices of the children and the stories that they were capable of generating based on the reality of their daily lives. Project ideology about childhood as a time of innocence seems to have been the motivating factor related to the censorship of *Preciso de Amor* as a theater performance piece.

One day while walking on the street with a friend, I noticed a sign that read: "Do not give alms: Many children live in the street because their parents are beggars. If you give alms, they continue requesting and soliciting. Offer opportunity in the form of work." It was acceptable for street youth to do honest labor for pennies (selling ice cream, shining shoes, washing cars, etc.), but not to beg. I bring this experience up as a way to demonstrate how social issues that affect the lives of the children are not addressed at Viva Crianças, in the large or small *rodas*, in the theater workshop, the theater news journal, or in the monthly newsletter that the project put together. Where are the voices of the children and youth discussing the social and political issues that affect them so directly? If the children had not discussed them with me, I would be less inclined to press for an extension of their voices. However, it was not uncommon for me to be told by a working child at the project how difficult it was to work on the streets because people did not treat them with respect. The children of the elite were idle, but, nonetheless respected. This was confusing to the project youth, who often talked about the difference between the way they lived and the ways in which privileged youth lived. Project youth also discussed with me the issues of domestic violence, hunger, illness, and the fear of losing their parents. However, the use of theater as an aid to understanding the social problems and daily life experiences of the youth was not encouraged at Viva Crianças. I learned shortly after arriving that Roberto Silva was the director of an excellent theater group called *Ponto de Partida* (Point of Departure). One weekend I attended one of their performances, and came away with the desire to expose the children at the project to such finely tuned artists. I discussed this possibility with Roberto Silva who responded by telling me that the children at the project did not have the capacity and attention span to watch such a complicated theatrical group.

Music Group

My music class met every weekday afternoon. One of our first projects was for the youth to write stories on any topic that interested them. Writing stories was difficult, and I discovered that tape recording their stories as they told them allowed them to express their ideas more freely. Creating stories about themselves proved difficult, and the youth frequently used the themes of familiar fairytales to build stories. From these stories we designed and created puppets and marionettes for use in theater pieces (which would also be accompanied by the musical instruments that the children were to make). I was at first surprised by the children's lack of familiarity with simple tasks such as holding scissors and using a glue bottle. I later understood that they rarely participated in making the toys that the project claimed as the work of the children because they refused to allow the youth to handle power tools or to apprentice with the men working in woodshop. In their own homes, they were even less likely to have access to paper, glue, crayons, and other creative materials.

Over the course of a year, my music group designed and constructed twenty unique musical instruments. Among the instruments were wooden and metal xylophones, wooden slit drums, rawhide drums, shakers, water gongs (using cut and hollowed gourds placed in bowls of water and struck with mallets), stringed African cellos, thunder claps from sheet metal, cut bamboo tubes hit with the soles of rubber sandals, a variety of scrapers and rasps, tin-can drums, and tube drums from PVC pipe of graded diameter sizes.

Usually, when a group of people, young or old, who are non-musicians are presented with percussion and string instruments, there is a period of time where chaos and a profusion of noise is produced. In my music group the youth drew designs of the instruments they hoped to make and then participated in their construction. They were less enthralled with the sheer volume they could produce than with the quality of sounds and their possibilities. Hence, over time the group and I jointly developed a series of exercises using their instruments (among other things) as a way to develop rhythmic proficiency and voice. My class began working with sound as a sense. I wanted to encourage the children to give descriptions of sounds that contained rich emotional and perceptual information. Are sounds dark, bright, cold, warm, hot, happy, angry, and neutral? Are they rough, harsh, hard, cold, cool, smooth, sharp, warm, comforting…? What images do the sounds produce, what kinds of feelings do they stimulate? I wanted to encourage them to draw pictures of these impressions, to design puppets and marionettes, to write stories about their feelings, and to create theater and performance art from these impressions. In this way, I too, expected the project youth to fit into a creative process that was outside of their experience; talking about themselves and their lives, their experiences, and their feelings.

The creation of a non-verbal cohesive exchange using non-traditional instruments for the production of sound qualities in a patterned form is a daunting task. The youth at the project were willing participants, but also presented the usual forms of resistance to creative improvisation: embarrassment, shyness, bravado, incomprehension, confusion, and disruption. The section that follows describes some the exercises developed by myself and the youth in the music group.

One exercise I used in the early stages of my group before the individually designed musical instruments were completed consisted of the development of an imagined machine that was to be made up of several people, each responsible for creating a movement and sound as part of the machine's function. We chose a machine that would make dry dog food pellets. The creation and production of the machine required teamwork and precision of gestures and sounds. One person was the mechanical bucket that creaked and turned and dumped the dry grain into a large imagined vat. His movements were accompanied by a series of sounds that included something like the following: Iiiirrrrrkkkkkk! Ssssshhhhhhhhppppppppp! Plunk, Splunk! Iiiirrrrrkkkkkk! Ssssshhhhhhhppppppppp! Plunk, Splnk! This was repeated over and over without stopping or, for that matter, laughing or breaking the rhythm created by the movement and sounds. Each person created a part of the machine, which in the end was united into one grand performance of body gestures and sounds producing the effect of the dry dog food factory.

As odd and strange as this was (and it was initially received with laughter, hysterics, and at times resistance in the form of "I will not do this!"), the eventual result was a strengthening of friendship and the development of trust between participants and me. Looking odd, acting strangely, and still relating to others by being odd and strange for the purpose of creating a harmonious whole actually worked. The result was larger and more encompassing than the exercise. Over a period of time, the music group began to investigate not only sound through their innovative instruments, but also through the ambiance of their environment, both on the streets and in the pulsing sounds of nature as the myriad of insects took to flight and song as the sun began to descend. We recorded traffic sounds while walking through the city, sounds of shoppers while standing in various stores (supermarkets, street markets, clothing stores), car sounds, horses' hooves on cobblestones, babies crying, people talking in passing, blaring speakers from stereo shops, and loudspeakers on top of cars and buses spewing propaganda. All these sounds were worked with as background for musical improvisation and vocalizations. Such exercises and explorations created, over time, a close-knit group. Project youth began to talk more freely about their family life, their street activities, their fears and aspirations. Eventually, the group began to compose songs. Diego wrote the following song:

> Once upon a time in a forest that was full of little beasts,
> These little beasts always lived in harmony and with lots of care,
> On a certain day there appeared a very wicked man.
> He destroyed nature and imprisoned the animals.
> The animals tried to find a solution
> They wanted to show to the man
> That to be destructive was not good.
> With a lot of united force,
> They made the man think,
> The man that lived to destroy,
> Became a man that preserved and built.

Elisa wrote the following song:

> The project you and I really like
> You and I like my desire and my flower
> Is with you and with you I will understand
> To sing and to play instruments
> That the students make.
> And *a dona* Marcia and Catrina
> Will go and teach us to play

> The strings and the drums.
> Go, go there to the project
>
> For a better life
> Go, go there to the project
> For a better life.
>
> I guarantee that there it is really good
> You will understand how to work and to play.
>
> For a better life
> Go, go there to the project
> For a better life.

Vinicius wrote the following song about the music group:

> Here in the project there is a lot of playing
> There is a lot of friendship, there is a lot of longing
> Let's go guys, and do a little hand clapping
> What a pretty thing is this young little girl
> What a cool thing this recycling shop
> There is a lot of wood, bottles, and cans
>
> With four small round ones and a can
> A cool toy you will soon have
> For here, in the project we can play

Eventually, the music group wrote their first joint composition and called it *Preciso de Amor* (*I Need Love*).

Preciso de Amor

> Ever since I was little
> I was abused at home
> Beaten by my father and mother

I suffered condemnation

I need love

I never went to school
Nor can I write my name
I'm the fruit of society
That wants to see me dead

I need love

The police beat me
To carry and use drugs
At night no one gives me love
Because of this I'm in this situation

I need love

I wish that my life
Were different
With rights and liberties
So that I could grow with contentment

I need love

I wish that the world
Were full of love
That everyone was happy
Without thoughts of pain

I need love!

The composition of this song was a turning point for me as a participant in the project and for the youth, in that they began to talk about and compose music that reflected the reality of their lives. This composition was eventually selected by the youth in the theater group to be turned into a theater piece about the hardships experienced by street children in Brazil. Even though most of the children in the project lived at home, they were aware of the hardships of poverty and the responsibilities placed upon the children of the poor. As the music group continued to practice and gain a sense of unity as an improvisational group, we were invited to perform at various functions and to present our work at other projects in Morro de Santana. Our performances included improvisation pieces and traditional children's *roda* songs suggested by the project coordinators and the youth.

In addition, the music group performed for the youth at the project at various times throughout the year, principally in the *roda grande*. One of the activities the youth enjoyed was performing for the project Mother's Day party. Several youth in the music group, guided by Diego, collaborated in the creation of music for this event. The title of the composition was *O meu coraçao bate felizi* (*My Heart Beats Happy*), and was descriptive of the love and care a mother gives her children. A typical performance by the music group at Viva Crianças went something like this:

> Our presentation to mothers at the project went very well on the fourteenth, and yesterday, the fifteenth we presented for half an hour for the seminar on education at the local public school. There were approximately 50–60 people present. Alana introduced me and my work. I talked about the class, our daily ritual of working with rhythms in a small *roda*, and demonstrated each instrument, the children introduced themselves. I asked that the audience participate with us in our demonstration of our daily rhythmic exercises, which they did gladly. The group of nine children and 50–60 adults clapped rhythms together, beginning with one child who chooses a rhythm, then at my cue, changes

the rhythm and everyone must follow. This happened around the *roda*. Then the *roda* is divided into two groups of four children each. The audience was divided into two groups as well and the two groups played two different rhythms chosen by the children. Two rhythms are occurring simultaneously; each group changes its rhythm and the rest must follow. Diego demonstrated his exercise of using the voice and body gestures. He produces a sound with his voice and we must imitate it, he changes and we must follow, he usually modulates from slow to very fast sounds and it is a real challenge to keep up with him.

It was during the period of time when the music group was asked to perform at another project, Bom Jesus, that I was informed by Alana that the theater based on *Preciso de Amor* was not really acceptable because it did not represent what Viva Crianças was about. Unlike the majority of the coordinators at the project, Alana was completely devoted to and invested in the ideology of Viva Crianças. Hence the presentation of controversial material, such as the theater and music of *Preciso de Amor*, was not acceptable. *Preciso de Amor* came from the children in Viva Crianças and rapped about their difficulties with consistent attendance at school, their illiteracy, and their knowledge of the stereotypes about street children that frequently prefer them to be dead than alive. Police brutality, drugs, lack of love, and lack of human rights are themes in *Preciso de Amor*, and as such, these themes did not fit the image of childhood embraced by the project. Since discussions about racism, inequality, poverty, and human rights abuses were not encouraged in the daily *rodas*, *Preciso de Amor* was seen as controversial and inappropriate material to be presented to the public at large by the children. However, it was the children, in the instances of theater performances at other projects and within the community, who insisted on presenting *Preciso de Amor* numerous times. Their activism was effective and I was told by several children in my music group that this experience has encouraged them to speak out in the future if and when they feel unheard.

As mentioned, it was through my participation and daily life at the project that I came to see that the ideology of Viva Crianças was deeply rooted in middle-and upper-class notions that idealize childhood. Thus, the reality of the racism and poverty experienced by youth at Viva Crianças were shrouded by the project name and its ideology. Such ideologies tended to render the project's clients voiceless while promoting organizational aims. Such dedication to an ideology can mollify and sublimate deeply entrenched social issues; in this case the issues of racial and class inequalities.

Bornal de Jogos

The *Bornal de Jogos* is a program that was initiated approximately two years before I joined Viva Crianças in 1997. According to Roberto Silva, the *Bornal de Jogos* was created as a by-product of the daily work within the project. It was Maria Vitória's job to coordinate, select, construct, and design the games that constituted the *Bornal de Jogos*. I made it a point to spend time working and participating in all the activities. My early notes about the *Bornal de Jogos* and my participation in their creation are quoted here:

> I worked with the coordinator (Maria Vitória) who made games today and with an Afro-Brazilian boy while we turned the used boxes into a collage using colored paper made by the children at the project. I found out that the project gets materials donated by local businesses, and when I asked how the businesses found

out about the project, I was told that the children go to the stores and tell them about the project. Most stores seem to donate what they can (boxes, tubes, plastics, excess wood, etc.). Maria Vitória tells me that she goes into the schools with materials made at Viva Crianças to present these games and materials to the teachers and children. She informed me that she returns later, at intervals, to do a kind of informal survey about the children's responses to the games, which ones they like the most, which ones they do not, and obstacles the teachers had to face in learning and presenting the games. I was told that the teachers do not want to have training workshops on the weekend (the tradition for about a year) because they do not want to work on weekends. Instead, the coordinators and the teachers met with the city (this project is funded by the city) and it was decided that the coordinators would go to the schools during the week. This saves the teacher from having to have meetings on weekends. Maria Vitória visits each school once a month for training. The teachers also rate the games and are encouraged to discuss their reactions to the process of learning new material. Maria Vitória indicated that the teachers were not interested in the games in the beginning because the games were new and unfamiliar. Feeling threatened, the teachers resisted the program and in the beginning, this process was very difficult for the coordinators.

According to the project's historical literature on the creation and development of the *Bornal de Jogos*, the initial questions that led to the creation of games came from the following concerns: 1. What happened to the books read to children and to reading in general? 2. Have we lost our enchantment with books? 3. Have the public schools stopped telling children about books? From these questions Viva Crianças began to respond to the need to develop a more creative, lucid, and investigative relationship with learning through books as well as games. The ideology of Viva Crianças states the following: "It is a fact for us at Viva Crianças, that to play and to learn are versions of the same process" (Viva Crianças, 1997). The written literature published by the project about the *Bornal de Jogos* continues by saying:

> In the meantime, we remembered our personal experience of school and observed on a day to day basis the difficulties and the boredom that children felt with their school responsibilities, where happiness was not present and many fled the school. Therefore, we have gone out to look for this child who is not able to be a child and who is a person without grace.

The *Bornal de Jogos* is theoretically born from the same ideology that created Viva Crianças. Essentially, the root of Viva Crianças's ideology is anchored in the words *brincar e cultura popular* (play and popular culture). According to Roberto Silva, transforming the work that children must perform in school into games and toys via the use of popular culture is a way to enrich the dialectic between play and learning by absorbing and using the popular culture of the diverse regions of Brazil. However, the processes used to create and develop the *Bornal de Jogos* were antithetical to the project's methodology. Indeed, through my participation in the project I came to see how the games were selected and where they originated. Ironically, many of the games were photocopied from American educational journals, cut and pasted onto cardboard, and then hand colored. The selection process was in the hands of Maria Vitória, who selected the games she thought were interesting. The youth at the project were not consulted. Hence, the youth participated in the hand coloring of the games and in gluing the colored paper onto the game boards. The culmination of this process was a series of games, such as "Chutes and Ladders" and their accompanying game parts (metal bottle caps covered in colored paper, game pieces made from caps from medicine bottles, cut pieces of hand-colored cardboard), which were placed in handmade patch-work quilt bags.

As I interviewed the children of the project, I found that their experience with the creation and construction of the games was indeed limited. Joana, a nine-year-old girl, put it this way:

> *Marcia*: The *Bornal de Jogos*....
> *Joana*: Ah, the *Bornal de Jogos*....
> *Marcia*: Do you play with these games?
> *Joana*: Yes I do.
> *Marcia*: And have you created or helped to create some of these games, or do you just play with them?
> *Joana*: I just play with them. Up till now, I have not been able to make any games.
> *Marcia*: Do you know any youths at the project that have made some of these games?
> *Joana*: No. I know Adice, but she is no longer a child. (This is a girl in her late teens who helps out at the project. She used foreign educational magazines from the US and France to get ideas for games to make from cardboard and reusable trash items like plastic bottles, old tins, fabric pieces, buttons, etc.).
> *Marcia*: Do you think that the kids at the project are making a lot of these games or are they just using the games that Maria Vitória and her helpers (Adice) make?
> *Joana*: I think it is that they are just using them.

In conclusion, the *Bornal de Jogos* offered the youth at the project various games that had the potential of assisting them in language, math, and possibly history subjects at school and in this sense, provided a valuable resource. In truth, my observations of the youth at Viva Crianças on a daily basis revealed minimal use of these games, which were mostly played or used in the school demonstrations or when visitors (usually potential funding sources) arrived at the project to observe the activities of the youth. During these times, the project prepared the youth in advance to be on their best behavior and to use the materials present in the toy workshop as well as the games.

Bornal de Jogos: Teacher Workshops

Projects based on popular culture tended to focus on *brinquedotecas* (areas that promote play and are filled with toys). During my fieldwork in 1997, I attended the third *Intercâmbio Entre Brinquedoteca* in São Paulo. Dr. Denise Garon (Ph.D. Psychology from the University of Quebec) stated during a workshop she presented that:

> …free play is non-hierarchical. Children learn how to choose a toy, wait for a toy, and share toys. These are small things but important in the life of a child. Children have the freedom in the *brinquedotecas* to choose their play item and to terminate playing with it when they wish. In addition they learn to apprehend (learn) spontaneously by telling stories and having social interactions. In the *brinquedotecas* we witness didactical, intellectual, and creative learning all occurring together. In addition we witness personal responsibility and democratic play. Play helps children learn how to adapt to the world, and helps children integrate their culture

(dances, games, foods, stories, and songs). In this sense, play is a culturally specific experience and it reinforces and develops culture (1997).

In the presentation above, Dr. Garon exemplifies the elite view of childhood as a time of freedom, play, and self-construction while living in relative freedom from poverty, hunger, and violence. Here, it is clear how little awareness exists of the reality lived by Brazil's poor children and youth. By creating projects that promote private schools receive large quantities of public money through direct and indirect transfers from federal and state governments. On the other hand, the fees that private schools charge parents are subject to regulation by public authorities. play without changing the economic, educational, and political environment of the country's social and racial inequality, educators unwittingly continue to oppress the children they seek to serve. By placing children and adolescents in idealized environments, often with substandard equipment and entrenched ideological approaches, project directors and staff ignore the very issues that could, if addressed through community education and civil and political social activism, alter the course of Brazil's class and race inequalities.

The essence of the *brinquedotecas*, while admirable in intent, imports the free school ideology of the Summerhill Schools in the 1960s, where free play without competition is seen as an essential tool for the growth of intelligence. While this is perhaps true (and is beyond the scope of this research to argue), this philosophy and more current child development theories do little to prepare poor children of color to enter higher education and hence move toward even a small degree of upward mobility. By offering daycare centers, parents of poor children are assisted, alleviating their concerns for their children, who would otherwise be left unattended while they work at whatever type of employment they can find. In addition, daycare projects do provide

CHAPTER SIX 215

necessary nutrition to the children they serve. However, beyond these kinds of assistance, daycare projects fall far short of providing viable educational skills and exposure to educational materials that will effectively alter the life possibilities of street children and youth.

The *Bornal de Jogos* did provide a valuable service in the public schools in Morro de Santana, where low-quality educational practices are rampant.[23] Maria Vitória, Alana, and a couple of adolescents from the project went to the public schools in Morro de Santana on a monthly basis. One of their main objectives was to lessen the authoritarian mode of Brazil's educational system.

> Schools need to have a happier face, a face that is friendlier and a heart that is more generous. It is not necessary for schools to be synonymous with an authoritarian vision, closed and scowling in order to have respect and to be valued. We believe that schools have to be an ideal locale in order to form happy and competent people who are curious and restless, people who search for what interests them, and who search for their desires. (Viva Crianças, 1997)

I attended workshops held by Maria Vitória in the public schools. I found the public school teachers to be receptive to the ideas presented by Maria Vitória, who worked toward bringing the teachers to a remembrance of their own childhood. A total of thirteen schools were presented with the *Bornal de Jogos*, and included both municipal and state schools. Reinstating a sense of play within the teachers was an admirable goal, and to some extent Viva Crianças and the *Bornal de Jogos* achieved a small victory. The teachers attempted to take their training back into the classrooms and to introduce the games to the children. In addition, the teachers were encouraged to make their own games. The extent to which teachers built upon their training from the *Bornal de Jogos* in the classroom is unknown to me and would be a valuable future research area for educational anthropologists.

The goal of the *Bornal de Jogos* project was to work with approximately twenty teachers for a total of forty hours broken into the following activities:

1. Ten hours devoted to demonstrating how to make and use the toys (made from the reuse/recycle area in the project)
2. Twenty-two hours devoted to demonstrating how to make and use the games in the *Bornal de Jogos*
3. Eight hours in discussion, debates, evaluations, and elaborations

In their final evaluation, Viva Crianças found that the teachers felt more liberated and satisfied in their work by the end of the workshops, and that they had developed a better relationship to Viva Crianças because of the workshops. In addition, and perhaps most important, the teachers came to see that authority and rigid teaching (usually by rote) were not necessarily the best tactics for the creation of a dynamic learning environment. The project found that the state schools were more satisfied with the workshops than were the municipal schools, in part because the first phase of the *Bornal de Jogos* met with the teachers during the week and added to their work load. Subsequent workshops (to be held the following year) were scheduled on the weekends.

My notes on some of the activities of the workshops will help orient the reader to the kinds of activities presented and the spirit in which they were delivered.

> The games materials used: (all from the local community), cardboard, paper (reams of paper), paper made by children, game pieces (made from bottle caps, dice from

wood, players' pieces from cardboard, etc.). Crayons and magic markers were used for coloring. The group I was in discussed a letters/numbers game, somewhat like bingo. A sack with letters or a box with letters (or numbers) was drawn from. First we made the letters by cutting up a cardboard box and making approximately 1 × 1 pieces, and then one of the coordinators wrote the letters and the vowel sounds with consonants on each piece. The pieces were put into a round cardboard box made by the coordinator. We each used the process of scissors, rock, paper hand signs to decide who went first. I won. We began by drawing a cardboard piece with a letter or a sound (consonant and vowel: ba, be, bi, bo, bu, etc.). The player must use a word that begins with that sound and create a sentence using the word. If they can do that, they progress forward one place. The first one to reach the center wins.

After the word/body game, the coordinator who constructs most of the games (math and language) demonstrated her work. She had prepared a large hand-sewn bag that was full of games. She took out each game, puzzle, and toy, and described it and discussed how it was used. There was an airplane, a hand puppet, a marble game, math games, color games, and word games. Each game had a game board and a box with playing materials. The boxes are covered with colored paper that is glued onto the boxes. The materials are passed around and the mothers look at and at times test the materials.

Game #2 was a mathematics game: a board with dots in a very specific pattern that determined the direction of moves. A number problem for multiplication or division is chosen. The player must give an answer and if successful, can move to a higher position. The turn then passes on to another child.

Game #3 was a language comprehension game. The purpose of this game was to learn the difference between an opinion and a fact. There was a board and reading material. The child read a passage and determined if it was an opinion or a fact. Examples: "I really like brown eyes, they are very pretty." "Eggs are oval and have a smooth surface." If the child is correct, they get to move their pieces forward.

In the final evaluation of the first year's work within the municipal and state schools, Viva Crianças conducted informal interviews with children in the project and with the public school teachers who had participated in the *Bornal de Jogos*. The following table summarizes Viva Crianças's evaluations of the *Bornal de Jogos* and compares the informal interview data between the project youth's responses to the games in the *Bornal de Jogos* and the municipal and state school teachers' responses to the workshops presented to them by Viva Crianças.

Child and Teacher Evaluation of the *Bornal de Jogos* Project

Viva Crianças Youth	Municipal/State School Teachers
• Helpful • Entertaining • Playful • Cool • Calming/ Relaxing • Fun • Allows you to win • Have to think fast • Gives me confidence • Makes me happy • Learning to read • Helps me learn • Makes learning easy	• Feel less tense • Children play differently • Good relations between project and schools • Teachers participated in the workshops • Teachers were interested in and valued workshops • Teachers used the materials presented • Teachers exchanged experiences • Teachers made the games • Good relations between schools • Want to produce more games • Want to produce more music • Want to produce more theater • Teachers validated the use of recyclables as materials • State schools were more satisfied with workshops than municipal schools were

It is important to note that the data were collected by Maria Vitória, the game coordinator at Viva Crianças. Teachers' evaluations were selectively published in the final report that I was consequently given; hence, negative evaluations were not included in the report. In addition, I was not given the interview instrument used in the evaluation that asked participating teachers to evaluate the use of the games in their classrooms. Further research is suggested in order to determine the efficacy of the *Bornal de Jogos* within the public school system in Morro de Santana. However, the project's evaluation of teachers and youth are presented here in order to demonstrate one of the effective and positive programs under development by Viva Crianças. While the project youth did not seem to play or work with the *Bornal de Jogos* materials with regular frequency, they did enjoy assisting Maria Vitória in making the games.

Conclusions

It was to become clear to me after my year with the project that the constructions of childhood integrated into the project were importations of Western European and North American post-industrial nations. I came to see how Montessori's notions of the child and her descriptions of the child's love for order were incorporated into the ideology of the project, as were her notions on freedom of choice. Montessori postulated that children, when given the necessary tools (materials) within a prepared environment, would by nature maintain the order and integrity of the materials they used. In addition, Montessori theorized that children would demonstrate qualities normally assigned to adults and would demonstrate these qualities through their spontaneous participation in cleaning and caring for their creations, and replacing the materials they used. By offering children a prepared environment, it was possible to witness the spontaneous love of freedom that each child was prepared to demonstrate. By incorporating the ideas of Montessori (whose work was with the poor children of the Italian slums) along with upper-class notions of childhood that expect children to be irresponsible and immature, the project unwittingly created an arena for the explosion of class tensions. After five months at the project, I made the following observation:

> Here, childhood is even more defined as a time of innocence and children are coddled, treated as simpletons, and kept in a state of ignorance about almost all social processes, about the injustices of the adult world. Poor children are kept ignorant and are not coddled, but rather are often hit or beaten. They learn to keep quiet around adults and to not think for themselves. They play hard and rough, they enact between themselves the harsh treatment they receive at home and in society in general. Hitting with fists, swinging sticks, and screaming rage are common sights at the project.

Poor Afro-Brazilian children are expected to be hard working, emotionally tough, and physically independent. Yet the project, in its philosophical and methodological practices expected the youth to be adult-like and at the same time child-like according to the constructions that define privileged youth. That is, they were to be free yet docile, while also being directed and motivated by the same educational goals offered to lighter-skinned upper-class youth. Education and opportunity are qualitatively and quantitatively different for the upper classes, where education most often offers financial rewards in terms of professional jobs. Yet the reality of the children conflicted with the conceptions the project had of them. The coordinators themselves were conflicted, and outwardly attempted to act in concert with the project's ideology, while privately (and confidentially in conversations with me) expressed their disagreement with the project's daily activities and treatment of children and youth.

Poor children's education is inferior to that of privileged youth, who overwhelmingly attend private schools. Street children are not allowed leisure or economic and emotional dependency upon their parents; they are not expected to be docile and child-like at home or on the streets. Indeed, they are used to taking what they need and are used to fighting physically and emotionally to survive both at home, on the streets, and in the projects. Hence, Viva Crianças and numerous other projects, including all three types described by Flávia Impelizieri (see the beginning of this chapter), often fail to alter the life possibilities of the children they seek to serve. It is not possible to change the sensibilities of the children in projects without changing the social conditions that create their marginality (and hence the street-wise and adult-wise sensibilities they possess), which include economic inequality, racism, and class distinctions, not to mention government corruption and the social and economic system of clientelism.

The following chapter will discuss the coordinators views, experiences, and perceptions of Viva Crianças. I discuss the tensions experienced by the coordinators who work there, and explore the reasons Viva Crianças isn't more effectively working with their clientele. Finally, I present the conceptual maps drawn by the coordinators as we discuss how they view relations of power within the project.

CHAPTER SEVEN
VIVA CRIANÇAS: COORDINATOR SELECTION PROCESS

This chapter presents the views, feelings, and experiences of the coordinators who work directly with street children. The coordinators voice their conflicting reactions to the project's ideology and discuss what actually takes place in Viva Crianças on a day-to-day basis. They describe tensions and relations of power among themselves, the children they serve, and the project's administrative staff. They draw conceptual maps that illustrate the hierarchy of their organization. The coordinators' conceptual maps serve as a basis for discussion of the gap between Viva Crianças's ideology and daily practice.

The ten coordinators hired by the city of Morro de Santana for Viva Crianças were women in their twenties. Most of them lived in the *favela*s of Morro de Santana and grew up in poverty. Only one woman was an Afro-Brazilian; the rest were fairly light-skinned. As I continued to work at the project on a daily basis, my relationship to the coordinators became more casual. I became good friends with a few of them, and easily interacted with the rest. However, it was not until I began interviewing them during the fifth month of my fieldwork that I came to understand fully what their responsibilities entailed. As the daily life of the project became routine for me, I came to see the underlying currents that rippled under the general flow of daily activities that both combined with and produced the harmonious and discordant events that occurred each day. The coordinators brought with them their unique histories, including their experiences as students in the Brazilian public school system. In addition, some of the coordinators had taught in the rural schools, the only teaching jobs available to them with their high school diplomas. Hence, the attitude of authority over children and the accompanying need for respect from them often followed the coordinators into their work at Viva Crianças.

The experience of one coordinator was typical. She told me how she was selected by the city government to work at Viva Crianças, how excited she was during the training period, and how disappointed she was once she arrived at Viva Crianças:

> I took a test at city hall and passed it. Then I taught in the rural schools. All the coordinators at the project also worked in rural schools, and we all complained to the *prefeitura* because we were dissatisfied because we had all received good grades and ended up teaching in the horrible rural schools. So they placed us at Viva Crianças. I had never heard about Viva Crianças. It was not known by any of us. Isadora and Roberto Silva wanted us to do a training for fifteen days, which we did. Then we went to the project and saw that it is very different from any classroom or any school. When they talked (Roberto Silva and Nona) we would go crazy. It was beautiful: children learning a profession! Being able to use what they learn in their life! We

thought it was great! When we got there, I was startled! Lazy children that think they are only going to eat. My adolescent group was very bad. My group activities in the vegetable garden...no one wanted to do that work.

Some of the undercurrents of dissatisfaction that the coordinators felt came from their own childhood and personal educational experiences both as students and subsequently as teachers. In applying for employment at the project, half of the ten coordinators I interviewed were looking for a way out of teaching in the rural areas, where poverty, hunger, and inadequate teaching facilities (not to mention the poor pay) were unattractive. In addition, the ideology of the project seemed to offer an exciting new potential in the field of education. A theme that ran through all my interviews with the ten coordinators hired by the city of Morro de Santana was that of initial enthusiasm for the project's ideology quickly dissolving into frustration and disenchantment. Incidentally, I was surprised to hear the coordinators at Viva Crianças using the term "ideology" when they described the projects roots. I came to learn that Roberto Silva used the term "ideology" in his training workshops for the coordinators. Initially, the coordinators were reticent in sharing their criticisms of the project with me. In part, they were afraid that what they told me might, in some way, get them dismissed from the project. Unemployment rates were high in Morro de Santana and to find work that paid more than one minimum salary was rare. Here, the coordinators were paid close to two minimum salaries ($R257 per month) while working part time (five-hour shifts, five days a week. Store clerks averaged $R130 per month for eight hours a day, five and a half days per week). However, over time their complaints began to emerge in our conversations.

This section will discuss the ways in which the coordinators described their daily experiences at Viva Crianças and will display, via diagrams, their perceptions of the organizational structure of the project. The coordinators' diagrams of the project's structure will be compared to the ways in which Roberto Silva and the upper-level staff conceptualized the organization's structure. Coordinators joined the project full of expectations that they would be able to talk to a child with problems and be able to influence them in some way. One coordinator put it this way:

> I felt a great disappointment…I've had so many disappointments at Viva Crianças. I thought the project was going to be one way, but now I'm seeing that it is really another way. Those things that we were told in the initial fifteen-day workshop, the things they preached at us about the way the project worked and about their ideology…well, they do other things. It is different from what they said and we're disappointed.

Workshops and Training

During my year with Viva Crianças, I attended four training workshops with all the coordinators. The workshops were designed to sensitize the coordinators to the project's philosophy of childhood and align the coordinators with the ideology of popular culture. Below are several examples of the kinds of activities and exercises presented in the training:

> I arrived at the project around 7 in the morning. We began with an exercise designed to heighten one's awareness of personal judgments about others. There are fourteen coordinators present (ten coordinators from the *prefeitura* and four coordinators from Viva

Crianças). We are told by Alana that there is a person in the *roda* who is very dangerous and who has committed many crimes and has many victims who have died. One person in the *roda* is a detective who must protect a lot of people. Alana passes a plastic container filled with small pieces of paper. Each piece of paper has one of the following words written on it: victim, detective, assassin. There is only one assassin and only one detective. The group is instructed to get up and walk around but not to talk to each other. We must discover who the detective is and who the assassin is among the victims. We walk for quite some time, trying to guess who the assassin is, who has committed the horrible crimes, and who the detective is. Both the detective and the assassin will act in ways that are suspicious, and the victims will also have manners. How we judge who is who is the point of the exercise.

The next exercise was taken from the story *O Rei Que Só Queria Comer Peixe* (The King Who Just Wanted to Eat Only Fish), a popular folk story passed on through oral traditions and published in children's books. Essentially, the story is about a king who loves to eat fish, and will eat *only* fish. He eats so much fish that the rivers are empty of them and eventually run dry. All the fishermen in the villages throughout his kingdom unsuccessfully try to find more fish for the king. One day a fisherman arrives at the gates to the city and asks to see the king. He talks to a guard whose name is Yaco-Zarolho who tries to convince the fisherman to sell his fish to him, but the fisherman refuses. The fisherman tells Yaco-Zarolho that he must meet the king in person and give him the fish he has. He does not want to sell the fish. Eventually Yaco-Zarolho changes his tactics and convinces the fisherman to sell him half of his fish. The other half he will let him take to the king. The fisherman agrees and is told the guard's name, Yaco-Zarolho, so he can ask for him the next day. When the fisherman meets the king he gives him the fish and the king asks him what he wants in payment. The fisherman tells the king that he only wants twelve lashes from the stick. The king is dumbfounded and asks again what the fisherman wants, and hears the same reply. He orders the lashes but tells the guard who will give the punishment not to hurt the fisherman and not to draw blood. Before the fisherman receives the twelve lashes, he tells the king that he sold half of his fish to the guard Yaco-Zarolho and gave the other half to the king. The king, upon hearing this, grows angry at the guard and gives Yaco-Zarolho twelve lashes with the cane but orders the guard to hit Yaco-Zarolho with full force and to hurt him. The king rewards the fisherman.

We were asked in this training *roda* to be the fisherman, the guard, or the king. We then met in groups of about four people each and created a short theatrical play about our assigned character. What kind of person is each character?

I enter a group that must make a play about the guard. We must depict what kind of person the guard seems to be to each of us. Is he deceptive, bad, cunning, or simply intelligent? We decide that the king is in a position to deliver punishment, is in the upper class, and is concerned only with his own needs. He has the power to decide who can fish in all the rivers of his kingdom, and has no thought for his subjects. The guard is just trying to acquire as many fish as he can, and uses tactics that will ensure that he and his family have plenty to eat. His actions do not make him a bad person, but rather a person who is capable of thinking of ways to survive. He uses his intelligence and cunning to outsmart the king, who, after all, is using and abusing his people for his own purposes.

In this manner each group develops a plot, a kind of theme that describes and justifies the actions of each character. The king is seen as a child who was trained to think that he is better than all others. He must act in ways that benefit him and his power, his family, and his relatives. He must take care of all the poor people who do not know how to think for themselves. He is the most special of all people, the most important person in the community, the country, the state. His word is law and he has the power to make all laws. Therefore, he should always think about how to increase his power. The fisherman is seen as a clever expert, a person who knows how to use the wisdom of the people, the wisdom of the street, to outsmart the upper class. He is not bad, just trying to survive.

The coordinators were asked again to reevaluate the characters of this fairytale and to put them into the context of class/political struggle, a play of survival. The questions we must face involve social, political, and psychological constructions that sometimes subtly rule our lives and perpetuate inequalities and class power. Later, a paper is taped to each of our backs. The papers have a line drawn down the middle and are labeled fisherman, guard, and king. We are to walk around and write on one side of the paper all the good qualities of each character. Later we are asked to write all the bad qualities of each character. The fisherman is creative, intelligent, perceptive, hard working. The guard is intelligent, decisive, hard working. The king is changeable for the better, has justice. And the fisherman is deceptive, sly, cunning. The guard is a liar, disloyal, untrustworthy. The king is egotistical, selfish, persuadable.

We are asked to think of one of the bad qualities that we possess in ourselves and to write it on a paper and put it into a can. Then we are asked to write one good quality that we possess and put it into another can. Later the "bad" can is passed around and drawn from and we are asked to write a few lines to help a person with the bad quality we have drawn. How would we help them become aware of the bad quality and how would we help them change the bad quality?

After each activity, we move into the *roda grande* and discuss our reactions and feelings. It is Alana who brings up the most insightful points, such as Paolo Freire's suggestion that both the poor and wealthy play roles that create oppression, and that we need to recognize our contribution to oppression if we wish to alter it.

This workshop occurred in my third month at the project. I was aware of the significance of the exercises as well as some feelings of discontent and resentment from the coordinators. It took me several more months to develop relationships with the coordinators that were substantial enough to allow me access to them and to have in-depth discussions with them about their feelings and conceptions of the workshops and the project in general. My field notes were filled with my thoughts and observations of these early trainings.

> We are filled with preconceptions that tell us who is good, who is dirty, who is nice, who is honest, who is trustworthy. All these notions are constructions that in the end label others, segregate and categorize "the other." Of course, the children at the project experience this kind of social segregation in the negative every day, and the coordinators are trained to examine their own constructions of the children they work with. Even though the coordinators are from the same *favela*s, the same class as the children they work with, they absorb the social constructions of the middle and upper classes about who is "normal" and who is "deviant."

I later learned that in addition to the preconceptions held by the coordinators about the children in the project (their unruliness, outbursts of anger, undisciplined characters), they also resented the ways in which the project's organizational structure eliminated the coordinators from participating in the creation and development of project activities, workshops, and programs. In essence, I came to see that the balance of power within the project was skewed toward the top. Before presenting three of the diagrams representing those drawn by nine of the ten coordinators hired by the city, further examination of other coordinator workshops will reveal patterns that reflect the project's concerns with the coordinators' training and, hence, their performance at Viva Crianças.

At another weekend workshop, Alana had selected what she perceived to be the most pressing problems occurring at the project. The coordinators were to work with these problems and find ways of solving them that reflected the project's ideological concerns:

> The coordinators were asked to create a "tree" of problems, placing pieces of paper that described the problems existing in Viva Crianças on the tree. We were asked to go and think, in pairs, of solutions to these problems and to write the solutions on a piece of paper. We then put the solutions on another tree. The coordinators acted out, one being a child, the other a parent and the other a coordinator, problems between children, parents, and coordinators. This particular skit was about a child who had her sandals stolen by another child at Viva Crianças. The theme of stealing or robbery is a common concern at Viva Crianças.

During another workshop, an exercise based on the game musical chairs was intended to encourage cooperative work relations. Each time the music played, a chair was removed. However, instead of having the person left standing leave the circle, she was asked to share a seat with another person. The object of the game was to demonstrate how to work cooperatively instead of competitively. No one seemed to find the game particularly interesting, and I did not feel that anyone tried to solve the problem of how to sit jointly in one location without a chair, which Alana said we should think about.

The workshop continued in this fashion, with Alana presenting the various exercises followed by the creation of a *roda* and a kind of forced discussion of the meaning of the games and their intended objectives.

> In general, the meeting continued in this way, playing games and then trying to discuss issues, but everything is directed by Alana who does not ask for any input in the organization or construction of the workshop. The coordinators were passive, waiting for her instructions, and discussions were instigated by Alana who asked questions that she felt were important. After this last exercise we took a break and Dona Larissa had made a cake and juice for a snack. At the end of the training, we returned to the *roda grande* and were told to write an evaluation of the project using the following questions: What is the ideal project? What kind of child do you want to work with? What kind of space do you want to work in? What problems do you want to write about? Again, the coordinators' responses are limited in the sense that questions are prepared in advance. The evaluation apparently ended here. There was no discussion of problems, no explorations for solutions, no development of new programs with the coordinators, and no discussion of individual problems as experienced by the coordinators.

The coordinators' ideas and suggestions were never solicited other than in the form prepared by Alana, nor were the project children participating in the development of new programs, games, or materials. Community participation, especially with the parents of the children attending the project, and the numerous *favela* organizations (of which there were thirty-seven) was entirely absent, as was actual discussion that focused on local problems. Indeed, during an interview with Lívia Matta, the financial director for Viva Crianças, the topic of poverty and its relationship to the project was discussed. I quote Lívia:

> The institution is not there to resolve the problems that people have because I think that this is not the responsibility of an NGO. Do you think that Viva Crianças will be able to resolve the problems of misery in Morro de Santana? Never. If you think it is possible to resolve these problems that would be beautiful, if we could resolve the problems of misery in Morro de Santana, right? But we cannot. We can validate the life, the folklore, the traditions of the people. We can help them feel proud of who they are, just as they are.

One of the fundamental platforms of Viva Crianças's ideology is that culture is the most sacred aspect of a population. It is culture, according to Roberto Silva, that reveals the essence and the potential within the contradictions of a community. Education, according to Roberto Silva, cannot close its eyes to this reality and must embrace the rich popular cultures of Brazil's diverse regions. Education and pleasure must be linked, according to Roberto Silva, for real learning to take place. Popular culture is the primary raw material of Viva Crianças and is the raw material from which Roberto Silva expects to contribute to the development of Brazilian society.

The basic aims of Viva Crianças, as stated by Roberto Silva are as follows:

1. To propose research that will create new and concrete alternatives for the development of social and cultural expressions.
2. To participate in the process of local community culture through interactive projects with other organizations in Minas Gerais.
3. To work for the dissemination and propagation of knowledge and the development of regional culture.

One of Viva Crianças's aims is to change schools into community cultural centers and transform the concept of schools from an elaborate, physical administrative structure to an open space where it can reinvent itself on a daily basis. Here we can see the direct influence of A.S. Neill's New School and Free School movements of the United States (founded in 1921) but made popular during the 1960s. Yet, the incorporation of Neill's Free School ideas into Viva Crianças created an unusual clash between the city un-indoctrinated coordinators, the project youth, and the project's indoctrinated coordinators. In addition, this fundamental rift between coordinators, project, and youth exposed the deeper class, race, and social inequalities that lay under the surface at Viva Crianças. Ironically, the popular culture the project sought to validate exposed the wide differences between the social constructions that define poor street youth and the youth of the elite. "To be a child" depends on the context of what defines childhood. The ideological gap between social classes in Brazil that defines what it is to be a child was unbridgeable at Viva Crianças. I found the other four projects where I worked to be more in touch with the everyday realities faced by the children they served.

The Coordinators' Views: Work and Viva Crianças

Prior to 1996, four coordinators (Alana, Rayssa, Giovanni, and Maria Vitória) worked at Viva Crianças. In 1996, Viva Crianças expanded the number of coordinators through a program funded by the city of Morro de Santana. At the time of this study, there were fourteen coordinators, ten paid for by the city, and four whose salaries were paid by Viva Crianças itself. In exchange for the ten coordinators, Viva Crianças agreed to give (through Roberto Silva) various workshops on education to teachers in the public schools in Morro de Santana. In addition, Roberto Silva's theater company *Ponto de Partida* came to Morro de Santana for an evening of theatrical performance.

The expansion of the number of coordinators at Viva Crianças seemed to hinge on the *Bornal de Jogos* project and Roberto Silva's vision for altering the public educational system in Morro de Santana from a system based on rote learning and authoritarian teaching practices into a system where children learned from community centers based on local popular culture. The new coordinators were an experiment in altering the ways in which adults interact with children and youth, and Viva Crianças was Roberto Silva's laboratory. The ultimate vision of Viva Crianças was to have all who worked there as adults—be they servants, cooks, directors, parents, or students—act as teachers. This vision was to be achieved without leveling the playing field, where most parents were illiterate and without the luxuries that the upper-level staff possessed. The daily reality at the project was far from its proposed goals. Contact with parents and community was minimal at best.

Several themes became apparent when talking with coordinators who were dissatisfied with the project and the work they were doing. I interviewed all ten of the city-sponsored coordinators (the un-indoctrinated), of whom eight clearly revealed their disenchantment with the project's ideology and daily practice. The following themes emerged from my discussions and describe the most difficult aspects of working at Viva Crianças. Many of these thematic statements reveal the distance between the project's ideology and practice. The Thematic Differences chart demonstrates the split between the project's ideological Free School roots, the on-the-ground practice of the project (suggestions at workshops), and the coordinators' personal views. The main thematic differences between Viva Crianças coordinators and Alana:

Thematic Differences: Viva Crianças Coordinators and Alana

Coordinators	Alana
Seeking Respect: Coordinators seek autonomy and respect as participants in the creation of project programs, rules, and practices.	Roberto Silva is the head of Viva Crianças, and she (Alana) is responsible for coordination, training, and directing coordinators. **Disrespect:** City coordinators are not of "good" quality and were the "worst" candidates picked by the mayor's office to work at Viva Crianças. The mayor's office sent the worst educators because they did not understand or respect the project's progressive ideas about childhood and/or education.
Discipline of Children: Coordinators want repercussions for bad behavior of children in the project (broken toys, stealing, aggressive behaviors, violence).	**Discipline of Coordinators:** It is the coordinators responsibility to make sure the children do not misbehave or destroy project material. Coordinators are held responsible for "bad" behavior of children and there are no repercussions for the children.

Children and Accountability: Coordinators want children to be responsible for "their" responsibilities: cleaning bathrooms, washing floors in the project, working in the garden.	**Coordinator Accountability:** Alana holds the coordinators responsible if children do not complete their tasks. The children are not disciplined, but the coordinators are. Many lectures are given to them regarding their lack of compliance (finding a way to make the children carry out designated tasks).
Pride in Traditional Education: Coordinators take pride in their completion of primary and secondary public education.	**Lack of Respect for Traditional Education:** Alana does not respect the traditional education system, public or private.
Dependable and Interested: Coordinators feel they are dependable and interested in working at the project, even though they were frustrated by the way in which they were treated.	**Undependable and Disinterested:** Alana stated that the coordinators worked at the project because it was "easy" money. They did not have to report to anyone and they were not dependable.
Children and the Real World: Coordinators stated that the children at the project need to develop behaviors that will help them in the work world now. They need to learn responsibility and control over their behaviors.	**Children and Popular Culture:** Alana stated that popular culture is where project youth and their families should be educated and that pride should be developed in their "folk" roots. Training on effective social action for social change is ineffective, and hence unimportant.

Coordinators' Voices

On many occasions I sat and talked with various coordinators about their work at the project. During these discussions the coordinators talked about their feelings of frustration, particularly about the problems they were having with the youth and the sense of powerlessness they felt at the project. Catrina became a close friend and a primary informant, revealing many issues that would have remained hidden or unnoticed by the casual observer. In conversation with Catrina, we began to draw a conceptual map of the organizational structure of Viva Crianças. We found that the act of giving form to her sense of the project's structure was helpful in clarifying her feelings of discontentment and frustration with her work at the project, and that the map was a useful tool, assisting both of us as we attempted to explore the ways in which the project worked and did not work. According to Catrina, the project's organizational structure was top-down, with the coordinators in the middle of the map, and the parents of the youth at the very bottom. Catrina felt that she was voiceless and powerless and essentially useless at the project. During

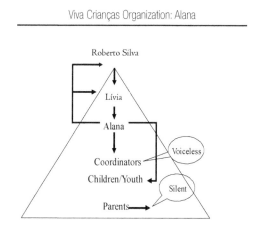

workshops she felt that the problems she raised for discussion were dismissed and unappreciated. She was frustrated with the project in many ways. There were constant problems with supplies. When she requested materials, she did not receive them. When she did receive a few materials, the children did not respect them. There were no rules of conduct or responsibility. She does not agree with Paulo Freire's notions of liberty and freedom, at least not the way it is interpreted at the project. For example, Catrina repeatedly told me about incidents where project youth broke or destroyed project materials such as pencils, scissors, paper, tape, and such. According to Catrina, Freire's discussions about liberty and freedom from oppression included taking responsibility for one's actions. Indeed, Freire's discourse on freedom from oppression makes many references to the development of dialogical and analytical skills to be used for the express purpose of self-observation in order to discern the ways in which the oppressed participate in their own oppression. In this sense, Catrina stated that the project youth did not have to be responsible for their actions when they destroyed supplies and acted out destructive and aggressive behaviors toward their peers and co-ordinators. In this way, Catrina told me, that the project youth were oppressing themselves by developing behaviors that would further alienate them from society at large.

Another coordinator, Natália, also felt voiceless during workshops, stating, "When we're going to say something, make a suggestion on how to work differently, she (Alana) laughs in our faces." Natália drew the following organizational map.

To Natália, the project's ideology and practice were far apart. She pointed out that what she had originally thought the project was about (her impressions from the initial fifteen-day training) was very far from her daily experience.

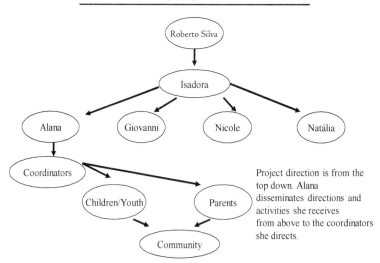

As I explored the difficulties of communication between the coordinators and Alana more deeply with Natália, we talked about the ways in which communication could be improved and expanded. She expressed ambivalence about a suggestion that I made in reference to talking with the office staff, in particular to Roberto Silva and Isadora about her feelings. Was it not possible to arrange a meeting with them and share her ideas about possible solutions to the everyday problems with the youth? Was it not possible to discuss her feelings about Alana with them? Natália implied it was a dangerous thing to do and could result in losing her job at the project. I came to understand that open discussion about the project's ideological framework was not welcomed. As we talked, Natália timidly stated that the power to instigate and initiate change within the project lay with Alana, and added that most of the coordinators did not agree with Alana's point of view about the problems of discipline, responsibility, rules, respect, and order.

Natália's views on children and childhood were as follows:

> A child is a person that is developing and needs our help because it is going to become what we pass on to it. It is a person that depends very much on us, but it already brings with it a weight of knowledge, the culture, its culture…the only thing is that it does not know all that culture consciously. Because we have to develop it, bring it out. It is a very important phase of the child's life, because it is there that it will create its self-esteem. That it will learn. It is in this way that respect is created and it is through respect that a child will be formed to become a responsible adult, an honest citizen.

I asked Natália if she felt that Viva Crianças was helping to create responsible, honest citizens.

> *Natália*: Sometimes I do not think so.
> *Marcia*: Can you tell me why?
> *Natália*: When we (the city coordinators) came here there were those children who had been here for a while…the older ones, for example. They have been here for years (in Viva Crianças) and I did not know them before they joined Viva Crianças. But by what we see, it does not seem that much has changed. They are disrespectful, they throw all the work and the responsibility onto the smaller ones, the younger ones. For them, it is the law of the stronger one. It is all that matters. I think that the adolescents here have a lot of freedom. I think that's why they are not respectful with us here.

It is interesting to note how Natália perceives the freedom given to the youth at the project. Here, she seems to be reflecting her social class norms about the appropriate ways in which children and youth should be viewed, which include the working-class notion of childhood responsibility. Yet in her previous statement, Natália seems to reflect the upper-class views of childhood as a phase of life in need of protection and guidance. These two statements seem to be ideologically in conflict and may, in part, reflect the wide gap between the project's upper-class views of childhood and the coordinator's lower-class experience of childhood as a time of hardship and participation in the adult world.

Yet as Natália and I probed more deeply into the reasons for her silence and her sense of being voiceless within the project, she confessed that she lacked the confidence to express her ideas. When I asked Natália to describe in her own words what she thought the ideology of Viva Crianças was, she became confused and struggled to put her words into form. I was curious to see if Natália, like many other coordinators, also knew and understood what the term "ideology" meant in the context of the project. "We were told that the ideology at Viva Crianças was to form a citizen so that the child will become respectful to others and to themselves. I do not know—it is not happening here." Natália told me that she understood the term "ideology" to mean a set of beliefs about who children are and how they become adults. This ideology was used by Roberto Silva to create Viva Crianças.

Natália had an interesting suggestion for involving the adolescent youth who were so difficult for her to work with. Her idea comes directly from her cultural inheritance of having been a child of poverty herself. When she was a child her mother sent her to live with a wealthy woman. In exchange for being the woman's domestic servant, Natália would be fed, clothed, and sent to school. Hence, Natália grew up with the knowledge of what it meant to work and be responsible as a child. She stated that, "The adolescents that are there (at Viva Crianças), fourteen years and up, I think that they should not stay here (in the project). I think that they should have more responsibility—like a little factory for them, where they can work and be responsible and earn some money."

Here, it is possible to see part of the conflict between the un-indoctrinated coordinators and the project's ideology of freedom, leisure, and protection. Poor children are introduced into the world of the adult at an early age and are expected to be tough, resilient, and productive. To Natália, the project opened the door to a world of freedom and irresponsibility not experienced by these children, and as a consequence, they were running wild and uncontrolled; they were disrespectful and defiant. Poor children are not coddled, and at home they are often expected to respond when spoken to and to respond with downcast eyes and submission. The project was out of compliance with the reality of both the coordinators' experience of their own childhood and the experience of the children they worked with.

Good communication between coordinators and project staff (upper-level staff) was essentially nonexistent because of the distance between the project's imported constructions of upper-class privileged childhood and the coordinators' inability to assimilate and relate to these constructions. In addition, the problems of discipline, anger, robberies, and disrespect at the project were an inevitable outcome of the project's ideological base that ignored the extreme class, race, economic, and social inequalities experienced by the children they sought to serve. The upper-level staff (project directors and general office staff), when compared economically and materially to the youth and the coordinators, lived in opulence, with cars, satellite dishes, VCRs, CDs, cell phones, trips abroad, and the ability to send their children to private schools and private tutoring to assure their entrance into university degree programs.

These differences create extremely different ways of being in the world. For Natália, talking about her feelings was foreign and uncomfortable, as it was for the children in the project. Talking about inequality, injustice, and unequal relations of power was dangerous and unthinkable. We talked about the relative wealth and opulence of the upper-level staff in comparison to her living conditions and those of the children at the project. I asked her if she thought it was a good idea to begin talking about racial and economic inequality at the project with the children and youth:

> *Marcia*: The children's theater sometimes talks about social injustice and racism, but it is not a matter of just talking, but to do concrete things about how to change things. What can we do, even in small ways that might begin to make people more aware of social injustices? Do you think it is a good idea to encourage the children to think about, to talk about these social problems?
> *Natália*: I think it is a difficult question. It is dangerous…
> *Marcia*: Why is it dangerous?
> *Natália*: Because people are going to mess around with something and people are going to try to change the heads of people who have a fixed idea (about racism). "Oh, black is no good." And so on. It is dangerous as soon as they talk about change.

To Natália, as with the parents of the children, the most common solution to suffering and misery is to pray for a better life, and continue to serve your master. Keeping quiet and maintaining good social relations as well as a good reputation is one of the major strategies for economic security poor people have to ensure their survival.

Sophie

Sophie is a twenty-six-year-old woman who had also been teaching in the public rural schools when she went to the *prefeitura* and asked to be transferred to a school in Morro de Santana. Like Natália, Sophie was chosen to work at Viva Crianças, and like Natália, Sophie also went to the fifteen-day training meant to prepare the new city coordinators for work at the project. Sophie was a very frank woman, and talked openly about her feelings and frustrations related to working at Vi*va* Crianças. Indeed, she was often very vocal at meetings and training weekends, so much so that I was often startled at her ability to be so direct and articulate about her opinions. She was well liked by the other coordinators, even though she was seen as confrontational by the main coordinator. Sophie became an articulate and faithful informant and greatly assisted me in my attempts to understand life at the project. In addition, I found her to be not only articulate about her opinions and feelings, but also to be an astute and insightful observer of others. Because she was aware of her own opinions and felt confident enough to express them, she was also able to think about and analyze events and occurrences with some insight. During our interview, Sophie and I began comparing notes on the number of children attending the project and the number of children in each coordinator's group. Sophie told me, "Many kids do not come. I'm not sure how many children are missing in all the groups. But, I think that the children are missing a lot of the time. Today, the *roda grande* was very small. Today it was actually—actually every day it looks like that."

I wanted to know if Sophie had any insight into the reasons that attendance at the project was inconsistent. Instead of giving me concrete reasons children would not come for days at a time, Sophie revealed to me the nature of her frustrations with the project. Instead, she stated what many of the coordinators had tried to tell me, specifically that they felt that Alana blamed them for the children's absences:

> *Sophie*: I understand everything and I do not understand anything, and I tell you the truth, many are missing, but not only in my group but they are missing at the project. In the whole project.
> *Marcia*: I find that many children are missing many of my music classes. Alana told me it must be related to the way I'm presenting my class. Do you think this is so?"
> *Sophie*: Did Alana say this? I do not think that they stay a short time…but her question has a manipulative part in it…to demerit your work.

Sophie states that coordinators are blamed for the children's actions and for their absence from the project. In reality, I came to learn that children frequently missed consecutive days at the project because they were needed at home either to work or to attend to younger siblings. Again, when children were aggressive or when they took advantage of their freedom (often the only experience they had of free time) and became unmanageable, the coordinator was seen as being out of compliance with the project's ideology, and hence it was understood that it was the coordinator's behavior that instigated negative behaviors in the children.

In another conversation with Sophie during a period when the project had several visitors who were potential funding sources, she discussed her frustration about the lack of cohesive communication between the head coordinator and the general coordinators on a daily basis. Sophie felt that her contributions as a coordinator were not valued and did not matter.

> They (the project) maintain appearances. Mostly, I do not know if you noticed when there is a visitor. It is very different. They wash, they clean everything. They are very concerned on the days when there are visitors, with cleanliness, with lunch, with everything. Why are not they concerned about it every day? Why do not they ask me every day what I'm going to do? Only on a day when there are visitors do they want to know what I'm going to do. On the day that there are visitors, they are worried about disciplining the children and what the children are doing. Every day it is freedom with confusion here. That's not freedom. It is confusion, because discipline means responsibility. If there is no responsibility, there is not any real freedom and respect.

I asked Sophie when she began to feel that the project's ideology and practice were inconsistent, and I was curious to know if she felt there was a difference between the ways in which Viva Crianças constructed its views of childhood and the ways in which she viewed the nature of childhood.

> It did not take me long to figure it out. We always had them.... Oh, since the beginning we had controversies. I'm noticing that people are more...how should I say it, in the beginning people were paying more attention to things, but not giving them value. It is only valued... what somebody does. What Giovanni does, what Natália does...who is better. What we do (the general coordinators), nobody says anything about. It is no good and it has no value. And they never speak about us (the general coordinators). Any place they go, anything that

happens, any video they have made about the project, they never say that they have ten coordinators. Only them (Alana and Giovanni, and often Natália). Only them, do you understand? The work that we do is never singled out. When I went there (to Viva Crianças) I would do things that I liked doing and that were linked to the kids. So they said Sophie did this and Sophie did that, but they constantly compared me to the others, understand? Sophie did this well, and you did not. It has always been like that. But that was because I saw what was happening and I would not say anything. Then there was a time that passed, that I started seeing the things that were wrong. I would go there and talk. Now, it is over with me. I'm not fooling around anymore. There is no more Sophie this and Sophie that. I can do what I can do, but it was because I finally complained about the rights of others, the things that I would see that were wrong. Understand? I always say things. I really started talking. Everything that I see that is wrong, I will say it. When it happens, right then and there I say it. I have to say it because one cannot stay quiet.

If there was such dissatisfaction among the majority of the city coordinators, why did they not work as a group and designate a spokeswoman who would take their complaints to Alana, Lívia, and Roberto Silva? Sophie could not find an answer to my question. "I do not know—I do not know what it is," she replied over and over again. I probed her for reasons. Was it because they were afraid of losing their jobs? Were they shy and not used to talking to authorities? "I do not know—I do not know what it is" was the only reply that Sophie could give me. Did she and the other city coordinators have contact with Nona, the director of programs for the youth? Sophie stated,

"No, none—no contact at all." The lack of communication between the organization's upper-, middle-, and lower-level employees (which includes the city coordinators) was a major problem within Viva Crianças. Coordinators felt undervalued and powerless to effect change within the project. Indeed, they felt oppressed by the project's mix of ideological methods. Sophie expressed it this way:

> It is my experience, because you understand that the ideology that was preached is like that. If anything happens, if there is any problems with any child, I'm going to check it out. You see? If anything happens with any kid, you go and take care of it, all right? To talk to me, to my group...it means that I have to watch my group and anything that happens in this group that is wrong, it is my fault. You understand? If a boy went into the *horta* (vegetable garden) and stepped on the vegetables, it is all my fault. The fault is not the boy's—no, it is mine. It is because of your group—yes, that's what it is. And I think that this is wrong. It is wrong for sure. There is no doubt about it.

During our interview, we explored ways in which the coordinators could begin to instigate changes that would aid them in participating more directly with the upper-level staff, including Alana. The following discussion is quoted at length because it reveals the complexities involved in making such changes:

> *Marcia*: Imagine if all the coordinators have the opportunity to talk about their problems in a group meeting with Alana and Roberto Silva.
> *Sophie*: But if we say something, we are not respected.
> *Marcia*: But imagine...just imagine if you talked, I talked, and someone else talked...and then there is

another person to write it all down. Then I think that you will all see that everyone is trying to deal with the same problems, and are all trying to resolve these problems.

Sophie: OK, but I think, but I think that a lot of things would have to change for us to do this.

Marcia: What things would have to change?

Sophie: The type of rules, rules for everyone.

Marcia: For the coordinators?

Sophie: Yes and the children and everything. Mostly the children. We should start with the children, you know?

Marcia: But what changes need to be done? Tell me what kind of changes need to start with the children.

Sophie: More responsibility—it has to start there. To do the things, for example…the boys know that today is the day that I need to work in the kitchen. "I do not have to go there (to the kitchen)." "Hey you there, you have to do it (says a coordinator)" "I'm not going! I'm not going! (the boy at the project)" He knows that he has to go—he knows. "Today I have to go." But, if he cannot because he is sick, then that's OK. Everything is fine. He is not going because he is sick, not just because he does not want to. Now those boys that say, "Ha, I'm not going because I do not want to," if others have to do it, why should not he have to as well? So we have to change things like this.

Not only did Sophie feel that rules needed to be enforced for the children, but she also felt that the coordinators needed to have some autonomy in their role as coordinators and teachers in negative behaviors.

Marcia: Do you have any ideas about this kind of problem and how to start resolving this kind of violence?
Sophie: Well, then there is the business of the kids knowing that they cannot do that, and they know it. They do it anyway, but they know it. A lot of this comes from the home. Many of them, if not all of them, because we really do not know the reality of every kid, but the parents are violent with them, they hit them, they often beat them. They are used to this kind of thing.
Marcia: But how are you going to change the violence the kids have against one another, what type of rules?
Sophie: I think that by instilling in the kids the respect for the human being, and talking like that—who knows?
Marcia: Only talking?
Sophie: Working with the kids. You're asking me—I do not know, because the project always demands this talking. The problems with thefts and so on, "How are we going to resolve this? We ask Alana, "Oh, we have to sit down and talk." They never said, you resolve it in this way. It is been more than a year that we've (the coordinators) been asking them for more guidance and for more guidelines. Problems with thefts and bad language (*palavrões*), with fights—it is not easy. But one thing is for sure, there are no consequences for these actions for the kids. That's why things do not change. This is why when we (the coordinators) got here (at Viva Crianças) we were kind of lost, without knowing what to do. Understand? When we want to do something different, we have to ask and sometimes you

actually get to talk to someone, and then you have to wait, wait, wait—so you give up what you wanted to do.

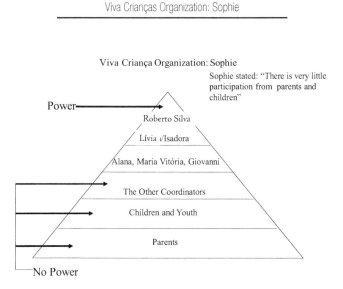

Viva Crianças Organization: Sophie

When I asked Sophie to draw a diagram of the project's organizational structure, she drew the following picture:

In conclusion, Sophie felt that the project was not helping the youth because it was reinforcing negative behaviors by offering the youth unlimited freedom, without consequences for their actions and without requiring them to be responsible for daily activities and routines. In addition, Sophie felt that the project needed to "develop something for the adolescents and the younger ones who want something more challenging…different. Something where they can make some money (the boys), and where they can create and learn about responsibility while they do it." According to Sophie, the project built a base, an idea, and the project is this idea, but the idea is not what happens.

> And they maintain this "idea." All the places where they talk about the project, they say the same things. So, the people on the outside have a very different idea, an image of the project, but the reality is not this image that they are painting. The way it is right now, I do not think it is very good, no. It is not forming anything in the children. They just continue in the same way—the way that they come from the house, they go to the project, I think very little has changed, but I think that we can influence them in some good ways. Generally we chat, maybe—I do not know, relations with the coordinators and with the children—we can influence something good, we can change something—not in all of them though.

Nine of the ten city coordinators at the project drew diagrams of the project's organizational structure. While presenting interviews with all the coordinators would be informative, it would be repetitive. I selected the three coordinators shown in the diagram because their views were descriptive of the rest of the coordinators interviewed.

Although the organizational maps presented are drawn differently by each coordinator, they all share with Sophie a similar view of the project's organizational structure, which is universally diagrammed as top-down. The premise that the larger NGO and Viva Crianças were conceived with the intent of validating the culture and traditions of the poor children they sought to serve was severely hindered by the lack of two-way communication between upper-level staff and coordinators, children, and parents.

The ten city-hired coordinators at Viva Crianças struggled with the memory and knowledge of their childhood, which had required most of them to work at an early age in order to ensure their family's survival. Their expectations of the children and youth at the project were markedly different from the project's notions about childhood. While they expected the children to act as they did at home when they were children—that is, with fear of and respect for adults—they found the youth at the project to be angry and resentful when faced with the assumed authority the coordinators felt they earned by having entered adulthood. Indeed, the project youth *were* different at home. They were subdued and expected to receive harsh treatment if they were not compliant with the wishes of their parents. By encouraging the children's freedom, and eschewing physical punishment, the project had unwittingly created a type of "twilight zone" where behaviors were strangely undefined and unregulated, leaving room for explosive feelings to find expression. Instead of learning to talk about social problems among peers, youth employed aggressive behaviors that reflected the confusion they felt as they moved between home, the streets, and the project. Indeed, their aggressive behaviors were adaptive, giving them an advantage both in the project and on the streets.

The next chapter presents the additional four NGOs I participated in that work with poor children in Morro de Santana and briefly compares their ideologies and organizational structures. While all the projects molded their programs around the popular culture model, each project had unique ways of dealing with very similar problems among youth, parents, coordinators, upper-level staff, and with conflicts between ideology and practice.

CHAPTER EIGHT
FOUR ADDITIONAL PROJECTS

After spending nine months at Viva Crianças, I came to see that my fieldwork would be enhanced if I worked with other NGOs within Morro de Santana that represented different ideological points of view in relationship to street youth. In the end I worked in a total of five NGOs, each representing a different segment of Brazilian NGO culture. This chapter will briefly present the four additional NGOs I came to know in Morro de Santana: Curumim, COV, APAE, and Bom Jesus.

Curumim
(Director Marco Antônio, Coordinator Yuri)

Curumim was developed by the secretary of sports, Morro de Santana's leisure, and Morro de Santana's tourism and supported by the governor of Minas Gerais. It was first developed in the city of Belo Horizonte in 1986 with the principal intention of getting street children (up to the age of twelve) off the streets and back into school. Curumim is intended to be an apolitical entity, according to its director Marco Antônio Mourthé Edmundo (hereafter referred to as Marco Antônio);

> *Marcia*: Could you explain the system or the philosophy?
> *Marco Antônio*: OK Courvelians—look, it is like this. When the program "Curumim" came to Morro de Santana, it needed to be a program that was not tied to politicians. It is a program that's apolitical—it is not political—it is apolitical. It could not benefit from the work of the city councilmen (*vereadores*) of the *prefeito* (mayor and local politicians who often benefit from being involved in programs that would "deal" with poverty, without actually changing the economics of poverty). This Curumim, here in Morro de Santana, it is a kind of model, a way to make a project for poor kids really work. So, it has become the foundation for a series of courses in the "superior course" here at the *faculdade* (college)—the *faculdade de Ciencias Humanas* (College of Human Sciences) (which is conveniently situated next to Curumim). The project was brought to this *favela*, because it is a *favela* with a lot of problems, our purpose is to transform this community. It is like I was saying about the question of being apolitical. The secretary had to put this program in place in a city in the interior, so that it would transform the politics of *cabide emprego* (*cabide* literally means hanger or hat-stand). Curumim was not aligned with local politicians who frequently use current political and popular problems to get votes and then do nothing to solve local problems.

The project is designed to provide care, academic support (tutoring by monitors whose function is identical to the coordinators at the project, Viva Crianças), civic training, and the development of social and community skills for poor children living in the *favela*s of small and large cities. I quote from their statement of purpose, and then from Marco Antônio:

> The Projeto Curumim has as its objectives the integration of the children they work with into society through sports; to awaken the interest of children through *futebol* (soccer); to develop the experience of working in a team setting that is sustained by friendship and cooperation; to prepare the child for society and competition; and to create the most favorable social, cultural, and physical environment for the development of the children attending Curumim. (Programa Curumim 1997)
>
> The first Curumim was started 11 years ago…it was created to provide street youth with sports, leisure and recreation. In the city of Belo Horizonte (BH), where Curumim was created, the reality is different than here in Morro de Santana. They began to implant other things into Curumim. They created the following: education, work themes, and these things began to function. And then Curumim worked OK, because it works on a low budget…here (in Morro de Santana) the kids work, for example part of the responsibilities of the children is to clean up the classrooms…and the monitors are work study students from the college. We earn very little, we work more here in philanthropic ways. We do not have a lot of finances. So, Curumim is a low cost process. We were taking the children off

the streets and returning them to school. We knew that sports and leisure were important and that just the privileged classes have the means to put their children into a school of soccer, or in a private class for music or tutoring classes. So these kids' cognitive development (kids of the upper classes) develop[s] faster. So, today the work market is for the kids of the upper classes. So, Curumim was created to try to meet these necessities. The college knows that to change the community, it needs to enter the community and work directly with the people.

It is through their methodologies that Curumim attempts to create this environment . Associating themselves with informal education, the use of *aulas práticas* (practical classes or classroom tutoring), physical education, collective training, theoretical classes, lectures, and videos as well as offering workshops for parents and children on creating micro-businesses such as a small home-sewing studio, a child-care facility in a home, or a home-based car repair business. Finally, children at Curumim were instructed on their civil and legal rights as children based on the ECA.

Daily Activities

The day at Curumim began with staff meetings between the monitors and the project director. Children slowly arrived at the project and waited for the *roda*. A typical morning at Curumim would unfold in the following manner. I quote from my field notes:

> Curumim has sessions at 7:30 am to 10:30 am and another from 1:00 pm to 3:30 pm. Every day, so I'm told by Marco Antônio, begins with a planning session

with monitors (same as coordinators) Camila and Yuri. Activities for the day usually begin with a *roda*, singing, and prayer. The *roda* takes about 45 minutes, during which time the children also talk about problems they had over the weekend, occurrences, and marriages/births/birthdays and the like. Homework is given on every day but Monday. The kids do not have homework over the weekend. After working on homework, the youth play *futebol* (soccer) and/or work on theater projects. The theater, about the daily difficulties experienced in the daily family life of the children at the project, will be presented to public schools. The theater will focus on daily problems, activities, and citizens' rights.

Rodas differed between projects. How they were conducted, who was in charge, and what was deemed appropriate for discussion determined the physical, emotional, and intellectual climate of each *roda*. At Curumim there was a great deal more control by the monitors than at Viva Crianças. Indeed, Bom Jesus, Curumim, APAE, and COV had similar *roda* management styles by project directors and monitors/coordinators. Ground rules outlined what kinds of behavior were expected from participants, and included not interrupting, not fighting, not yelling, and generally respecting the emotional, physical, and intellectual space of another. Topics of discussion were open at Curumim (and somewhat more limited at Bom Jesus) and I attribute this openness to the calmer atmosphere within the *roda*, especially when compared to Viva Crianças. In the *roda* at Curumim, they frequently focused on child rights and community improvement and involvement. There was a sense of order that made it clear when behaviors were not seen as productive or were viewed as destructive, and there were consequences for the continuation of destructive behaviors. Being suspended from the project, keeping in close contact with the families of the youth, and consistent monthly meetings ensured that parents and youth were informed about the project activities and the children's involvement within the project.

Tutoring, Homework Assistance

Like Viva Crianças, Curumim provided tutoring to the children attending their project. Unlike Viva Crianças, Curumim provided a higher quality of tutoring, in that their monitors were students at the local college who were studying to become teachers. In addition, their work at Curumim was part of their training. Regular meetings with the teachers, discussions about the students' progress, and training on children's rights and community-building were all part of a monitor's job. School work, as at Viva Crianças, was rote memorization with little focus on understanding the process of problem solving and creative interaction from the student. My field notes provide an example of the all-too-common educational experience for poor children:

> Like Viva Crianças, Curumim uses games imported from the US and a European school model to teach language, math, history, and science. Letter Bingo was a popular game and made from used materials. Children and youth tended to actually use the games and to play them to conclusion while working in a more harmonious manner. There were times when chaos erupted and screaming along with hitting occurred, but such instances were mediated by the coordinators who used concrete methods to interrupt aggressive and potentially abusive behaviors. Again, small *roda*s were formed and discussions about anger and its causes actually resulted

in peaceful resolutions. Issues of poverty, abuse at home, limited resources, and anger management were discussed. If solutions were not reached and unacceptable behaviors continued, the child faced suspension from the project for a specified amount of time. Parents were included in these deliberations. In this way, Curumim was having an impact on the "culture" of the parents, who tended to see their children as solely available for service and work.

I witnessed the monitors at Curumim working with the youth in ways that empowered them to be responsible for their actions and for the materials and supplies provided to them. If game pieces were left out, scattered on the ground or on a table, they were called back to put them away and to account for all the pieces. In addition, the children participated with the monitors in cleaning and organizing the project on a daily basis. Sweeping, stacking supplies, and helping in the kitchen were all daily activities shared by monitors and children alike.

Games and Activities

Curumim, unlike Viva Crianças, did create and design a large number of games with the children and youth attending their project. Literacy, mathematics, science, and human rights were subjects for which games were created. All game pieces, as at Viva Crianças, were made from reused materials, yet at Curumim all learning materials were selected, cared for, and put away by the youth at the project. Hence, materials lasted longer even though they were more consistently used than at Viva Crianças. In addition, because the daily routine at Curumim was more regulated and more consistent, time for homework, games, gardening, theater, and play were all well organized and the youth were more fully attentive and participated in activities with less sense of confusion and less aggression. Curumim gave special attention to children's rights and had developed game boards based on the Statute of Children and Adolescents (ECA).[24] The game focused on the inherent citizenship rights now legally available to children, which include the right to physical, intellectual, emotional, social, and cultural development. In addition, no child could be arrested simply for being on the street, unattended by adult supervision. Any child or adolescent arrested had to be charged with an actual crime. I watched as the youth at Curumim played the ECA game with ease, clearly understanding and expressing their rights as Brazilian citizens and as children.

Another avenue for the development and use of the ECA was through the production of small theater skits, often created, written, and co-directed by the children and the monitors at Curumim. Common themes for theatrical productions were the right to education, the right to be treated with respect by the public at large and by their parents, their right to work (after the age of fourteen), and their right to medical treatment and adequate nutrition. The following is an excerpt from a play written by the children regarding their right to an education and the need to educate their parents about the importance of education:

> *Mother*: "Hey kid, go get a bottle of *pinga* for me, you *moleque*!"
> In the margin of the text it states that the boy has the right to protection. Another child enters and announces that the boy is nine years old and has never been to school and his mother does not know what's up or how he will survive in the future. How will he matriculate?

> *Mother*: "School! Why do you want to go to school?"
> *Boy*: "But mother!" he cries. "All my friends are in school."
> The boy says his friends' names.
> *Mother*: "Look here, boy! I'm old and I never went to school! I work all the time doing services for others. I never needed school! Get out of here and go get the clothes for me to wash, now!"

After the rehearsal, the children and monitor stop to discuss the various meanings and themes of the play. I ask if the story is true, if the children know others who live this reality. I'm told by five out of six children (all between the ages of eight and twelve), that they have friends who must stay at home helping their mothers. They tell me it is a "...bad thing, very difficult for us, and for the kids that have to stay home. We need both things, because we learn one thing at home and another at school. But, we need school to be able to survive in the world." This is in contrast to Viva Crianças, where disdain for formal schooling seemed to dominate the project's ideology. It was common to rehearse such theatrical productions for about 10 to 20 days, after which they were presented to the college, public schools, and ultimately to the parents of the children.

Nutrition and Gardening

Curumim, like most of the other projects I came to know in Morro de Santana, worked effectively at a local and individual level on the more basic issues of better nutrition for children and their families. Curumim, more than Viva Crianças, worked closely with the parents of the children and youth, having consistent monthly meetings and frequent lecture/discussion groups on how to improve the local *favela* da Passaginha. Discussion focused on ways to develop viable work for youth, especially girls, via sewing classes and training for childcare. Classes were being arranged for girls to take with their mothers in these areas, in order to bring a sense of collaboration and cooperation between parents and children. In addition, most projects tried teaching their students (and sometimes parents) gardening skills, encouraging them to plant small garden plots at home. However, one youth I interviewed told me that planting a garden in his *favela* was futile because everything he tried to grow was stolen by his neighbors. This situation was not unlike the accounts I heard at Viva Crianças.

Child Behavior: Home and Project

I was told by the monitors at Curumim that the children are "naturally" aggressive because no one at home respects them as individuals. They are not talked to, and mutual discussions are rare. It is common for them to be hit, yelled at, ridiculed (*xinga*), and beaten. The monitors were aware of the different constructions that define the childhood of poor children. I was told by project monitors in all five NGOs how the children of the rich are protected and expected to be children, while poor children do not have toys and must fight, often physically and certainly verbally, to attain even their smallest needs. They have learned that those who yell loudest and are the most persistent and aggressive often get what they want. Attitudes and behaviors of aggression that often appear disrespectful, particularly to the more affluent, are common. Hence, street youth are often stereotyped by those in the middle and upper classes as deviant, dangerous, and marginal. During discussions and individual interviews with local elites, I was frequently told how amoral and frightening street youth are. Ironically, middle- and upper-class adolescents are expected to be on the streets during the weekends, drinking beer and hanging out with their friends until the early morning hours. Nothing negative, indeed, nothing at all is thought of this behavior. Yet a dark-skinned and poorly dressed street youth who is begging or working on the streets is despised and avoided, conceptualized as marginal and dangerous. Once, while interviewing a prominent businesswoman on the veranda of her exclusive restaurant, a group of street youth approached us for money and/or food. Her response was harsh and abrupt:

> *Businesswoman*: Look, many of them have homes, in the periphery of the city. But they stay in the street. I think the tendency is for them to be violent. Right? Because they don't have work, they don't study, they don't have anything except staying in the street begging and robbing. I think the tendency [their character] is for the worst.

As I came to know business owners and professionals in Morro de Santana and we discussed street children in their city, such comments were very common.

In general, I found Curumim to be immensely closer to a useful intervention into the lives of the poor than Viva Crianças is. Like Viva Crianças, Curumim does provide a few hours each day for play and leisure, but the youth return each day to inferior schools, experience social stereotyping and racial profiling, and still have to work on the streets in order to help their families survive. At Curumim the notions of childhood are more balanced with awareness of everyday realities. Finally, the ideological platform from which Curumim is built is one of human rights and children's rights. This foundation alone has enabled them to more effectively address the life needs of the children, their parents, and the community in which they live.

Their attempts to present the ECA to the children and their parents are a step in the right direction.

Popular Culture versus Technology

Curumim, like the four other NGOs I came to know, focused on popular culture as a way to enter the lives of the children and youth they served. In so doing, the educational opportunities and advantages (attending well-provisioned/-funded private schools, attending tutoring schools for taking the *vestibular* test, a college entrance exam similar to our SATs) offered to upper-class youth were ignored, and assumed to be irrelevant.[25] Here, we can see how the concern with good citizenship and family morality are the focus, implying a stereotypically negative evaluation of the morality that accompanies poverty. Educational tutoring is provided at Curumim, and the monitors offered a higher level of educational expertise because of their affiliation with the college. Their dedication to and affection for the children and youth at the project were admirable, but in and of themselves, were powerless to affect the curriculum. Like Viva Crianças, Curumim also had a theater group, but unlike Viva Crianças, their plays were written by the children.

What concerns me most is the assumptions that poverty and lack of educational skills automatically exclude economically disadvantaged youth from access to technological and computer skills, which, in and of itself, would afford them more access to the marketplace than all the rudimentary educational tutoring they receive via the various projects they attend. The following excerpt from a discussion with Marcos Antônio, the director of Curumim, was typical of the lack of interest and hence, lack of knowledge about their ability to provide computer and technological access to poor youth:

> *Marcia*: Do you have access to computers here?
> *Marco Antônio*: Here at Curumim, no.
> *Marcia*: Is this something that you would like to have access to?
> *Marco Antônio*: Yes.
> *Marcia*: Because here in Morro de Santana there are now at least two providers in order to use e-mail. You could develop a program here, for example, where the kids have the ability to talk to other kids in Rio de Janeiro, where there is a huge movement organized around and by street kids.
> *Marco Antônio*: I did not know this.

I would like to stress that the directors of the projects with whom I worked had access to computers, either in their offices or in their homes. In the case of Marco Antônio, the college situated next door had computers available for staff and professors. Knowledge about the availability of e-mail providers certainly existed, for it was a service that was growing rapidly in Morro de Santana during the late 1990s. During the same conversation with Marco Antônio, the topic of globalization became a focus through which the ideology of Curumim was again reiterated.

> *Marco Antônio*: In our program we look towards working with the reality of Morro de Santana, but locating it within the process of globalization. I do not agree with globalization either, but globalization is here and it is not a process that's going away. Globalization is not a new process, you understand? There is no way to go back. So, what is it that we can do? Now, I'm OK, your children are OK—but what about these children? Are they going to have a place to go? Or are they going to be thrown back into the masses living in misery?

> *Marcia*: You're going to develop and produce another generation that has the same problems or you're going to develop a population that has a way to participate and has a better life.
>
> *Marco Antônio*: A better life—better their quality of life. So, returning to this, we work inside of these five areas: arts, recreation, communication and expression, integration, and sports.
>
> *Marcia*: But not with computers?
>
> *Marco Antônio*: No.

Yet, Marco Antônio understands the implications of not having access to technologies that will link the poor to the marketplace. Indeed, the problems of linking equal educational opportunities to current computer and web technologies are intimately related to the ability to speak both English and Spanish:

> *Marcia*: So, if you had this capacity you could e-mail this organization and develop many ideas. Now, for only $30 per month you can have access to people far away. It is not impossible now. This is an interesting possibility; perhaps you could develop this if you had a computer and a little course on how to use the computer. How to use the Internet.
>
> *Marco Antônio*: Yeah, sure—today information—I would like to say that we do not work with computers or with "foreigners." Because as an educator, I'm worried—because Mercosul/Mercosur has come here.[26]
>
> *Marcia*: How are these children going to enter the market without speaking Spanish? Brazil is the only country inside Mercosul that speaks Portuguese. How are these kids here in Brazil going to enter the market

> without speaking English or Spanish, until they have access to e-mail?
>
> *Marco Antônio*: That's not the answer.
>
> *Marcia*: What is the answer?
>
> *Marco Antônio*: Popular culture—give them pride in being who they are.

Marco Antônio always returned to his notion of the informal school that is based on popular culture as the way out for the poor, and in this way, without intending it, Curumim and many other NGOs keep the population they seek to serve in poverty. Marco Antônio continues: "...interaction is an exchange. Here you enter the process of school, because Curumim is an informal school."

Undeniably, learning literacy and proficiency in language and basic mathematics are important tools that will aid in an exit from poverty. Brazil has initiated educational reform in its public school system for over sixty years. The effectiveness of these reforms has been based on enrollment, illiteracy rates, dropout levels, school failure, and teacher qualifications, revealing depressingly poor performances in all the above areas (Carnoy, Werthein, and Levin. 1987). As Professor Francis Musa Boakari, from the *Universidade Federal do Piaui*, in Teresina, Piaui, stated,

> Despite numerous efforts to improve and make the educational system more adequate, education has to satisfy two conflicting demands: to act as an instrument for socioeconomic mobility (access to economic capital) and as an imperceptible tool for excluding the poor while maintaining the status quo of the dominant social classes (1994:109–133).

Such dichotomies make effective educational reform for public education almost impossible and place an unrealistic burden on NGO tutoring programs to educationally empower their clientele.

Without changing the basic structures that limit access to a higher quality of education that includes working with crucial technologies used in all areas of the new marketplace, poor children have little chance of upward mobility. In this way racial inequality is linked to Brazil's poor educational system, which lacks resources available to middle-and upper-class children and youth who most commonly attend private schools. Short of revolution, these changes will come about only through government mandates and civil rights activism. However, as we have seen in the case of other Brazilian mandates, these will be insufficient if policies and infrastructure are not designed to implement them.

Citizens for Life Options (COV)

Before introducing *Cidadania Opção de Vida* (Citizens for Life Options), it is necessary to briefly discuss the Brazilian sociologist Herbert José de Souza Betinho. Lovingly referred to simply as Betinho, de Souza Betinho devoted his life to the analysis of social inequality and to the creation of effective campaigns against hunger and misery. Born with hemophilia in 1935 in Minas Gerais, he experienced almost constant illness. Later in his adult life, he contracted AIDS as a result of his medical need for frequent blood transfusions. In 1964, Betinho was a student leader and adviser to the government of João Goulart, and, during the military regime, he left Brazil and lived in exile in Argentina; Glasgow; Toronto, Canada; and Mexico. He returned to Brazil in 1979, founded the Brazilian Institute of Social and Economic Analysis (IBASE), and brought to Brazil his capacity for analysis of social, political, and economic issues. While abroad, Betinho worked with the then-new technology of computers. Upon his return to Brazil, he introduced to his institute computer technology, which had previously been accessible only to state and federal offices, and large corporations. IBASE worked to understand social inequality, racism, and historical political processes in Brazil that perpetuated poverty and misery. His campaigns against hunger, misery, and human rights abuses used market research techniques that successfully recruited millions of people to support his efforts. It was through Betinho's campaign against hunger that COV found its inspiration and structure. Betinho died in 1997 of complications from AIDS.

Cidadania Opção de Vida (COV) is a relatively new NGO in Morro de Santana, founded in 1995. It was initiated by a group of workers at the *Caixa Econômica Federal* (Federal Economic Bank) in Morro de Santana based on the ideas of Betinho. Its constitution, written by its board of directors, states that it is an *entidade civil sem fins lucrativos, de caráter beneficente, com personalidade jurídica própria, de duração por prazo indeterminado* (a civil non-profit entity of a beneficent character with individual judicial personality with a duration of indeterminate span).

At the Morro de Santana branch of the *Caixa Econômica Federal* (CEF) there was enough interest in assisting street youth that Betinho's work, especially his compassionate work toward eliminating hunger and misery among the poor, was embraced and COV was created in July 1996. Yet the founders of COV wanted to create a project with different characteristics that did not follow the established directives set up by the central *comitê* of the CEF for the following reasons:

1. They resolved to create a committee with an individual legal personality, one that allowed for the possibility of collecting resources using tax deductions from the paychecks of those

donating. This idea would not have been possible inside the central *comitê* scheme.
2. Unlike Betinho, the founders of COV did not want their work to be simply giving food and resource materials (clothes, medicines, financial assistance) to needy people. They believed that their work was deeper, and in this sense needed to work with the moral and social rehabilitation of those who are marginalized. They understood that it was better to teach people to be fishermen than give them fish. Hence, COV was deeply imbedded in the religious ideology of the Catholic Church. COV explicitly stated that, "The needy population needs more cultural, religious, and educational support than the usual *cesta de alimentação* (basket of food)."

Gilceu Ferreira da Costa (hereafter referred to as Gilceu), the director of COV, told me that the most difficult part of the creation process came after the ideological formulation for COV. As he put it, after COV became a legal entity, the real work began:

> The most difficult part came when we had to figure out how to put our ideology into practice. What were we actually going to do? How were we going to begin? Where were we going to start? It was incredible, this kind of inquiry…but in a society that is so dismal, where there is so much need, it was difficult to know how to begin this work. We began therefore, to accidentally help needy people, but this was not the work that we wanted to execute. There were anxious periods where we wanted to give to the first person we saw without observing our path. It was here that we got to know about the existence of the newly created group *Grupo de Evangelização* (The Group of Evangelics) that met

on Sundays in the big *Paróquia Santo António* (Parish of Saint Anthony). Every Sunday, poor children came to *Paróquia Santo António* to learn the word of God. We decided to direct our work toward needy children such as these. We resolved to work jointly with poor children in the following way:

1. To work with to the *Grupo de Evangelização*, and they would present to the children their teachings about God, education, respect, etc., and on the other side, our committee took charge of giving financial, moral, and cultural support to the children and their families.
2. We began in this way, to get to know each child that participated in the project, and we began to detect the bigger problems. We began to see the principal necessities of the group or of each individual child, by talking with these children on Sundays and by visiting in their houses and talking with their parents. It was in this way that we were trying to supply or substitute the necessities of each one of the children and/or their families.

Gilceu was a practicing Catholic, whose involvement in the church through weekly meetings and groups led him to become part of the newly created group *Grupo de Evangelização*. Hence, it was Gilceu's religious proclivities that guided and directed COV.

The COV Project

The resources to develop this work, according to Gilceu, came "providentially from spontaneous donations and promotional events," where board members talked with co-workers and recruited volunteers to work with the project. Besides recruitment of volunteers, there were clothing drives with boxes for collection placed in various locations throughout the city as well as in stores. In addition, public service announcements on local radio stations, sponsored by various businesses and civil service organizations, helped to spread the word. These forms of assistance were part of Betinho's original work and were absorbed into the COV project. The booklet published by the committee describes its early efforts:

> We worked with children we'd find on the streets, and eventually we were working with children who did not have homes. We resolved to redirect our work, this time concentrating our forces on *crianças de rua*. We approached these children and began to work with them, with the intention of re-educating them to live inside the margins of society, because these were children and adolescents that stayed in the street, slept in the street, and in the end, were children of the street that had all the peculiar habits of these children.

In June of 1996, COV began to develop the project with street children, meeting every Tuesday at 7:30 pm where they and the board would talk, trying to "turn the kids into our friends, and at each meeting we noted that each one opened up more and that their confidence in us was growing." The board visited and talked with the parents of participating children who had family members willing and able to talk with them. During meetings with the children, the board discussed what they had learned from the parents, and also discussed the attitudes and lifestyles practiced by the youth on the streets.

In early 1997, after the board had won the confidence of the youth and convinced them to return to school, arrangements were made for them to matriculate and enroll in a public school in Morro de

Santana. It was agreed that the youth would maintain contact with the board and continue meeting every Tuesday evening. Of the eight children and adolescents the board came to know during this initial stage, four returned to their families. The remaining four became the first youth in the project. Gilseu, the director told me,

> We began to put together a way to get a place for them to live. On the 22 of June, 1997 we rented a small house and finally these children had a place, a house where they could live with the necessary comforts and various activities. Our major objective has been to take all the children in Morro de Santana off the streets. The committee works with these types of children (street children who are lacking in morality, spirituality, and correct social behavior), doing everything that's possible to turn them into respectable men.

Since the placement of the youth into a rented house in 1997, two of the youth have completed their studies up to the fourth grade, and two have passed into fifth grade. My participation in the project included observing the boys on a daily basis, talking with their school teachers and private tutor, as well as meeting with the boys and talking about their life histories. Teachers and tutors struggled daily with the boys' lack of literacy and low self-esteem. Homework and studying were extremely difficult for them since their reading level was very elementary, and in one case nonexistent. All the boys had been evaluated by a local mental health practitioner, and one boy had been put on an anti-depressant. The attention given to their educational and emotional life was admirable and consistent, yet their sensibilities about themselves and their way of life were not successfully altered to conform to middle- and upper-class norms about childhood.

In a recent phone conversation, Gilceu told me the following: "Today, we are a group who is aware of what we are doing. Poverty, lack of spirituality, and street behavior are ingrained in street children and it's very difficult to change them." In this sense, Gilceu identified what he felt the committee had learned through their work with street youth. As we continued our discussion, Gilceu talked about the difficulties of re-educating street youth in order to alter their sensibilities about appropriate social behavior for children and adolescents in Brazilian society. The streets were seen as a dangerous environment, and no children of any age are allowed to spend unsupervised time on them. In addition, the types of clothes and shoes worn by street youth were also a marker that marginalized them, as was their linguistic style (street lingo) and social mannerisms. For the youth in the project, restrictions placed on their way of life by the project were a constant irritation. Staying up late, going out at night, sleeping late, missing school, not wearing clean clothes, and acting aggressively had become a way of life for the project youth. COV's attempts to bring them into compliance with middle- and upper-class behavior were essentially not successful. Brazilian social scientist Flávia Impelizieri points out that the home life of street children is often filled with violence and indifference.

> The repeated absence of one or both parents because of work; an early responsibility for domestic tasks which are more suited to an adult; the rejection by stepfathers or stepmothers; the violence practiced by physically or mentally stressed parents: all these factors contribute to the failure of the home as a place where the child can find shelter, care, guidance, social and leisure activities. More often than not, it becomes a place of conflict, risk, loneliness and servility; a place where childhood is taken away instead of being promoted (Impelizieri 1995:37).

In contrast, the street offers a perceived liberty, a space that holds almost unlimited freedom. "There are no fixed times for eating, sleeping, working, studying or coming home. The satisfaction of material needs is insured by strategies that go from begging to assaults...life in the streets is also characterized by a strong solidarity among the gang members" (Impelizieri 1995:37–38).

Unfortunately, COV folded in 2000, lacking sufficient funds to continue providing support for their shelter, food, education, and health care. Since COV closed, the three youth living in the rented house returned to the streets. It is difficult to know if the goals of the project could have been achieved had the project continued longer than three years.

Associação de Pais e Amigos dos Excepcionais (APAE)

The Association of Parents and Friends of Those with Disabilities (APAE) was founded in 1962 in São Paulo, Brazil. Today throughout Brazil there are 2,000 APAEs that attend to approximately 200,000 people with disabilities. Approximately 37,000 professionals working in the areas of special education (including dyslexia and other learning disabilities), daily living needs, rehabilitation, health, and training for employment in the marketplace teach and train people, from infants through adulthood, who are living with disabilities.

While APAE does not work specifically with economically disadvantaged children, the majority of children attending the APAE in Morro de Santana were poor children of color who, because of difficulties at birth (usually lack of oxygen), were born with brain injuries. The second most common reason for brain injuries or physical deformities was mothers' poor nutrition and lack of prenatal care, as well as a high incidence of alcoholism among poor women. Ana Livia, a psychiatrist working for APAE, reported that,

> A majority [of the children at APAE], we can observe… that they needed oxygen at birth and it was not provided. The question of bad nutrition [is also an issue]. Unfortunately, most of the children that come here are very poor children. So, they have all the problems that come with bad nutrition, poor health care, and frequently, poor medical care during birth.

My tenure at APAE was less intensive than the four other projects identified here. I became involved with APAE because several of the children I came to know in the other projects (Viva Crianças and Bom Jesus) also attended APAE. I was curious as to the kinds of attention they were receiving, the types of intervention and therapy they participated in, and in general, how they were classified among the children served by APAE.

Nicolas, a nine-year-old boy, attended Viva Crianças and also participated in APAE. Instead of attending regular public school, he received special educational training via APAE, where he was attempting to learn how to read and do basic math problems. When Nicolas was about two years old, he was kicked in the head by a horse as he played in the streets. His mother eventually abandoned him and he was being raised by another woman who had several children of her own. To all appearances, Nicolas was normal except that he had difficulty focusing his attention, particularly when doing schoolwork.

In Brazil, there is (largely through the efforts of APAE) an emerging social movement dedicated to guaranteeing the efficacy of social rights for people with disabilities. However, APAE in Morro de Santana still felt that children with disabilities should be separated from "normal" children, and they referred to Nicolas and all children with disabilities as *deficiêntes* (deficients).

As one progressive parent stated in an interview by Bárbara Amelia Vampré Xavier (International Relations for the APAE Institute in São Paulo), "We [as parents of children with disabilities] have learned to put aside the notion of a charity organization, created to give help to those children who were called 'fools,' without human value, an idea which, unfortunately, still prevails..." (2000 webpage article). At Viva Crianças, Nicolas frequently was treated as a child with deficiencies who talked nonsense and acted "like a fool" by both project coordinators and project children. At APAE, he was provided with additional attention, both educational and psychological. On a daily basis he received speech therapy, physical therapy, and counseling, and his progress was monitored on a monthly basis through the use of standardized testing protocols.

Bearing in mind the unfortunate stereotypes concerning disabilities that still prevail in Brazil, APAE offered training in various handicrafts, principally needlepoint, weaving, baking, cooking, and various manual dexterity tasks that could be used in repetitive nonintellectually demanding factory and assembly jobs. It is interesting to note that these activities are similar to, if not identical to, various activities offered at the five NGOs working with street youth. Again, the popular culture model prevails, and in addition, at APAE these activities are considered appropriate for people who are living with disabilities. In this way, street children are perceived in very similar ways throughout the NGO community, which frequently presents the popular culture model as the only viable form of economic employment for poor children. Just as children born with disabilities have traditionally been viewed as "fools without human value," so have street children often been described as disposable human waste, as vermin, as a plague on society, and as worthless garbage that needs to be removed from view and discarded by more privileged Brazilians. In a survey I conducted in Rio in 1994, two thirds of my sample of fifty individuals from five distinct areas of the city stated that street children were violent and dangerous and should be removed from the streets using whatever means possible; that included placing them into FUNABEM institutions or even placing them into the adult prison system. One woman in downtown Rio who consented to an impromptu interview stated the following about street children:

> On the streets these children do things that appall us…they steal sometimes to eat, some have animal tendencies, and do things out of meanness…these kids aren't that hungry! They have no shame because of the freedom they have to do what they want and there is no punishment for them.

I was invited to have dinner with a well-off family one evening in Morro de Santana. Seated around the table were my host, her husband, two adolescent male children, and her grandmother. During dinner, I was asked what I thought of street children now that I'd had time to study them. I stated that that was a difficult question for me to answer because I was trying to understand who street children are and how they lived. I decided to ask my host what she thought about street children, and she stated that street children were less than animals and should be destroyed. I found that such sentiments were not uncommon among many Brazilians.

The following incident illustrates how Afro-Brazilian street children are viewed by many Brazilian elites:[27] I was invited to the home of an adolescent boy named Olívio who had quit school in order to sell mangos along the side of the highway. Olívio, Evelyn (his mother), and I sat talking about the 1997 murder of a *Pataxó Ha-ha-hae* Indian man named Galdino Jesus dos Santos in Brasilia. Five white upper-class youths were riding around the city in a car that belonged to the father of one of the boys. It was after midnight (according to Galdino, who survived for a short while after he was attacked) when he woke and found his body on fire. Galdino had been a leader within the *Pataxó* tribe of *Ha-Ha-Hae* and he had been staying in a hostel in Brasilia, whose policy was to close and lock the doors after eleven at night. He had come to Brasilia from a village in the Amazon to participate in the commemoration of *O Dia do Índio* (The Day of the Indian). Galdino had arrived back at the hostel shortly after midnight and found that he was locked out. He walked the streets for a while, looking for a place to sleep, and chose a bench at a bus stop, covering himself with newspapers. The five youths between the ages of seventeen and nineteen drove by and saw Galdino, whom they described as a *mendigo* (beggar). When the youth saw Galdino lying on a bus stop bench, they apparently thought up a prank. They went to a nearby garage, bought a two-liter bottle of alcohol, poured it over the sleeping Indian and set fire to him. They were heard laughing hysterically as they ran to their car. The man died at a hospital shortly afterwards, with 95% of his body burned. Only the soles of his feet escaped the flames. The trial judge handling this case declassified the seriousness of the crime from homicide to one of bodily harm resulting in death. Two of the five youth are sons of high officials in the Brazilian justice system (de Roupre, *Revista* CONSULEX 1997). Evelyn and Olívio shared their feelings with me about their lack of faith in the Brazilian justice system:

> *Olívio*: Remember the case of the Indian here in Brazil?
> *Marcia*: Yes, the case of the Indian…that happened in 1997, right? Ah…they burned him because they thought that he was a *mendigo* (beggar).
> *Evelyn*: And those three adolescents, they weren't punished…they weren't.

Olívio: No…they weren't.

Evelyn: Why weren't they punished? Because they were the sons of parents that are part of society…if they were people from the lower classes, poor, black… they'd all have been put into FUNABEM! They'd be in FUNABEM because it's just the poor and dark skinned that are castigated. They weren't poor, they were from the middle and upper class, and they aren't punished.

In the same article from the 1997 *Revista CONSULEX*, the upper-class youth stated that they were simply ridding society of its garbage.

The Arts

The arts played a very important role at APAE, especially singing and dancing, in that both activities stimulated motor and sensory systems. In addition, APAE offered therapy in speech, auditory perception, motor coordination and sensory stimulation, and basic educational skills such as reading and mathematics. All teachers at APAE received advanced training in their specialized fields and collaboration between teachers, physical therapists, neurologists, speech therapists, and other professionals was key to reaching some level of measurable success with children born with disabilities. Working with parents was crucial, and I was told that without educating the parents, there was no hope of improving the lives of the children at APAE.

Again, as at Curumim, Bom Jesus, and COV, I was told by staff that children were treated harshly at home. One staff member at APAE stated,

> The majority [of children we work with] have grave neurological problems [usually resulting from problems at their birth, such as lack of oxygen, frequently

due to medical malpractice]. They are usually totally dependent on their care givers. If it is just us, the professionals who are working with these children, they will not get the stimulation they need. We try to work with the potential that each child has. We know that they have specific problems but they do not have any specifically defined stimulation for them. So we sit and talk with the psychologist and the physical therapist and we discuss how to work with the parents.

The skills and knowledge to give basic care for a child born with severe disabilities is most frequently lacking in poor mothers. The same staff member told me,

> My work also looks at guiding mothers in nutrition, how to change her child's clothes, because it is the mother who is with her child. If she does not have time, I will work with the child for half an hour for the mothers who have other responsibilities. So, I'm always struggling against things that exist…for example the moment of giving nutrition, the time to give a bath, the time to change clothes…because if I give adequate stimulation, she will learn to give it back.

Here, the half-hour's attention by the staff member accomplishes little or nothing. Yet, I was made aware of the difficulties that existed in educating poor parents who often cannot read, are undernourished themselves, and frequently are alcoholics. In addition, basic hygiene was a constant problem. Many children live in homes without running water, and frequently the only water available to them is river water that is polluted by raw sewage. Intestinal parasites, skin infections, and bronchial conditions were fairly constant among all the children I came to know in all five NGOs.

APAE has drawn extensively on sensory stimulation models to work with children born with brain injuries and physical disabilities, as well as teaching mothers how to play with their children, especially during daily activities. Yet, this same staff person told me that it was very difficult to get the parents to follow through on a daily basis.

> It is really difficult to bring the family here because the problems that they have, for them to talk about them they become afraid. So, the difficulties that we have are really big. But we try to work on top of all this, to bring them here so they will learn how to work with us.

When I asked various staff at APAE about parent–child relations, I was told what I had been told at Bom Jesus, Curumim, and COV: that parents do not talk to their children, nor do they treat them as individuals in their own right.

> *Staff member*: Ah! No…no there is not this kind of dialogue. "How was your day today?" No. There is not this kind of relationship and dialogue.
> *Marcia*: Do you think that the parents are *xingando* (chiding or scolding) their children a lot?
> *Staff Member*: Yes…yes…
> *Maitê (psychologist):* In the same way that they abuse them (*xingam*) there is the problem of how to begin working with them [the parents] initially. The parents, for example, understand that they need to be more of a friend to their child, but this is what happens. The parents are disoriented and perplexed, bewildered… until they understand that they need to put limits on their children. The only way they know how to do this is to *xingar* (scold) their child. They curse or ridicule their child. So, they feel a lot of insecurity when they

are asked to think about their child in a different way. To learn to see their child as another human being that they relate to as a friend or as deserving of respect and who has the right to be a full human being with feelings and the right to express these feelings. This is very confusing and disorienting to the parents. They resist this.

APAE's work in the area of re-education of parents and the rights of the children born with disabilities is extremely important and their impact within the community needs further research. Indeed, their work with disabled children could indirectly assist street children, who are symbolically linked to the negative stereotypes applied to children born with mental and physical disabilities.

Bom Jesus

Bom Jesus is formally called *O Centro Educacional Comunitário Bom Pastor* (The Good Shepherd Community Educational Center), the first entity established by the *Centro Social Achilles Diniz Couto* to work in the area of education. Bom Jesus states that their objectives are to: 1) make every effort to defend the rights of children and adolescents and 2) contribute to the integral development of the human being through the experience of community involvement. In addition, Bom Jesus seeks to protect the health of the families of the children with whom they work, to combat hunger and misery by developing horticultural activities with the children attending their project, to support and offer local cultural idioms, and to promote sports and leisure. Finally, Bom Jesus works to develop an interest in and increase involvement with issues related to ecology and the protection of the environment.

In many ways, Bom Jesus was similar to Viva Crianças, beginning each day with the *roda*; however, since Bom Jesus is a Catholic entity, every morning first began with a prayer and a blessing, in addition to a short talk about the importance of religion and spirituality in daily life. In this sense, propagating the mission of the Roman Catholic Church was the primary goal, though that is not listed in their statement of intent. After the morning *roda*, a nutritious breakfast of *pudim* (a corn or rice pudding) served with milk, *todi* (chocolate milk), or juice, along with bread and, at times, eggs was served. Then the children broke into their respective groups with their monitors and began working on the various activities offered by the project, which included weaving, drawing, woodworking, gardening, homework, cooking, and various handicrafts. The morning session began at 7:30 and ended at 11:30, when lunch was served. Again, the food at Bom Jesus was usually excellent, with casseroles often being served along with rice and beans, salad, and vegetables and more milk and bread. The afternoon session began at 12:30 and followed the same format and schedule as the morning session.

Bom Jesus, like Curumim, was highly structured and the monitors received a lot of support and training from the director, Sister Irmã Heloisa, who met monthly with all the monitors and staff, including the cooks, gardeners, and office support staff; she also met with the parents (usually the mothers) of the children who attended the project. In this way, there was a tight unity among all levels of the project, and communication flowed from the top to the bottom as well as from the bottom to the top. Discipline problems were handled by discussions between the child and the monitor on an individual basis first. Then, if necessary, a small *roda* was formed in order to discuss the problems that occurred among children. Irmã Heloisa was usually part of any *roda* discussion. If serious behavior problems continued, such as bodily harm to another child, the parents were called and a meeting was arranged between the monitor, the child, Irmã Heloisa, and the parents. In extreme cases, the child was suspended from the project for a designated period and the parents continued to meet with Irmã Heloisa in order to continue working on the problems. Monitors often visited the homes of the children in their groups and worked with their parents as well.

During monthly meetings, monitors often discussed issues related to poverty, racism, the use of *palavrãos*, aggression and anger by children and youth in the project, and their frustrations related to solving problems. When discussions were fruitful, which was more often than not, several monitors would encourage others to problem-solve, writing possible new tactics on the large blackboards that ran the length of several walls. In this way, new ideas were initiated and they originated from the staff themselves, rather than from a disembodied director. Irmã Heloisa was exceptionally good at facilitating these meetings and in encouraging the monitors to come forward and talk about issues that needed resolving.

Bom Jesus was clean and was housed in a newly built structure that was open to the air. It was situated on a hilltop in the *favela* of Bom Jesus, where all the children who attended the project lived. Irmã Heloisa felt it was important that the children attending the project live within the *favela* of Bom Jesus, because contact with their families was seen as essential to the successful integration of the project into the community. When the project began in 1996, there were approximately fifty children. During my tenure in 1997, there were over 150 children, and a long waiting list. Its reputation was excellent within the *favela*, and the children and parents expressed a high degree of respect for the project in general.

Like Viva Crianças, Curumim, COV, and APAE, Bom Jesus also offered tutoring for schoolwork; games that assisted in the learning of grammar, mathematics, history, and science; as well as theater and music. I created a more traditional musical group at Bom Jesus that focused on singing, and together we created a successful Christmas program that was presented to the parents.

Bom Jesus was highly integrated into the community where it worked, and insisted on and maintained contact with the families of the children attending the project. Staff, monitors, and director were in constant contact. Irmã Heloisa was at the project every day, without fail, unless she was traveling by request of the church. There was less aggression and anger at the project than at Viva Crianças and Curumim and more family participation. Bom Jesus was aware of and addressed the realities facing its clients, including racism. There was an atmosphere of support for the children who worked and attended school, and there was an abiding respect for them as individuals in their own right. In addition, the families were also treated with respect and confidentiality as well as compassion, while working to increase the rights of children within their families as well as within their community. Bom Jesus and Curumim were both actively involved in the *favelas* where project youth lived, had clearly defined rules that outlined acceptable behavior and consequences for infractions, provided meetings and other avenues for contact with parents, and offered a fairly high standard of educational tutoring. Curumim's monitors were college students, and in this sense, they provided the highest level of educated monitors. APAE and COV additionally worked with the families of the youth they served, especially APAE. Community involvement, parental involvement, educationally proficient monitors/coordinators, open meetings that encourage creative input from monitors and staff, clear rules of engagement and behavior consequences for infractions were evident in all projects with the exception of Viva Crianças.

In this sense, it is possible to conclude that some programs based on the popular culture model, when well-conceived, are more successful than others. Success in this sense can be defined as providing project youth with an environment that cohesively promotes their well-being and full citizenship. As we can see from the five NGOs discussed here, there is no "typical" street child or youth. I have attempted, primarily through my analysis of Viva Crianças, to address the complexities involved in creating effective programs for street and working children. In addition, I have attempted to present the children's views about Viva Crianças, while also addressing the reality of their life at home and on the streets. Finally, the four additional NGOs have been discussed here in order to contrast their programs, staff, and daily procedures with Viva Crianças. It is my intention through this analysis to make a contribution, however modest, to the literature on street youth and the NGOs that seek to serve them.

In conclusion, it is assumed that street children need help, and indeed they do, but the basic assumptions about the kind of help that they need are in conflict with the reality of their lives. Street children carry the negative social stereotypes often used by social scientists to describe those living in poverty. The symbols of the street versus the house, the public versus the private, the dirty versus the clean are very much alive in Brazil (da Matta 1991). Cynthia Sarti writes, "To ensure that one is in the 'good' realm, one has to construct an 'evil' realm and place counterparts there" (Sarti 1995:124).

Street children, I argue, are symbols of social conflict and targets of social angst. NGOs reflect, in some measure, the social confusion about where street children belong in society and how they should be treated. The next chapter discusses how street children struggle with their identity as Afro-Brazilians, and as children and adolescents at home, on the streets, and in NGO projects. I present data from my fieldwork on the low self-esteem street children expressed. My informants discuss their experiences with violence at home, frequent hunger, and constant poverty. Their experiences demonstrate how being a street child places them in a particularly vulnerable social position.

CHAPTER NINE
STREET LIFE AND SOCIAL RELATIONS

Low Self-Esteem

Racism and poverty are intricately linked in Brazil. While each condition generates debilitating life circumstances within society, together these socially explicit terms generate a particularly devastating internal condition that often leaves those who are socially marked and marginalized by them with an internal self-numbing silence. I have addressed both racism and poverty in order to demonstrate the impact that Brazil's silent racism has on the lives of poor Afro-Brazilian street youth.

While in Brazil, I found that, although poverty could be seen and was acknowledged in daily discourse, the linkage between racism and poverty was not a socially acceptable topic. There is a mysterious imperative to remain silent about racism and it was this silence that impressed me the most. Gerald Sider argues: "The creation of culture is also, simultaneously and necessarily, the creation of silence... we can have no significant understanding of any culture unless we also know the silences that were institutionally created and guaranteed…" (1997:74–75).

In this chapter, I argue that street youth suffer from the effects of Brazil's unique social and racial marginalization of them as a group. The marginalization of street children includes the silencing of their voices, despite the continuous efforts of many NGOs to bring their cause to the forefront of Brazilian and international society. Social consciousness of the racism directed toward street youth is, practically speaking, nonexistent. In this sense, cultural censorship enforces the compliance and further marginalization of those who are the most victimized. Low self-esteem is common among street youth, who remain ignorant or silent, about of the codified social discourse on their character. Keeping the appearance of honesty and goodness was uppermost in the minds of most of the children and families I worked with in Morro de Santana. Many were too poor to present themselves in public. In the absence of alternatives to torn and dirty clothes, their social reputations took on added meaning. What other people said about them, their friends as well as their *patroas*, formed their reputations and preceded them as they left their homes every day. Hence, struggling to counter the socially sanctioned and saturated discourses about their immoral character, poor Afro-Brazilians often internalize the silent social consensus in which they live.

Street children cling to an idealized sense of family and familial solidarity. Frequently, when discussing family life with the children at the projects, they wanted to assure me that while there were problems at home (hunger, alcoholism, disease, violence) their families were intact. Indeed, their sense of family was one of the most important elements in their lives. Not only was it important to be valuable to their family through their work at home and in the streets, it was important to have a family with a reputation for honesty and the willingness to work hard. While domestic violence and child abuse were common elements, the children I came to know struggled to create a picture of love and acceptance within their family. It was also equally important to have a good *patroa* who, given the hardworking and honest nature of a servant, would offer at least the hope of acquiring a few luxuries (schoolbooks, school uniforms, second-hand clothes). Such fantasies of normalcy, based on middle-class values and behaviors, were a common theme among my informants.

It took some work to excavate the reality of the children's lives and to move beyond the fantasized family life initially related by the youth at the projects. Sarah, a girl of twelve at Viva Crianças, found my questions about her family's economic status very difficult to answer. She very much wanted to convince me that they lived in a middle-class home and had a middle-class life even though they lived in the *favela* in conditions of extreme poverty.

> *Sarah*: The middle class is small in Morro de Santana…
> *Marcia*: The middle class is small? The upper class is big?
> *Sarah*: Yes, the big class here is the upper class…middle class is medium and the poor are many…
> *Marcia*: There are lots of poor here in Morro de Santana?
> *Sarah*: Yes, there are very many little people here (she refers to the poor as little people).
> *Marcia*: OK.
> *Sarah*: There are more little people here than the others.
> *Marcia*: If you were to put yourself in one of these classes, where would you say that you live? Upper, middle, or lower? Which one would say?

Sarah: Which one do I live in? I think I live in the middle class.
Marcia: You think that your family is in the middle class?
Sarah: (no response. Sarah is looking down at her feet)
Marcia: Do you think that your family is in the middle class or lower class?
Sarah: (whisper) *Grande*. (big)
Marcia: What? I do not understand.
Sarah: *Grande*.
Marcia: The upper class?
Sarah: Yes….
Marcia: You think that your family is in the upper class or the bigger class? That they have a lot of money?
Sarah: Yes…more or less….
Marcia: Your family has a lot of money?
Sarah: No…they do not have— (She is whispering, and I'm feeling really bad. I wish I had not asked this.)
Marcia: They have…
Sarah: Middle…
Marcia: Middle…are you sure?
Sarah: (she is nodding, indicating yes)
Marcia: Do you live in the *favela*, or in the center of the city?
Sarah: I live in the *favela*. (she is whispering)

There was little awareness of the causes of social inequality and class difference when mothers talked with me about their lives. Many described their childhood as ideal, even though there were often ten children in a family and there was continual hunger and struggle for survival. There is a desire to idealize or to re-create a past that erases poverty, discomfort, shame, and fear. They are very much like the children I work with who want to draw pictures using fairytales that create happy endings to their difficult circumstances. Yet even children who were able to talk about the difficulties of their lives (particularly the alcoholism and abuse of their parents) continued to see the goodness of their mothers and fathers, in spite of acknowledging their behavior to be ignorant and brutal.

> *Milena*: Ah…if I could change my childhood, I would ah…I would change the way my parents were, I would change my family…and I would change how ignorant they are…the way they drink and fight…I would change it more like a family more turned towards God, a family that would have gone to Mass, a caring family, a very religious family.
> *Marcia*: Do you think that you would choose the same parents or choose different ones?
> *Milena*: No…the same people, because my mother is very good to me and she is very honest. My father also. I would just change these bad things.

Nevertheless, when informants got to know me well, their detailed accounts of family life and the reality of their childhood presented a desperate and much more depressing picture. Milena continued:

> *Milena*: I suffered a lot, I used to be beaten a lot by my father and mother…they drank a lot and fought all the time. One time my mother took a knife and stabbed my father, and my father beat up my mother, he hit her with his fist and broke her nose, and my father's family revolted against my mother, and the entire family was ganging up and hitting her.
> *Marcia*: Yes, that's difficult, huh?
> *Milena*: Yes…

> *Marcia*: Did you see all this happening or did you just hear it?
> *Milena*: No, I saw it all…one time I even went to jail with my mother because they apprehended her.
> *Marcia*: What did you do?
> *Milena*: I cried…I cried and cried, and I tried to stop the fights, but I never succeeded…and me and my sister cussed at our father because we did not like to see our mother beaten up…we are both very traumatized by all this.

When describing the violence that they witnessed or received at home, from parents or older siblings, children commonly denied the severity of it. Many times children also told me that they deserved to be hit and at times, even beaten. Lucca told me the following story when I asked if his parents hit him, and if so, had they hurt him: "One time when I was very, very little, I do not even remember, my grandfather is the one that tells this story—I was wanting bread. I was making a nuisance in the street, she went, (my mom was drunk)—she hit me with the squeegee handle, a piece of wood and my arm got very swollen."

When I worked at Projeto Viva Crianças, Catrina, my teaching assistant and I became friends. Catrina was twenty-one years old, and was a very dark-skinned Afro-Brazilian who, through her hard work and natural intelligence, managed to pass the *vestibular* (exams similar to the SATs in the US) and graduate from the US equivalent of high school. Passing the *vestibular* meant that she could enter college, a rare occurrence for poor Afro-Brazilians. At the time I knew and worked with her, she had begun her higher education at the college in Morro de Santana. Catrina and I became good friends, sharing the frustrations of working at Viva Crianças. Over the course of several months we would meet to discuss the problems we were having as well as to brainstorm, looking for innovative ways to enhance the music class. My notes report what Catrina told me the about her life and the feelings she has about being black and poor in Brazil:

> When she was thirteen years old she began to work as a domestic servant in the house of *Dona Ana Laura*. At fifteen she worked for *Dona Yasmin*, who paid her R$20 per month. At that time, Catrina told me that the minimum salary was R$70 per month. She would wake up at 6:00 am to make breakfast for the four children and the mother and father and then clean, wash clothes, and cook lunch between 10:00 and 11:30 am. Catrina ate the leftovers from lunch and washed the dishes. Dinner was prepared as well and the kitchen was cleaned again and made ready for breakfast the following morning. At about 8:30 or 9:00 pm, she showered, dressed, and went to school until 10:30 when she returned home close to 11 p.m. She began to cry when she told me the story. I asked her how she felt always doing for others, making breakfast for other children who could go to school and come home and have free time. Catrina pointed to the tiles on my kitchen floor and told me that she used to ask herself why her house did not have pretty floors, why she had to live under the house in a cement room, why she had to eat alone, separate from the white family she worked for. She said her self-esteem was very low. When she was eleven years old, she wanted to die and tried to kill herself by taking some medicine. As she told me the story, she laughed, saying that the medicine did not do anything to her. She had written a note telling her parents why she wanted to die…they beat her all the time and the neighbor told her that perhaps she was not

their real child. She said that people always say that she is so happy, but that really she is filled with sadness and anger. She usually does not cry. "You do not cry here, you pretend that all is well, that all is tranquil."

Another coordinator, Beatriz, also twenty-one years old, worked at the Projeto Bom Jesus. During an interview with me about her life, her experiences with racism and social exclusion, she talked about the ways in which her *favela* is viewed by the elite:

> People have considered our *favela* here, a place that is not—that does not have money and furthermore if they do not have money they think that the people here are inferior, dangerous, that they do not have a good quality—that they are people that live practically isolated from the city and that are aggressive, from a place that is *terra de índio*s (land of the Indians) because of some of the things that have happened, and I have faced various difficulties because various places that I have gone, that I have gone to look for work, when I say that I live here, then I feel a certain lack of interest, or when we go to buy things at some stores, we give them our address (when we give our address to buy on credit), they ask also, right, where you live. Some places here in our *favela*, you know, have a kind of reputation for dangerous people, that do not like to pay and all, so there is this also.

One day while I was preparing to work with my music group at Viva Crianças, Nicolas (eight years old) came running up to me. I had promised him that we would meet and tape record our talk about his life. When I held up my hand to greet him, he flinched and quickly moved away from me. I noticed it and raised my hand again, and explained that I was just greeting him; he flinched again. Again, I tried to explain my hand action and he flinched. It was clear that a raised hand meant abuse. In Morro de Santana, I noticed that dogs are skittish in the same manner, running from an extended hand meant to pet them. Like the street youth, they too are often hit and abused, and very rarely treated with kindness.

I came to understand the sense of fear children in the projects and on the streets had of adults. Their sense of self seemed to be molded by parental authority expressed as everyday violence against their right to be autonomous. At the same time, my subjects remained devoted to their parents. Knowledge of violence and hope for love informed the children's efforts to support the very people who often abused them.

I decided to test the children's sense of class consciousness with a set of pictures that I cut from *Veja* (a weekly newsmagazine in Brazil similar to *Newsweek*). I chose seven pictures, each representing people in different settings, from the white, upper-class elites in city centers, to school children in public and private school settings, to *favela* residents in Rio de Janeiro and São Paulo. Lucas, a youth who lived on the streets and had recently been accepted into COV, responded to the picture of a white couple walking in the center of the city. "Ah, they are rich. They are walking on the street and smiling. They do not use drugs, or smoke, and they all read and write. I would not make friends with these kinds of people." In response to a picture of white children in a private school, Lucas said, "They are reading, at a school or library and they are rich. My school does not look like this because this looks like a rich place. They have tables." One picture was of a white adolescent male sitting on a bench in a park, and Lucas responded, "More rich people. I would not get to meet him." The picture of *favelados* brought this response from Lucas, "In the city—in a *favela*, they are like us, poor. I would have friends here." Another picture was of a mother and a young girl, both dark Afro-Brazilians from a *favela*, dressed in dirty, torn clothes in front of their slum dwelling. Lucas stated, "This girl, she lives in the *favela*. She is poor. I could have a friendship with her, if I met her." One of the last pictures was of a wealthy white man, and Lucas said with finality, "He's a rich man. He is not hungry." I present these statements by street youth in order to demonstrate the low self-esteem often expressed by them. Such low self-esteem works in tandem with the knowledge of their "place" within the social/racial hierarchy in Brazil.

Violence

It was not uncommon to hear about adolescents who turn against their parents, whose parents, in the end, often give their children to FUNABEM, the state-run juvenile institutions notorious for their mistreatment and even torture of street children. One day at Viva Crianças, I was eating lunch with the twins Enzo and Vitor and we talked about adolescent boys who were angry and aggressive. I was curious to discover if they were violent at home with their parents. Later I reconstructed the conversation in my field notes:

> *Marcia*: Do you think, at home, these adolescents that are violent against you all, do you think they have violence at home too?
> *Vitor*: They have, I think they have. The same as Lago, he hits his mother...
> *Marcia*: He is hitting his mother?
> *Enzo and Vitor*: Yes.
> *Marcia*: Do you think his mother hits him?
> *Vitor and Enzo*: No, she does not hit him, no. She put the clothes closet in front of the door so he would not

> come in and hit her, including until today, this is still happening, and she signed a paper to put her son in FENABEM in Belo Horizonte.

Upper- and middle-class informants often referred to the violence in the homes of the poor as a reason for street children leaving their homes and as a source of the violence that is attributed to youth who work on the streets. My informants recounted many instances of alcoholism, spousal abuse, and sibling abuse of younger children within their families. It was common to see children react with physical violence when angry at a friend. On several occasions I witnessed both children and adolescents at various projects pick up sticks and boards and hit a colleague hard in the back, legs, or head. The effects of such violence on the children and youth were varied. The following field interview with Lucas demonstrates the ways in which my informants came to deal with domestic violence and child abuse in their daily lives.

> With me it was like this: I would go out to the streets, get money, come back home, get beaten up by my big brother, go back to the streets. I would get food and get by. My brother would always take the money and hit me. So I did not want to continue getting hit. We are four brothers, and the oldest one always wanted to hit us. So I ran away, and I took trains, cars, and walked. Then the police found me and brought me back. I would stay in this house, that house. I did not know how to take the train or anything. The first day I jumped off and fell, and then I learned. I would sleep by the door of a building, selling things. Then people would come and buy them. With the money I would go get some breakfast, and

when I had a little time I would go play video games. Sometimes I spent all my money there.

On another occasion, during a meeting with two coordinators at Viva Crianças, I was told how powerful and indeed harmful a *palavrão* could be.

> I was told today in a meeting with Alana and Isadora that quite often fights occur at Viva Crianças when one child calls another child a really bad name. Apparently the worst name a child can call another child is a *filho da puta* (child of a whore). This kind of phrase is a *palavrão*. This is the worst kind of insult a child could use, and if they use it their mouth is washed out with soap by their mother. A *palavrão* is an immense obscenity, it is *muito pesada* (very heavy), and it is used to verbally *machucar* (hurt) another person, to symbolically beat them up with words full of misfortune or fatality, an insult accompanied by filthy language. No one wants to be called this, where here in Morro de Santana and in Brazil many poor children have only one parent, usually the mother with whom they live. Women, particularly mothers, are supposed to be pure, saintly…the worst thing you can say to someone is that their mother is a prostitute. It does not matter if your mother beats you every day or if she is an alcoholic. If a man is a *moleque* (black, frivolous, and unreliable person or street urchin), if he is a beggar or robber, it does not reflect on his character, but if your mother is a prostitute, if she is immoral, you are rotten to the core. Considered in the light of street children, or children who are at personal and social risk, this word takes on a

new kind of meaning: that street children and the poor in general in Brazil represent the dirt and the disorder people so often try to correct. Every day, in front of every house in the upper/middle class neighborhoods, maids are out sweeping, washing, and then squeegeeing the sidewalks and porches, until they shine. The paint on the walls may be smudged and streaked with age, but the streets and floors shine.

Otávio, from COV, talked about his parents and domestic violence in the following way:

> *Marcia*: You have a mom that hits you, and a father that you do not know that drinks. Do you feel anger at this? To what extent does this affect you?
> *Otávio*: I was never angry at my mom. Now my dad and my brother I do not know, it's different. My dad I cannot swallow. I start to remember things from the past, so I cannot have love towards him. I went through an angry period. But I developed, and now I feel more calm. I will not fight with them. Before we would fight about any little thing, and we would hit each other.

Kaique told me the following during a group meeting at COV when I asked him if his parents were alive:

> Yes, they live and work here. I know my father's face, I know his face, but I do not have much contact with him. He would hit my mom, and chase my brothers out of the house, sometimes through a window. So I cannot feel love for him. My mom took care of me. When she got worse with her drinking then I left. From when I was eleven, I was alone, did not even accept my own

mother. And then when she would get drunk and want to hit me I would even hit her back. So it was better for me to leave, or a tragedy was going to happen.

One day during my music class, I was able to encourage the children to talk about their home lives. I wanted to know if their parents talked to them, asked them how their day went, what they did with their parents, and if their parents were gentle with them, or if they punished them and, if so, how. Tomás (nine years old) told me that his father drew blood on his back "more than once" by beating him because he missed school. His brother told his father that he was missing school. When I asked if his father talked to him first, asking why he did not go to school, he said no, he just began hitting him. He told me he cried a lot. I was told by the coordinators at Curumim that this kind of treatment is common and that parents commonly ridicule their children and use *palavrãos* to humiliate them. Parents scream and yell at their children, but almost never talk to them. I saw most children being ordered to do tasks and rarely saw parents hugging, touching, or talking with their children when I was in their homes. The coordinators at all the projects told me the biggest problem the children experience at home and in the streets is that they are not treated with respect.

Vinicius, from my music class, saw his neighbor fighting with her son who drinks. She fights with him in the street, yelling and screaming, calling him names. One day he arrived home very drunk, stumbling and falling on the ground. Vinicius laughed as he told the story, and described the woman as very old and bent from a life of hard physical labor washing clothes, which she often did until well past midnight. She began screaming and hit her son. According to Vinicius, the son fell to the ground in the street. In his telling of the story, Vinicius put a lot of energy into reenacting each character, acting out the beating, falling to the ground, screaming (he laughed a lot as he told the story) and seemed to lack any feelings of empathy or sadness. He was just relating a factual event, one that is all too common in the everyday lives of these youth. Feelings of shock or fear seem to be absent. Indeed how could they be present when they constitute "the way things are" on an almost daily basis?

Other youth in my music class talked about home violence as a common occurrence and freely discussed their personal experiences. Maria Sophia said that her father used to beat her all the time. Now she is living with her grandfather. Maria Sophia's brother Raul said that his father hits him more than his mother does, and even though Maria Sophia is living with her grandfather, she said that her mother hits her more than her father now. Raul said his father is always hitting him. When I asked why, he gave me the example of wanting to play *futebol* and having his father say no. One day he defied his father and went out to play. Later that day, his father was waiting on the street for him and began to beat him publicly. When I asked if their parents talked to them, they did not understand my question. I asked if their parents asked how their day went, what their opinions were, what they were feeling when they came home from school or work on the streets. They looked confused. Everyone in my group became quiet while they thought about my question. Finally, Raul laughed, breaking the tension, and shook his head no. No, everyone agreed—nobody's parents talked to them.

Catrina, who was always present in my music class and had been listening to the youths' stories, tried to explain to me the kinds of everyday violence that occurred in the *favelas*. I had protested, saying, "But in Morro de Santana, there is not a lot of violence, is there? Everyone says how *tranquil* Morro de Santana is!" Catrina responded in the following way, emphatically and clearly supporting the students' stories of *favela* life:

> *Catrina*: Yes there is!

Marcia: What about in the center of the city?
Catrina: In the center they fight verbally, understand? Now in the *favela*, in the *favelas*!
Marcia: What type of violence is there in the *favelas*?
Catrina: Family, in the family! The father fights with his child, the mother fights with her children, you know? And then they call the cops. There is one (a woman) where I live that was kind of a prisoner in her home—the mother, because she beat up her child. This because people take justice into their own hands, the mother was afraid to go out of her house. Therefore she was a prisoner in her own home.
Marcia: Do they hit their children a lot?
Catrina: They hit a lot! They break things in the house, you know? They destroy the furniture.
Marcia: With women and men, is there a lot of violence between them too? Do they fight between themselves?
Catrina: Yes. This woman that was afraid to go out of her house, she drank a lot and did not have any way to care for her children. Understand? So I think that she takes that attitude (beating her children). She blames her children for her misery and takes it out on them. She blames the kids and beats them. She was a prisoner in her own house because of the pressure of the neighbors…because the police will not put her in jail. But the neighbors beat their children too….

Daily life for street youth is dramatically different from the life of their middle- and upper-class counterparts. Hunger, violence, domestic abuse, economic responsibility, and sibling care and discipline frequently define their childhood. Yet these children also carry the blame for local crime, carry the stigma of poverty that follows them into the streets where they labor, and earn pitiful wages that make the difference between sickness and health, hunger and malnutrition, and more frequently than not, life and death.

I found very little conscious anger, that is, anger that was easily accessed and expressly directed toward the inequalities (social, racial, and economic) that these youth face on a daily basis. Instead, like their parents, the children and youth I worked with were surprisingly placid when approached on this level. My informants often watched TV in shop windows or at home—most people knew someone who had a working TV. I began asking them how they felt when they watched *novelas* (a *novela* is a Brazilian soap opera) and saw the beautiful clothes, homes, cars, and furniture of the wealthy portrayed. Almost without exception, the answer was "Ah! I would like these things, but everything is in the hands of God."

Their silence, their acceptance of misery, poverty, and violence was addressed by Paulo Freire in his seminal works on the oppression of Brazil's poor. According to Freire, who fought his entire life to bring literacy to the "muted masses," and to bring voice and agency to those who he saw as almost pre-reflexive and, hence, without agency, participants in my research tended to demonstrate a muted silence. I agree with Nancy Scheper-Hughes when she sums up her experiences in the Alto Bom Jesus in the Northeast of Brazil:

> The hostile paternalism of traditional…boss-worker relations reproduces the violence of the asylum and of the *casa grande*, where dependency, silence, and passivity are rewarded and where loyalty to the patron-boss is the most valuable token of economic exchange for survival. The shantytown, like the mental asylum, exists as a "total institution," a satellite of the sugar plantation and sugar mills, and anonymity, depersonalization,

and surveillance are used…to create a climate of fear, suspiciousness, and hopelessness (1992:532).

Yet street youth are hardly without agency and are doggedly determined to help their parents and remain staunchly loyal to them. Their sense of self is created by a complex web of negative social stereotypes, scarcity of resources, familial erosion, alcoholism, and physical abuse, and, for those who attend the projects, intimations of an idealized childhood that they are not actually living. They are more literate than their parents, but they are deprived of social and economic literacy. They are denied the acquisition of skills that could lift them out of poverty by the dominant discourse on the parameters of "normal" childhood. Their experience of violence is both internalized and externalized. Its effects can be seen in the relations they have with their peers. Everyday violence in the projects and in the *favelas* was real and often extreme.

I asked Catrina if there are police in the *favelas*. Could such violence be left unattended?

> *Marcia*: Do you have police here in the *favela*?
> *Catrina*: No. The police say that there is not any gas to buy, understand, to put in their cars to come here. They just answer emergency calls. For example cases of murder. They come then. Fights, beating up children… they will not come and they say they do not have any gas to come out for that. This gas that I talked about in the case of the police that will not come, you know? The government does not give gas to them, no! Understand? They will not come.
> *Marcia*: Here in Morro de Santana they just stand on the street corners in the city center, doing nothing?

Catrina: Right! They just assist people here in the center of the city, not in the periphery.

Catrina's statement demonstrates another way in which street children learn to fend for themselves. Solving social problems between friends often leads to aggressive behaviors that frequently end in violence. Hitting with sticks, throwing rocks, and lashing with wire found on the streets was not uncommon, and such violence was frequently carried into the projects.

    I found that residents of the *favelas* derive their dignity from their ability to labor, and to labor long and hard. The future of the young people I came to know hangs on their need to be a person, to have an effective voice, and to have the ability to enact changes in their lives that bring immediate results. Yet, the paralyzing silence of cultural censorship adds to the enormous difficulties involved in lifting racism and poverty from the subaltern regions of social consciousness into the light of civil protest and effective activism. The patterns of being mute and muted come to an end through recognition of the processes that produce the extreme levels of social and economic inequality in Brazilian society. There is a great need for effective educational and organizational programs that will pragmatically invert the sanctioned cultural censorship that denies open discussion of racial inequality and social marginalization in Brazil. Currently, the miserable life circumstances of the children and youth living in poverty in Morro de Santana create a kind of external social violence among the poor, who compete for the limited opportunities and resources available to them. Attacking each other and the most sacred icon of street youth, the sacred and immortalized image of the mother, is a common practice.

    When a *palavrão* is used, it is used as a tool to verbally hurt another. Linguistic ammunition is used to attack self and others instead of revolting against the social inequality that creates the conditions of misery that so shame the poor, and that turn one against another. Debasing self and other prevents direct perceptions of the social conditions and raging inequality that keeps the poor in poverty, in social and intellectual deprivation. This is the cycle that keeps native intelligence battling itself while spinning an endless cycle of poverty, ignorance, anger, and simplemindedness.

Hunger

Descriptions of the daily lives of street children would hardly be complete without some reference to their diet, clothing, and shelter. Although pictures of *favelas* are widely distributed in appeals by organizations like Save the Children and UNICEF, the extent of the poverty is, nonetheless, hard to imagine. Hunger was a common subject, a theme of daily life among the children I came to know in the projects. One of the most important contributions of the NGOs was their practice of providing vegetables and occasional meat (mostly small pieces of chicken) five days a week. Without this nutritional support, I imagine the child mortality rate in Morro de Santana would be much higher than it currently is (28.4 per 10,000) (*Almanaque Abril 2000*:188).

I begin with a quote from my field notes of 1994 where I interviewed residents in the *favela* of Vidigal in Rio de Janeiro: "There are so many people suffering difficulties, there are kids who almost die of hunger but are not street kids," said an informant whom I interviewed in 1994. This statement stayed with me during my fieldwork in Morro de Santana, where I found these words to be a kind of mantra for the poor. In 1997, Catrina told me a story about hunger:

> Catrina was working in the rural schools outside of Morro de Santana as a teacher. She was instructed

to teach a class on sexuality while the students in her class were literally too hungry and tired to stay awake. She described a girl who came every day with head lice falling out of her hair, covering her clothing. Catrina described her as so listless she could only stare into empty space. She would often ask, "Oh, auntie, has lunch time arrived yet?" Catrina was angry that President Cardoso's new educational programs promoted only the appearance of education for the poor, while in reality the children of the poor and the poor themselves were unable to study and unable to learn because they were hungry, filled with disease, landless, and disempowered. She had to give a lecture on sexuality while the girl in front of her sat listlessly, staring into space, longing for the school lunch. The girl told her she could not sleep at night because her head was so infected with lice that Catrina bought medicated shampoo and went to the girl's house and washed the hair of everyone in the family, but this is a losing battle. Everyone has lice and intestinal diseases, and on her salary she could not afford to buy medicine even once, much less buy it again and reapply it, which is absolutely necessary because the eggs live on to re-infest.

Catrina knows firsthand the kinds of hunger that are experienced by the children at Viva Crianças. One day after my music class, she told me about her ongoing battle with hunger. I had asked her about food, what she ate at home, and how much and what kind of food a family could buy while subsisting on one or two minimum salaries a month. She began rather matter-of-factly to tell me what I wanted to know, but as she talked, she became more emotional, even desperate at times. I quote at length from the interview.

Catrina: Food—it is expensive.

Marcia: Can you tell me, more or less, how much money your family spends on food a month?

Catrina: There are times (Catrina laughs)…

Marcia: More or less, it doesn't have to be exact.

Catrina: About R$100 for four people—only for the basics like rice, beans, macaroni—just for the basics. With $R100 we do not buy vegetables and meat. Other things like cheese. No, only the basics.

Marcia: What else do you buy?

Catrina: Oil, *maizena* (corn starch), coffee, *fubá* (*mandioca* flour).

Marcia: Milk?

Catrina: No, no milk.

Marcia: What is the basic, what do you eat for breakfast?

Catrina: Bread and coffee.

Marcia: Do you have butter?

Catrina: No—sometimes just oil or margarine.

Marcia: Just bread and coffee. What do you eat for lunch? You eat here at Viva Crianças?

Catrina: Yes, at the project.

Marcia: For dinner?

Catrina: Dinner I eat at home.

Marcia: What is a typical dinner?

Catrina: Rice, beans, and sometimes a vegetable.

Marcia: What kind of vegetable?

Catrina: Potatoes, tomatoes.

Marcia: Do you eat chicken?

Catrina: Sometimes—one time a week, maybe…

Marcia: Is chicken expensive?

Catrina: Yes, it is.

Marcia: Do you prefer meat or chicken?

Catrina: I like red meat more. At home there are times that we eat rice and beans the entire week. Without vegetables or meat or anything. I say to my mother, "I'm really weak—I'm getting really weak because we do not have any vegetables or meat."

Marcia: Do you lose your appetite?

Catrina: Yes, many times I do. I lose my appetite because dinner arrives and it is just rice and beans and my mother complains, because she says there are people who do not have even this. You have to eat it. Understand? There are people who do not even have this! Sometimes the hunger is so intense, it does not matter. I do not care if I get just beans, I will eat it, just rice, I will eat that. The hunger is so great I do not really have a choice. Your stomach will not be choosy if it is good or not.

Marcia: Do you eat a lot of beans and rice and also *farina*?

Catrina: *Farina*, yes—*mandioca* (these are pure starch and give you the feeling of being full).

Marcia: Do you eat sweets at home?

Catrina: Juice—mainly juice, the kind in small packets with lots of sugar.

Marcia: How about fruits?

Catrina: Sometimes—no, not really, no. It is very expensive.

Marcia: Rice and beans are cheap?

Catrina: It is not very cheap either, but what are we going to buy?

> *Marcia*: But so you do not have any nutrition from fruit?
>
> *Catrina*: No…we do not worry about the nutritional qualities in our food. We want to eat! There are times that we do not have any vegetables for a long time—weeks!

Catrina was shaking as she tried to explain to me the reality of her constant hunger. I asked her if she was aware of her shaking, her *nervoso*, a condition that Nancy Scheper-Hughes (1991:167–215) discusses at length in *Death Without Weeping: Everyday Violence in Brazil*. She did not respond at first, but after reflecting on my question, she said that a woman or parent may be upset because of family problems, or because of trouble with children, and they would go to a doctor and ask for medicines. As I probed more, she agreed that lack of food produced symptoms that were described as nervous, such as shaking, trembling, and that the problem of hunger and basic nutrition were not solved by doctors or medications—they just prescribed drugs to make you less nervous. Like the children who take on the negative stereotypes that define them, like the violence that they have come to accept and expect at home, in the streets, and from life in general, hunger has also come to be an accepted norm. It is another social injustice that is conceptualized as a deficit within their bodies. As Scheper-Hughes points out,

> It is easy to overlook the simple observation that people who live by and through their bodies in manual and wage labor—who live by their wits and by their guts—inhabit those bodies and experience them in ways very different from our own. I am suggesting that the structure of individual and collective sentiments, down to the feel of one's body, is a function of one's

position and role in the technical and productive order. (1992:185).

In Morro de Santana, street youth and their families often saw themselves as inferior physically, as weak and scrawny. They "lusted" after red meat because it was indeed a symbol of wealth and, hence, also a symbol of health. Observing the difference between the ways in which the affluent perceive food (to please the palate and provide nutrition for the body) and the needy perceive food (to fill a constantly hungry stomach), I wrote in my field notes:

> I have come to know that the word "full" has a very negative meaning for the middle and upper classes. The word "full" is seen as vulgar and impolite. The poor are always trying to fill their stomachs, usually with a variety of starches (rice, beans, potatoes) and if they are lucky a piece of fatty meat. They long for the real food, the food of life: meat.

In this sense, the poor turn their bodies into their enemy, describing themselves as less than whites, those elites who are strong and healthy. It is not the social inequalities and racism of Brazilian society that they blame. It is their own bodies. Catrina was more articulate than most, in large part because of her unusual educational achievements. She expresses her anger at social and economic inequality through sarcasm, whereas most of the children and their parents saw the wealthy as superior, as patrons who would continue to ensure their survival if they worked hard enough and remained strong enough to continue laboring.

> *Marcia*: Do you think that rich people say that life is a bone that's hard to chew?

Catrina: They, just like I said…they worry a lot! But their problems are very different than ours…They say… for example, "Oh my God! I'm not able to travel to the Caribbean! What kind of life is this! I'm not able to travel to Paris this year!" So, they say this (life is a bone that's hard to chew) but their problems are very different than ours. Understand? "Oh my God! I'm not able to buy those pants that cost $R200 and I really want them!" Or, "Oh my boyfriend did not call me!" (Laughter) So their problems are very different. Our problems are about paying the light bill! Or, "Oh my God! I can't pay my bills! How can I buy gas to cook rice and beans with! It is all gone! How am I going to feed my children?"

Not surprisingly, children often idealized their family lives, describing the kinds of foods they imagined they ate daily. These food fantasies were based on their knowledge of what their parents' patrons had in their homes. Domestic servants (most mothers of the children I came to know worked as domestic servants in wealthy homes) arrive at their *patroas*' home early and prepare breakfast, which includes an array of cold meats, breads, butter, jams, cookies, chocolate milk, fruit, and strong sweetened coffee. The following is a description that Enzo (from the Projeto Viva Crianças) gave me when telling me about a typical breakfast that he made for himself and his four siblings. I later learned that they only have black coffee for breakfast and occasionally they will have some bread:

Marcia: What do you usually eat for breakfast?
Enzo: Yes, I make a biscuit for them.
Marcia: Tell me again how you make this biscuit for them. Are you using flour?

> *Enzo*: We use flour used for cakes (it has baking powder), sugar, salt, two eggs, and just this. I do not think you have to put in *fermento* (baking powder).
> *Marcia*: No, because the flour to make cakes has it in it. You do not put in butter or margarine?
> *Enzo*: I think you could put it...
> *Marcia*: Do you then whip it?
> *Enzo*: Yes, and then you make them into balls, using a spoon, and then put them onto the pan, and then they stay round, you put grease on the bottom of the pan and leave them to cook, and then you eat them.
> *Marcia*: How long to you cook them?
> *Enzo*: They stay cooking for about ten minutes.

In Enzo's home (the home of the twins discussed in the case histories) poverty was all-pervasive. On every visit to their home, it was clear that eggs, milk, flour, sugar, salt, and any other type of baking goods were not present. Their mother told me that Enzo's story was a fantasy of his, to be able to eat like the rich. He had created an accurate scenario based on the many times he watched his mother cook for her *patroa* as he stood outside, looking in. And Milena, when asked what she ate on a daily basis replied:

> *Marcia*: At home, what do you normally eat every day?
> *Milena*: We always eat—my mother will make a cake. We eat meat, vegetables, some kinds of vegetables.
> *Marcia*: Like?
> *Milena*: Carrots, little potatoes and *quiabo* (okra). I really like *quiabo*.
> *Marcia*: What else?
> *Milena*: Mandioca.
> *Marcia*: Rice?

> *Milena*: Yes, rice and beans, and there are times that we have a salad.
> *Marcia*: Do you eat meat every day?
> *Milena*: We have it every day. When I wake up do I have breakfast? Yes.
> *Marcia*: What do you have?
> *Milena*: A piece of cake or cookie with coffee, or bread with coffee and milk. Or coffee or a *todi*.
> *Marcia*: What kinds of bread?
> *Milena*: *Pão de sal* (salt bread), *pão de doce* (sweet bread).

I came to know Milena's mother and father and visited their house on several occasions. They lived in extreme poverty in a one-room mud shack. When it rained, we sat under an umbrella inside because the roof was full of holes. Her family did not own a refrigerator or stove and they often did not even have rice. It was Milena and her aunt I met on the streets begging. Milena described her food fantasies to me, not the reality of what she ate.

What is significant here is the detail with which Enzo and Milena talked about their fantasy meals. In Enzo's case, his mother is illiterate and when she works as a maid, her twin boys read her the recipes that she then memorizes in order to cook for her patrons. Enzo also memorized the recipes and created imaginary food from them.

Studying street youth put me in contact with hunger in ways that I, as a privileged American and an anthropologist, would never experience, except through extreme circumstances. I became sensitized to the linguistic phrases that clustered around the word "hunger" and gave it meaning to the poor. I also came to understand the ways in which food—its smells and colors and its presentation—took on meanings within the realm of social status among the wealthy. On more occasions than I can remember, I ate with the economically secure, in their beautiful homes, where I took special care to watch the way in which food was presented and consumed.

> There is an order to the way my plate is constructed or filled with food by my hostesses. First a layer of rice is put down so that it covers the bottom of my plate. Then a layer of beans is put on top of the rice, followed by a vegetable (squash, okra, green beans, etc.), then a kind of macaroni (a pasta salad usually made with mayonnaise and diced green peppers or spaghetti without sauce seasoned with garlic and butter), then a kind of diced salad. The salad plate is very pretty, usually arranged to display colors in intricate designs. Lettuce is cut very small, almost shredded, and placed usually in the middle of the platter and other vegetables arranged in rows outward from the lettuce, like bright red beets, orange carrots, green peppers, and cucumbers. The meal pivots around the daily portions of meat, usually heavy and fatty, and in abundance. Often there are several choices of meat, for example, beef, pork, and chicken. The meat is the last item to be placed on the plate and the most visible. The salad is a kind of decoration to make things look pretty, and is arranged around this constructed plate. This is the common plate, built like a sculpture to be viewed with delight and consumed.

Contrast this description with Antonella's, a maid who worked for me in my apartment. I had thrown away some moldy bread and rotted vegetables from my old and partially functioning refrigerator. Antonella left me the following note one day:

Dear Marcia,

When you do not want food any more, do not throw it way. Leave it for me. Everything that you do not want, leave it here for me. On Thursday, I will get it. I'm sorry.

(signed) Antonella.

I talked with Antonella later about her note. She told me that when you have hungry children at home like she does, you cannot throw anything way. Nothing is garbage…it can all be eaten. Antonella has had a very hard life…working from an early age doing domestic housework (she started at twelve), attending school only until the end of the first series. She was married at nineteen and has three children. She told me that many mornings her little girl wakes up hungry and there is no food in the house, not even bread. Milk is rare, a very precious luxury. She can afford the usual: beans, rice, macaroni. Sometimes, but very rarely, she can afford meat.

Living Conditions

The standard dwelling in the *favelas* of Morro de Santana is a mud and wattle hut with a tin roof and an old cloth hung in the doorway instead of a door. A typical home has one or two rooms, with dirt floors, no plumbing or running water. The stove is often an open pit or a mud stove that uses wood, or perhaps an old gas propane range. When there is enough money, propane is bought. Otherwise the mud stove is used. Washing is done in a pan with water hauled from either a public tap or a nearby polluted stream.

The following story was reported in the *Fólio de Morro de Santana* (Pages of Morro de Santana) on March 4, 1997, describing the conditions in Comunguem, one of the *favela*s that ring the city. I quote at length from this article titled, "The Misery in the Center of the Debate: Unemployment, Hunger, Sickness, Fights, and Drugs."

> Imagine a street of battered earth, dirty, full of holes, without a middle line, and with a fence of 40 shacks on each side, many of them of rotten timber. Imagine now, in each shack, approximately 8 people in the same family sleeping in a pile in a room of approximately only 9 meters square. If you imagined all of this and some more, you are certain to know one thing: this place exists and has a name. *Comunguem*, without a shadow of a doubt the *favela* is the most miserable in Morro de Santana, next to the *favela* Ponte Nova, where a majority of the people struggling to survive live on what they get in the streets or by going from door to door, begging *esmola* (charity). On the street *São José dos Campos*, the last street in *Comunguem*, in a shack of scarcely two rooms, we find the property of *Tereza Silva Vieira*, who lives here with eight people: Her, her husband (who is sick), two adolescent children (a boy and a young girl of presumably 16 years) and four children. These eight people sleep in the same room, on three single mattresses and to complete the room of misery in this shack they do not have a bathroom either. The physical necessities of the family are taken care of in the bush, during the day or night, in the rain or in the sun. The other room in the shack is used like a kitchen. The old stove with four *bocas* (burners), the old and worn out easy chair and some dishes, "all gotten from others" help to swallow up the space that practically does not exist. "How is it that you came to live in this shack of almost less than two rooms with more than

seven people?" asked the reporter. "We are accustomed to suffering. The worst things that we have here are the lack of food, lack of security, and sickness." "To take a bath, how and where do you do it with your children and adolescents?" asks the journalist. "The bath is in a basin or large bowl or in the stream in *Comunguem*. When they use a basin, they shut the door to the room. "While sleeping, how do you sleep with just three single beds in the same room?" asked the reporter. "The young man sleeps in the bed against the wall and I, the adolescent girl, my husband and the four children sleep in the other two beds…A little bit later, in the shack numbered 280, belonging to Ailton Mendes de Araújo, other surprises are revealed. Secondly Márcia Regina dos Santos, the wife of Ailton, says that the problems of the place are not confined just to the poverty of those living here, but also are the fault of security, sickness, and high consumption of alcohol, fighting, etc. The Shack of Márcia Regina also does not have a bathroom. Close to 99% of the people living in Comunguem do not have bathrooms in the house because the streets do not have a sewer line."

I often walked to the Alto Bom Jesus, the *favela* where the Projeto Bom Jesus is located, from the city center. The walk is a long one, probably two miles, all uphill. During the first two months of my fieldwork, I found myself exhausted and sweating profusely after climbing the hill to Bom Jesus. I arrived in January, the dry time of the year. We had not had any rain for over four months, and the dust was almost unbearable when cars, dogs, children, or bikes stirred it up. All the *favelas* are unpaved and dusty. There is no sewage system. Electricity is available, but telephones must be bought and paid for, so no one has them. I came to the Alto Bom Jesus to visit the children I worked with in my music classes. A majority of the houses are just shacks, concrete walls with two or three rooms (kitchen, bedroom, room to eat and sit). Some houses have running water, some have bathrooms. There is no indoor plumbing, and hence no bathroom facilities other than a hole in the ground. There are no windows with glass in them in the poorest houses, just wooden shutters if they are lucky, or cloth draped over them if they are not. Holes in the walls are plugged up with broken bricks, plastic bags, paper—whatever can be found to fill the holes and stop the wind from entering during the cold nights of winter. The roofs are tin, some are cardboard, and for the least poverty-stricken, the roofs are red tiles that sit on the frame of the house, with an open space between the roof and the house. This affords good ventilation during the hot summer but offers no protection from the cold nights in winter. In Morro de Santana the winter is not cold, at least not by my standards, but at night it can get cold enough to see your breath.

During my walks through the Alto Bom Jesus, I was struck with the devastation in which Morro de Santana's poor live. People live in structures that are constructed from broken mud bricks with open sewage running past doorless entryways. Women wash clothes in streams polluted with sewage and I watched children drink water from a trickle of underground water flowing into the polluted stream. Garbage is everywhere, floating in the water, blowing by in the dust, and swirling in dust devils. Poverty is difficult to describe, but one thing I'm certain about is that poverty is created and enforced. To survive the effects of poverty requires enormous energy, a will to survive in spite of a daily destiny of drudgery and misery. To survive this kind of poverty demands dreams of another world. As with Sonya (a mother and a domestic servant), this other world is her evangelical religion, where everything in her life is "in the hands of God." I came to theorize that material needs are actually shunned; working for a better material life is an attack against the construction of this other world, where real power lies in your ability to survive. In this sense, one works to maintain poverty, and poverty becomes a badge of honor and courage. It seems that for those living in hard poverty, real power lies in their knowledge that the rich, while they have what they need to live in comfort, will never reach this other land, this land of spiritual promise. There is a kind of pride in being poor and in suffering, a kind of knowledge that the possessors of real power are the poor. Furthermore, if your faith is strong enough, you will in the end triumph over the ignorant materialism of the rich.

The presence of the Catholic, Pentecostal, and Protestant churches can be felt, particularly in relation to the social constructions that define what "goodness" is. The promise of the Sermon on the Mount, that the meek shall inherit the earth, is one that has never been fulfilled. Indeed, religion has been complicit in the production of servitude by the poor in the name of "goodness, purity, meekness, righteousness, and persecution." Andrew Chesnut, in *Born Again in Brazil: The Pentecostal Boom and the Pathogens of Poverty*, writes about the inexplicable schism between poverty and privilege as played out in the daily lives of *favelados*. "As servants of God, believers must forswear the earthly vices that circulate freely through the streets of the *baixadas*..." (bottomlands) (Chesnut 1997:108).

Interviews with eight youth (four females and four males between the ages of sixteen and nineteen) from the upper classes in Morro de Santana showed how unaware upper-class youth are about the degree of misery within their midst. One day, while talking with a group of upper-middle-class youth, an adolescent girl told me how flabbergasted she was by the poverty that she has seen during her infrequent passage through a *favela*:

> What you will see there is something unbelievable! Little houses like this. I saw a family, what most impressed me, or had an impression on me was there were six people that lived in a little house like this, it was minuscule and everything was of cardboard! They did not have anything to secure it with. It was just cardboard. Whenever it rained, everything came apart! Everything!

During this same meeting, it became clear to me, that no one present had friends in the *favelas*. Furthermore, it was made clear that it was not necessary or even advisable to have such friends. Why would they want to go into the *favelas*? Everything they wanted or needed was in the city center. It was the *favelados* who were coming into the city center in order to steal and commit robberies.

> *Marcia*: So, I need to disentangle these relations of power. And we now, now we are exploring together. Observe…no one has friends (that they go out with) who are poor and live in the *favelas*…. To change this situation, I think that we need to begin here. We need to have contact…but if you do not have this in your life, this kind of attitude or opportunity, how will we change? I think it is difficult. Could we talk about this? *Resp*: I think the following. Many times you do not have to go to the *favela* to try to change this because people are living together here in the center of the city. There is a situation that for example, the people leave the *favelas* to come here, because they do not have anything to eat, they come looking to rob these things, steal these things from us.

During this meeting, we pushed into territories not often discussed in Brazil. I asked if they thought there was a lot of poverty in Morro de Santana, to which they replied:

> *Resp 1*: We have a lot of poverty, but misery we do not have.
> *Marcia*: Can you give me a definition of misery?
> *Resp 1*: Misery is total poverty…when a person does not have anything to eat when you have to go to the streets. There is some of this here, but very little….
> *Marcia*: I do not agree, just because of my work here. Each day I have met kids that do not have anything to eat in the house….
> *Resp 2*: But they have a house!

It was difficult to understand how these youth were so out of touch with the degree of poverty and misery that surrounded them. Poverty, hunger, and basic misery were visible on every street in every area of the city. I asked them if they had friends in the *favelas*, not just someone they casually know, but someone they are close friends with who lives in the *favelas*. They responded unilaterally in this way:

> *Marcia*: I have another question. Who among you has spent time in the *favelas*?
> *Resp 1*: I go by it all the time.
> *Marcia*: You just pass through it? And you, do you just pass through it too? Does everyone just pass through?
> *Resp 2*: I rarely go, I rarely pass by…very few times.
> *Marcia*: Do you have friends that live there?
> *Resp 3*: I have…
> *Marcia*: You have…
> *Resp 3*: I have…
> *Marcia*: Have you spent time in their home?

Resp 3: No...!
Marcia: Why? Why not?
Resp 3: I just know them, understand? Not as a friend that I go around with (go out with), or do things like this with, I just know them.

When our discussion turned to economic inequalities, there was a general consensus about their need to have domestic servants and how difficult it was to pay them more than one minimum salary per month. If the servant did not like their wages, they could look for other work!

Resp 1: I think it is useful...there has to be someone, if a person has the means to have someone helping them, helping them in the home...then they can have that. There are people who have money and those that don't. That is the way it is!
Resp 2: I agree with Ryan, because it would be hypocritical of us to say that it is absurd. I agree with that—in the home of everyone here we need to have maids.
Resp 1: It is a reality that we live.
Resp 3: I think, Marcia, that it exists, I think that the situation of this girl you were talking about, I think that it is exploitation, you know. I think that it is rare today that the person that works in a home earns less than a minimum salary because that person that is the maid, just like Ryan said, for us to do what is practical or utilitarian, it is useful for us because we need them in our home.
Resp 2: If you stay around washing cups, washing clothes, ironing, you'll never get to do anything important!

Resp 3: Because the time that I go to study, or go to the university, I will not be able to go because I will have to clean my house! So, it is useful.

Resp 2: The life of the middle and upper class today is very busy, and no one has time to stay home. Also, to do these things we need someone to do them. And, I think, Marcia, just look, in a lot of families $R100 or the minimum salary (she did not know what the minimum salary was) is, many times it is all that they have available for that kind of service. And sometimes I think that, there it is, if this family cannot give $R100, it is true that it is a small amount, but it might be all I have, but I would prefer that this person (the maid) earn a little so they will not be unemployed. Understand?

Resp 3: I also think that the work relationship there is a lot that prevails around the people involved. For example, the boss and the employee. Do you agree to earn $R100? I agree. You want to work? The service you will provide is this—is this OK for you? Or no? Well, then go look for another job! You know, do you understand?

Such indifference toward economic inequality was common among upper-class youth. Looking for another job, one with better pay exists for professionals with college degrees, not for those who are essentially illiterate and uneducated for a global economy.

Health, Illness, and Substandard Medical Care

Frequent illness and poor medical care are constant problems for the poor of Morro de Santana. As discussed earlier, Nancy Scheper-Hughes (1992) proposes that a commonly used term has been developed to describe the state of mind of a person who lives with constant hunger. Further discussion of the term *nervoso* will be helpful in clarifying how the body acts as a receptacle for the suffering endured by hunger. The term *nervoso* described a physical condition previously unknown to the medical profession. Here, hunger is reconceptualized by the poor as a condition that presents a variety of symptoms not commonly related to poor nutrition. People suffering from constant hunger, in turn, seek medical aid and medications for their symptoms. In this sense, Scheper-Hughes suggests that the medical profession has, in turn, reconceptualized the folk idiom *nervoso* to inappropriately diagnose and treat poor nutrition and malnutrition with various forms of medications, including tranquilizers. Hence, hunger and malnutrition and their social, racial, and economic causes remain unaddressed (Scheper-Hughes 1992:213). When I questioned Cauê, a thin and lethargic teenage boy about how to improve the quality of his life, he used *nervoso* to describe and delineate the most difficult problem that he faced. Cauê had a difficult time describing what *nervoso* was, but in general it centered on his stomach and a constant ache he felt along with dizziness, anger, fear, and shaking. Cauê had dropped out of school because of a sense of hopelessness he felt about his future and because he had trouble concentrating and focusing in class. He said he was not learning anything, and felt that nothing would ever change for him.

Because of the raw sewage that runs down the middle of the streets and gathers in dangerous pools where children often play or drink from, sickness and disease are a daily reality. For Cauê, health problems related to poor diet as well as constant exposure to environmental contaminants is a serious problem. Cauê, like many poor youth I came to know, was unaware of the causes of his physical problems, often relying on the belief that he was simply of "bad stock" because he was poor. One mother, a woman I will call Betina, talked with me about the difficulties she has experienced with the medical care system for the poor (INSS) in Morro de Santana:

> That's right, we arrive at the *Pronto Socorro* (emergency care) with a really sick child and because we cannot pay, they make us wait. If the kid has to die it will die because it takes too long, because it is for free, you know how it is. They tell you to go to a clinic, but if the kid gets sick at night, how can I go get the form to go to the clinic (this allows her to get free medical care). So what you have to do is run to the hospital, because sometimes it is late at night when a child gets sick, so you cannot go to the clinic. Now, when I have to go, I have to wait, then go get the *ficha* (certification paper for free medical care), and then return home and get my sick child in the middle of the night, and then take him to the hospital and then I can finally see the doctor. Other than this, there is not a way—what else can I do if I have a sick child? If I do not do this, I will have to wait for another day yet, to get a *ficha* they look at you. It is very complicated!

I came to know the look of poverty, which was not simply poor housing and tattered clothing. The vast majority of the children and youth at the various projects where I worked tended to be physically smaller and thinner than children of the middle and upper classes. As I came to know the children at the projects and as we spent time working together and talking, I found that many of them had suffered various kinds of accidents as well as illnesses. The most commonly reported illnesses were intestinal parasites, pneumonia, bronchitis, serious cuts, burns, and malnutrition. Also common were accidents that occurred in the streets. One child discussed earlier (Nicolas) had been playing in the street next to a horse that was tied to a cart. The horse had become startled and kicked the child in the head, resulting in brain damage. Another child told me that when her sister was an infant, her mother had placed her in a hammock. Her younger brother was playing with a large metal stake and wandered over to the hammock, where he accidentally dropped the stake on their baby sister's head. Again, severe brain injury was the result. Dog bites, burns, broken bones (often from child abuse), and serious cuts were also common forms of injury to children. Medical malpractice and medical indifference to poor infants during birth who are in need of oxygen is the most commonly stated reason by nurses and social workers for brain-injured babies.

I came to know Lorena, a social worker in the public health clinic in the center of the city. We had several discussions about poor children and the constant health problems that plagued them and their parents. According to Lorena, based on her almost twenty years' experience, the most common illnesses for the children of the poor were the ones I've listed, as well as dehydration, yellow fever, cholera, dengue fever, hepatitis, and polio; but Lorena had also found an alarming rise in the rate of children's cancers:

> *Lorena*: Inside the health clinic, I think that I've seen cases that shock or startle us, like cancer in children. It is very common, you know.
> *Marcia*: What kind of cancer?
> *Lorena*: Ah—leukemia, it is in the blood. And so this really shocks us. When I did some work for INSS, I also observed a lot, problems during delivery. Mothers, for

example, without help. I do not know if this is the reality today, understand? But, for example some years ago a large number of mothers, right, had their children without assistance.

Marcia: During their pregnancy?

Lorena: During delivery, during their pregnancy. Right? So, today I think this is getting better.

Marcia: Do you think this is because of negligence on the part of the doctors? You will see a large number of children with problems, with deficiencies? Do these problems come from negligence during delivery?

Lorena: Yes. And because of little attention during the woman's pregnancy, and a badly done delivery. So, we saw a lot of this.

Marcia: So, this kind of mental problem is connected to bad deliveries and the lack of care the woman received during her pregnancy?

Lorena: Yes, this is certain.

Marcia: And it is also connected to misery and poverty?

Lorena: Yes, we say this, "The health system is not good—the public health system. It does not offer citizens what they need." So, I want to say that if the health system leaves things like this, clearly the one to suffer is the patient, the citizen that is not getting what they need.

I wanted to know if the increase in childhood cancers crossed economic classes or was primarily being found among children of the poor. Lorena gave me the following information:

Lorena: When I worked in public service, the majority of cases were in poor children.

Marcia: Do you think this is because of the lack of nutrition and good diet, or the environment in which they are living...?
Lorena: I think so.
Marcia: That there is a lot of pollution?
Lorena: I think so.
Marcia: That their immune system is very stressed?
Lorena: I think so—I think that it is all this. I would like to have a scientific base to say this. I'm not a doctor, right? But I've observed this, I think that it is a little bit part of the environment, the kinds of care that the children receive, the kind of family that the child has, right? I think that this is able to generate this situation. I do not know anything in terms of the numbers of children with cancer here, or if the number has risen but I would like to say that these children that are presented to us, the very fact that they are children they create a lot of emotion in us. The cause of this high rate of cancer in children here, I do not know any work being done on this, any research being done on childhood cancer in Morro de Santana.

For those who are lucky enough to arrive at a *Pronto Socorro* and be seen, buying medications is a constant problem. Frequently, the patron of a parent will pay for medications and deduct the cost from their workers' salaries. Catrina told me about her experiences with health care and paying for medications:

Marcia: Does the government pay for the medicine and treatment at the hospital?
Catrina: No, because here it is difficult here in this town. For this, when we find medicine, when we cannot find medicines we go there (the clinic) with the

prescription, but come back with our hands empty. Like the prescription without the medication. You do not have any money.

Marcia: The doctor will write a paper with the prescription and you must pay for it?

Catrina: That's right, I have to pay for the medications.

Marcia: But you do not have money to pay for it?

Catrina: When we do not have the money, we have to ask a relative to loan it to us.

Marcia: But the government will not pay for it?

Catrina: No, sometimes the government sends it, but here there are so many children that need medicines—a lot of the time because of the weather, because of the place also. I do not know if it is because of these things. So, we cannot get the medicines and then sometimes the clinic says they do not have the medication. The government sends it but sometimes we cannot find where it is. It gets lost at the clinic.

Marcia: Why?

Catrina: There are more people than there is money. The ones that have money never have to deal with lines. Sometimes we have to get up very early in the morning (3 or 4 am) and stand in line to get medications. So…that's what they do…they just go to a pharmacy (the rich people) and buy it with money. Now we, who do not have money, have to be in line, and we wait to see if we get the medications. So, here there are more poor people than people with good stable financial situations.

During part of my tenure in Morro de Santana, I lived in the house that was rented by Viva Crianças for the production and sale of products made by the cooperative *Dedos de Gente* (Fingers of the People). The cooperative produced and sold sweets, liqueurs, jams, and wooden toys. During my short stay in the house, I had the opportunity to watch the women of the co-op work as they cut, cleaned, cooked, and bottled their products. They were always dressed in white with white face masks, and the room was full of bees that were attracted to the heavy smell of boiling fruits and the sweet syrup used to preserve them. Their hands and arms were swollen from bee stings and the screen-less windows were kept open because of the heat. I was struck by the contrast of the poverty of the women working in the co-op and the appearance of a sterile work environment. All of the women live in the surrounding *favelas*. Their houses are often damp mud hovels with cloth over windows and doors, and bushes for toilets, with raw sewage running down the middle of their streets. Yet, here they sat, day in and day out, cooking on restaurant-quality stoves, boiling fruits in huge, expensive pots, and working with blenders and kitchen utensils they will never be able to use for their own purposes, much less hope to buy for themselves. All the women in the co-op wear spotless white aprons. Their hair is tied up and their heads are covered in white scarves. They sit at the tables filling the jars of fruit while their faces are covered with masks. This is hygiene. They go home to houses made of mud wattle and discarded lumber and cardboard, if they are lucky, or they go home to a shelter made of garbage bags. Their windows do not have screens. Flies are common and constant. Ants are always there, too. The poor are not hygienic because they cannot afford to be. But here, the appearance of lab technicians covers their poverty while they prepare the delicious fruits that the rich will buy for prices above and beyond the means of those who produce the delicacies. They are paid a paltry one-half minimum salary, $R60, per month for eight-hour days. Each jar of canned fruit costs what it takes them a half day to earn. Of course, these women never eat the fruit they prepare. Their tongues cannot savor the sweetness of candied and sweetened fruits, but their arms and hands feel the sting of bees and their fingers crack and peel at the joints and cuticles from immersion in water and lemon juice.

A story told to me by a woman (whom I will call Betsy) who worked at APAE (The Association of Parents and Friends with Intellectual Disabilities) is an appropriate summary of poverty in Brazil. I had asked if she could tell me what the most common health problems were of the children who attended their institution. Betsy told me the following story: One day a child of about five years of age was brought to APAE and she had the appearance of an animal. She was covered in dirt. It had built up in the cracks of her skin and her hair was matted and caked with dung. The child could not stand in an erect posture, but rather stayed hunched over despite the fact that there was nothing congenitally wrong with her spine. When the child was evaluated for intelligence and neurological development, it was found that she was at the level of a two-year-old. This child had been born in the country, in the poor rural areas outside of Morro de Santana to a poverty-stricken family. Her mother worked in the fields on a small farm. After the birth of this child, the mother had to return to work and had no one to care for her child. Using her ingenuity, she dug a deep hole in the ground and put her baby in it, leaving her there for hours at a time while she worked. The child had grown up living in a hole in the ground with pigs roaming the ground above as her playmates. The child was neither mentally deficient nor physically deformed from natural causes, but rather was physically stunted and mentally undeveloped because of the life conditions into which she was born. The ignorance and poverty of her mother, the indifference of her country, the loneliness of her existence, the horror of poverty and inequality formed her hunched body and stunted mind. Such lives are common in Brazil, and hence such indifference and social inequality constitute the most common health problem for poor children, who overwhelmingly are Afro-Brazilian.

Stereotypes of Danger and Immorality: *Pivetes e Ladrões* (Thieves and Bandits)

Differences based on race and class in Morro de Santana cause dark-skinned children to be viewed as immoral and dangerous by the mostly light-skinned elite. During the focus group I discussed, held with upper-class youth, the following exchange revealed the wide gaps that exist between the reality of street youth and the images and stereotypes held about them by youth in upper-class Morro de Santana:

> *Resp 1*: Another thing that I wanted to say is that, was that I also see families, I see families here downtown, in the streets of downtown Morro de Santana. The families come down, the mother, the children come down, they all come down and they encourage the children to beg. They go and do all the things we've been talking about. I've seen this. They get the little kids and the youngest is two years old, and even the oldest—and they talk and they go here and there begging, they go all over with one or more of the children. If their parents would say, "No, my child, let's find something to do, some work." They do not have this.
> *Resp 2:* No, no.
> *Resp 1*: That's it—it is a lack of instruction.
> *Resp 3*: It is a lack of instruction, people. It is not everyone who has someone supporting them, instructing them to look for work, to look for something to do.

> *Marcia*: In other words, he was instructed to do what?
> *Resp 1:* To ask for handouts, to beg. So the parents ask for handouts and all the kids will too. And so they are sort of directing them to do this, and they are going to grow up doing this.
> *Resp 3*: What I want to say is, it is sure that, I think for me in my case if I were going to sum up this whole problem, I think I would sum it up—to sum up the question of education, the person who has an education for example—it is not education like that. Instruction, the base of an education, is to have principles.

Here, the privileged upper-class youth who view begging mothers and their children as amoral and without principles do so based on the premise that poverty equals immorality. This assumption leans heavily on the physical appearance of the poor: dirt, the smell of sweat, lack of upper-class gestures based on social etiquette, and stereotypes that define poverty as a state of laziness and indolence.

Privileged youth in a beautiful home in the city center told me about their perceptions of street youth as dangerous and immoral:

> *Marcia*: Do you all agree that the numbers of street kids here in Morro de Santana are growing?
> *Resp 1*: Yes, I agree, this is evident.
> *Resp 2*: Yes—it is visible.
> *Resp 3*: That's right.
> *Resp 1*: Yes, it is the same in terms of violence.
> Resp 2: Assaults, things like these—exactly.
> *Marcia*: Assaults are increasing?
> *Resp 3*: Yes, actually there are a lot more.
> *Resp 2*: I was almost assaulted (laughter and confusion with everyone talking), by a *pivete* from the *favelas*.

> *Resp 1*: This is evident here in Morro de Santana. People like that, who go through the streets, downtown in Morro de Santana. You're seeing, you know, lots of crazy kids, running around, here and there, taking advantage of you. You know?
> *Resp 3*: Also, I heard that the number of, someone said that the number, it was on the radio today, that there are many *pivete* (street urchins) here, already, that there were not three years ago.
> *Marcia*: When you say "*pivete*," could you give a definition of what you mean?
> *Resp 3*: A *pivete* is a street kid who robs, that assaults, you understand? It is a kid, generally a minor.
> *Marcia*: Normally it is a young boy or adolescent?
> *Resp 3*: Generally a minor.
> *Marcia*: OK. That assault you?
> *Resp 3*: There are a lot like that, that knock on people's doors and beg.
> *Resp 2*: No, this is a *pivete*, a street kid.
> *Resp 1*: No, this is also a street kid, you guys! (Everyone talking at once)
> *Marcia*: One person at a time.
> *Resp 2*: I think that a street kid and a *pivete* are the same thing.
> *Resp 3*: A *pivete* robs! A *pivete* is one who does bad things, you understand?

When I asked them to be specific about the types of crimes that they felt street youth committed, they stated crimes that fit the stereotypes they held about the poor youths who inhabited the streets:

> *Marcia*: You said that violence and crime is growing. What type of crime do you think is growing?

Resp 1: Here in Morro de Santana?

Resp 2: In Morro de Santana—assaults, muggings, I think.

Marcia: Assaults, against?

Resp 1: In the home.

Resp 2: And direct assaults on people too.

Resp 3: I think, and in businesses too.

Marcia: You said businesses?

Resp 3: In businesses because I think that robbery like that, armed robbery is like that.

Resp 2: I think that we have not yet had the *trombadinha* (orphaned or abandoned street youth who steals) of the big cities yet, it has not happened here yet. For example, the kid who is a *pivete* that shows up and who runs into you, I do not know, throws stones in your face – —he is here!

Marcia: Look, the people that are doing these things, are they people from all classes or are they just poor people?

Resp 2: The people who rob are only from the lower classes.

Resp 1: The poor classes!

Resp 3: Yes, that's certain.

What is striking here is the certainty that it is only the poorer classes that commit crimes of assault and robbery. Such entrenched notions of the poor, who one must remember, are also mostly Afro-Brazilians, mark the perceptual faculties of many elites, who project onto the poor characterizations that define them as deviant and dangerous. It is as if the actual activities of many working youth are not perceived by those whose existence precludes them from struggle, hence when they see a working street youth they see a symbol of danger from which they must move away:

> *Marcia*: Going back, with respect to the children, what type of activities do you think that street kids do in the streets?
> *Resp 1*: I've seen them stealing, smelling glue. I've seen them smelling glue and bothering people in the streets, understand? Provoking, hurting, asking for handouts, begging. Also asking for handouts is what's practically—it is only asking for *handouts—that's all I've seen.*
> *Marcia*: Just asking for handouts?
> *Resp 2*: I've seen them asking for work also.
> *Resp 3*: The hunger that most of them, the majority of the street kids, the *pivete*s have—I'm going to generalize now—they say "give me real food," this kind of thing. They threaten you to give them money. Do you understand? "Oh, give me a real, or else." Understand?
> *Resp 1*: They just want to be free without responsibility.

Street youth were seen as lazy, dirty, and without morals, and at times even equated with trash on the streets, thrown there by their families and discarded by society:

> *Resp 1*: It is knowing how to live with society. You do not act like trash in the street, you know? People who have an education, people—it is like street kids, like they do not have an education, they do not have the least amount of knowledge when it comes to principles, nothing!
> *Marcia*: When you say education, do you mean such things as reading, writing?

> *Resp 1*: No. I mean that they do not have principles, understand? Moral principles, do you understand? For the street kid, it is a lot easier to go into the street and beg and hang on people instead of going out to work, or to try to shine shoes. Understand?

I found these statements to be commonly held by elites, who have been protected from the complexities and hardships of social injustices and social inequalities. These negative perceptions and stereotypes of working youth were very far from the reality of their daily lives. Yet, one girl in the focus group told me how an experience she had was what marked a change in the ways in which she perceived street children. Her story, especially since she was willing to share it among her peers who were opposed to contact with street youth, suggests a potential for social change at the individual level. Perhaps this is, in the long run, the only way in which social change actually occurs:

> I wanted to make a comment. This happened two times with me. I had a girl, a street girl, she must have been at most twelve years old and she was tormenting me. I was working in a store and she kept bothering me, you know? She was always bothering me and the more things that she did, I was becoming more and more angry with her. I was becoming very unsympathetic with these things and becoming very negative about this situation. And she was always coming at me, swearing at me, so she insulted me and I insulted her. What I was saying is that I realized this, that from the moment that I began to treat her in a better way. I said to myself, "either I'm going to fight with her for the rest of my life, or I'm going to find a better way to win her over." And

it was from the time that I really changed with her, my attitude about her, that I started talking to her, little by little. I started initiating conversations, chatting with her, treating her better. So what happened is that she stopped coming in the store to fight or to swear at me and she started coming to visit and to tell me about something that happened in her neighborhood. She started gaining confidence in me. She started trusting me. I really could see that she was changing that she was changing the way that she acted with me. The same thing with another little boy who was about six years old. He used to come in (to the store), and one time I had to practically explode with him there. I fought with him. It was horrible. Then, one day I got this idea, and I said to myself "wait a minute. I'm going to start to be really patient with this kid. And then I started to talk with him, to ask him where he lived, what he did. Every day that he came by we would start talking, so much so, that today, well, before when he used to come by, he would mess up things in the store, but now he comes in and, like I say to him "Oh, wait a minute, wait there, and when I'm done helping this person I will talk with you." And then from the time I started doing that, you know, he stopped messing up things because I asked him not to mess with things. Really, because I asked him not to mess with things, he would wait for me there right in the doorway of the store, and if I had asked him a while back not to come into the store, he would have said something nasty to me and come into the store anyway, and thrown things on the floor. But from the moment I started changing the way I acted with him, when I changed with him, he would come on in and I would say "Oh, wait there at the door" and he would not come in the store, he would really wait for me and I started to realize this. That it was really in the way I handled things. Two times. From that moment, when you give a chance, when you start, when I started to change with him, with those two people, they changed with me.

One day, while in a pharmacy on the plaza, I was talking with the store clerk about a program that worked with street youth, through the *Caixa Econômica Federal*. As the clerk was telling me about the program, a girl about eight or nine years old came into the store and stood quietly looking around, perhaps preparing to beg for money. The clerk turned to the girl and said, "Ah, but these kids prefer the street to working, right, girl?" The girl heard the remark and she quickly looked at the ground and turned toward the exit. Then, in a quick movement, retreated out the door. I thanked the clerk for her information about the program, and left. I looked for the girl, but she had fled the area. I took a seat at a table on the street in front of a local ice cream store and watched the activities on the street in front of me. My gaze moved to a group of white, well-dressed, upper-class boys riding their bikes and playing in the park across the street from me, and I wondered at their freedom and liberty. While white youth get up to a breakfast made by a black girl, they do not clean or pick up after themselves, they do not help in the home. Indeed, in comparison to poor children, they have an excess of leisure time. School is only from 7:30 am to 11:30 am every day. Children from privileged families come home from school and typically watch TV and play. They have toys and technology to learn and grow from (computers, games, etc.). They can spend time on the street, in very restricted ways, time that is respectable—buy an ice cream or a toy, ride their bikes, or move through the streets while they go to a friend's house.

I wondered at the words of Professor Ricardo (see Chapter Five) who told me that when street kids are young, people feel for them, but when they get older and become adolescents, people hate them and perceive them to be lazy violent beggars. He made it very clear that the street is where adults negotiate. This is a world constructed and maintained by adults and it was an inappropriate place for children. This social space is a place reserved for adults, and if children, especially poor children who spend a great deal of time in the streets, cross the boundary from child spaces into adult spaces, they will be polluted, corrupted, mistreated, and abused.

The street is a forbidden space for children and a liminal space for adolescents who could, at any moment, turn into dangerous social animals. Morality and values are found in the home, in the church, and in God. Those who are poor and black are in special need of social assistance because they inhabit the world of the street, of the dirty, of liminality, a place between sanity and insanity, between order and chaos. They are untrustworthy, dirty, lacking in discipline, raw, without education, teetering on the brink of pervasive illogic and outright craziness. These people, especially the youth, require more discipline, more surveillance, more religious education, and more lessons of morality and compassion. One day, after our work in the music class at Viva Crianças, Catrina and I took a walk to the plaza. As we walked, she told me how she had come to understand the negative stereotypes leveled at her, because of her poverty and because of her dark skin:

> I think that the majority of poor people are not violent. But there is this impression. But this is a stereotype that they've created (rich people) that it is just the poor that rob, and it is just the poor black person that kills, just

the poor black person that, you know? Everything that is bad, it is just the poor blacks that do it. So, it is like this, the rich kids, the rich, they do not do this. They do! But it is just covered up! They fight, they kill too! But money covers up their crimes! It is like I said, many rich people, you know, kill, and they rob a lot, and they do terrible things but they can keep things covered up, you know? But I think that many times people that have a lot of money, I think that many times they just care about what they need and what they do, because they have access to many things that are good, and with all these "good" things, they still kill, you know? The way of the poor—they have a heavy weight. A person that does not have any money, many times it is so heavy because, it is good to wait, but they've waited and waited—because—Oh, my God! How am I going to pay the light bill? Or pay my rent? There is not any way to pay for my children's school things, you know? So, I think that many times people say that they just wait, wait, wait, and wait some more for more to come. It is really difficult. You know? A person takes another and kills them, they rob, understand? Some rich people do this too, but I think that many times there is no justification for their actions (rich people), because they have access to school, they have access to many things so why are they robbing? I do not know. I do not think that they have a motive. I do not understand these acts of violence by the rich. But I think that they cannot justify their actions, like these boys that killed the Indian. They are from upper-middle-class families—they have everything! Why, why did they kill this Indian? For pleasure? There is no justification! Understand?[28]

Juxtaposing the words of Catrina with those of Professor Ricardo, it is clear how the two worldviews, one of poverty and the experience of discrimination and social injustice, and the other of privilege and opportunity, collide. The violence of social injustice born of economic and racial inequality is both concrete and subtle, both obvious and hidden, both rejected and accepted.

> *Professor Ricardo*: I think the question of street kids, I think that they are not in a place where they should be. Even for me, seeing these kids on the street has become an established fact. Because one has different sorts of feelings; repulsion, fear, pity—there is all this. There is practically acceptance of a group that is excluded. So these kids are going to stay there at night, and I do not know how we're going to resolve it. The kids living on the streets have become an institution. There is a normality about it. It is not even noticed anymore. They are unseen, yet they are hated.
> *Marcia*: The children stay on the streets the whole night, they are changing the construction of childhood because they are staying in a reality that is reserved for adults?
> *Professor Ricardo*: I need to make sure that I'm understanding you when you say the constructions of childhood. There are constructions of childhoods, right?
> *Marcia*: Right.
> *Professor Ricardo*: So inside the reality of Brazil today, this is a different construction of childhood today, one that is a childhood in the streets. And this construction

of the street, it disturbs (*incomoda*), it gives pain and anger and fear. It is full of the most diverse feelings and sentiments. These feelings create a kind of acceptance of these children as a way to avoid them. This acceptance strengthens all the other feelings. Getting used to it is as strong as all the other feelings in my opinion.
Marcia: Do you think that these kids that stay on the streets should be working or must work?
Professor Ricardo: No, I think that they must have a way to study.
Marcia: How can they do this, how can they have the conditions to study with the life they have?
Professor Ricardo: I do not know. I do not know how many there are. The solution must be resolved and corrected. But they cannot stay in the streets. The streets bring about behaviors that are not acceptable to society.

It is in the world of the street where images meet, where worlds collide, and where battles are fought, both with real violence and with the subdued violence of averted looks. City centers in Brazil signify wealth, access to services and luxuries. *Favelas*' streets signify poverty and marginality. Like childhood, the streets are delineated and circumscribed. Certain people, certain ages, certain activities are allowed and others prohibited. The life experiences of working children and youth collide with the social consensus of what constitutes normal childhood for the dominant classes in Brazil. The upper-class youth in my focus group could not see the discrepancy between their privileged lives and the lives of the young people who worked as servants in their homes. They needed to study and go to the university—they could not wash their own clothes, cook, and clean house too. They needed someone to do that for them. But it is the fault of the poor, who are ignorant because they did not learn, regardless of the fact that as a child and adolescent, they could not study or even go to school because of their need to labor in order to survive on a daily ration of rice and beans. Indeed, Vitor told me, "I think that my mother has a lot of responsibility. If we arrived at some point where we are begging on the streets, it would be because there was absolutely no other way, no other way."

Children from poor homes tend to have a lot of unsupervised freedom. The lack of individual attention at home means that these children and adolescents must turn to their ingenuity in order to construct a sense of value. The sooner they become independent and financially reliable, the more they are valued in their own right (Veloso 2012: 667–71). In addition, these children experience more physical and emotional violence at home, see more substance abuse, particularly alcoholism, and have little if any privacy. The lack of privacy and personal space creates a sense of collective property that often clashes with project ideologies about ownership of property. As discussed, robberies were common in the projects, and I came to see that stealing was the result of larger issues. Poverty and lack of resources as well as small living quarters and large families have created ways of being that demand the constant sharing of available resources. Lack of privacy and personal space tend to encourage impersonalization of property.

While children were frequently treated by their parents with what seemed to be particularly harsh (if not insensitive) actions, my informants (both parents and children) made me aware of the deep love and commitment they have for each other. Nancy Scheper-Hughes has written extensively on the lack of expressive motherly love among *favela* mothers for their sickly infants in Brazil (1992:268–339 and 340–399). Similar to Scheper-Hughes' findings about parental responses to sickly infants, I found that parents' apparent coldness or harshness toward their surviving children is, in reality, a strategy used by parents to prepare their children to survive day-to-day life in the *favelas*. I have shown how parents' expectations of their children in the *favelas* contradict the constructions that define normal childhood. Indeed, it is the parents' apparent harshness toward their children, which is, in truth, born of love, that prepares them to survive more successfully, not only on the streets of their *favelas*, but also in the broader world of Brazil's extreme poverty.

This chapter has shown the reality of street children in Morro de Santana: The ways in which they view themselves, the ways in which they are viewed by their neighbors, and by their parents. The contributions, (both emotional and financial) that children make to their families are impressive when viewed alone; however, when those same children are juxtaposed to the negative stereotypes and social exclusion that they experience daily, their tenacity and survival become extraordinary. Truly, then, daily survival in *favelas* for both adults and children are a joint effort in which both sanguine and fictive families must actively participate.

The final chapter summarizes my findings on street children and NGOs in Morro de Santana. I discuss the theoretical contributions made by this research to social science literature and to the anthropological research of children and childhood. I examine Brazil's poor public educational system and its effects on street children and address the lack of technical computer training for street youth in public schools and in NGO projects. Finally, I offer suggestions for changing NGO practices and policies and I discuss differences between the NGOs where I worked.

CHAPTER TEN
SIGNIFICANCE OF FINDINGS

Introduction

I have postulated that imported modern Western European social constructions that define childhood in idealized terms have been absorbed and practiced by the middle and upper classes in Brazil. As this study has demonstrated, such idealized notions of elite childhood emphasize its innocence and fragility. These constructions collide with the realities of Brazilian street children, who work daily on the streets among adults in the informal market. Such social constructions contribute to the complexity of social conditions affecting street children. When these constructions are combined with other social inequalities in Brazil, the result is the marginalization, stereotyping, and abusive treatment of street children in general. For example, the spaces children inhabit (streets, projects, inferior public schools, and mud huts, to name a few) and the activities in which they engage (informal market labor, care-taking of both siblings and parents, robbery) are linked to several factors: poverty, racism, clientelism, and educational inequality. Further compounding the problems faced by street children are the NGOs themselves. In addition, NGOs are largely created and directed by middle-and upper-class Brazilian elite who have absorbed the Western European idealized notions of childhood. I therefore contend that NGO programs, based on the popular culture model, are largely helpless in alleviating the conditions of this social inequality.

This research has discussed each of the above issues as they relate to the daily life experiences of street children. I have examined the practices, policies, and ideologies of NGOs serving the street children of Morro de Santana through a case study of one NGO and comparison to four others. The voices of street children, their families, and NGO project directors and coordinators are my principal data. I have discussed how NGO ideology is intimately tied to certain elite social conceptions of childhood, while the bulk of NGO coordinators come from poverty and hardship similar to their clients. While four of the NGOs with which I worked in Morro de Santana were able to work more effectively with their clients than Viva Crianças was, they were also struggling to find ways to address social, economic, and educational inequality within the communities that they served. I argue that the split between project directors (usually middle-to upper-class Brazilians) and project coordinators (usually people from the *favelas*) exists, in part, due to the extreme differences between their life experiences. The dissonance and disconnect between project ideology and practitioners' experience needs to be addressed if there is to be improvement of NGO efficacy in their stated missions. There is a serious need for innovative programs that incorporate coordinators' perceptions and practical input.

In this final chapter, I present a brief discussion on my contributions to anthropological theory and research, and I make suggestions for changing established ideas about who street children are. I discuss the gaps within social science literature about street children and offer potential solutions for developing more effective NGO programs. I follow this discussion by investigating NGO practices and policies, and I make suggestions for developing a new model that can assist street children in their expressed life needs. I then offer a discussion on the economic, educational, and racial inequality experienced by street children, and I offer the practical suggestions for community activism that were made to me by the children I worked with. Many of the street children I befriended told me of their desire to learn how to use computers. In addition, they wanted to know if there were ways for them to be eligible for international educational exchange programs currently available only to more privileged youth. Because the children expressed these ideas to me, I explore options for training in computer literacy, job training, and international exchange programs for street children. I conclude by making suggestions for further research into the life circumstances of street youth, their families, and NGO programs.

Contribution to Anthropological Research

Anthropological research about street children and NGOs focuses on the types of NGO programs in Brazil, understanding poverty in Brazil, and identifying the types of street children to be found in urban centers. This book examines three areas that are usually not addressed when discussing Brazilian street children and their life circumstances: racism, the social constructions that define street children differently than the children of the middle and upper classes, and the life experiences and daily economic and labor contributions of street children who still live at home. In addition, in order to determine if their programs effectively address the needs of street and working children, this research examines five NGOs that represent a range of NGO types in Brazil. This research provides quantitative and qualitative data on street children's activities in the streets and the income they earn. Street children who live at home and work on the streets have been understudied, with most research focusing heavily on autonomous street children. By studying children who still live at home, attend school, and work on the streets, a different picture of Brazilian street youth is beginning to emerge. This population of poor children constitutes a large percentage of what is currently defined as street children, and their daily life experiences redefine poor children as responsible citizens who make valuable contributions to their families, both economically and emotionally.

My research findings on NGOs and street children agree with, expand upon, and, at times, contradict current anthropological literature about street children. In particular, my research widens the discourse on street children's right to work, and provides concrete evidence of their contributions to household income and maintenance of family stability. The chapter on the economy of daily life describes how street children are viable actors, who perform daily tasks not commonly associated with the developmental models that define normal childhood. In this sense, some of my findings contradict current theoretical discourses that define normal childhood, and make a contribution to the growing literature that is redefining childhood in social science literature (Oldman 1991; Nic Ghiolla Phádraig 1990 a and b; Shanahan 2007). Indeed, street children must perform adult-like tasks as they deal with the extremes of life's hardships. This raises the question: if a large group of children, under any circumstances, consistently responds with abilities previously thought to be beyond their capacity due to their biological and psychological development or immaturity, then are the constructions that define who they are and what they can do in need of revision? Such a question needs to be examined and must include the pressing issues of poverty and substandard educational practices that have forced street children to redefine themselves, and hence to potentially redefine childhood in general. Indeed, not too long ago, definitions that previously defined another group, (i.e., women) underwent intensive examination by feminist scholars and activists. I would like to suggest that street children are the activists who will, through their need to function in the adult world and their desire to participate in it, make significant contributions to reinventing childhood as they work the streets, go to school, assist in family maintenance, and work as activists for children's rights in Brazil.

Theoretical Contributions

My findings agree with and expand upon current social science constructionist research on children who are defined as active social agents. I provide further examples of how children are not only active social agents but are also constructing new perceptions about who they are as individuals within their society at large. Indeed, my findings demonstrate that street children are fully endowed social agents, not passive recipients in the cultural soup that constructs their society. As I have demonstrated, street children participate actively and creatively in their society at large (in the informal marketplace, and at home with siblings and parents) while they participate in forming the constructions that define how they view themselves and their society. They do so by playing a rather large part in shaping the way in which they learn about themselves and others. In this sense, they are also constructing the knowledge base that will constitute future social norms for poor children in Morro de Santana. Thus, the findings of this research differ from the classical sociological and anthropological findings about children and childhood. I have shown that the childhood of street children is far from a protected sphere of childhood bliss that is a prelude to entering the real arena of social life: adulthood.

Social science often positions children outside the margins of society and conceptualizes their transition into adulthood as a series of progressive stages. Further, it defines and delineates appropriate social spaces and activities for them throughout these stages. In order to position children and childhood outside of society (or at best subsumed within a protective social sphere) the field of social science made an assumed distinction between socialization and society. Socialization has been conceptualized as shared knowledge, while society has traditionally been deemed to be constituted of coordinated, replicated, and negotiated patterns of interactions; hence, one knows how to interact only after being socialized (Herskovits 1948; Mead 1963; Schwartz 1976). The difference between modern classical theories (constructions of childhood born out of the industrial revolution) and constructionist views of childhood are striking. Classical theory disempowers children by excluding them from participation in the everyday world of adults, while the constructionist theory empowers them to enter and participate in activities that have been socially sanctioned only for adults. Hence, these two theories create a dissonance that is hard to rectify: acceptance of one implies the rejection of the other. Such conflict forces social scientists, especially anthropologists, to seek a new and more accurate understanding of who children are, what they want, and what they are capable of. The constructionist view that I advance here, particularly for poor children, holds that children are propelled at birth into the actual center of the social world and are socialized accordingly. Hence, as street children have shown us, they (and children at large) learn in order to **make** their way in the world, not to gain entry into it. Street children contradict how childhood and its various activities have been constructed in the modern world. Ironically, I argue that constructionist theories reach back into pre-modern constructions of childhood to the time when children participated in the adult world, working alongside adults, but not viewed as full social agents with social and human rights. The twist here is that in the constructionist view, children are finally seen as complete social agents, and not powerless, exploited, underdeveloped humans.

I have attempted to demonstrate how street children are indeed powerful, self-actualized social beings with a body of legalized and sanctioned rights. Poor children in Morro de Santana are reliable informants and articulate orators who can talk about the more subtle aspects of their lives with emotional intelligence and psychological facility. In this sense, this research suggests that social scientists continue to change their views about the reliability of children as informants in social science research, and to expand their research agendas to incorporate children and youth alongside adults in the collection of data about real life events. Given that street children are the best informants about who they are and what they need, it is indeed *their* expressed needs that can substantially alter the ways in which the public at large views them. I contend that researchers, when studying children and childhood, need to turn their attention to new methodological practices that include street children as their main informants. It is time to collect systematic information on the *experience* of street children's lives from street children themselves, and not from adults describing them. By working with street children as informants, social scientists will assist in empowering them. Such research will indeed empower all children by examining and questioning the constructions that currently cast them into the realm of idealized and/or silenced social spaces. The eventual result of such research can assist in decreasing the invisibility of children within society at large, hence helping to ameliorate the unequal power relations that currently exist between children and adults. Such results can profoundly impact educational systems and curricula, from kindergarten to universities, and eventually impact the ways in which children interact with the world.

Changing Established Ideas About Street Children

Stereotypes (Social Class and Racism): Street children come from a specific segment of Brazilian society: the socially and racially underprivileged. To address that central fact, established notions and ideas about street children must be challenged. Until Brazilian society at large understands and addresses the causes for street children being on the streets, there is little hope that street children's life possibilities will improve. They will continue to lack proper housing, education, leisure, consumer goods, decent wages, and effective health care.

The stereotypes and the common terms that define street children are pejorative. Such linguistic markers as *moleque* (a black slave child), *trombadinha* (an orphaned or abandoned child or teenager pickpocket), or *pivete* (which roughly translates as "urchin") were used to describe freed slaves and their children, and their usage continues today (Buarque de Holanda Ferreira 1975:1413). Even the relatively neutral description *crianças de rua* (children of the street) underscores the fact that children on the streets represent a deviation from the norm.

The distinction between house and street in Brazil has been minutely discussed and analyzed by Robert da Matta and Sandra Lauderdale Graham, among others (da Matta 1991; da Matta 1985; Graham 1988; Scheper-Hughes and Hoffman 1991). The street is a social space designated for adults and, at least from the elite perspective, children are appropriate there only if affiliated with an adult. I argue that dark-skinned children on the streets present an extremely negative symbol for Brazilian elites for two reasons: 1. street children are linked to racially negative stereotypes about slaves and their children and 2. constructions of childhood innocence collide with the presence of unsupervised children working in the streets (Mikulak 2011; Wood, de Carvalho, and Guimarães 2010). Yet, street children inhabit the streets out of poverty, which forces them to work. Contrary to the negative stereotypes that define them, and defined their slave ancestors as *vagabundos, pivetes, ladrão,* and *moleque* among others, they contribute significantly to their families' incomes (Emerson and Knabb 2006).

National Education Campaigns on Poverty and Race

In order to redefine who street children are, I suggest it is society at large that needs to change its sensibilities about the nature of childhood for poor children, rather than attempting to change the sensibilities of street children to match elite notions of privileged childhood. For such a change to occur, an educational campaign about who street children are needs to permeate society at large. Indeed, effective change for street children will occur only once society effectively addresses the serious economic and social inequalities that have historically defined and delineated Brazilian society. Such a campaign must be addressed and funded at the national and federal level, and make the provisions for economic, educational, medical, and racial equality provided in the 1988 Brazilian Constitution a reality. In order not to create a and-aid approach to these serious economic, educational, and social inequality issues, federal mandates need to be put in place. Such mandates need to include programs based on civil rights laws, similar to those initiated in the US. Examples of such programs could include educational quota systems, early childhood education programs such as Title One Food Programs and educational tutoring programs in public schools, and Title One Summer School Programs for Migrant Workers' children in the US (the equivalent in Brazil would be families with incomes below the poverty line). Such programs as Headstart and Upward Bound, developed in the US, could be modified to work within Brazil's public educational system. In addition, public school districts in rural and urban areas need to receive federal funds for food assistance and tutoring programs based on parents' incomes. Funds need to be allocated according to the expressed needs of parents and their children within public school districts. NGOs working in local communities can greatly assist in drawing parents and children into functional and successful community educational activism. Finally, such educational mandates, along with federal funding, could greatly assist NGOs in providing quality educational tutoring and vocational and computer training to street youth.

Gaps Within Literature on Street Children

There is a lacuna in the literature about street children who are living at home but working on the streets. This population, which constitutes the majority of working street children in Brazil, needs in-depth study in order to comprehend the degree and depth of their social exclusion, and the social issues described that create negative stereotypes about them. There is also a pressing need to understand their actual household economic contributions. My research addresses the paucity of information about street children's incomes by providing actual figures and percentages that demonstrate the importance of their economic labor.

My findings contradict popular social perceptions about street children (the majority of whom still live at home part-time or full-time) in Brazil by demonstrating that they are not, for the most part, dangerous deviants. In this sense my research demarks yet another irony by demonstrating how street children defy the normal social discourses about what children are actually capable of. Here, street children demonstrate their developed sensibilities of economic responsibility, emotional depth, sophisticated knowledge of the hardships of daily life, and their dedicated concern for the survival of their parents and siblings.

My findings demonstrate that NGOs have been largely ineffective when attempting to change public perceptions about street children because they have focused on altering the sensitivities and sensibilities of the children and their families, instead of focusing on altering the sensibilities of the public at large. Issues related to street children that address their social marginalization and poverty need to be studied and linked to race and discrimination in Brazil because Brazilian popular notions about racism state that "there is no racism in Brazil." Brazilian racism is a crucial factor in economic, educational, and social inequality. Indeed, Brazil's position within the global economy is compromised by its continued social and economic stratification. For Brazil to enter the global market, racial discrimination and its connection to educational, economic, and social inequity must be addressed.

Suggestions for Changing NGO Practice and Policy

NGO Directors and Social Class Differences: NGOs are traditionally organized by the middle- and upper-class elite in Brazil, who have frequently been perceived by various governments as politically leftist. During the military regime of the 1960s to the late 80s, the communist and socialist parties were disbanded by the government because of their pro-nationalistic or anti-capitalist ideologies. Many leftist political leaders were incarcerated, tortured, and made to disappear, while others sought exile in other Latin American countries, Canada, and the United States. Today, NGOs are most often created and directed by elites, who strive for social change. However, because of their positions of social privilege, the founders of NGOs often prefer to ignore race and racism due in part to their acceptance of Brazil's historical notion of a racial democracy. To complicate matters, the liberal elite have absorbed the social constructions that define childhood as a time of innocence and purity. These constructions ironically contradict the elite, leftist positions that kept social inequalities (racial, economic, and educational) high. I postulate that many liberals are not aware that they have absorbed constructions of childhood that are in conflict with the realities that define the childhood of poor children. When NGOs attempt to bring their ideas about assisting street children into social programs, they construct programs that are based upon their notions of who and what children are. Therefore, many NGO programs are based on the popular notion of the culture of the poor by designing programs that offer theater, craft making, and popular folklore, rather than basic literacy, mathematical, and computer skills. Such programs leave street children unprepared to achieve even a modicum of economic and educational success. Hence, poor children must work on the streets to survive.

Community Activism and Education: At the community level, NGOs need to work with street children in creating educational programs that work on a multiplicity of levels:

1. With public schools (improving the public schools),

2. With parents (involving parents in their children's education), and,
3. With other NGOs (working with other NGOs on improving civil, political, and human rights).

Such programs could include letter-writing campaigns to local senators, educational secretaries, and local politicians, demanding increased public funding of public schools, the creation of parent–teacher associations that can begin to influence local school performance and teacher accountability, and the creation of classes that teach parents and their children what their civil, economic, and political rights are in Brazil as provided for in the 1988 Brazilian Constitution. It is important to point out that school boards are a relatively new phenomenon in Brazil. The 1988 Constitution empowered states and local governments by delegating them more responsibility and eliminating the transfer of a large portion of educational funds to the capital, Brasilia. There have been many difficulties and pitfalls for local governments as they try to manage local educational budgets in effective ways. Hence, empowering communities to control local educational expenditures and raise educational quality is a major challenge, one in which NGOs need to play a part. In addition, local governments have been resistant to overcoming the long tradition of corporatism and practices of patronage (Birdsall and Sabot 1996:117–141).

As briefly touched upon in Chapter Five and Chapter Nine, politicization of individuals, regardless of age, can set in motion the social skills and tools necessary to push for civil rights. Indeed, children in the various projects discussed in this book were eager to begin programs that would empower them to write letters, gain access to local radio stations, and provide entry to local politicians as well as access to computer training. They took these ideas home with them, and their families and friends often discussed the need for such activism within their communities.

Differences Among NGOs

I found differences among NGO programs in Morro de Santana. Viva Crianças had fully absorbed imported constructions of childhood innocence and purity, such that its ideology conflicted with the daily reality of the children it sought to serve. The additional four NGOs studied and discussed had a vision of childhood more appropriate for the children of the poor, but one that nonetheless included notions of childhood innocence, purity, and protection. In general, I found the other NGOs to be more in touch with the realities of street children's lives. In the case of Bom Jesus, Irmã Helosia was able, in part, to discuss the everyday realities of poverty, racial discrimination, social class, and interpersonal conflicts between the children of the elite and the children of the poor.

Community Involvement: One of the most important differences between Viva Crianças and the other four NGOs was Viva Crianças's lack of involvement with the communities from which the children came. Unlike Viva Crianças, the other four NGOs were located in the communities and had frequent and ongoing contact with parents. These NGOs incorporated accountability and consequences for inappropriate behavior by children and youth in their programs. While interviewing parents of street children, individuals in the business community, and local teachers, I found that many people in Morro de Santana had never heard of Viva Crianças. In these same interviews, I found that the other NGOs discussed in this research were widely known. In addition, the other projects often described Viva Crianças as a project that did not wish to collaborate with other entities in Morro de Santana (even though this was expressly stated as part of their mission goals), and in this sense was most often perceived as isolationist. Hence, paradoxically, the programs of the more traditional NGOs were actually less arrogant, even though their ideological roots were similar to Viva Crianças's, because of the ideologies they did NOT choose. Viva Criança isolated itself from the communities it served, and tended to ignore the real-life circumstances of the children in their program. In this sense, the NGO with which I worked the longest and came to know the most intimately was the least functional because its ideological base was highly reified and rooted in extreme notions of childhood innocence, while at the same time embracing popular cultural notions about the poor. Their leftist views resulted in a program that was less community-based, less comprehensible by children, parents, and other NGOs, and more theoretical than more traditional NGOs that were working with Morro de Santana's street children. In short, Viva Crianças's ambitious and reified ideology isolated it from the children it sought to serve, as well as from other local NGOs. The most effective NGOs were those that were less theoretical and more concretely linked to the everyday realities of street children and their families.

NGOs and Ideologies: If NGOs are able to create flexible and permeable ideologies that allow for the real needs of street and working children and their families, the realities of Brazil's social inequalities can begin to be addressed. NGOs need to create programs that define who street children are, based on the ways in which the children describe themselves and their needs, and their families, friends, and communities. By working with street children in this way, NGOs can more realistically impact the inequities of Brazil's social service system.

Contribution to NGO Practice and Policy Regarding Street Children

After working in five NGOs, I began to question their actual non-profit status. Their financial records are not a matter of public record, and they seemed to lack standardized reporting protocols. According to Brazilianist Vera Sylvia Branco, there is a pressing need for a revision in the laws (established in 1935) that define the ways in which NGOs conceptualize the notion of "public interest," which entitles them to receive the status of a tax exempt organization.

> …[T]he law does not specify the extent of this concept, [hence] many private institutions with no real commitment to public service have benefited from tax privileges in the past…certification of tax exemptions should be transferred from the Ministry of Justice to the Brazilian IRS in order to eliminate political criteria…the 1988 Constitution leaves the door open to the traditional practices of clientelism and patronage unless present certification requirements [for NGO status] and procedures are radically modified…corporatist and clientelistic interests bravely resist necessary structural reforms…. (2000 paper presentation).

I am wholeheartedly in agreement with Branco in calling for more stringent certification requirements for NGOs, so that they must demonstrate through yearly accountability reports how, where, what, and when their funding is used.

NGOs must address the real-life needs of the children they seek to serve. In this sense, the most pressing social agendas in need of attention by NGOs that work with street youth include strong and forceful lobbying for decentralization, public funding for public schools, effective educational tutoring, computer literacy training for street youth, educational training in civil and political rights, and abandonment of folk or popular culture models for training in productive work skills.

Addressing Economic, Educational, and Racial Inequality

Economic Inequality: Addressing social inequality would, by its very nature, require a systems approach to addressing the daily life of those living in poverty. Alcoholism, racism, child abuse, illiteracy (principally parental), hunger, and lack of money all produce an environment that is lacking in support for street children. A systems approach for the allocation of funds assisting street children requires that a structural change occur within the political arena in Brazil. Currently, federal money does not exist for school supplies, reading materials, and uniforms, not to mention adequate training for teachers in the public education system. Hunger, illness, and exhaustion are constant deterrents to educational success. Street children and their families experience the effects of poverty on an ongoing basis.

Hence, NGOs need to address the entire family system in their programs. Assisting parents by providing adult education on supportive parenting (talking and discussing with their children instead of hitting and beating them) and alcoholism (AA and other alcohol programs were just getting started in Morro de Santana) and its effects on the life possibilities of both parents and children would go a long way in assisting street children to stay in school while they worked part-time. I agree with Brazilian social scientist Flávia Impelizieri who writes, "...[poor families] should...be assisted in order to overcome their most urgent material needs, especially those concerning their children's welfare, while receiving psychological counseling" (1995:115).

Educational Inequality: This research cannot address the multiplicity and complexity of the problems existing in the Brazilian educational system. Suffice it to say that NGOs can play a part in improving the public schools attended by street children by promoting parental and community involvement in public schools by *favelados*. In addition, I suggest that NGOs work at the state and federal level by advocating that public funds be funneled into public schools. In addition, NGOs need to work in tandem with parents and street children in order to raise teacher proficiency and expand curricula so that street children's needs are met. Finally, NGOs that work to build a higher quality of education for street children need to provide effective tutoring by well-qualified teachers in their programs. Parents of street children, who tend to be illiterate or functionally illiterate, need to be made aware of the importance of creating an atmosphere that supports study habits at home. Most importantly, NGOs need to provide effective tutoring in all subject areas.

I conclude that NGOs frequently reproduce the inadequate public education offered to poor children. It could be stated metaphorically that NGOs have been trying to rearrange the deck chairs on the *Titanic* without addressing the causes and effects of social inequality. The significance of this finding (the disconnect between NGO policy and education) is imperative for effective communication and cooperation between NGOs and public schools. These two entities need to at least recognize and to utilize each other in order to achieve the goal of improving the life possibilities of street children in Brazil. My research attempts to demonstrate that NGO practices will not be substantially more effective without becoming involved in the Brazilian educational system. While one of the main objectives of NGOs has been to champion the rights of street children and to alter the negative popular perceptions about them, they have failed to do so because they have not addressed the fundamental issues discussed here.

Racial Inequality: Since NGOs tend to focus on altering the sensibilities of street children and their families, there has traditionally been a disconnect between the social issues faced within the communities where they are located and the programs they offer. Throughout my fieldwork with street children, I became increasingly aware of the need for NGO programs to address what racism is and what it does to people. During my music class, my students and I gradually developed a dialogue about racism and its effects on their lives. The children frequently requested that we talk about why their dark skin color marginalized them. In addition, only one NGO program was willing to discuss the development of programs that explored the nature of race and racism in the lives of their clientele. Hence, I argue for an increased awareness among NGO directors and staff on race and racism in Brazil and its effects on street children and their families. Through an increased awareness of the effects of racism on street children, NGO directors and staff can begin to design programs that address racism.

Higher Education and Human and Civil Rights Programs: Research and teaching institutions in Brazil and abroad need to include the topics of racism, social inequality, and street youth on their agendas and in their curricula. Research findings need to be published in newspapers and magazines, and broadcast on radio and TV, in order to keep Brazilian society informed and aware. The Constitution of 1988 and the ECA of 1990 provide for the right to life, liberty, health care, education, economic liberty, and happiness for every citizen. With such documents in place, social action and activism can, over time and extended effort, succeed.

Educational curricula on race relations, African history, and black pride need to be part of the mandatory curriculum in public, private, and university settings. Higher education institutions (colleges and universities) are attended mainly by middle-and upper- class youth. Exposing youth from the middle and upper classes to civil rights issues is an important element in the campaign against racism and inequality in Brazil.

I argue that Brazil should consider the implementation of a quota system in their private primary, secondary, and higher educational systems. Such a quota system would reserve a certain percentage of allotted spaces for people of color living in poverty. A recent article in *The Chronicle of Higher Education* (Easterbrook 2002) discusses a quota system currently being considered in Brazil at the college and university level. Given the difficulties of clearly identifying Brazilian racism and the plethora of terms used to describe skin color, a model that links social class, poverty, and skin color may be the only way in which the cycle of inequality can be broken.

Computer Literacy and Exchange Programs

Computer Training: I found a serious lack of attention by NGOs to computer literacy for poor children. NGOs could, through federal funding and international funding, provide access to computers, computer literacy training, and use of the Internet. Computers are a powerful organizational tool that, when used in conjunction with basic educational skills such as literacy, writing, and computing, can potentially lift poor children into higher reading levels, and hence, into better income-earning positions. Access to technology and training in computer literacy will help to improve poor children's life possibilities. I suggest that public schools expand their curricula to include technical training for poor children and youth to develop marketable skills that include computer literacy. Currently, public schools in Minas Gerais do not provide access to computers or computer literacy. Lack of funding from the federal government is, in part, responsible for the absence of computers in public schools. However, public schools can and do work with the business community, providing an alternative to the long and often futile process of requesting funds from the federal government. A good example of an existing program in the business community is Task Brazil, an organization that seeks to provide street kids the opportunity to learn vocational skills by providing them with computer training, and the CEARA Urban Development and Water Resource Management Project titled ABC, funded by the World Bank.

> The goals of ABC are to improve the living standards of poor children and adolescents between the ages of seven and seventeen, furnishing through professional training (in basic computing, auto mechanics, electrical engineering, culinary arts and other skills) and development activities (sports and cultural events) the tools and opportunity to escape extreme poverty. (http://www.worldbank.org/education/economicsed/finance/demand/case/ceara/ceara_index.htm)

One final example is the City of Knowledge project, directed and run by São Paulo University's Institute for Advanced Studies and the Education Faculty Foundation. This project focuses primarily on literacy, education, and the development of computer skills. The City of Knowledge is backed by several media corporations that include the daily newspaper firms of *Folha de São Paulo* and *O Estado de São Paulo*, and by such corporations as IBM, *Banco Santander*, and the Boston Bank. It is the expansion of the Internet in Brazil that is beginning to fuel such programs along with a growing awareness within the business community that the wealthy must participate in assisting the poor. Gilson Schwartz (2013) from the University of São Paulo's Institute of Advanced Studies states,

> Millions of people, many of them wealthy, have realized that poverty can lead to drug dealing that could threaten their own children... Many business people now understand that supporting professional training programmes is the way to get children off the street, where they might otherwise fall into a life of crime that could threaten their businesses. (Brener, Jayme http://www.unesco.org/courier/2001_06/uk/doss23.htm or http://www.gamesforchange.org/festival2013/speakers/ilson-schwartz/)

Exchange Programs: Additional suggestions for improving the life possibilities of street children include funding of exchange programs for poor children to spend time in English-and Spanish-speaking countries. While this suggestion may seem idealistic or perhaps surreal, there is a growing movement, tentative as it may be, to bring the opportunity for foreign educational exchange to poor youth. A good example of such a program by a private citizen in the US is that of Greg Kiddy, the husband of history professor Dr. Betsy Kiddy. Mr. Kiddy has created a non-profit organization designed to fund street youth in Brazil to come to the US for a six-month period. During this time the youth would live with an American family, attend language school, and receive intensive tutoring in basic academic subjects and computer training. Upon return to Brazil, assistance is provided to readapt and integrate into the marketplace.

English and Spanish skills vastly improve the economic upward mobility of people living in poverty. With Brazil as a pivotal member of Mercosur, Spanish and English language skills will become increasingly important in the 21st century. Funded international exchange programs would open educational doors for street youth previously unavailable to them.

Right to Work

Job Training and Education: My research found that the vast majority of street children interviewed wanted the right to work *and* go to school. Impelizieri found that older teenage street youth in Rio who had become autonomous would not return home even if threatened with placement in an institution. Instead, they "repeatedly expressed during…interviews their wish to become self-supporting, working adults" (Impelizieri 1995:115; Veloso 2012:665). I found that even young street children have the same desire to work and be an active participant in their families' survival. Hence, job-training programs that work in tandem with local businesses need to expand in Morro de Santana in particular, and in Brazil in general. Such programs must include offering opportunities to poor youth by including them in training programs that prepare them for work in banks (such programs existed in Morro de Santana, training boys to be "boy Fridays," with the potential for higher-paid positions, such as bank clerks and tellers), local businesses, teachers' aids, assistants in city government work, and more.

Corporatism and Clientelism: However, none of these suggestions will have much impact if Brazil's political culture of clientelism, state centralism, and corporatism is not addressed and changed. As Branco states,

> American society has developed a political culture deeply rooted in community and voluntary action throughout its history. In contrast, Brazilian society has

had its political culture impregnated by state centralism, patronage (clientelism) and, corporatism. More than three hundred years of our history can be resumed in three words: plantation, monoculture, and slavery (2000 paper presentation).

Brazilian social worker and professor Vincente de Paula Faleiros notes that in Brazil, citizenship and state of law are often in conflict, leading to the

> …law of the powerful, with no respect for rights, where private groups act in their own self-interest. Such groups replace the state-of-law culture with "regulation" stemming from the private sphere. The privatization of ideology preached by liberals is taken to its logical extreme when the public order is violently controlled by private interests. Legitimate violence—by definition the role of the state—is replaced by illegitimate violence (de Paula Faleiros 1994:179).

Faleiros suggests that the murder and disappearance of street children is rooted in Brazil's history of social, political, and racial inequality, and hence linked to relations of power that go beyond the state of law and beyond the constitution. Such relations of power are part of Brazil's history of economic and political clientelism (de Paula Faleiros 1994). NGOs can, through educational programs like those suggested herein, along with their clientele (street children and their parents) put pressure on the federal government, for example, to pay attention to the resolution to investigate the murder and extermination of street children during a special Congressional Investigation Committee of 1992.

Discussion of Areas for Further Research

The World Bank (2000) published the following primary objectives for changing Brazil's history of social and racial inequality:

1. Equalizing opportunities for access to education of adequate quality for Afro-Brazilians in order to break the intergenerational trap of low education that hinders their socio-economic mobility.
2. Improving primary level education for Afro-Brazilians.
3. Raising awareness, enacting and enforcing laws against race discrimination in the labor market in order to enhance social equity in Brazil.
4. Providing cash incentives to poor families in order to keep Afro-Brazilian children in school.
5. Promoting dialogue and reflection among government officials and other social actors in Brazil on how the social exclusion of Afro-Brazilians compromises Brazil's development prospects and social equity.

These findings correspond, in large measure, to my research findings on racial inequality in Morro de Santana. I suggest that further research needs to done in the area of Brazilian NGO certification and accountability. In addition, national and international organizations that fund NGOs may be influencing the types of programs that NGOs develop. Such influences may be part of the problem NGOs face in creating effective programs, especially in the areas of civil rights. I suggest that this is an area that needs in-depth research. Findings should be widely published in Brazil in order to assist NGOs to effectively deal with the pressing issues of racism, poverty, hunger, human rights violations, and political corruption.

Finally, NGOs in Morro de Santana need to be more involved in the communities they serve. Community solidarity was not a common occurrence in the *favelas* of Morro de Santana, and this is an area where NGOs could effectively work to improve the quality of community life. Indeed, the level of poverty is such that Foster's notion of "limited good," as opposed to Janice Perlman's organized social support networks, discussed in Chapter Five, is applicable here. Solidarity needs to be addressed through a consensus within each *favela* that improvement must be forthcoming, and must be so as a basic civil right. Here, NGOs can work to educate *favelados* on their civil, economic, health, and educational rights. One effective avenue toward social change is to develop education programs for children and their parents in dealing with local, on-the-ground issues such as the construction of sewage systems, running water, and medical assistance, as well as advocacy for parental involvement in public school improvement. Many of my informants and their families were ignorant of their basic rights as Brazilian citizens. Letter-writing campaigns to local newspapers, public demonstrations, and mass withholding of votes for political candidates could be organized by projects and include children and their parents in social and political action for change, while simultaneously teaching basic literacy and organizational and thinking skills. Effectiveness could be increased through the use of e-mail, the internet, and web pages, all of which could easily be created and managed by the youth in the various projects they attend. Although this idea may seem utopian, it is by no means so. Street youth consistently discussed the need for computer training, something they were not likely to be able to pay for, in order to help them enter the job market in the future. Indeed, the two most frequently stated needs of street children were good educational tutoring in computer training and basic math, reading, and writing.

Vera Sylvia Branco points out that common, everyday people in Brazil are beginning to demand their rights instead of the favors of clientelism, requesting action instead of good intentions, and accountability instead of excuses (Branco 2000). Hosana Heringer quotes Fernando Gabeira in her doctoral dissertation regarding the extermination of children and adolescents in Brazil noting that; "The image of children wrapped in grey blankets, participating in the burial of their street companions, has become a symbol of an historic moment in the history of Brazil" (Heringer 1997:271). This quote embodies the urgency that NGOs face in addressing the most pressing social issues experienced by street children in Brazil.

> NGOs went through an expansion and consolidation phase between the end of the 80s and the early 90s and in recent years have been in crisis. Many NGOs have profoundly questioned their institutional mission and political role in Brazilian society as a result of a decline in international funding that is linked to the government's incorporation of proposals and projects that used to be run by the NGOs. Recent national and international circumstances have obliged NGOs to adapt to new realities and challenges and take action through innovative strategies. (Heringer 1997:271).

Brazilian NGOs need to reinvent themselves and their mission in order to play a significant role in improving the lives of the growing number of Brazil's urban poor.

Conclusion

This research has provided new insights into the realities of life for Brazilian street children in Morro de Santana, including the daily experiences of poverty and racism, as well as economic and educational inequality. I have shown how NGOs that are set up to address these many problems are only partially successful in their efforts. One of the principal reasons for this limited success is their incorporation of elite social conceptions of childhood, which have little relationship to or utility for the realities of these street children. Rather than enjoying a protracted and idyllic childhood, they must daily address the necessity of making contributions to their families' subsistence needs, as well as often caring for siblings and even parents. Thus, for the street children, there is a strong value on being able to work and to earn an income. Most of the NGOs investigated in this study failed to recognize these realities, and thus their programs of service to these children contributed little in the way of long-term practical skills. Taking my argument further, Brazilian anthropologist Leticia Veloso argues that Brazil's Child and Adolescent Statute of 1990 (a critical document used by NGOs) unintentionally reproduces existing inequalities while seeking universalist ideals of equal citizenship for all children. Street children and children of the middle and upper classes are conflated such that social, economic, and ethic discrepancies are ignored. Veloso argues that "…this universal ideal of rights-bearing childhood is being imposed upon a profoundly unequal, exclusionary, racialized, and class-stratified social world" (Veloso 2008:48).

I have made suggestions for improving the programs offered by the NGOs as well as modifications in the public educational system that would particularly benefit these children. Perhaps most importantly, I have shown how these children are active social agents, very much in command of their own lives and vigorously involved in constructing their own social identities. My work is, however, but a first step, and as I have pointed out, there remains a great deal more research to be done on these questions. It is my hope that both Brazilian and North American scholars will be inspired by my work to investigate further, while those involved in the practical provision of educational, social, and economic services will find useful ideas for improving their programs. More permanent solutions to poverty, racism, and educational inequality in Brazil are beyond the scope of this research. However, I have stressed the need to empower street youth in ways that will make it possible for *them* to improve *their* own lives and the lives of their families through individual agency and community activism.

Endnotes

1. See the article *Nonprofit Sector in Brazil* by Vera Sylvia Branco, University of Texas at Austin, Institute of Latin American Studies.
2. Ariès' work has been criticized for being Eurocentric in terms of juxtaposing notions of Western European historical processes that developed childhoods of protected, protracted worlds of innocence set apart from the world of adults. I recommend Suzanne Shanahan's "The Sociological Ambivalence Toward Childhood" in the 2007 Annual Review of Sociology. Shanahan's article provides a good overview of recent literature on constructionist perspectives of childhood within a global perspective.
3. The term "Afro-Brazilian" is used throughout this book to denote street children of various degrees of darker skin color. I have chosen to align myself with contemporary Afro-Brazilians, the street children in my sample, and with social scientists who declare that race and racism play a key role in Brazil's historical economic and social inequality. Rebecca Reichmann points out that the color line,

as perceived in Brazil, is one of the greatest areas of contention that continues to divide those "...who believe that Brazil is a racial democracy from those who perceive discrimination based on color" (1999:7). Reichmann points out that (skin) color in Brazil is THE dominant category for social classification of individuals, while one's racial or biological ancestry are underemphasized by elites (1999:7). Such a fluid color line is a product of miscegenation that describes skin colors from darkest to lightest. Hence, the darker the skin color, the more stigmatized the individual.

Throughout its history, Brazil has adopted several national discourses on race. During the late 1800s. abolitionists embraced the notion of miscegenation and the mixture and fusing of races. During the 1920s, scientific notions about race that validated racism were embraced and the official doctrine became one of "whitening" through encouraging immigration of European immigrants and prohibiting immigration of darker-skinned races. Brazilian anthropologist Gilberto Freyre, in later decades, developed the notion that Brazil's racial democracy was developing a "meta-race" that would in the end unify the Brazilian people into a new racial identity (Reichmann 1999:8). During the 1950s, UNESCO sponsored a series of studies on race in Brazil. Anthropologist Marvin Harris participated in the UNESCO study and found that the plethora of terms used to define color in Brazil was in actuality linguistic markers that avoided the identification of a person's skin color. Since Brazil has never legally enforced racial segregation policies, civil rights movements based on the color of a person's skin have never occurred. Indeed, dark-skinned people at times do move vertically upward in social status dependent on their income. Hence, the expression "money whitens" is a common one in Brazil. The wealthier a person becomes, the whiter they become; however, The 2000 Global Justice Center reported that "Of the 146 million inhabitants [of Brazil] in the 1991 Census, approximately 51%

declared themselves to be white and 5% black, whereas 42% considered themselves brown. If we consider that most people designated as 'brown' have black African blood, Brazil's black population ranks second only to that of Nigeria." Brazilians of color (*preto, pardo, moreno*) do not proportionally share in Brazil's wealth. The 2000 Global Justice Center report stated that "According to the 1990 Census, whites earned 2.12 times the average salary for *pardos* (browns) and 2.41 times more than *pretos* (blacks). That same census indicated that while 18.9 percent of whites had eleven or more years of schooling, only 6.0 percent of blacks (*pretos*) had reached this level" (http://www.global.org.br/english/annual_report_documents/annual_report_inequality.htm). In 1995, one of Brazil's leading survey organizations, the *Datafolha* found that 89% of respondents to a survey on racial discrimination in Brazil stated that whites were prejudiced against blacks (*Sabia como É a Escala. Folha de São Paulo*. June 25, 1995). In 1999, The United Nations Development Program ranked Brazil 74th among 174 nations based on income per capita, literacy, and education level. This ranking places Brazil in the mid-range for development. However, if only the black population was counted and analyzed, it would put Brazil 108th among 174 nations. If the white population was counted and analyzed alone, it would put Brazil in 49th place among 174 nations. This analysis would place the Afro-Brazilian population lower than such African nations as Algeria and South Africa (Federation of Agencies for Social Assistance and Education (*Justiça Global,* Human Rights in Brazil. *Federação de Órgãos para Assistência Social e Educativa, or FASE).*

In this book, racism in Brazil is based on current research data by Brazilian researchers whose social inequality indexes are cited herein. In addition, racism as defined here, is based on my fieldwork with street children who experienced frequent discrimination based on the color of their skin as well as their poverty. It was their stories about racism that informed this research.

4. Cunningham (1991) points out that the climbing boys, who were made black by the soot of chimneys, were the most visible and pitiful of England's working children. They were easily recognizable on the streets of towns and cities. Through their visibility, they brought public attention to their plight, and to their potential future. "Climbing boys were regarded as villains ripening for the gallows rather than as objects of compassion"(Cunningham 1991:53). But for some in the upper classes, the climbing boys' plight became a popular sentimental distraction and they attempted to assuage the suffering of these children with yearly dinners and festivals. Climbing boys became central players in May Day celebrations, traditionally the province of the Milk Maids, who represented purity and fecundity.

5. See "Orphans and the Transition from Slave to Free Labor in Northeast Brazil: The Case of Campina Grande, 1850–1888" in the *Journal of Social History*, Vol 27, N. 3, 499–515 for a clear description of the Brazilian legal codes of inheritance and property rights as related to children with legitimate parentage, and the treatment of children who were considered orphaned and property-less. See also, "Slavery and Social Life: Attempts to Reduce Free People to Slavery in the Sertão Mineiro, Brazil 1850–1871" in *Journal of Latin American Studies*, Vol 26, Part 3, October 1994, 597–619, authored by Judy Bieber Freitas, assistant professor of history, University of New Mexico, Albuquerque.

6. The development model adopted by the Vargas regime and its followers up through the 1980s was statist. It was only in the 1990s that Brazil adopted a neo-liberal globalistic model of development with massive capital outflows. The worst period of international debt formation in Brazilian history occurred during the military dictatorship and to some extent during the Kubitschek government, when the development model was centralistic and statist.

7. The word *favela* is often used in Morro de Santana synonymously with *barrio* and *periferia*. *Barrio* in its most accurate sense means neighborhood, while *periferia* signifies the outlying areas of the city where *favelas* have sprung up.
8. See David Baronov's *The Abolition of Slavery in Brazil: The "Liberation" of Africans Through the Emancipation of Capital*, 2000. London: Greenwood Press, 117–143. Baronov puts the figure of "kidnapped" Africans for slavery within the Americas at 10–15 million over a 400-year period, with 1.5 to 2 million perishing in the transatlantic voyage. According to Baronov, 80 percent of the slave population entered the Americas during the 18th and early 19th centuries. Brazil and Spanish America absorbed two thirds of all slaves brought to the Americas. By the end of slavery, Brazil had imported 3.6 million Africans as slaves.
9. The largest group of immigrants came from Italy, and the second largest group came from Portugal and then Spain. See *Brazil: Five Centuries of Change*, Thomas Skidmore, 1999, New York: Oxford University Press, 71–73.
10. Thomas Skidmore, in *Black into White: Race and Nationality in Brazilian Thought* (1993) richly documents the degree to which Brazilian immigration policy between the years of 1887 and 1914 prohibited the entrance of Japanese and African immigrants as well as anyone deemed to be a beggar or an indigent. Creating a new national image based on the superiority of the Western European Anglo-Saxon race became a prominent focus for the Brazilian government. See pages 124–144.
11. If the slave owner did not want to continue using the services of the child, the government would pay a fee to the slave owner. However, there was not enough money to pay for these children—so only 118 out of 400,000 slave children had been given to the government (Del Priore 1991; Conrad 1984, 341–350).

12. Before the abolition of slavery (May 13, 1888), the black labor force was excluded in large part from paid labor. Afro-Brazilians were referred to as *desocupado*. A statistical survey in 1882 of the provinces of São Paulo, Minas Gerais, Bahia, Pernambuco, Cerará, and Rio de Janeiro demonstrated the demographic breakdown of working people: Free Workers (1,433,170), Slave Workers (656,540), *Desocupados* (Idle Workers—freed black slaves) (2,822,583). See *Slavery and Beyond: The African Impact on Latin America and the Caribbean*. Edited by Darién J. Davis, 1995: 246.
13. In Morro de Santana, households headed by single women were common. I estimate that close to 40 percent of the families living in the favelas were composed of single women raising several children. My estimate is based on the ten informal interviews I collected from parents of children in projects in Morro de Santana where four out of ten were single women with children.
14. See pages 38–77 in Thomas Skidmore, *Black into White: Race and Nationality in Brazilian Thought* for a comprehensive discussion of race in Brazil in the late 1800s. Skidmore discusses Brazil's complex system of racial classification based on phenotypical characteristics. The middle category (between white and black) for race has always been the mulato in Brazil, where hair texture, dress, and undertones and degree of darkness of skin color all play a part in categorizing where a person is within the social structure. As Skidmore points out, the degree to which a person looked European and not African determined in large measure the social class of the person. "The limits of his mobility depended upon his exact appearance. The more 'Negroid', the less mobile and the degree of cultural 'whiteness' (education, manners, wealth) he was able to attain" (Skidmore 1993:40).
15. I have included here an article published June 21, 2002 by Kevin Hall, Free Press foreign correspondent for the *Detroit Free Press* in order to provide a clear description of the current climate of Brazilian thinking on race, racism, and the legacy of slavery that

continues to affect Afro-Brazilians today. (http://www.freep.com/news/nw/ebrazil21_20020621.htm , or http://www.highbeam.com/doc/1G1-86535936.html).

MAINARTE, Brazil—Brazil is promising an aggressive affirmative action program for tens of millions of descendants of African slaves in an effort to make amends for the gross racial inequality that persists 114 years after emancipation. Twenty percent of all federal government jobs would be reserved for Afro-Brazilians in the nation now home to the world's largest black population outside of Africa. President Fernando Henrique Cardoso announced outlines of the program in May, with details to follow in July. Though Brazil has little overt racism, Afro-Brazilians lag behind their white peers in income, education and almost all social indicators. Urban Afro-Brazilians are more likely to be victims of police brutality, are more frequently incarcerated and are more likely to be killed by police. "Just as South Africa had racial apartheid, Brazil has social apartheid," Congressman Aloizio Mercadante, a leading member of the leftist Workers' Party in Brazil, said of the country's gaping racial divide. Political activists are suspicious about motives for the program, coming just five months before a presidential election. But it has also created a sense of optimism and has yet to spawn any white backlash. "It's a huge stimulus, because a black today will feel motivated to study, to participate. If he wants to be a lawyer, he can study because he knows he will now have a number" of positions reserved for Afro-Brazilians, said Adalgimar Gomes Goncalves, an aspiring novelist and schoolteacher in the small town of Mainarte in Minas Gerais. The state has one of the largest black populations in Brazil because gold-hungry Portuguese conquerors brought slaves there about 350 years ago. In the nearby colonial-era city of Mariana, Jesus Antonio de Oliveira Lino, a dark-skinned university student studying history, hoped proposed racial quotas would fuel a growing black-awareness movement. "The history of the United States is very different from here in Brazil," said Oliveira Lino. "African Americans were able to organize much more quickly and actively. In Brazil this process is just beginning." Between 1532 and 1850, an estimated 3.6 million slaves were brought to Brazil, the world's leading recipient of slaves. Today, Afro-Brazilians comprise an estimated 45 percent of Brazil's population of 173 million. Yet there are few black politicians of national stature and only a handful of powerful black businessmen or sports figures. Soccer legend Pele, whose face appears on every imaginable form of advertising, remains an exception to the rule. On the 2000 census forms, where individuals note their skin color, only 6.2 percent identified themselves as preto, or black. The other 39 percent are mostly mixed-race Afro-Brazilians who historically have cited dozens of different tones in describing their skin color. To qualify for consideration under the quotas, Brazilians will not be asked to describe their skin color but whether they are Afro-Brazilian. "It's pretty easy to know who is black in Brazilian society, that's not really a problem. The police seem to know that well," said Marcos Pinta Gama, the chief adviser to Brazil's human rights secretariat, which is overseeing implementation of the federal government's efforts to promote racial diversity. In the countryside, many descendants of Africans say they think they aren't much better off than back in the slave days. "Everybody treats us badly. They still think we still are slaves," said Jose Celso Martins, a dark-skinned ranch hand in Mainarte, a town of about 500. Martins said ranch owners pay him just $2 a day, and work him from 5 a.m. until 7 p.m. If he complains, he goes hungry." What can we do about it? "he asked. Gama Pinta, the government's human rights adviser, hoped the affirmative action effort would be copied by Brazilian and foreign businesses. "This is a concrete measure that can be followed not only in the public sector but also in the private sector," he said. US automaker Ford Motor Co. is one of the only foreign companies with a publicly announced affirmative action program in Brazil. Prominent Afro-Brazilian leaders complain the program has taken too long to gain flight. "If we had initiated affirmative action during Fernando Henrique Cardoso's first term, we would have a very different Brazil today, "said Benedita da Silva, who rose from the slums to this year become the governor of the state of Rio de Janeiro and first black governor in modern Brazil. Afro-Brazilians should not view affirmative action as a blessing from the government but "a right that is ours, "said the influential da Silva. Ana Liviar dos Santos, an activist who leads boycotts of stores that don't hire Afro-Brazilians, has called for racial quotas of more than 40 percent. "The 20 percent that the government has set aside attracts attention because it is so very little," he said. (Copyright 2002 *Detroit Free Press*).

16. See Clifford Geertz' discussion on ethnographic authority in *The Predicament of Culture: Twentieth Century Ethnography*. Cambridge, MA: Harvard University Press, 1988, 21–54.

17. Categorizing people into classes based on occupation and/or profession is complex and I do so here only as a way to distinguish the acquisition of capital among individuals who constitute larger groups often referred to as social classes, frequently categorized by race, gender, age, and so forth. See *Distinction: A Social Critique of the Judgement of Taste* by Pierre Bourdieu, 1984, especially pages 102–103.

18. The child Labour (Prohibition and Regulation) Act of 1986 designated a child as "a person who has not completed their fourteenth year of age." It is supposed to regulate the hours and conditions of some child workers as well as prohibiting the use of child labor in certain enumerated hazardous industries. However, there is no universal prohibition on the use of child labor, nor is there any universal minimum age set for child workers. The Bonded Labour System (Abolition) Act of 1976 is a very important act within the body of child labor rights laws. This act strictly outlaws all forms of debt bondage and forced labor of children. Such current legal safeguards mean little, however,

without the political will of countries to implement them (*The Small Hands of Slavery: Bonded Child Labor in India*, Human Rights Watch Publications, ISBN 1-56432-172-X, September 1996 < http://www.hrw.org/reports/1996/India3.htm>). In addition, if economic inequality in underdeveloped and developing countries continues to perpetuate social, racial, and economic inequalities, child labor will continue to grow with parents choosing to hide the economic contributions of their children.

19. Perlman surveyed 600 favelados in Rio de Janeiro, and found that 43 percent declared that "most" of their friends could be counted on for support and 70 percent stated that mutual help support systems were as great as or greater than in the rural areas. See "Social, Cultural, and Economic Marginality," specifically Table 18, page 134, *in The Myth of Marginality: Urban Poverty and Politics in Rio de Janeiro* (1976). Recently, Janice Perlman's work on megacities seems to substantiate my findings in Morro de Santana (http://www.megacitiesproject.org/perlman.asp). Perlman distinguishes between capital cities, world/global cities, and megacities. She defines capital cities as the administrative and political capitals of non-states, while world/global cities are financial capitals that command and control information, labor, and finances. Finally megacities "…may be capital cities and they may be global cities, but, primarily, they are the capitals of human beings. They're the places where people have decided to live—and voted with their feet—to come and settle. A megacity is defined less by its position in the global economy or its relationship to a nation-state, than by the number of people who live there, and consequently by their density, proximity, and heterogeneity" (www.megacitiesproject.org/interview). While Morro de Santana is not a megacity neither does it fall into Perlman's other categories. However, Perlman points out that many communities, regardless of size, often lack linkages between organizations and residents. This is indeed what I discovered in Morro de Santana, where *favela* residents were aware of their local

favela organization and citizen council, but lacked confidence in their ability to effectively work for improvements within their *favela*. Local leaders within *favela* organizations were not "politicized" and hence were not effective "activists." Rather, such leaders were viewed as corrupt politicians. In an interview with Paul Malamud from USIA, Perlman stated: "We need to move from a deficit-based approach to an asset-based one, analyzing of the potential to take advantage of the creativity of the people. The former approach only creates a kind of paralyzing despair and despondency rather than an energizing sense of hope." Studies on poor neighborhoods in the US also find discrepancies between the creation of helping networks. Carole Stack in *All Our Kin* found that in order to develop helping networks in poor communities, people needed to trust one another. Indeed, Stack developed the notion of non-kin or fictive-kin relations among non-related poor families that copied relations between extended family networks among sanguine family members. My analysis of the non-existence of *favela* networks in Morro de Santana is not based the fact that I didn't look for creative asset-based behaviors; I simply did not find them.

20. See Thomas Skidmore's *Brazil: Five Centuries of Change* for a thorough discussion of over 500 years of development, political instability, military dictatorships, and horrific human rights and environmental abuses. In addition, Eileen Stillwaggon's book *Stunted Lives, Stagnant Economies: Poverty, Disease, and Underdevelopment* discusses the living conditions of the poor in Latin America. Debt crisis and structural adjustment policies are discussed, demonstrating how difficult it is for the poor to escape a fate of illness and poverty (Skidmore 1999; Stillwaggon 1998).

21. Pierre Bourdieu has described the accumulation of symbolic capital as a set of social rituals or as an "inevitable sequence of miraculous intellectual acts..." that lead to the conversion of social acts into a

form of symbolic capital. See the preface to the *Logic of Practice*, page 16, and Chapter Seven, 112–121 (1980:16).

22. Rebecca Reichmann in *Race in Contemporary Brazil: From Indifference to Inequality* (1999) discusses patron–client relations as related to female domestic servants in Brazil. Poor women of color have been able to achieve some upward mobility due to the generosity of their *patroas*. See pages 234 through 249.

23. See *Opportunity Foregone: Education in Brazil* by Nancy Birdsall and Richard Sabot, eds. 1996, Published by the Inter-American Development Bank and Distributed by The John Hopkins University Press for a good discussion on Brazil's failing educational system. In addition, *Social Change in Brazil: 1945–1985 The Incomplete Transition* (1989), Edmar L. Bacha and Herbert Klein, Eds., has a good chapter on education in Brazil, 263–309.

24. *The Estatuto da Criança e do Adolescente* was created on July 13, 1991 and nationally enforced on October 14, 1991. The Statute of Children and Adolescents (*Estatuto da Criança e do Adolescente, ECA* (redefined children as citizens endowed with rights: physical, intellectual, emotional, social, and cultural development). The ECA abolished the former Minors' Code (*Código de Menores* of 1970), which conceptualized children and adolescents (particularly darker-skinned poor children) as "minors" subject to legal and punitive intervention by targeting children in "irregular situations" (abandoned children, street children, and poor children on the streets in general). See "Children in Brazil: Legislation and Citizenship, in Children" in *Brazil Today: A Challenge for the Third Millennium. Rio de Janeiro*: Editora Universitária úrsul, 105–115. Irene Rizzini, ed. 1991(b).

25. See Chapter 16 in *Opportunity Foregone: Education in Brazil* by Nancy Birdsall and Richard H. Sabot for a discussion of the educational opportunities offered to children in private schools in Brazil.

26. January 1, 1995 was the beginning of a dynamic economic zone between Brazil, Argentina, Uruguay, and Paraguay. Mercosur, The

Common Market of the South, is an economic bloc in existence since January, 1995 uniting Brazil, Argentina, Uruguay, and Paraguay.

27. Again, I need to restate that I refer to Brazilian street youth as Afro-Brazilians because most street youth are children of darker skin coloring. Street children are most often offspring of a black (ancestors of African slaves) and mulato union, and are most often referred to as *cablocos, mulatos escuros,* and *preto*s (Stephens 1999:555 and 561). In addition, I refer to street youth as Afro-Brazilians in deference to the street youth I knew who took pride in their black heritage.

28. In 1997 an Indigenous man from the Pataxó Ha-Ha-Hae tribe was burned to death as he slept on a bench at a bus stop in São Paulo. He had arrived in the city that day and registered at a hostel. He was in São Paulo to attend a convention about Indigenous rights and had returned to the hostel past eleven o'clock, and found that's when the doors are locked. Not knowing the city, he decided to sleep on a bench under the shelter of a bus stop. Several boys, driving their father's expensive car, saw him. They bought a bottle of alcohol and returned to the bus stop where they threw the alcohol on him and set him on fire. They left him there burning. He died the following day with over 90 percent of his body covered in third-degree burns. The upper-class youth were not sent to jail, and they described their act as doing the job of a good citizen. They were cleaning up the city by burning human trash. See Greenleft Weekly1997 (https://www.greenleft.org.au/node/13546)

GLOSSARY
BRAZILIAN PORTUGUESE TERMS

Associação de Pais e Amigos dos Excepcionais (APAE): The Association of Parents and Friends of Those With Disabilities.

Acidrola: A fruit, similar to rose hips, rich in vitamin C.

Aulas Práticas: Practical classes or individual classroom tutoring.

Bairro: In Morro de Santana, informants used the term to refer to Neighborhood and *Favela*.

Basílica São Geraldo: Basilica Saint Gerald.

Boa Patroa: A good boss, usually used by a female domestic servant (maid) to describe the woman of the house who is her boss.

Bom Jesus: Good Jesus.

Bonita de Mais: Really pretty.

Bornal de Jogos: Bag of Games. A project developed by Viva Crianças to develop board games and take them into the public schools, training the teachers how to use play as a learning tool.
Brancos: Whites.

Brincar e Cultura Popular: To play and popular culture.

Brinquedoteca: Play environment for children that is 'scientifically' prepared.

Cabide emprego: Hanging occupation or part-time work that is uncertain in duration.

Caboclinhos: Little Brazilian "half-breed" of white and Indian mix. A copper colored person of both Indian and Portuguese mixture who is acculturated.

Cafuzo: Offspring of a black and a *mulato*, or the offspring of a black and an Indian. A very dark-skinned, nearly black mulatto.

Capoeria: An Afro-Brazilian martial art Form.

Caixa Económica Federal: Federal Economic Bank.

Centro Nacional de Preferência Cultural: The National Center of Cultural Choice or Preference.

Centro Social Achilles Diniz Couto: Social Center *Archilles Diniz Couto.*

Cesta de alimentação: Basket of food given to poor people by churches, the city, and NGOs.

Cidadania Opção de Vida (COV): Citizens for Life Options (COV).

Comitê: The Committee (Board of Directors for COV).

Comitê de Cidadania Contra a Miseria e a Fome: Citizens Committee Against Misery and Hunger.

Cozinha: Kitchen.

Congos: Black people who have come to Brazil from the Congo, Africa.

Conselho Municipal de Assistência Social de Morro de Santana, Controle Social e Participação Popular: Municipal Council for Social Assistance in Morro de Santana, Popular Social Control and Participation.

Criança de rua: A Street child or children of the streets.

Curumim: No direct translation. Name of an NGO in Morro de Santana working with street children.

Dedos de Gente: Fingers of the People.

Deficiêntes: Term used in Brazilian Portuguese to refer to people with either physical or mental disabilities.

Delegacia de Mulheres: Delegation for Women.

Derrame: Hemorrhage.

Derrame cerebral: Cerebral brain hemorrhage.

Desesperado: A desperate person, one who has lost hope.

Desocupado: An unemployed person who was idle and irresponsible.

Direitora: Director.

O Dia do Índio: Day of the Indian.

Dona: Owner of a business or mistress of a house.

Entidade civil sem fins lucrativos, de caráter beneficente, com personalidade jurídica própria, de duração por prazo indeterminad: A civil non-profit entity of a beneficent character with individual judicial personality with a duration of indeterminate span.

Escola: School.

Esmola: Charity or hand-outs.

Estatuto da Criança e do Adolescente: The Child and Adolescent Statute (ECA) of 1990.

Faculdade: A school within a university or a college. Also used to refer to the faculty within a university or college.

Faculdade de Ciências Humanas: The department of Human Sciences within a college.

Farinha: Flour made from manioc root.

Farofa: Flour made from manioc or cassava root.

Favela: Slum, shantytown, or ghetto.

Favelado: A resident of the *favela*.

Faxina: Cleaning woman.

Fermento: A leaven or yeast product used in cooking bread or baked goods.

Ficha: An index card or record book, or a certification paper from a doctor or nurse in a clinic.

Filho de Puta: Child of a whore.

Folclore: Roteiro de Pesquisa: Folklore: Summary of Research.

Folio de Morro de Santana: Pages of Morro de Santana (the name of a local newspaper in Morro de Santana).

Foz do Córrego: Mouth of the stream, river, or narrow mountain pass.

Fubar: Mandioca flour.

FUNABEM: *Fundação Nacional do Bem-Estar do Menor* (National Foundation for the Well-being of Minors).

Futebol: Soccer.

Grande: Large, big.

Grupo de Evangelização: The Evangelical Group.

Groupo de fraternidade Inrmão Luizinho: The Fraternity Group of Brother Luizinho.

Horta: Vegetable Garden.

Incomoda: Disturbing or emotionally painful.

INPS (Instituto Nacional de Presiência Social): A governmental low quality health care system, similar to medicare in the US.

Intercâmbio Entre Brinquedotecas: Exchange between play spaces. Brinquedoteca refers to a scientifically prepared play space or area for children where they learn through playing.

Irmã: Sister, as in a sibling or a nun in the Catholic Church.

Ladrão: A robber or thief.

Madrasta: Stepmother.

Mandioca: Manioc or cassava root.

Machucar: To hurt or harm someone physically or verbally.

Maizena: Corn starch.

Mendigo: Begger.

Meninos: Boys.

Minino-Problema: Problem boy.

Ministério: Ministry

Muito Pesado: Very Heavy, either physically or emotionally.

Moçambiques: A term that refers to black people, usually slaves, from Mozambique, Africa (Stephens 1999:612).

Moleque: Street kid. This word is used to refer to street children. The word refers to a "young black, usually a slave" (Stephens 1999:613). The term is also used to refer to any street kid regardless of skin color.

Moreno/a: A dark-complexioned (brown skinned) person.

Mulato/a: A person who has dark skin color. An offspring of a black and white union. Also used to describe the offspring of a black and white union that produces a person with "...pretty features and clear complexion, but of indolent character" (Stephens 1999:632).

Nervoso: The term *nervoso* described a physical condition previously unknown to the medical profession.

Novela: A Brazilian Soap Opera on national television.

O Centro Educacional Comunitário Bom Pastor: The Good Shepherd Community Educational Center.

O Dia do Indio: The Day of the Indian.

O Meu Coração Bate Feliz: My Heart Beats Happy.

O primeiro: First through fourth grade in comparison to U.S. primary school grades.

O Folclore do Povo: The Folklore of the People.

O Rei Que Só Queria Comer Peixe: The King Who Just Wanted to Eat Only Fish.

Palavrões: Course words, foul language.

Pão: Bread.

Pão de Queijo: Cheese Bread.

Pão Doce: Sweet Bread.

Pão de Sal: Salt Bread.

Pardo: A term used frequently to refer to a *mulato* person, but that also further defines the color of brown skin as a brownish or dun-color with reddish tint.

Paróquia Santo António: Parish of Saint Anthony.

Pataxo Ha-Ha-Hae: Indigenous tribe from Brazil's Amazon.

Patroa: Female boss.

Patrão: Male boss.

Picolé: A Popsicle or an ice-cream bar.

Pinga: *Cachaça*, a strong liquor, made from sugar cane.

Pivete: A street urchin.

Por causa do lugar: Because of the place.

Preto: Black.

Prefeito: The Mayor's office.

Prefeitura: City Hall.

Pretinho: Little black person.

Preciso de Amor: I Need Love.

Pronto Socorro: Emergency room in a health care clinic.

Ponto de Partida: Point of Departure. The name of Roberto Silva's theater group.

Puta: A prostitute.

Quiabo: Okra

Rainha Perpetua do Congado: The perpetual queen of the Congo.

Rapariga: A young girl, used in the context of being a 'child' without responsibility.

Revista: Magazine.

Roça: A plot of land without resources where the poor eek out a living.

Roda: Circle.

Roda grande: Large circle.

Roda pequena: Small circle.

Satisfieta: Satisfied. In Brazil, 'satisfied' is used to indicate that one is 'full' after eating.

Viva Crianças: Hooray Children.

Se Essa Rua Fosse Minha: If This Street Were Mine.

Serra do Criado: Mountain range.

Sítio: A small farm.

Sucata: Recycling bin or recycling center.

Rainha Perpetua do Congado: The Perpetual Queen of the Congo.

Tia: Aunt.

Tia Gorda: Fat Aunt.

Todi: Chocolate Milk.

Uma Filha de Criação: A foster child This term is used to delineate a child who is taken in and raised by a family who is not blood related.

Uma historia é muitas vidas: A History is many lives.

Um lugar bonito: A pretty place.

Universidade Federal: Federal University

Vereadores: Councilmen.

Vestibular: Standard achievement test in Brazil similar to the SAT tests in the U.S.

Vagabundo: A vagabond.

Xinga/xingar: To ridicule, shame, or curse a person.

BIBLIOGRAPHY

Abebe, Tatek, "Earning a Living on the Margins: Begging, Street Work, and Social Spacial Experiences of Children Addis Abebe," *Geografiska Annaler. Series B, Human Geography,* 90:3. Geographies of Children and Youth (2008): 271–284.

Almanaque Abril 2000
2000 Almanaque Brazil 2000: O seu Guia de Pesquisas Prático, Rápido e Atualizado. Pp. 188.

Amnesty International. 1994. "Beyond Despair: An Agenda For Human Rights in Brazil." EMBARGO, 14 September, AI Index: AMR 19/15/94

Amnesty International. 1998. AI Index: AMR 19/08/98. http://web.amnesty.org/ai.nsf/Index/AMR190081998?OpenDocument&of=THEMES\CHILDREN+JUVENILES

Amnesty International UK Blogs, "Children's Human Rights Network. Amnesty AGM – A Proposed Resolution on the Rights of Street Children," 2013, accessed March 9, 2014, http://www.amnesty.org.uk/blogs/childrens-human-rights-network-blog/amnesty-agm-proposed-resolution-rights-street-children

Ariès, Philippe. *Centuries of Childhood: A Social History of Family Life.* New York: Vintage Books, 1962: 119, 412, 413.

Aristide, Jean-Bertrand. *Eyes of the Heart: Seeking a Path for the Poor in the Age of Globalization.* Monroe: Common Courage Press, 2000: 53.

Atkinson, Sarah; Medeiros, Regianne Leila Rolim, Lima Oliveira, and Paulo Henrique, "Going Down to the Local: Incorporating Social Organization and Political Culture into Assessment of Decentralized Health Care," *Social Science & Medicine*, 51:4 (2000): 619-36.

Austin, Joe & Willard, Nevin, Michael, eds. *Generations of Youth: Youth Cultures and History in Twentieth-Century America.* New York: New York University Press, 1998.

Azedevo, Thales, de. *Cultura e Situação Racial no Brasil.* Rio de Janeiro: Civilização Brasileira. 1966: 121–123.

Azevedo, Thales, de. *Democracia Racial: Ideologia e Realidade.* Petropolis: Editora Vozes

Bacha, Edmar, L. and Herbert S. Klein. *Social Change in Brazil: 1945–1985 The Incomplete Transition*. Albuquerque: University of New Mexico Press, 1989:16, 263–309.

Baer, Werner. *The Brazilian Economy: Growth and Development. 5th Edition*. Westport: Praeger, 2001: 4, 12–13

Bakhtin, Mikhail, "Forms of Time and the Chronotope in the Novel." In *The Dialogic Imagination*, edited by Michael Holquist. Austin: University of Texas Press, 1937. Pp. 84–258.

Bandeiro, Beato, Lucila, "Inequality and Human Rights of African Descendants in Brazil," *The Journal of Black Studies*, 34: 6 (2004) Pp. 768–774.

Barickman, Bert. *A Bahian Counterpoint: Sugar, Tobacco, Cassava, and Slavery in the Recôncavo, 1780–1860*. Stanford: Stanford University Press, 1998.

Baronov, David. *The Abolition of Slavery in Brazil: The "Liberation" of Africans Through the Emancipation of Capital*. Westport: Greenwood Press, 2000: 117–143.

Barros, Ricardo; Fox, Louise, and Rosane Mendonça, "Female-Headed Households, Poverty and the Welfare of Children in Urban Brazil," *Economic Development and Cultural Change*, 45:2 (1997): 231–257.

Baxter, Eva, Jane, "The Archaeology of Childhood," *Annual Review of Anthropology*, 37 (2008): 159–175.

Behar, Ruth. *The Vulnerable Observer: Anthropology That Breaks the Heart.* Boston: Beacon Press, 1996: 2–3

Benedict, Ruth. *Patterns of Culture.* New York: New American Library, 1959.

Berndt, Angelika, "Children at Risk: a Socio-Political Profile of the Circumstances that put Children at Risk in Brazil's Urban Centers," 2009, accessed March 9, 2014, Action for Brazil's Children Trust. 53 Firth Street, London W1D 4SN, T++ (44) (20) 7494–9344 www.abctrust.org.uk

Bieber, Judy. *Power, Patronage, and Political Violence: State Building on a Brazilian Frontier, 1822–1889.* Lincoln: University of Nebraska Press, 1999: 21–22.

Bieber, Judy, "Slavery and Social Life: Attempts to Reduce Free People to Slavery in in the Sertão Mineiro, Brazil 1850–1871," *Journal of Latin American Studies* 26: 3 (1994):124, 597–619.

Birdsall, Nancy and Richard Sabot. *Opportunity Foregone: Education in Brazil.* Inter-American Development Fund. Washington, D.C. Inter-American Development Bank. Baltimore: Johns Hopkins University Press, 1996: 7–44, 124, 117–141.

Boakari, Francis Musa, "Educational System Reform as Legitimization for Continuity: The Case of Brazil." In *International Perspectives on Education and Society.* 4 (1994): 109–133.

Bourdieu, Pierre. *The Logic of Practice*. Stanford: Stanford University Press, 1990: 16, 81, 112, 114–121

Bourdieu, Pierre. *Distinction: A Social Critique of the Judgement of Taste*. Cambridge: Harvard University Press, 1984: 102–103.

Branco, Sylvia, Vera. "Nonprofit Sector in Brazil" (paper presented at Fundação Getúlio Vargas, São Paulo by Vera Sylvia Bronco). Published by the University of Texas at Austin, Institute of Latin American Studies.

Brener, Jayme, "Brazil: Taking Up the Social Slack," *Courier UNESCO*, June, 2000, accessed September 22, 2014, http://www.questia.com/library/1G1-76472426/brazil-taking-up-the-social-slack and http://unesdoc.unesco.org/images/0012/001227/122747e.pdf last accessed on 9-22-14

Brick-Panter, Catherine and Malcolm T. Smith. *Abandoned Children*. Cambridge: Cambridge University Press, 2000.

Brody, Eugene, B. *The Lost Ones: Social Forces and Mental Illness in Rio de Janeiro*. New York: International Universities Press, 1973.

Buarque de Holanda Ferreira, Aurélio. *Novo dicionário da língua portuguesa*. Rio de Janeiro: Editora Nova Fronteira, 1975: 1413.

Burdick, John. *Blessed Anastácia: Women, Race, and Popular Christianity in Brazil*. New York: Routledge, 1998.

Burgess, M. Elaine, "Poverty and Dependency: Some Selected Characteristics," Journal of Social Issues 21: 1 (1965).

Burns, Bradford, E. *A History of Brazil.* New York: Columbia University Press. Third Edition, 1993: 41.

Butterworth, Douglas, B. *Peasants in Cities*, edited by William P. Magnin. Boston: Houghton Mifflin, 1970.

Carnoy, M., J. Werthein, and H.M. Levin. *Escola e Trabalho no Estado Capitalista*. São Paulo: Cortez, 1987.

CEARA Urban Development and Water Resource Management Project, ABC, "Street Children Pilot Scheme: A Case of Demand Side Financing" 1994, accessed September 14, 2014, http://www.worldbank.org/education/economicsed/finance/demand/case/ceara/ceara_index.htm last accessed 9-14-14

Chesnut, Andrew, R. *Born Again in Brazil: The Pentecostal Boom and the Pathogens of Poverty*. New Brunswick: Rutgers University Press, 1997: 108.

Clemens, Benedict, "The Real Plan, Poverty, and Income Distribution in Brazil, in F&D: Finance and Development," September, 1997. International Bank for Reconstruction and Development, Washington, DC.

Clifford, James. *Predicament of Culture: Twentieth-Century Ethnography, Literature, and Art*. Cambridge: Harvard University Press, 1998: 22

Clifford, James, & Marcus, George, E. *Writing Culture: The Poetics and Politics of Ethnography*. Berkeley: University of California Press, 1986.

Conrad, Robert, Edgar. *Children of God's Fire: A Documentary History of Black Slavery in Brazil*. Pennsylvania: The Pennsylvania State University Press, 1984: 100, 341–350.

Conselho Municipal de Assistência Social de Morro de Santana Controle Social e Participação Popular, January 27, 2000.

Cunningham, Hugh. *The Children of the Poor: Representations of Childhood Since the Seventeenth Century*. Oxford: Blackwell, 1991: 29, 69, 71, 151–152, 154, 166.

Da Costa, Emilia Viotti. *The Brazilian Empire: Myths and Histories*. Chapel Hill: University of North Carolina Press, 2000 re-published.

da Costa, Gilceu Ferreira. *Comitê de Cidadania Contra a Miséria e a Fome* Morro de Santana, Minas Gerais. Xerox bound manuscript, privately published, 1981.

DaMatta, Roberto. *A Casa e a Rua: Espaço, Cidadania, Mulher e Morte no Brazil*. São Paulo: Brasiliense, 1985.

DaMatta, Roberto. *Carnivals, Rogues, and Heroes: An Interpretation of the Brazilian Dilemma*. Notre Dame: University of Notre Dame Press, 1991: 64.

Da Silva, Benedita. *Benedita da Silva: An Afro-Brazilian Woman's Story of Politics and Love.* Oakland: Food First Books, 1997.

Da Silva, Martins, Sérgio; Carlos Alberto Medeiros and Elisa Larkin Nascimento,
"Paving the Road from Racial Democracy to Affirmative Action in Brazil," *Journal of Black Studies*, 34:6 (2004), African Descendants in Brazil, Pp. 787–861.

Da Silva, Wilson, "Black Conscience in Brazil," 2009, accessed August 14, 2014, http://www.migrazine.at/artikel/black-conscience-brazil-english

Davis, Darién, J. ed., *Slavery and Beyond: The African Impact on Latin America and the Caribbean.* Wilmington, Del.: SR Books, 1995: 264.

Degeler, Carl. *Neither Black Nor White: Slavery and Race Relations in Brazil and the United States.* Wisconsin: The University of Wisconsin Press, 1986. Quote from Azevedo as a footnote citing Nogueira and Bastide, from *Relacoes raciais* p. 175.

de Moura Castro, Cláudio, "What is Happening in Brazilian Education?" *In Social Change in Brazil: 1945–1985 The Incomplete Transition.* Edited by Edmar L. Bacha and Herbert S. Klein. Albuquerque: University of New Mexico Press, 1989: 263, 523–552.

de Paula Faleiros,Vincente, "Violence and Barbarism: The Exermination of Children and Adolescents in Brazil." *In Children in Brazil Today: A Challenge For the Third Millennium.* Edited by

Irene Rizzini. Rio de Janeiro: Editora Universitária Santa Úrsula, 1994: 177–191.

Del Priore, Mary (org.); Laura de Mello e Souza, et al. "O Abandono de Crianças Negras No Rio de Janeiro," in *Historia da Criança no Brazil*, edited by Mary del Priore. São Paulo: Editora Contexto: CEDHAL. 1991:67, 70.

de Roupre, Denise, Revista CONSULEX, Maio 1997, Ano I – No.5.

Diamond, Timothy, J. and Judith A. DiIorio. *The Status of Children Under Advanced Capitalism: A Critical Perspective* (1978). Circulated by the Red Feather Institute for Advanced Studies in Sociology as part of The Transforming Sociology Series. Sent to me by author.

Dodge, C. P. and M. Raundalen. *Reaching Children in War Sudan, Uganda, and Mozambique*. Norway: Sigma Forlag, 1991.

Douglas, Mary. *Purity and Danger: An Analysis of the Concepts of Pollution and Taboo*. New York: Routledge, 1966:50–51.

Douglas, Mary. *Implicit Meanings: Essays in Anthropology*. New York: Routledge, 2003. Pp. 50–51.

Durigan, Giselda, "Restoration of 'Cerrado' Vegetation in Degraded Areas," SE Brazil XI World Forestry Congress Vol. 2, Topic 7. 1997, accessed September 30, 2014, http://www.researchgate.net/profile/Giselda_Durigan/publications/3 last accessed 9-30-14

Easterbrook, Michael, "Brazil Considers Quotas to Bridge Racial Divide in Higher Education," *The Chronicle of Higher Education,* March, 2002, accessed September 17, 2014, http://business.highbeam.com/434953/article-1G1-146964605/brazil-considers-quotas-bridge-racial-divide-higher

Elson, Diane, "The Differentiation of Children's Labour in the Capitalist Labour Market," *Development and Change,* 13 (1982): 419–497.

Emmerson, Patrick, M and Shawn D. Knabb, "Opportunity, Inequality, and the Intergenerational Transmission of Child Labour," *Economica,* 73: 291 (2006): 413–434.

Ennew, Judith *The Iconography of Street Children.* Paper presented at Department of Social Anthropology, University of Oslo, 1990.

Ennew, Judith (a) "Parentless Friends: A Cross-Cultural Examination of Networks among Street Children and Street Youth." In *Social Networks and Social Support in Childhood and Adolescence.* Edited by Frank Nestmann and Klaus Hurrelmann. Berlin: Walter de Gruyter, 1994: 409–426

Ennew, Judith. *Time for Children or Time for Adults? 1994. Edited by* Qvortrup, Jens, Bardy, Marjatta, Giovanni Sgritta, and Helmut Wintersberg. Aldershop: Avebury.

Escola Magazine *ano Xi, 94 (*June 1996): 30–31.

Estatuto da Criança e do Adolescente. http://www.planalto.gov.br/ccivil_03/leis/l8069.htm (1990). Accessed September 29, 2014.

Evans, P., Rueschemeyer, D., and T. Skocpol. *Bringing the State Back In.* London: Cambridge University Press, 1985:71.

Evans, P. *Dependent Development: The Alliance of Multinational, State, and Local Capital in Brazil.* New Jersey: Princeton University Press, 1979.

Faleiros, Vicente de Paula, "Violence and Barbarism: The Extermination of Children and Adolescents in Brazil." In *Children in Brazil Today: A Challenge for the Third Millennium.* Edited by Irene Rizzini. Rio de Janeiro: *Editora Universitária Santa Úrsula, 1994.*

Ferreira, Windyz. 2000. Brazil wants all children in School: Government initiatives and reality. In *Enabling Education Network.* Ferreira is a lecturer in Special Education at the Federal University of Paraiba, Northeast Brazil ferreira@hotmail.com.

Foster, George, McClelland
1967. *Tzintzuntzan: Mexican Peasants in a Changing World.* Boston: Little, Brown. Pp. 122–152

Foucault, Michael.
1984 *The Body of the Condemned* (From Discipline and Punish). In the Foucault Reader, by Rabinow, Paul (Ed.). New York: Pantheon Books. Pp. 170–178.

Freire, Paulo. *Pedagogy of the Oppressed*. New York: The Seabury Press, 1970: 75–118.

Freyre, Gilberto. *The Masters and the Slaves: A Study in the Development of Brazilian Civilization*. New York: Knopf, 1946.

Furtado, Celso. *The Brazilian Economy: Growth and Development*. 5th Edition. Westport: Praeger, 2001: 12–13.

Fyfe, Alec. *Child Labour*. Cambridge, UK: Polity Press, 1989.

Garon, Denise, Dr. 1997. Third *Intercâmbio Entre Brinquedotecas*, São Paulo, Brazil. Unpublished Paper

Gay, Robert. *Popular Organization and Democracy in Rio de Janeiro: A Tale of Two Favelas*. Philadelphia: Temple University Press, 1994.

Geertz, Clifford, J. *The Predicament of Culture: Twentieth Century Ethnography*. Cambridge, Mass.: Harvard University Press, 2002: 24–54.

Glauser, Benno. 1997. "Street Children: Deconstructing a Construct." In James, A. and A. Prout, (eds.) *Constructing and Reconstructing Childhood*. London: Falmer Press.

Global Justice Report. 2000. "Summary of the Civil Society Report on Brazilian Compliance with the International Covenant on Economic, Social, and Cultural Rights," accessed June 23, 2002, http://www.global.org.br/english/annual_report_documents/annual_report_inequality.htm

Goffman, Erving. *The Presentation of Self in Everyday Life*. New York: Doubleday, 1959.

Goffman, Erving. *Frame Analysis: An Essay on the Organization of Experience*. Boston: Northeastern University Press, 1974.

Graham, Lauderdale, Sandra. *House and Street: The Domestic World of Servants and Masters in Nineteenth-Century Rio de Janeiro*. Austin: University of Texas Press, 1988.

Guadalupe, Salazar, "Second-Class Citizens in the Making: The Rights of Street Children in Chile, *Latin America Perspectives*, 35:4 (2008). *Youth and Cultural Politics in Latin America*. 30–44

Hall, Kevin, G., "Brazil Program Will Set Aside Jobs for Blacks: Government Plans to Address Inequities," Detroit Free Press, June 21, 2002, accessed September 29, 2014. http://www.freep.com/news/nw/ebrazil21_20020621.htm or http://www.highbeam.com/doc/1G1-86535936.html

Hammel, Eugene & Laura Nader. 1979. *Will the Real George Foster Please Stand UP? A Brief Intellectual History*. Anthropology Emeritus Lecture Series at U.C. Berkeley. *Kroeber Anthropological Society Papers, 55–56 : 159–164*.

Hasenbalg, Carlos, Alfredo. 1979. "Discriminçáo legi e desigualdades raciais no *Brasil. Rio de Janeiro: Editações Graal*." In, *Racism in a Racial Democracy: The Maintenance of White Supremacy in Brazil*. New Brunswick: Rutgers University Press: 8.

Healy, Barry, "Brazilian Indian Burned Alive," Greenleft Weekly, October 22, 1997, accessed September 30, 2014. https://www.greenleft.org.au/node/13546

Hecht, Tobias. *At Home in the Street: Street Children of Northeast Brazil*. Cambridge: Cambridge University Press, 1998: 4–6

Heringer, Rodrigues, "Rosana, Extermínio de Crianças e Adolescentes no Brasil: Construção e Análise de uma Categoria Social" (Ph.D dissertation, Doctor in Human Sciences: Sociology, 1997: 271).

Herskovitz, M. J. *Man and His Works*. New York: Alfred A. Knopf, 1948.

Higgins, Martha. *From Slavery to Vagrancy in Brazil*. New Jersey: Rutgers University Press, 1985: 63.

Human Rights Watch Publications
The Small Hands of Slavery: Bonded Child Labor in India. ISBN 1-56432-172-X, September. http://www.hrw.org/reports/1996/India3.htm. (1996) Accessed September 30, 2014.

IBASE (*Instituto Brasileiro de Analises Sociais E Economicas*)
Translated Edition,
"1992 Survey of Boys and Girls on the Streets of Rio de Janeiro."
Pereira, Almir, Junior & Heringer, Rosana. Cadernos do IBASE
6. Projeto "Se Essa Rua Fosse Minha" ("If This Street Were Mine"
Project). FASE/IBASE/IDAC/ISER March. Pp.7

IBGE (*Instituto Brasilero de Geografia e Estatística*)
1992 *Seção: Características Demográficas e Socioeconômicas
da População. Anuário Estatístico do Brasil.* Rio de Janeiro:
Fundação Instituto Brasileiro de Geografia e Estatística. Table
22.2:261

IBGE (*Instituto Brasilero de Geografia e Estatística*) 1996 *Contagem
da População.* Rio de Janeiro: IBGE

IBGE (*Instituto Brasilero de Geografia e Estatística*) 2000 www2.
ibge.gov.br, Census Page

IBGE (*Instituto Brasilero de Geografia e Estatística*) Population
Figures for Morro de Santana, Minas Gerais, Brazil. Luiscarlos@
ibge.gov.br

IBGE (*Instituto Brasilero de Geografia e Estatística*) www1.ibge.gov.
br,census page (2001).

IBGE (*Instituto Brasilero de Geografia e Estatística*) http://www.
ibge.gov.br/english/estatistica/populacao/caracteristicas_raciais/
default_pdf.shtm (2008). Accessed March 9, 2014.

Impelizieri, Flávia, "Street Children and NGOs in Rio: A follow-up Study on Non-Governmental Projects," Rio Janeiro: AMAIS Livaria e Editora; IUPERJ (1995): Pp. 37–38, 69–73, 101–103, 115.

Inhelder, Bärbel. *De la logique de l'enfant á logique de l'adolescent.* English. *The Growth of Logical Thinking.* Milgram. New York: Basic Books, 1958.

Jahoda, Gustav. *Images of Savages: Ancient Roots of Modern Prejudice in Western Culture.* London: Routledge, 1999.

James, A.; et al. *Theorizing Childhood.* New York: Teachers College Press, 1998: 1,4.

James, Adrine, L., and Allison James, "Tightening the net: children, community, and control," *The British Journal of Sociology,* 52: 2 (2003).

James, Allison, "Giving Voice to Children's Voices: Practices and Problems, Pitfalls and Potentials," *American Anthropologist,* 109: 2 (2007): 261–272.

James, A. and A. Prout. *Constructing and Reconstructing Childhood: Contemporary Issues in the Sociological Study of Childhood.* London: The Falmer Press, 1997.

Justiça Global 2000 Human Rights in Brazil. *Federação de Órgãos para Assistência Social e Educativa, or FASE).*

Kader, Asmal, Minister of Education to the Human Sciences Research Council (HSRC) 2000 Seminar on *Transforming the State and Society: Reflections from the Water and Education Sectors*. Monday, 5 June 2000, at the HSRC, Pretoria.

Kerstenetzky, Celia, Lessa. 2001. "The Violence of Inequality." *Instituto Brasilero de Análises Sociais e Econômicas (IBASE).* (Brazilian Institute for Social and Economic Analysis). *Instituto del Tercer Mundo—Control Ciudadano: Uma rede ONG de monitoreo y vigilancia de los compromisos realizados por los gobiernos en la Cumbre Mundial de Desarrollo Social y la IV Conferência Mundial sobre la Mujer* observatorio@ibase.org.br.

Kiddy, Elizabeth, "Brotherhoods of Our Lady of the Rosary of the Blacks: Community and Devotion in Minas Gerais, Brazil" (Ph.D. thesis, University of New Mexico, 1998.

Kilbride, Philip, Suda, Collette, and Enos Njeru. *Street Children in Kenya: Voices of Children in Search of a Childhood*. Westport: Bergin & Garvey, 2000: 1–4.

Kuperman, Diane, "Stuck at the Gates of Paradise," *The Courier, UNESCO*. September 2001. Pp. 1–4. http://connection.ebscohost.com/c/articles/5222166/stuck-gates-paradise. Accessed September 12, 2014.

Lamphere, Louise. 1997. "Work and the Production of Silence." In *Between History and Histories: The Making of Silences and Commemorations*, edited by Gerald Sider and Gavin Smith. Toronto: University of Toronto Press, Pp. 74–75, 263, 271.

Leite, Costa Ligia and Aberu Esteves de Martha, "Escola Tia Ciata: A School for Street Children in Rio de Janeiro," *Environment and Urbanization*, April, 3 (1) 1991.

Lewis, Oscar. *The Children of Sanchez: Autobiography of a Mexican Family.* New York: Vintage Books, 1963.

Louzada, Affonso. *O Problema da Criança: A Ação Social do Juízo de Menores.* Rio de Janeiro: Imprensa Nacional, 1940:18

Lusk, Mark, W. "Street Children Programs in Latin America," *International Social Welfare*, 16:1 (l989): 66

Lusk, Mark, W. and D.T. Mason. 1992. "Fieldwork with Rio's Street Children. In *Children in Brazil Today: A Challenge for the Third Millennium*, edited by I. Rizzini. Rio de Janeiro: Editora Universitária Santa Ursula

MacKay, R. 1973. "Conceptions of Children and Models of Socialization." In, *Dreitzsel, Childhood and Socialization,* London: Collier-Macmillian

Marcos, Alen, P, "Sex, Color, and Geography: Radicalized Relations Brazil and Its Predicaments," *Annals of the Association of American Geographers*, 103:5 (2012): 1282–1299. http://www.tandfonline.com/loi/raag20. Accessed March 20, 2014.

Marcus, George, E. *Rereading Cultural Anthropology.* Durham: Duke University Press, 1992.

Marteleto, Leticia, "Educational Inequality by Race in Brazil, 1982–2007: Structural Change and Shifts in Racial Classification," *Demography*, 49 (2012):337–358.

Márquez, Patricia. *The Street Is My Home: Youth and Violence in Caracas*. Stanford: Stanford University Press, 1999:2.

Marx, Karl. *Capital. Volume One*. New York: Vintage Books, 1997: 353–359.

Mattoso, Katia de Queiros. 1991. O Filho da Escrava. In, História da Criança no Brasil, edited by Mary del Priore. São Paulo: Editora Contexto CEDHAL

May, Margaret, 1973, "Innocence and Experience: The Evolution of the Concept of Juvenile Delinquency in the Mid-Nineteenth Century," *Victorian Studies*, 27:1 (1973):7–29

McDonald's, George Sir Gibbie. Whitethorn, Calif.: Johannese, 1996.

Mead, Margaret, "Socialization and Encultration," *Current Anthropology 4 (1963):184–188*.

Metcalf, Alida. *Family and Frontier in Colonial Brazil: Santana de Parnaíba, 1580–1822*. Berkeley: University of California Press, 1992:499.

Meznar, Joan, Ellen, "Orphans and the Transition From Slave to Free Labor in Northeast Brazil: The Case of Campina Grande, 1850–1888," *Journal of Social History*, 27:3 (1994):499-515, 504–507.

Mikulak, Marcia, "The Symbolic Power of Color: Constructions of Race, Skin-Color and Identity in Brazil," *Humanity & Society*, 35:1 and 2 (2011): 62–99.

Morss, John, R. *The Biologising of Childhood: Developmental Psychology and the Darwin Myth*. Hove: Lawrence Erlbaum, 1990.

NACLA: Report on the Americas, "Disposable Children: The Hazards of Growing up Poor in Latin America." National Alliance for Children in Latin America. 27:6 (1995):16–40.

Nascimento, Abdias, do. 1995. "Afro-Brazilian Ethnicity and International Policy." In *Slavery and Beyond: The African Impact on Latin America and the Caribbean*. Edited by Darién J. Davis. P. 246.

Nesbit, E. *The Enchanted Castle*. New York: Puffin, 1995.

Nic Ghiolla Phádraig, Maíre. (a) "Childhood as a Social Phenomenon." National Report. Ireland. Eurosocial Report 36/8 (1990). Vienna: European Center for Social Welfare Policy and Research.

Nic Ghiolla Phádraig, Maíre. 1990 (b) "Daycare: Adult Interests Versus Children's Needs? A Question of Compatibality." Draft Chapter for publication in *Childhood Matters: Social Theory, Practice and Politics*. Aldershop: Avebury. Published in 1994.

O'Connell, Alison. Brazilian Society: The Year Ahead. *Pulsa MericaI* (2013). http://www.pulsamerica.co.uk/2013/01/06/what-does-2013-hold-in-store-for-poverty-and-social-inequality-in-brazil/. Accessed March 20, 2014.

Oldman, David. "Childhood as a Social Phenomenon." National Report. Scotland. Eurosocial Report 36/9 (1991). Vienna: European Center for Social Welfare Policy and Research.

Oliveira, Cleide de Fátima Galiza. *Se Essa Rua Fosse Minha: um Estudo Sobre a Trajetória Vivê dos Meninos de Rua do Recife*. Recife, UNICEF, 1989.

Ortner, S, "Theory in Anthropology Since the Sixties." In *Comparative Studies in Society and History*. 26: 1 (1984):159

Ozmon, Howard and Samuel Craver. *Philosophical Foundations of Education*. New York: Macmillian, 1990.

Patai, Daphne. *Brazilian Women Speak: Contemporary Life Stories*. New Brunswick: Rutgers University Press, 1993.

P. Bourdieu and J.D. Wacquant. *An invitation to Reflexive Sociology*. Chicago: University of Chicago Press, 1990: 9.

Penha-Lopes, Vânia. 1997. "An Unsavory Union: Poverty, Racism, and the Murders of Street Youth in Brazil." In *Globalization and Survival in the Black Diaspora: The New Urban Challenge*. Edited by Charles Green. NY: State University of New York Press.

Perlman, Janice, E. *The Myth of Marginality: Urban Poverty and Politics in Rio de Janeiro*. Berkeley: University of California Press, 1976. 242–243.

Perlman, Janice, E. 2000–2002 The Mega-Cities Project, headquartered at Trinity College in Hartford, CT. A non-profit organization with 501 (c) (3) tax status. www.megacitiesproject.org/interview. Accessed September 15, 2014.

Postman, Neil. *The Disappearance of Childhood*. New York: Delacorte Press, 1982.

Prawat, R.S., and R.E. Floden, "Teachers' Beliefs About Teaching and Learning: A Constructivist Perspective," *American Journal of Education*. (1992): 354–395.

Programa Curumim. 1997 Programa Curumim: O Direito de Centro Basileiro. Centro Brasileiro para a Infância e Adolescência. Informações: Secretário de Estado de Esportes, Lazer 3 Turismo. Belo Horizonte, Minas Gerais. Tel: (031) 271-2344

Public Policy Statement. 2007. "The Rights of Children," *Medical Anthropology Quarterly*, 21:234-238 (2007). Doi: 10.1525/maq.2007.21.2.234

Raphael, Alison, and Joanna Berkman., "Children Without A Future," Brazil Network, September, 1991: 22–33

Raskin, Marcus, G., Bernstein, Herbert, J., and Buck-Morss, Susan. *New Ways of Knowing: The Sciences, Society, and Reconstructive Knowledge.* Totowa, NJ: Rowman and Littlefield, 1987.

Redfield, Robert. *The Folk Culture of Yucatan.* Chicago: University of Chicago Press, 1970.

Reichmann, Rebecca. *Race in Contemporary Brazil: From Indifference to Inequality.* University Park, PA: The Pennsylvania State University Press, 1999: 234–249.

Reiter, Bernd, "What's New in Brazil's 'New Social Movements'? *Latin American Perspectives,* 38:153 (2011).

Richards, M. ed., *The Integration of a Child into a Social World.* Cambridge: Cambridge University Press, 1974.

Richards, M. and Light, P. eds., *Children of Social Worlds.* Cambridge: Polity Press, 1986.

Rizzini, Irene. (a) *A geração da rua: um estudo sobre as crianças marginalizadas* no Rio de Janeiro. CESME/USU. Série Estudos e Pesquisas-1, Rio de Janeiro: Editora Universitária Santa Úrsula, 1986.

Rizzini, Irene. (b) *Children in Brazil Today: A Challenge For the Third Millennium.* Rio de Janeiro: Editora Universitária Santa Ursula, 1991.

Rizzini, Irma, "In Praise of Science, or the Concept of 'Minors' in Legal Practice." *In Children in Brazil Today: A Challenge For the Third Millennium*, edited by Irene Rizzini. Rio de Janeiro: Editora Universitária Santa Úrsula, 1991:83–101, 179.

Robertson, Michael Owen, "Strategies on the Streets and in the Shelters: Transactions of Homeless People and Service Providers" (Ph.D. thesis, University of New Mexico, 2002).

Roca, Tião *Folclore: Roteiro de Pesquisa. Edição: Centro Popular de Cultura e Desenvolvimento—CPCE (1997).*

Rogers, Stainton. *Stories of Childhood: Shifting Agendas of Child Concern.* Toronto: University of Toronto Press, 1992: 89, 100.

Rosaldo, Renato. *Culture and Truth: The Remaking of Social Analysis.* Boston: Beacon Press, 1989: 25–45, 130–131.

Rousseau, Jean-Jaques. *Émile.* (Charles E. Tuttle, Vermont: Everyman, 1991). First published in 1762.

Sangren, Steven, "Anthropology of Anthropology? Further Reflections on Reflexivity," *Anthropology Today*, 23: 4 (2007):13–16

Saporiti, A., Sgritta, G.B. , "Childhood as a Social Phenomenon," *National Report. Italy.* Eurosocial Report 36:2 (1990). Vienna: European Center for Social Welfare Policy and Research.

Sarti, Cynthia, "Morality and Transgression Among Brazilian Poor Families: Exploring the Ambiguities." In *The Brazilian Puzzle: Culture on the Borderlands of the Western World*. Edited by Roberto da Matta and David Hess, New York: Columbia University Press: 124.

Scheer, Monique, "Are Emotions a Kind of Practice (And is that What Makes Them Have a History)? A Bourdieuan to Understanding Emotion," *History and Theory*, 51: 2 (2012).

Scheper-Hughes, Nancy. *Child Survival: Anthropological Perspectives on the Treatment and Maltreatment of Children*. Dordrecht: Reidel, 1989.

Scheper-Hughes, Nancy. *Death Without Weeping: The Violence of Everyday Life in Brazil*. Berkeley: University of California Press, 1992: 167–215, 268–339–399, 532

Scheper-Hughes, Nancy and Daniel Hoffman, "Kids Out of Place," *NACLA Report on the Americas,* 27 (1991): 16–23. Journal Code: NACLA Rep Am

Schwartz, Gilson, 10th Anniversary Games for Change Festival. June 17–19, 2013, New York City. http://www.gamesforchange.org/festival2013/speakers/ilson-schwartz/. Accessed September 29, 2014.

Schwartz, T. *Socialization as Cultural Communication*, introduction. Berkeley: University of California Press, 1976.

Shanahan, Suzanne, "Lost and Found: The Sociological Ambivalence Toward Childhood," *Annual Review of Sociology,* 33 (2007): 407-428.

Sheriff, Robin, E, "Exposing Silence as Cultural Censorship: A Brazilian Case," *American Anthropologist,* 102: 1 (2000): 114–132

Sider, Gerald and Gavin Smith. *Between History and Histories: The Making of Silences and Commemorations.* University of Toronto Press, 1977: 74–75.

Silva, Tião. Seeding Citizens. English Translation Version. Unpublished paper provided by the author.

Skidmore, Thomas. *Black Into White: Race and Nationality in Brazilian Thought.* Durham: Duke University Press, 1993: 38–77, 124–144, 199

Skidmore, Thomas. *Brazil: Five Centuries of Change.* New York: Oxford University Press, 1999: 17, 71–73

Skinner, B.F. *About Behaviorism.* New York: Knopf, distributed by Random House, 1974.

Slotkin, J.S. , "The Status of the Marginal Man," *Sociology and Social Research,* 28:1

Solberg, Anne. "Negotiating Childhood: Changing Constructions of Age for Norwegian Children" in *Constructing and Reconstructing Childhood: Contemporary Issues in the Sociological Study of Childhood*. London: The Falmer Press, 1997.

Solberg, Anne
1987 The working life of children. Report no. 15, Trondheim: Norwegian Center of Child Research

Stack, Carol, B. *All Our Kin: Strategies for Survival In a Black Community*. New York: Harper and Row, 1975.

Standing, G. *State Policy and Child Labour: Accommodation Versus Legitimization. Development and Change.* 13:4, London: Sage Publications, 1982.

Stephens, Sharon, ed., *Children and the Culture of Politics*. (New Jersey: Princeton University, 1995). 12.

Stephens, Thomas, M. *Dictionary of Latin American Racial and Ethnic Terminology*. Gainesville: University Press of Florida, 1999: 352, 362, 563, 583.

Stillwaggon, Eileen. *Stunted Lives, Stagnant Economies: Poverty, Disease, and Underdevelopment*. New Brunswick: Rutgers University Press, 1998.

Stocking,George,W. Jr. *Race, Culture, and Evolution: Essays in the History of Anthropology*. Chicago: University of Chicago Press, 1968: 126.

Strauss, Anselm and Juliet M. Corbin. *Basics of Qualitative Research: Grounded Theory Procedures and Techniques.* SAGE Publications, Inc. 2nd Edition, 1990.

Summerville, John, C. *The Rise and Fall of Childhood.* Beverly Hills: Sage Publications, 1982.

Tolman, Jon, University of New Mexico, Iberian Institute, personal communication, 2001.

Twine, France Winddance. *Racism in a Racial Democracy: The Maintenance of White Supremacy in Brazil.* New Brunswick: Rutgers University Press, 1998.

UNICEF. *State of the World's Children Report.* http://www.unicef.org/sowc2012/pdfs/SOWC%202012-Main%20Report_EN_13Mar2012.pdf. (2013). Accessed March 8, 2014.

UNICEF. *State of the World's Children Report* (1996).

Valladares, L. and Impelizieri, F. *Invisible Action: A Guide to Non-Governmental Assistance for Underprivileged and Street Children of Rio de Janeiro.* Rio de Janeiro: IUPERJ. (1992):16–23

Vargas, Costa, João, H, "When a Favela Dares to Become a Gated Condominium: The Politics of Race and Urban Space in Rio de Janiero," *Latin American Perspectives*, 33:4. Race and Equality in Brazil: Cultural and Political Dimensions. (2006): 49–81

Vawda, Ayesha, "Human Development, Network Educational Development." December 1, 1997. http://www.fordham.edu/economics/mcleod/Brazil-Bolsa-Escola.pdf. Accessed September 30, 2014.

Veloso, Leticia, "Child Street Labor in Brazil: Licit and Illicit Economies in the Eyes of Marginalized Youth," *South Atlantic Quarterly*, 111:4 (2012): 665; 667–71.1

Veloso, Leticia, "Universal Citizens, Unequal Childhoods: Children's Perspectives on Rights and Citizenship in Brazil," *Latin American Perspectives*, 35:4. Youth and Cultural Politics in Latin America. (2008): 45–59.

Viva Crianças. *Bornal de Jogos: Brincando Também se Ensina (Brincando Também se Ensina)*. *Fevereiro*. Annual Organization Report, Unpublished (1997).

Watson, John, Broadus and Rosalie Alberta Rayner Watson. *Psychological Care of Infant and Child*. Norton: New York (1928).

Weyland, Kurt, "Social Movements and the State: The Politics of Health Reform in Brazil." *World Development* 23 (1995).

Winn, Peter. *Americas: The Changing Face of Latin America and the Caribbean*. University of California Press: Berkeley, 73. 1992.

Wood, Charles, José Alberto Magno de Carvalho, and Cláudia Júlia Guimarães, "The Color of Child Mortality in Brazil: 1950 – 2000: Social Progress and Persistent Racial Inequality." *Latin American Research Review* 45:2 (2000):114–139

Woodhead, Martin, "Psychology and the Cultural Construction of Children's Needs." In *Constructing and Reconstructing Childhood*, edited by A. James and A. Prout London, 39. Falmer Press, 1990.

Woodson, Stephani. Exploring the Cultural Topography of Childhood: Television Performing the "Child" to Children. Bad Subjects: Political Education for Everyday Life 47(1999):14–17. Accessed September 29, 2014. http://bad.eserver.org/issues/2000/47/woodson.html.

Xavier, Maria Amelia, Vampré.
2000 *The Process of Inclusion in Brazil and in Latin America* federacaonacional@apaesp.org.br) International Relations, Instituto APAE SP; Chair, Communications Division Inclusion Interamericana Disability World: A bimonthly web-zine of International Disability News and Views. Issue no. 1, March

Zelizer, Viviana A. Rotman. *Pricing the Priceless Child: The Changing Social Value of Children*. New York: Basic Books, 1985.

INDEX

A

abandoned children 43, 392
abolition of slavery in Brazil 42
Abolition of Slavery in Brazil, The 385
Act for Children's and Adolescents' Rights 49
activities, daily 261–263
activities, educational 186–204
activities, games and 264–265
African slave trade 37
Afro-Brazilian 1–2, 14–15, 34, 40–41, 48–50, 151, 166, 192, 210, 222, 225, 282, 291, 293–297, 339, 342, 377, 381–386, 396
alcoholism 34, 64, 71, 84, 88, 149, 280, 294–295, 303, 310, 351, 369–370

Amnesty International 1–3, 49–50
Ariès, Philippe 7, 11–13, 26, 381
Associação de Pais e Amigos dos Excepcionais (APAE - the Association of Parents and Friends of Those With Disabilities) 7, 56, 146, 261, 279–284, 338, 395

B

behavior modification 22
biological immaturity 23, 29
black 14–15, 19, 38–39, 44–45, 304, 360, 372, 383, 396, 401, 403
Bom Jesus 7, 56, 77–78, 85, 107–108, 113, 119, 125, 143–144, 209, 257, 261, 280, 284–286, 300, 309, 324, 366, 396

boom–bust economy 36, 46
Bornal de Jogos 170, 187, 196, 210–215, 237, 396
Bourdieu, Pierre 60, 389–390
bourgeoisie 13, 16
Brazilian economy 45–46, 158
Brazilian inequality 45–48
Brazil's educational system 154, 190–191, 216, 272, 352, 370–371, 392
brown 14, 47, 383, 401, 403

C

caipira preto 39
capitalism 16–17
changing NGO practice and policy 363
cheap labor 18–19, 37
child abuse 64, 132, 295, 303, 333, 369
child behavior 266
childhood 4, 7, 11–22, 38, 98, 124, 141, 147–149, 154–155, 173, 183, 197–198, 209, 215–216, 221, 227–228, 236–237, 243–249, 266–267, 277, 296, 308–309, 334–335, 349–358, 380–381

child idleness 16
child law 48
children as economically useless 20
children as emotionally priceless 20, 29
children's income 57, 126
child rights 48, 261
Christianity 16
college 3, 258–259, 265–267, 290, 298, 330, 372, 399
colonial project 16
computer 54, 83, 100, 198, 268–270, 346, 352, 355, 362–365, 372–373, 378
computer literacy 355, 369, 372
concentration and penetration of capital 13
constructionist view of childhood 23–25, 33
constructions of childhood 11, 25, 29, 32, 38, 154, 183, 221, 349, 358–362
constructions of childhood innocence 361, 366
contribution to anthropological research 355
coordinators 9, 56, 80, 100, 111–112, 134, 139–140, 160–179, 208–210, 218–

220, 225–240, 259–261,
281, 290, 304–305, 354
COV (Citizens for Life Options) 7,
56, 272, 397
criadeiras (nannies) 43
criança de rua 39, 397
Curumim 7, 56, 115–116, 257–
263, 284–286, 306, 397
Curvelo 3–6, 30–31, 34–35,
51–52, 55–56, 65–66,
71–72, 84–86, 93, 98, 102,
107, 111–129, 153, 176, 181,
192, 208, 216, 221, 225–226,
235, 247, 256, 257–258,
265–273, 295, 298–306,
322–331, 352, 354–356,
366–368, 375–377, 385,
390, 395, 397, 399

D

daily life of children 33, 60–61,
111–113, 148, 161, 165, 187,
201, 210, 308, 312, 354–356,
363, 369
definitions of childhood 13
dependent development 38
development 6–7, 12, 26–27,
33–34, 35–37, 46, 52, 64,
132, 154–156, 165, 190, 198,
204, 211, 215, 221, 232–234,
241, 259, 264, 287, 338,
356, 371–374, 383–384,
391–392
division of labor 27, 178
drugs 207–208, 301, 316, 323

E

economic contributions 20, 362,
390
economic inequality 8, 34, 35, 132,
223, 246, 311, 317, 330, 369,
390
economic relationships between
parents and street children
112–114
economy of street life 57, 110–130
education 3–4, 13–18, 30–32, 109,
129, 132–135, 158–159,
166, 190–191, 197, 208,
215–216, 222, 237–238,
260, 264, 271, 272–280, 298,
313, 340, 343–344, 360–375
educational opportunities 55,
268–269, 392
elite 25, 37, 40, 45, 60, 69, 102, 149,
152, 190–192, 197, 201, 215,
236, 266, 282, 300–301, 317,
339, 342–343, 353–354,

360–362, 380–381
Emile 13
English Factory and Education Acts of 1802 20
English Poor Laws of the 1800s 16
epistemology 58
ethnographic method 58–60
everyday life 33, 151
exchange programs 355, 372–373

F

family income 30–31, 52, 112, 126, 136
favela(s) 3, 9, 38, 54–56, 78–79, 85–86, 101–104, 111, 118–121, 129–138, 179, 225, 232–233, 258, 266, 289, 295–298, 307–309, 322–324, 337, 340, 350–351, 354, 378–379, 385, 390, 395, 399
fazendas 40–41, 134
fieldwork 7–8, 35, 50, 53–54, 61, 68, 84, 118, 123, 134, 159, 214, 226, 257, 291, 312, 324, 371, 383
filho de criação 39
folk culture 175–176
folk traditions 159, 166
food 32–33, 37, 42, 53, 58, 75, 96–102, 122, 132–140, 176–180, 215, 267, 274, 279, 288, 303, 313–318, 343, 362, 397
forced migration 40
Foucault, Michael 93
freed slave children 15, 37, 42–43
Freud 20–21
FUNABEM (National Foundation for the Well-Being of Minors) 3, 44, 48, 282–283, 302, 400

G

games 76, 109, 123–124, 159–160, 170, 173–174, 187, 192, 196, 210–215, 234, 262–263, 304, 346, 374, 396
garden 83, 98–99, 150, 161, 176–180, 227, 239, 251, 266, 400
gender 23–25, 33, 38, 60, 63, 69, 158, 173, 389
Gini coefficient 5
grounded theory 58–59
Grupo de Fraternidade Irmão Luizinho 56

H

health, illness, and substandard medical care 331–335
household expenses 122–123
household income 6, 9, 99, 111, 118–119, 157, 356
household violence 34, 78–79, 169, 201, 253, 278, 291, 302–307
human rights 5–6, 47–48, 85, 106, 209, 263, 267, 273, 359, 365, 377, 388–389
hunger 4, 10, 43, 78, 98, 104, 142, 146, 151, 166, 184, 201, 215, 227, 272, 287, 292, 294–295, 308, 312–317, 328–330, 343, 369–370, 377

I

IBGE 3, 7, 47, 128
ideologies 2, 57, 83, 152, 194, 210, 256, 351–352, 364–366
ideology 9, 69, 98, 141, 154–155, 161, 165–166, 173, 179, 184, 192–196, 209–211, 221–222, 225–228, 235–236, 241–248, 265, 269, 274, 354, 366–367, 376
illiteracy rate 150, 191, 271
improvisation 194, 200, 203, 208
income 5, 9, 30–31, 43, 52, 57, 99, 111–120, 136, 149, 157, 356–357, 361, 372, 380, 382, 387
income inequality 120
Indian and African slavery 39
industrial revolution 13, 18, 36, 358
industrial schools 17
inequality 5–6, 15, 34–35, 47, 52, 58, 68, 86, 120, 131–132, 154, 166, 170, 191, 209, 215, 223, 246, 272, 296, 311–312, 317, 330, 338, 349, 354–355, 361–362, 369–380
innocence and purity 7, 12, 364–365
institutional goals x

J

Jean Piaget 21
juvenile justice systems 20

K

Karl Marx 17
kitchen 102, 166–167, 176–181, 252, 263, 299, 323–324, 337, 397

L

lack of support networks 109, 140
latifunda culture 37
latifúndios (large landed estate) 40
Lei do Ventre Livre (Law of the
 Free Womb) 41
limited good 130–131, 378
living conditions 10, 22, 246,
 322–326
low self-esteem 277, 291, 293–297

M

marginalization 2, 38, 294, 311,
 353, 363
Marx, Karl 17
medical care 154, 180, 280,
 331–332
methodology 58–59, 212
methods 8, 29, 52, 53, 58–61, 112,
 251, 262
methods of analysis 63–64
military dictatorship 6, 384, 391
military police 3
Minas Gerais 3, 7, 36–37, 54, 128,
 133, 154, 157, 236, 257, 272,
 373, 386–387
minor 3, 22, 28, 48, 107, 341, 392,
 400

Minors' Code 22, 28, 48–49, 392
moleque 38, 117, 136, 264, 304,
 360–361, 401
monitors 57, 116, 140, 259–263,
 288–289
morena 47
mulata 39
mulato 14, 39, 45–46, 386, 393,
 396, 401, 403
music 57, 61, 71, 100, 105,
 111–113, 139, 145, 162, 168,
 174–176, 184, 194–202,
 220, 233, 248, 260, 290,
 299–300, 306–309, 325,
 347, 371
musical instruments 202–203
music group 111, 139, 162, 168,
 194–195, 199–204

N

national education campaigns 361
National Movement for Street
 Children (MNMMR) 49
negative stereotypes 10, 28–29, 65,
 287, 316, 347, 352, 361
NGOs 2–6, 25, 33–34, 49–50,
 53–59, 160, 166, 199, 256,
 257, 266–268, 281, 285,
 291, 294, 312, 352–354,

362–371, 397
non-governmental organizations (NGOs) 2
'normal' childhood 12, 141, 350–351, 356
nutrition 150, 184, 216, 264–265, 279–280, 285, 316, 331–332

O

old Minors' Code 50
oligarchic political systems 36
organizational structures 256
orphanages 44

P

paper making 182–183, 193
patroa 103, 109, 133–137, 294, 318, 392, 395, 403
performance 94, 174, 194, 200–202, 208–209, 233–234, 271, 365
Peter Pan fantasy 17
Piaget, Jean 21
Pierre Bourdieu 60, 389–390
Pivetes e Ladrões (Thieves and Bandits) 339–345
popular culture 83, 154, 157–159, 166, 199, 212–213, 228, 235–237, 256, 268–269, 281, 290, 354, 369, 396
popular culture versus technology 268–270
poverty 3–4, 16–17, 24, 45–47, 56–57, 65, 68, 74, 78, 87, 98, 105, 109, 112, 123, 129–131, 136, 142–147, 165, 170, 191, 197, 208–209, 215, 225–226, 235, 244, 258, 263, 268–270, 278, 289–290, 293–295, 308–310, 319–328, 347–352, 361–371, 391
practice theory 58–60
praxis 165
preta 47
preto 14, 39, 156, 383, 388, 393, 403
programs 2, 5–7, 12, 24, 33–34, 50, 53, 58, 83, 111, 144, 159, 166, 221, 233–234, 238, 245, 250, 256, 258, 272, 290–291, 311–312, 354–355, 361–370
psychology 20–21, 26
public school dropout rate 30
puppets 193–195, 202
Puritan 12
purity 7, 13, 129, 173, 326, 364–365, 384

R

race 4, 7, 12, 23–25, 33, 35, 38, 45–46, 52, 56, 60, 63, 154, 158, 215, 236, 245, 339, 361–362, 371–378, 389–390
race relations 8, 35, 47, 372
racial inequality 215, 272, 311, 349, 355, 369–370, 376, 387
racism 1–2, 8–9, 14, 34, 35, 47, 52, 58, 68–69, 86, 105, 133, 166, 209, 223, 246, 273, 289, 293, 300, 311, 317, 353–354, 360, 363, 369–378
recommendations for the creation of NGO programs and social policy 10, 363–371
reflexive 65, 309
reformatories 17
relations of dependency 133
removal of children from the urban workforce 20
removing children from the street 15, 27
right to work 82, 107, 123, 127, 264, 356, 375
Rio de Janeiro 6, 53–54, 102, 112, 129, 269, 301, 312, 386–389
roda 157–166, 183, 194–195, 200, 208–209, 229–231, 247, 260–261, 288–289, 404

S

Scheper-Hughes, Nancy 6, 27, 309, 316, 331–332, 351, 360
secondary education 3, 190
Se Essa Rua Fosse Minha (If This Street Were Mine) 53, 404
self-esteem 10, 243, 277, 291, 293–294, 299–300
Ser Criança 7–8, 54–55, 65, 71, 74, 80–81, 98, 111, 115, 139–140, 145, 150–151, 153–186, 225–240, 257–262, 280, 288–290, 295, 298, 300–301, 313–314, 318, 336, 347, 354, 366–367, 396, 404
significance of findings 353–371
Skinner, B.F. 21
slave children 15, 37, 41–42, 385
slavery 2, 8, 15, 34, 35–41, 83, 134, 376, 385
slave trade 37, 41
social class 6, 24, 34, 60, 93, 120, 133–134, 148–149, 236, 243, 271, 360, 363–364, 372, 386, 389
social constructionist view of

childhood 25
social constructions of childhood:
    historical framework 11, 29
social relations 13, 26, 61, 134, 246, 293–320
statute for children and adolescents 23, 28
stereotypes 4, 10, 14, 28–29, 65, 83, 151–152, 209, 281, 287, 291, 310, 316, 339–345, 360–361
street children 1–5, 12–14, 23–29, 35–43, 53–58, 84, 108–115, 151, 153, 160–163, 184, 197–198, 208–209, 216, 223–224, 257, 267, 276–283, 294–295, 302–307, 344, 352–367, 392, 397, 401
street life 57, 111–130, 293
street youth contributions to household expenses 122
sugar plantations 36, 46
super children 4
surveys 56–57, 112

T

tables xv, 119
technology 24, 54, 191, 268, 273, 346, 372
the arts 284
theater 34, 83, 117, 194–195, 199–200, 207–208, 220, 237, 246, 261–262, 268, 289, 364, 404
thematic differences 238
the minors' court 22, 28
The National Movement for Street Children (MNMMR) 49
theoretical contributions 352, 357
theory 12–13, 20, 29, 58–61, 354–355
the World Bank 5, 30, 373, 377
Tião Rocha 9, 150–156, 165, 178–179, 194, 202, 210–211, 226, 235–236, 242–243, 250–251, 404
training 5, 18–19, 34, 40, 57, 69, 166, 197, 211–212, 216, 226–229, 238–240, 247, 259–262, 279–280, 284–285, 352, 355, 362, 365–371, 396
tutoring 166, 189–190, 245, 259–260, 268, 272, 289, 362, 369–370, 374, 378, 395
twins 67, 71–84, 109, 163, 302, 319
types of work 8, 111, 124, 182
types of work done by working children 124

U

UNICEF 1–2, 24, 312
university 6, 36, 59, 145, 156, 214, 245, 330, 350, 372–373, 381–384, 399, 405

V

violence 6, 10, 31–32, 48, 52, 65, 78–79, 87, 112, 162–163, 169, 201, 215, 238, 253, 278, 291, 294–295, 301–305, 316, 340–341, 348–349, 376

W

Watson, J.B. 21
Western European conceptions of childhood 7, 12
whitening 40, 47, 382
working children 2, 18–19, 33–34, 38, 57, 112, 119–123, 291, 350, 355, 367, 384
workshops 57, 211, 214–217, 227–234, 260
World Health Organization (WHO) 24

CPSIA information can be obtained at www.ICGtesting.com
Printed in the USA
LVOW04s1923270515
440148LV00001B/1/P